Learning to See

Learning to See

Historical Perspective on Modern Popular/Commercial Arts

Alan Gowans

Bowling Green University Popular Press
Bowling Green, Ohio 43403

Acknowledgements

Picture Number

12, 12a	Printed with the permission of The Oriental Institute, University of Chicago.
25a	Reprinted with the permission of Ryksmuseum van Oudheden, Leiden, the Netherlands.
30a	Copyright reserved, Royal Library, Windsor Castle.
38a	Reproduced by Courtesy of the Trustees of the British Museum.
83	Reprinted Courtesy of The Boston Globe.
100a, b	Reprinted from Miguel Covarrubias, *Indian Art of Mexico and Central America*, by permission of Alfred A. Knopf, Inc.
102b	Reproduced by permission of the University Museum, University of Pennsylvania.
109a	Reprinted by permission of the Chicago Tribune—New York News Syndicate, Inc.
113	Artist: Ronald Searle. Reprinted with permission from *TV Guide* Magazine. Copyright © 1975 by Triangle Publications, Inc., Radnor, PA.
117c	The Metropolitan Museum of Art, bequest of Mrs. H.O. Havemeyer, 1929. The H.O. Havemeyer Collection.
124	Reproduced with the permission of the Architect of the Capitol.
125	Reprinted with the permission of the Museo del Prado, Madrid, Spain.
127a	Reprinted with the permission of Musees Royaux des Beaux—Arts, Brussels, Belgium.
133, 133b	Reprinted from *Mad* Magazine with the permission of the publisher. Copyright © by E.C. Publications, Inc.
138b, 184a	Reprinted from Henry Glassie, *Patterns in the Material Folk Culture of the Eastern United States* with permission from the University of Pennsylvania Press.
158a, c	From *Art As Design: Design As Art* by Sterling McIlhany Copyright © 1970 by Litton Educational Publishing, Inc. Reprinted by permission of Van Nostrand Reinhold Company.
160b	Reprinted by permission of the London Express News and Features Services.
160c	On extended loan to the Museum of Modern Art, New York. Reprinted with permission.

TO

the members of
Uppsala Universitets Konstvetenskapliga Institutionen

and especially its head, Professor Allan Ellenius
this study is respectfully dedicated. I was encouraged to
rewrite and complete it thanks to the stimulus of an invitation
from one of the world's great universities to lecure for three
months (March-May 1978) as a Fullbright scholar on what in
all too many places still is regarded as no serious study,
Popular/Commercial arts and architecture—and by the kind
reception of those lectures there.

CONTENTS

III. *Traditional Forms and Functions of
Illustration in Modern Popular/Commercial
Arts*

VI. *Toward an Expanded Art History*

Preface

SEVEN OR EIGHT years ago *The Unchanging Arts* was published. Its theme was to identify the fundamental differences betweeen what in our time have come to be called "avant-garde" and "popular/commercial" arts. Its basic argument was that whereas popular/commercial arts carry on four basic social functions of traditional arts (hence deserve the title "Unchanging"), avant-garde art carries on only one, namely "artistic expression" and furthermore, has erected this one function into a self-justifying activity which has therefore no effective connection, certainly no objectively measurable connection, with historic arts. Instead of objectively analyzable social functions, avant-garde arts have, rather, a subjective social purpose: to inculcate a certain way of seeing in ethically relative, and hence politically harmless, terms. For this reason governments everywhere, with the sure instinct of the powerful and would-be powerful throughout history, have patronized and encouraged and thereby created that self-contradiction, our avant-garde Establishment.

This present study has other concerns. It starts on the assumption that popular/commercial arts are in fact a different kind of activity from avant-garde arts today; but that they represent the same kind of activity that we identify as "arts" historically. It proceeds then to investigate how popular/commercial arts carry out the social functions of historic arts. And it claims that, once we can thereby understand how historic arts worked in and for society, art history becomes a significant new tool for objective historical research as never before.

1

Toward an Expanded Art History

The Theory of Social Function and Its Implications
for Study of Popular/Commercial Arts

BUT THEY'RE NOT *ART!* And even if they *were* art, they'd still be frivolous! Could really serious scholars study "arts" like comics and political cartoons? Proper architectural history is concerned with cathedrals and mansions, not with trailers and hamburger stands. Dilettantish at best, trivial always...

Anyone with even peripheral interest in popular/commercial art of the later 20th century knows lines like these all too well; knows, too, how often they come from well-meaning self-elected defenders of something called High Culture who haven't thought through their assumptions that the Leo Castelli gallery is somehow freer of crass commercialism than advertising and package design, that Conceptual Painting somehow must have higher ideals than newspaper photography, that it's nobler to take public money and raze whole city blocks in the name of vague collectivistic visions of controlling chaos than it is to build cheap split-level ranch development houses for single families to buy and live private lives in. Unthinking attitudes, easily disabused by a few moments' reasoned reflection about the actual state of High Culture and the actual nature of popular/commercial arts nowadays. But what in fact is the positive case for serious study of popular/commercial arts? How and to what extent can it be considered a field for serious research? That is what this book is about.

Its concern is not primarily with the forms of popular/commercial arts *per se,* nor with evaluations of sociological qualities or cultural impact. Its concern is, rather, to define the functions of popular/commercial arts in society, to analyze what kinds of things are done by which, and thereby gain an understanding of how popular/commercial arts function in modern society. Once understand them, and you understand how all historic arts, High as well as Low, functioned in and for society; for their social functions were similar. And further: so understanding historic arts makes them instruments for historical research of a truly objective kind. In treaties and treatises and other written documents, people in the past set down what they thought they were doing, and claimed to believe. The social function of their historic arts, properly read, reveals far more truly what they actually did, where their real values lay. Arts and artifacts so considered in terms of social function become, then, major instruments for research into the past. Art history which uses its data in this way becomes a principal discipline for the study of history in and through art. And it is with the study of social function in the popular/commercial arts that all this begins. Not a field for serious scholars?

Implications of the Theory of Social Function for Art History Generally

"RECORDED HISTORY" is said to go back some six thousand years. For most of those years, the "record" consists principally of artifacts of one kind or another, made by diverse human beings, for various purposes. For many of them, such artifacts are all the record there is. One of the commonest places you find these artifacts is in art museums. Many have been classified as art. Some count among "art treasures of the world."

You might suppose, then, that anyone wanting to study the past would turn first to the discipline of art history, and rely heavily upon it. Wrong. For serious historians, art history seems to have been just about the last resort, something for which they have apparently had almost no use.[1]

That orthodox political history, working by custom with written documents, would tend to use arts and artifacts primarily or only as illustration (when at all), is perhaps understandable, if not altogether excusable. Yet intellectual history has made hardly more use of them.[2]

What accounts for so unnatural a state of affairs? Primarily, perhaps, the methodologies that art history has employed.

Art history has defined its data and perceived relationships between these data (arts and artifacts) and society (history) in three ways: by an aesthetic line-of-progress, as cultural expression, and by social function. These methodologies have developed successively and cumulatively: cultural expression building on aesthetic line-of-progress, social function representing a step beyond cultural expression, not its antithesis. With social function, which considers arts and artifacts not only as aesthetic objects or reflections of the spirit of their times, but also as instruments furthering the ideological foundations of society, art history has finally become the effective and prime instrument for historical research that it should always have been, revealing and analyzing those fundamental attitudes and presuppositions by which any age lives, and on which all the institutions of every society must ultimately rest.

But this methodology has come into use so recently that all too few historians yet realize its uses. As for art historians, some still are reluctant to broaden the definition of art to the extent that social function requires—to accept as legitimate areas of study in their discipline chipped flints as well as Altamira bison, political cartoons as well at those Papal commissions to propagandize theological propositions which we call the Sistine Ceiling and the Vatican Stanze—in short, to understand "arts" in the historic sense of "skills," activities with measurable ends and objectively evaluatable products.

It's not easy to surrender three or four centuries of aristocratic pretensions, as democratization of art history requires. Yet on analysis of the three methodologies of art history, the necessity and inevitability of broadening art history to include popular and vernacular arts, past and present, becomes self-evident.

Aesthetic Line-Of-Progress

OLDEST AND MOST BASIC of art history's methodologies is aesthetic line-of-progress. This was the reference by which relationships between arts and society were perceived by Ghiberti in the 15th century and Vasari in the 16th[3]; it remained the framework employed by the 1920's best known art historians— Bode and Berenson.[4] David Hackett Fischer in *Historians' Fallacies* charged that still in the 1970s,

a glance at the syllabus of an art history survey course or the contents of a text in this field suggests that more than a few art historians are still chugging along Berenson's main line, pulling passenger cars full of culture-hungry coeds. The main line isn't quite as narrow-gauged as it used to be, there are more side excursions, and the locomotives are a little more powerful. But the trip itself is much the same.[5]

This is more than a little unfair to H. W. Janson and Ernst Gombrich, whose *History of Art* and *Story of Art* respectively are the butts of Fischer's derision. Neither of these scholars is narrow; both have written powerfully, as scholars, against narrow aestheticism.[6] Yet no matter what they have written elsewhere, their surveys are the only idea most people ever get of art history (Janson's book has sold over two million copies; Gombrich's less, but still a lot), and if a book starts with caves and ends with Cubis by David Smith, then as far as the public is concerned, art history is a "line of progress" from there to here. And for publishers, too—try submitting a survey text constructed along other lines, and see how far you get!

Central to this aesthetic line-of-progress is the complex of assumptions that nowadays goes under the rubric "avant-garde." It structures the history of art as a series of avant-garde masterpieces—i.e., works of Artists who are "ahead of their times." Being ahead of their times is what makes them and their works Great, achievements to be imitated by a succession of later and lesser artists—the later, the lesser—until such time as

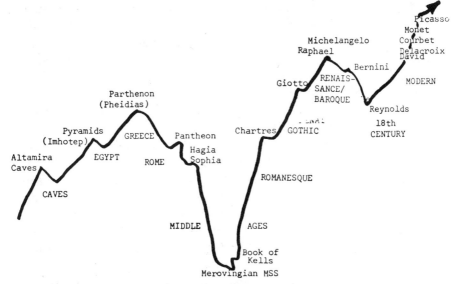

1. A heights-and-depths, hills-and valleys, aesthetic line of progress. Of course location of given highs and lows must vary with the ultimate high.

another Artist comparably ahead of *his* time comes along and gives the world the next avant-garde masterpiece. Diagrammatically, this aesthetic line-of-progress history can be rendered by a peaks-and-valleys pattern. Over several centuries, relative heights and depths have changed somewhat, and the system has developed modifications labyrinthine as the French verb system; but in essence it works very simply: the worth of any work of art is determined by how avant-garde it is. Thus, Raphael's style in the 1510s was a shade less avant-garde than Michelangelo's (proof: figures from M's Sistine Ceiling appear in R's *School of Athens*; cf. 22), hence the "Prince of Painters" stands just a shade lower in connoisseur esteem than the Climactic Renaissance Artist. That same style practised in the 1550s is retardataire and correspondingly less prized, lower priced. By the 1610s, backward and provincial, by the 1710s so kitschy and vulgar that you can buy Raphaelesque German statues in ordinary antique shops. Through the 19th, even into the 20th century, the style survives still, but now as "Catholic popular art" in plaster statuettes and lithographs that even in inflated currency cost only a dollar or two.[7]

Monet by Monet in the 1870s commands ransoms. Monet rendered by 1930s art students sells by the yard of used canvas. And so on.

Architectural historians for some reason (wood, perhaps?) seem to prefer tree diagrams. So Banister Fletcher set out the aesthetic line of progress on the title page of his *History of Architecture on the Comparative Method,* first published in London in 1896, far and away the most widely used textbook for architectural history until edged out c1945-55 by Siegfried Giedion's *Space Time and Architecture,* but still popular enough to warrant an 18th edition as late as the 1970s!

This time the aesthetic line-of-progress is a Grand Trunk: Greek to Roman to Romanesque to Renaissance ("Roman Influence," it's generalized here) to Modern. Everything else is on spur lines, branches now out of service: Egypt and China, India and Persia, Byzantine, "Saracenic." The moral, for architects trained on this kind of architectural theory: find the main line, and your buildings will live. Miss it, and you vanish from history. Once International Style modernism got identified as the "avant-garde" in the 1920s, the aesthetic line-of-progress assured its Establishment by the 1950s. Questions of merit are immaterial in

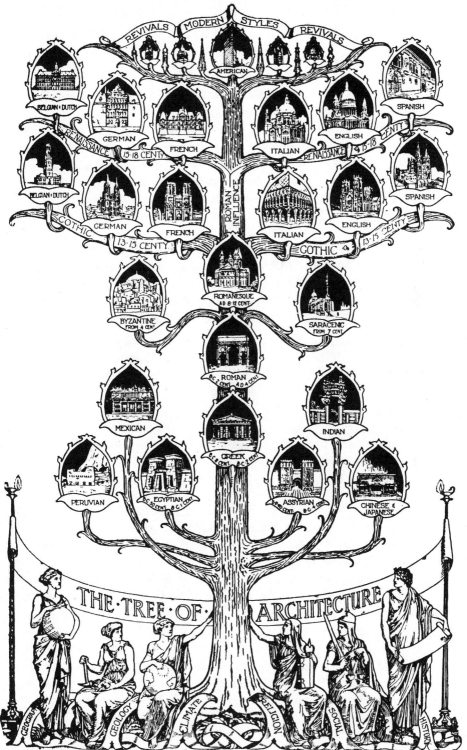

2. "This Tree of Architecture shows the main growth or evolution of the various styles, but must be taken as suggestive only, for minor influences cannot be indicated on a diagram of this kind."
Banister Fletcher's own drawing, frontispiece to his *History of Architcture on the Comparative Method.*

this scheme; there is only avant-garde—the good, the living—and non-avant-garde—the less good, the dying.[8]

Over the last couple of decades, influences from the 1960s' and 70s' egalitarian enthusiasms have been evident in aesthetic line-of-progress schemes. So in the newest editions of Helen Gardner's *Art Through the Ages* charts are provided with a somewhat different emphasis from the original 1926 edition's text. Hills and valleys are levelled out into more of a continuous chain. No matter; the text still tells us which are the peaks and which the foothills; the survey places Bronzino and Rosso as far below Leonardo and Michelangelo as ever a Berenson or a Bode did. There is no fundamental difference in principle between this line-of-progress-Through-the-Ages and Berenson's dictum which Fischer cited as a prime specimen of the fallacy of presentism:

"Significant events are those events that have contributed to making us what we are today.... Art history must avoid what has not contributed to the main stream, no matter how interesting, how magnificent in itself. It should exclude, for instance, most German and even Spanish and Dutch art. It should dwell less and less on Italian art after Caravaggio, and end altogether by the middle of the eighteenth century with Solimena and Tiepolo. Except for Ribera, Murillo, Velasquez and Goya in Spain, and Schongauer and Dürer and Holbein in German lands, the painters of those countries are neither in the main line of development nor of universal appeal to cultivated Europeans."

About this the historian comments scornfully, "Bernard Berenson was an art critic of splendid gifts. But he wasn't a historian—which was unlucky for him, and unhappy in its consequences, for he wrote several fat volumes of what is commonly called 'art history'."[9]

Now who is Us, to whom all history so leads? Us is of course 20th-century art generally, but more specifically those trends in 20th-century art which the aesthetic line-of-progess critic happens to admire; most specifically of all, whatever trends currently (i.e. when said writer is writing) have got themselves labelled "avant-garde." Since the current avant-garde is constantly shifting, aesthetic line-of-progress history must shift accordingly, and whereas in Berenson's time the main stream was composed of painters whose work might be seen as leading up to, say, John Singer Sargent (Mrs. Jack Gardner's favorite painter, as Berenson was her favorite picture-agent-cum-expert), now it must be revised to take account of antecedents of, say, Christo or Warhol—by no means the same masters! It follows that each critic in effect brings his own personal order out of the chaos of conflicting past events, an act only comparable to God's on the day of creation. Such acts were regularly performed by Berenson, Bode, Wölfflin and their epigones, magisterial figures who stepped forth on cue from the wings onto center stage with dramatic judgments: not Giorgione after all, but still Titian under Giorgione's influence; Amico di Sandi o whom We created, We shall destroy, etc., etc. In the process, they also resolved the otherwise baffling flaw in the logic of all aesthetic lines-of-progress: namely, how and by what standard those masterpieces are to be defined, whose past and present sequence constitutes the line. "What are masterpieces, as distinct from ordinary art? Masterpieces are what Great Masters, as distinct from ordinary artists, do. Who are Great Masters? Great Masters are artists who do masterpieces." Circular argument? Only if you don't add, or won't acknowledge, the coda: "...and the way you identify great masterpieces and so determine who Great Masters are, is to consult Great Authorities, such as...." It is a line of argument that stands in logical succession to the "What is great art? Great art is what great artists do. Who are great artists? Great artists are people who do great art—namely Me," on which was premised (however unacknowledgedly) the earlier "art histories" by Ghiberti the sculptor, Vasari and Reynolds the painters.[11] Only, authority now shifts from practising artist to critic, a process beginning with Johann Winckelmann[12] around 1750—at that moment, i.e. when the element of personal self-expression began to override all other considerations, so that the relationship of Fine Art to society got correspondingly more tenuous, its criteria correspondingly less objective, and artists, as a result, more and more dependent upon what was written about them by critics (to give them their proper name; they were not historians). The temptation for these critics to play god and create Great Artists by their praises and expositions was irresistible. Whence, ultimately, our present scene: the "Painted Word" that Tom Wolfe described; the total confusion between "Great Artist" and "Great Celebrity" that Warhol exemplifies; the creation of a faceless architecture that destroyed the past, by a "tiny handful of professors of the history of architecture" that Norris Smith describes[13]—and our present pressing need for an expanded art-history methodology.

10   Learning to See

Not that the Berensons and Bodes were without lasting impact. Far from it. "Influenced by the demands of the market and the growth of new museums—" to cite James S. Ackerman[14], they

were primarily interested in identifying authorship. Yes, they made mistakes, crossed themselves, but step by step they zeroed in on the artists responsible for the works to the point that all major artists are far better known than they were before, and other techniques are now needed for identification. It is important to distinguish Giogione from Titian even if you are not a connoisseur; a study of patronage would also need access to information of that sort. It is like information gotten from stratification in an archaeology dig; if it establishes fact, one can't sniff at it.

Furthermore, the stylistic terminology worked out for aesthetic line-of-progress, especially as refined by Heinrich Wölfflin[15] between 1888 and 1915 in *Renaissance and Baroque, Classic Art,* and above all the *Principles of Art History,* remain art history's indispensable vocabulary.

Unfortunately, however, there are some debits to set alongside the assets aesthetic line-of-progress bequeathed to art history. Pricing for dealers and collectors of art, for example, is still as much determined by avant-garde positioning in the aesthetic line-of-progress as when Berenson authenticated for Duveen. Most university curricula are organized by reference to this now two-centuries-old line of progress from Greek to Roman to Renaissance to Us, so that Renaissance still keeps pride of place at the core of art-historical faculties at all major universities, next in importance come its direct antecedents and successors—Ancient, Baroque, Modern—with Gothic and Byzantine revolving close around this axis; Oriental and primitive farther out; fartherest of all, away off in deep reaches of outer cold and darkness, arts with effective impact on modern life like television and industrial design and speculatively-built development houses. Slide collections are categorized by "major" and "minor" arts, in terms of this antiquated scheme.

Aesthetic line-of-progress theory too retains some sturdy, even passionate, spokespeople.[16] But increasingly they are on the defensive. The inadequacies of the old theory are just too obvious. To limit the study of art history to those few select objects defined by critics-qua-art-historians not only makes much art criticism in modern times totally meaningless, but also leaves effective use of arts and artifacts in studying the past for cultural anthropologists and geographers. To see in art history no more than a record of alternating ups and downs in artistic taste— "classical to anti-classical to classical again"—is to declare it pointless, and incidentally waste all the very real insights of Wölfflin's principles.[17] For, while aesthetic line-of-progress art history provides lots of picture-books wherewith any so inclined may marvel at how "taste" could differ so much amongst mankind's diverse civilizations, as to why taste should so differ, it offers no clue. This is unsatisfactory. Plainly, there was more to historic arts and artifacts than the expressions of artistic taste which "art" has come to be so predominantly in our times. They also expressed the culture that produced them. Whence art history's second major methodology.

Cultural Expression

ALTHOUGH SIR KENNETH CLARK'S *Civilization* is undoubtedly, at this moment, the best-known exponent of art history as cultural expression, its general principle has been an established art-history methodology at least since the 1920s[18], under the formula *Kunstgeschichte als Geistesgeschichte* ("Art History as Intellectual/Cultural History").[19] Elements of it are detectable, even prominent, already in Winckelmann's mid-18th-century concepts of Greek art and in Giambattista Vico (1668-1744)'s *New Science* of history (1725-30); and Georg Friedrich Hegel (1770-1830)'s cosmological history relies considerably upon art as cultural expression.[20]

The pivotal principle of art history as cultural expression is *Zeitgeist,* "the spirit of an age." All cultures and civilizations at all times have a recognizable essence or controlling spirit which is expressed in everything from clothes to philosophical theories, but most perceptively by Great Artists—those Great Artists, i.e., on whose successive masterpieces across the ages aesthetic line-of-progress art is history is built. The art historian's business thus expands beyond appreciation and identification of masterpieces, to recognizing and expounding how these masterpieces express the culture of their times; one methodology builds on the other.

Arts of many more sorts necessarily come into the art-historian-as-cultural-historian's ambience. Retardataire arts, excluded from aesthetic line-of-progress schemes, become important and interesting kinds of cultural expression. Late Gothic, for instance, is no longer just a dead-end branch off the main line; it's an expression of the persistence of medieval courtly society and Church power alongside the rising mercantile city-state culture which contemporary Renaissance art comparably expresses (though of course never as "good art" as the Renaissance's, which leads to Us). For early American architecture and furniture—a classic case—cultural expression not only justifies any study of the field at all (aesthetic line-of-progress sees the American avant-garde of 1950-75 as culminating a European, not an American, development), but the spread between avant-garde and retardataire styles over the 1700-1860 is an admirable cultural expression of the shift in balance of power which made the North's victory in the Civil War so inevitable.[21]

How far down the scale historians go with retardataire arts varies, of course. Sometimes the methodology is taken to justify studying low arts like folk painting or metalwork or porcelains. Sometimes, only expressions of High Culture have been deemed worthy of study; Aby Warburg's notion of "significant art," for instance, hardly differed from Berenson's.[22] But the principle of cultural expression makes expansion at least theoretically possible.

When "art" is employed to "illustrate" history, cultural expression in varying degrees is usually the methodology. So, for instance, in Weidenfield and Nicholson's *Milestones of History* series; in Holle's *Welt- und Kultur geschichte* series; in *de luxe* editions of Toynbee. Herein, the limitations as well as the advances of cultural expression methodology appear. The problem is, there's still no effective connection between pictures and text—that is to say, no integral connection between art and history. Toynbee illustrated is no more and no less convincing than Toynbee unillustrated; the pictures are merely there, they don't in any way prove the argument. Even when "art" is not something merely added to history books, like the "art, music, and washing extra" of the Mock Turtle's school curriculum, even when genuine efforts are made to use art causally, cultural expression affords no effective means of doing it. Spengler's is the classic case. Spengler was one of the few historians who really knew something about art history. He wrote the *Decline of the West* in Munich, while Wölfflin was at his magisterial height there, and it's quite possible that Spengler's "morphological method" owes something—perhaps a great deal— to Wölfflin's concept of inexorable cyclic progression (if it's inherent in the nature of Art to go through the Renaissance/Baroque cycle, why not the same biological inexorability in all aspects of culture?)[23] Yet Spengler's *Decline*, for all its apparent reliance upon statues as cultural expressions of the Apollonian spirit, music as cultural expression of the Faustian soul, and so forth, in fact uses art chiefly to illustrate points already made, rather than as documentation or evidence for them. The pattern is: first define a cultural characteristic, then find an illustration of that characteristic from art interpreted as cultural expression:

The Egyptian soul saw itself as moving down a narrow and inexorably-prescribed life-path to come to the end before the judges of the dead. Hence the most characteristic constructions of Egyptian architecture are not 'building, but a path enclosed by mighty masonry. The reliefs and paintings appear always as rows which with an impressive compulsion lead the beholder in a different direction.' For the Chinese too, life is a 'way.' But whereas the Egyptian treads to the end a way that is prescribed for him with an inexorable necessity, the Chinese wanders through his world...conducted to...his ancestral tomb not by ravines of stone...but by friendly Nature herself.[24]

Such an argument has no force, as long as it is based on a definition of arts or architecture primarily or largely concerned with "expressing" something, be it individual aesthetic sense, the nature of materials, or the "personalities of great societies." For to assume that arts "express the personality" of a civilization or society[25] presupposes that you already know what that society's "personality" is—in which case, artistic evidence for it is superfluous. Conversely, if you don't predefine a society's personality, you can never prove that what artists express is necessarily it—why should it not just as well be their own personalities or their own views of life? Those not only might well be quite different from their society's, but certainly must be if you equate "expression" in historic arts in any degree with "expression" in modern arts, where originality is automaticaly taken to mean dissent!

It follows that, for all its insights, cultural expression cannot be an effective tool for historical study. It has three basic flaws. First, it has too little concept of arts *doing* anything. It sees them too exclusively as "expressions," mirrors, something to be *looked* at.[26] Second, its internal contradiction: the artist as intuitive genius supremely gifted at perceiving the realities of an age and giving them form, versus the artist as "only an eye," reacting to his/her environment, expressing it in spite of himself/herself. Finally and fundamentally: cultural expression methodology uses a concept of "art" which has been too literally taken over from aesthetic line-of-progress and hence does not take account of the fundamental shift which has occurred since around 1750 in the nature of what is called "art."

Nowadays, "art" means any activity primarily or exclusively concerned with expression—expression of artists' personalities, or feelings, or tastes; expression of the nature of materials, of *Zeitgeist,* of moods. "Art" may therefore be anything claimed to express such things, whether man-made or not: found art, funk, figments of fancy, whatever. But this concept, like the concept of "artists" who "do art," is a relatively modern one. The very word "art" in our modern sense only comes into common use during the Romantic era, c1760-1840. Its origins go back somewhat further, to the later 17th-century development of those concepts of individual distinctiveness which puts words like "self-confidence," "self-esteem," "self-pity" into the language, and altered the meanings of "disposition," "spirits," "temperaments," etc.[27] Earlier, there were no "artists," only "picture-makers," "carvers," "builders," whose particular skills produced corresponding products: pictures, carvings, buildings. Vasari's history of art was not called "Lives of the Most Creative Artists," but "Lives of the Excellent Painters, Sculptors, and Architects" for the very good reason that there was yet no word like our "artists" or "art," and when "creation" was first used to describe what an artist was doing, an analogy was deliberately being made between the "divino" Michelangelo's activities and God's.[28] Earlier, cultural expression was no conscious activity. There was a good deal of personal expression, as Baxandall and others have shown,[29] but no artist in the Renaissance, say, ever sat down like so many modern ones with any deliberate intent to "express the spirit of the age we live in." Yet all too much writing about historic art has assumed they did—assumed, that is, historic art to be a similar activity, and similarly motivated, to what "art" now is. Endless confusions and distortions result.

One example: those constant citations of "twentieth-century art" (i.e., avant-garde Establishment art) as evidence of our civilization being degenerate, for our society going to pieces.

Crudity, barbarism, violence "expressed by the artists of our time," is contrasted to the high ideals "expressed" by Gothic cathedrals" or the orderly tranquillity "expressed by Renaissance painters," whence our dreary and decadent culture is contrasted with the confident exuberance of earlier times. The assumption is that Gothic cathedrals or Renaissance painting "expressed their times" in the same way that productions of modern avant-garde architects and painters do; that historic arts were the same kind of activity, doing the same kind of thing in and for that society in their times, as the 20th century's avant-garde Establishment's primitivism, minimal art, or the new Brutalism do in ours. But the assumption is false. Comparisons are totally irrelevant between a modern sculpture, say, made to be put in a museum and to enhance its creator's reputation for daring expression of the nature of materials or movement or whatever, and a sculpture made for a Gothic cathedral by some craftsman working in fundamentally the same anonymity as the designer of a modern aircraft—i.e. whose primary consideration was that the object work, functionally and symbolically, and for whom "beauty" or "expressiveness" was, when conscious at all, never more than adjuncts to that end. Renaissance artists were not in fact expressing realities of their times but its ideal expectations.[30]

There is nothing unique about an age which, like ours, seems desperate, chaotic, violent, out of joint to those who live in it; all ages have seemed like that to those who lived in them. Whenever people have undertaken to "express their times," the results have been about the same.[31] Conclusions based upon comparisons of modern avant-garde expressions with historic arts therefore distort history. Art can be used for objective historical research only by keeping firmly in mind that, whether or not there are differences between the forms of what we call "art" nowadays and historic arts, their functions were fundamentally different—in the same sense that a hoe is different from a golf-club, not because there is much difference in form, as because the two were made to do quite different things.[32] But this now goes beyond cultural expression. This is a methodology based upon social function. This is the third of the art-historical methodologies and the one whose proper business it is to relate artifacts to history.

Social Function

ART HISTORY employing the principle of social function is not different in kind from art history based upon the principle of cultural expression or aesthetic line-of-progress. It is simply a further step, an expansion of methodology. Its operative principle is the uses of arts and artifacts in society—what they were intended for by those who commissioned them, in addition to what significance they may have for us today, either as reflections of social values in the past or as aesthetic objects in the present; in addition to whatever component of artistic expression they may have.

Full recognition of social function as a new methodology came only desultorily. Its first real exponent was the mid-19th-century Swiss historian Jacob Burckhardt.[33] But for a long while thereafter art history, for a variety of reasons, went in another direction.[34] Burckhardt's great pupil Henrich Wölfflin revered him, dedicated books to him, but was frankly not interested in factors "extraneous to artistic creation" like patrons and social needs.[35] Wilhelm Worringer's 1908 *Abstraktion und Einfühlung* (Abstraction and Empathy) was a great sensation, extravagantly praised for showing how the factors determining how artists created form shifted from "19th-century materialist" (utilitarian purpose, raw materials, technics) to the 20th century's prime factor, an "impulse to abstraction."[36] Few objected, or even pointed out, that historic art forms were not and never could be solely determined by artists, no matter what factors were preeminent amongst them; that social circumstances and patrons' expectations have at least as much, and often more, weight. But such objections, and with them any systematic theory of social function, were not formulated until the mid-1950s, when Gregor Paulsson put out his little treatise *Die Soziale Dimension der Kunst.*[37] Therein was summarized Paulsson's *estetik miljömorfologie,* hitherto scattered through essays, mostly in Swedish, and his four-volume art-history text, also in Swedish, *Konstens Varldshistoria.*[38]

Paulsson, like most art historians of his day with serious interests in the relations of art to society, tended to equate social function in arts rather closely with leftish political programs.[39] More than others, he had begun to realize the central principle in the methodology of social function—that what we call "art" today is a different kind of activity from what we call historic arts. And this is the crux of the whole matter; this is the *pons asinorum* that must be crossed for any fruitful research in social function.

Effective use of art history based on social function for the study of history is only possible with a realization that what we call art today does not perform the social functions of historic arts·

With every passing generation the connection between the arts and art historian/critics has become ever more tenuous, since Winckelmann's time. But it took the avant-garde Establishment's extremes of the 1960s and early '70s to make the distinction decisively: "modern" art and "traditional" arts differ not in time, but in essence; in kind. It's not a matter of given arts or artifacts made by modern avant-gardists necessarily looking different from those made by artists in earlier times, but of their *doing* different things in and for society. Only when and as we are fully aware that the primary concern of historic arts, instead of being primarily or exclusively vehicles for the sensibilities and expression of artists, was with fulfilling certain specific and objectively recognizable functions and for society, can we begin to perceive historic arts more or less in the same way as their original makers perceived them (recapturing the exact and full outlook of earlier generations is of course impossible). And only then can historic arts and artifacts be seen as the invaluable instruments that they properly are for the study and recreation of history.

Historic arts had four social functions, easily and plainly recognizable once you look for them:

Substitute Imagery: Historic arts made substitute images of things or ideas whose memory it was desirable for some reason to preserve.

Illustration: Historic arts so related substitute images as to tell stories or record events.

Beautification: Historic arts deliberately shaped artifacts so as to make their function(s) plain to individual beholders, and thence to communities at large (i.e. the more intelligible, the more "beautiful"); and/or added substitute images, symbols, or illustrations to artifacts so as to link them to beholders' experience and to the historical experience of communities: in sum, historic arts "beautified" in the sense of humanizing artifacts in particular and environments in general.

Persuasion/Conviction: Historic arts deliberately "styled" artifacts so as to evoke associations with, or create metaphors of, ideologies and presuppositions (convictions) which underlie all social institutions. Historic arts thus were vehicles and instruments for transmitting those accepted values, ethics, belief systems, upon which ultimately depends the endurance of city, State and family. Historic architecture, especially, could be defined as the art of creating large permanent three-dimensional metaphors of "patterns of human interrelatedness." [40]

Historic arts had a fifth social function, equally plainly recognizable but not so easy to define with precision:

"Artistic Expression": This is not and cannot be a "social function" of the same order as the preceding four. It is not something objectively identifiable, that society cannot do without. Rather, it is a way of carrying out the other social functions, a particular skill or aptitude which becomes progressively more self-conscious as time and history move on.

Humanists of the 15th and 16th centuries, with whose writings modern art history begins, did not wrestle with the question of "What Is Art?" because for another two centuries to come no such word as art would exist, to cover the totality of activities like painting, sculpture, architecture, metalwork, etc. They described how painting, sculpture or architecture rationalized sight, ordered experience and so deserved to be called noble and humane activities rather than mere crafts; but they always, incidentally and implicitly, took for granted that these activities began as crafts; that artists began by learning skills; that it was by these skills and their products that "arts" were definable. Thus they talked about effective naturalistic representation; about story-telling; about pleasing spectators; about communicating with audiences. They talked on occasion too about personal styles, and about beauty; and they insisted that art which lacked these qualities, which had no other concern than to fulfil basic social functions, would be "mean." But they never thought of divorcing personal styles or beauty from the actual artifacts which embodied them.[41] When they said that painting or sculpture or architecture became "noble"—i.e. distinct from artifacts—insofar as they "revealed the mind of the artist," they did not mean that the artist's *only* business was to reveal his mind. Alberti, Leonardo, Michelangelo all agreed that in noble art "practise must always be based on sound theory"—

and vice versa. And so indeed for hundreds of years to come an obvious distinction could be and was made between Low Arts and High Art. Pamphlets and prints, limnings and signboards, and like images which did little or nothing more than reproduce appearances, or illustrate, or persuade at the level of a lowest common social denominator, were Low Arts. Distinguished from these were High Arts—not because High Art had no social function, or different social functions, but because it performed the same functions as Low Arts with whatever constituted "artistic expression" for the time and place—originality, moving masses, spatial composition, assisting iconography, brushwork, etc. The measure of the difference in the way these social functions were performed was the standard of Great Art. So it was until about a hundred years ao.

Then, very rapidly, just around the twenty years 1840-1860, assumptions about what "art" involved began to shift. "Revealing the mind of the artist" began to override all other considerations, and soon became an end in itself.[42] Theory superseded practise until "art" was concerned only with "art." Painters painted pictures to show other painters how to paint. Poets wrote poems only other poets read. Musicians arranged sound patterns to impress other musicians. Novelists began writing novels about novel-writing.

Obviously "art" of this kind has nothing to do with the older kind of "art" defined by social function. It dismisses substitute imagery and indeed all concern for an objectively perceived world. It abhors illustration. Since Courbet, it specifically abjures concern for beautification in favor of a quasi-scientific search for the Reality of things, conducted by intuition beyond the bounds of rational analysis. And its communication is of a radically different sort—the artist's personal views expressed in so allusive, incidental, accidental and solipsistic a way as to be for all intents and purposes private. Consummation of these trends comes in "art-as-art." In Renaissance times artists claimed higher social status than artisans because of their "philosophy." Mastery of both theoretical and natural philosophy—applied rational, visual symbolism and practical skills like bronzecasting, pageant-organization, perspective rendering and the like made them valuable to society. "Art-as-art" is the precise opposite: "a creation that revolutionizes creation and judges itself by its destruction. Artists-as-artists value themselves for what they have gotten rid of and for what they refuse to do."[43]

The forces behind such a drastic change are irrelevant to explore insofar as the methodology of social function is concerned. What matters for its understanding, is to realize that the change has occurred. Unless you understand what has happened—unless you grasp fully and finally that the difference between the activity called "art" today and what went on under that name in history has nothing to do with outward forms—nothing to do with abstraction and empathy versus naturalism and objectivity—but is a difference in what these activities *do* in and for society, all the otherwise brilliant insights in the world are wasted on futile conclusions drawn from comparing hoes to golf clubs, analyzing croquet-mallets in order to study sledge-hammers and maces. The change affects perceptions in every area of 20th-century arts. Most manifestly, and most crucially, it affects perceptions of those arts generally called "popular," but better, "popular commercial." For there, the four practical social functions of traditional arts survive.

For any understanding of 20th-century arts it is crucial to recognize that the traditional social functions of historic arts survive in modern popular/commercial arts.

Now that avant-garde arts have become an Establishment and taken more or less exclusive possession of the word "art," have the old categories all become obsolete, except for "artistic expression"? Has society dispensed with all those other needs which arts functioned to satisfy over the last six thousand years?

Of course not. Arts with those functions are no more dispensable frills now than they ever were. No more now than ever have their practitioners had to write treatises explaining their importance, because it has always been self-evident. Above all particular functions, historic arts had the primordial function of helping individuals find themselves, know who they are. That need is as basic as ever. From time immemorial, substitute imagery helped humans realize—in the original sense of "become aware of reality"—their world. It helps children do that still. We still need illustration to clarify experience, and suffer when we lack it. Only the barrenest of societies could dispense with beautification to bring order, hence meaning and pleasure, out of existential experience. No society could even survive without arts of persuasion/conviction to transmit established values from one generation to another. If what is called "art" cannot or will not satisfy these needs, other agents must and will be found.

So it comes about that the functions of historic painting, sculpture and architecture are still being carried out in modern times, but by other, popular/commercial, arts.

And this is the crux, the very foundation, of an effective methodology for art history based upon social function. Many art historians of great stature and learning cannot, for some reason, yet bring themselves to admit that any art wherein "artistic expression" is not paramount, can be "art" of the sort art historians ought to be concerned with. They point—very justly— to the fact that historic arts, what they study in the past, always had this quality. What they cannot point to in the past is any arts which had this quality and nothing but. They cannot, in other words, point to any past art which is the same kind of thing as avant-garde Establishment arts have become. By contrast, it's obvious that popular/commercial arts *are* the successors of historic arts in every respect *but* artistic expression (and in some case they have that too). Inescapable conclusion: what defenders of High Art call art today is no more a descendant of historic High Arts than popular/commercial arts are. What defenders of High Culture call culture today—avant-garde Establishment arts, i.e.,—no more constitute anything like the High Cultures of historic ages than popular/commercial arts do. Without an acceptance of this fact, and of its implications, there can be no genuine understanding of the methodology of social function.[44]

Conversely, with that understanding, all sorts of hitherto vexing problems fade into disposable side issues. The problem, for example, of always having to end art history on some anticlimax, i.e., the lastest fad in the avant-garde art world. If art history were not only the story, as it is now, of artistic expression from Ur to Raphael to Rauschenberg (O! What a fall is here, Horatio!), but also of pictorial symbolism from Pyramids to photography, or patronage from Perikles to PBS, it would be a lot better balanced than it is. Instead of a uniform precipitous decline from a glorious past, art history would have diverse endings, sometimes with arts which perform traditional social functions better than ever before. Our society has available, in photography and photographic processes of exact reproduction, substitute imagery of unprecedented power and accuracy. We get scientific and cultural information disseminated on a mass basis with a clarity and speed unheard-of before: movies, TV, newspaper illustrations.[45] (That they can deceive with unprecedented plausibility is of course also true; but that's the converse of advance in all ages.) As William Ivins was among the first to point out,[46]

The historians of [art] printing have devoted their attention to the making of fine and expensive books, and in so doing they have overlooked the great function of books as purveyors of information ....in the 19th century informative books usefully illustrated with exactly repeatable pictorial statements became available to the mass of mankind in western Europe and America. The result was the greatest revolution in practical thought and accomplishment that has ever been known...."

Pursuing the same line of thought, television and movies are obviously far more effective vehicles for drama than the legitimate stage could ever be (everyone in the audience can have closeups and long shots, intimate emotions as well as rhetorical gestures, etc.). Political cartoons are far more effective instruments for promoting social cohesion than clumsy Baroque allegories. Modern superhighways are far greater instruments for binding States together than the old Persian Royal Road or the imperial Roman Roads could ever be.[47] And so on. Or at least modern popular/commercial arts could do all these things better, were their social function more clearly understood and means of accomplishing them explicitly taught.

First, we'd have to get over the everlasting But-is-it-Art? syndrome. Are these arts—well, you know, *creative*? Well, if by creative arts you mean vehicles exclusively or primarily used for artistic self-expression, obviously not. But if by creative you mean prolific in invention of new forms—well, photography has been since its inception the chief source for new forms for avant-garde painting.[48] Whatever humane proportions and meaningful shapes have survived the desolation of our urban environments by the last couple of generations of self-elected Form-Givers and Planners[49] have been transmitted by those far less pretentious Form-Finders who have devised our Popular/Commercial arts and architecture.[50] Only recently have we begun to recognize that the modern culture expressed in arts like these is very far from the inexorable disintegration which Wölfflin's or Spengler's or Toynbee's laws, derived from avant-garde cultural expression, suggest.[51]

But popular/commercial arts are far more than cultural expression. Precisely because whatever artistic expression they manifest is subordinated, as in traditional arts, to social function, it is in them that records of our times are to be found comparable to the records of the past which historical arts provide. For insistence upon social function as the foundation of anything called "Arts" has been typical of all societies, at all times, at all places, until ours. It is *our* concept of art as expressive activity with no specific social function that is unique. Only in our times could someone have written like Robert Motherwell in 1951, "Every intelligent painter carries the whole culture of modern painting in his head. It is his real subject, of which everything he paints is...a critique, and everything he says is a gloss." Obviously painters of this sort, however intelligent, are not going to satisfy the kinds of needs and functions in and for society which in other times and places were handled by Reynoldses or Raphaels or Sung scroll painters or stained-glass-makers or Greek vase-decorators. That social function is handled now by popular/commercial artists whose work, because it so satisfied the 20th century's social needs, constitutes the record of 20th-century life corresponding to those earlier arts.

You can see this change of function reflected in the kind of arts useful in illustrating history. Still in Louis XIV's time painting and sculpture in Versailles performed their traditional functions, and so they can be used as a record of his age. By the Revolution of 1789 this situation is already beginning to change; by the revolutions of 1848 and 1871 it has changed completely and nobody thinks of using anything other than prints, posters, pageantry of all kinds, to illustrate them.[52] Avant-garde arts belong in histories *of* art. If you want to write about history *in* art, then for our times, the documents to use are its popular/commercial arts. Proper understanding of popular/commercial arts begins with full and constant realization of the fact that they perform different social functions from avant-garde art. Thus, the faint praise one sometimes (all too often!) hears for this or that popular/commercial "artistic expression"—i.e., grudging admissions that they might sometimes in some respects be comparable to avant-garde art— puts them in a totally false position, judged on wrong-headed premises. Whereas artistic expression is incidental to them, it's all that avant-garde arts have. Whenever I hear confessions like,

"Well, maybe some TV commercials are art; they have a lot of originality sometimes   ...." it reminds me of a young Louisiana graduate student who picked me up hitchhiking many years ago now, and said in conversation, "Y'know, I don't mind *all* nigras. I'd even give one of 'em a ride—a'course, so long's he wa'nt *too* black...." This is not really an open-minded attitude.

Nor are popular/commercial arts significant because they happen to catch the eye of some avant-garde Establishment figure and get used as a motif. "Pop art" has nothing to do with any appreciation of the real significance of popular culture. It's just a whim, a toying with yet another novelty, another variety of formalism, a minor manifestation of the art-is-what-artists-say-it-is syndrome. Popular/commercial arts are significant because they perform significant social functions in and for society—*that* is the beginning of all serious study of them.

Even if their functions in contemporary society were their only interest, study of popular/commercial arts would be a serious scholarly occupation. But they are much more. The implications of their social functions for the present-day practise and theory of arts and architecture are fundamental and far-reaching. Likewise for art history; for all history.

Understand the social functions of popular/commercial arts, and it becomes obvious how the later 20th century has come to have two kinds of art, each deficient in the other's qualities. A remedy for this situation becomes obvious, too. On the one hand we have an avant-garde art of extraordinary sensibility, fine feel for materials and spatial relations and optical effects, but, for all intents and purposes, lacking any really effective relationship to society.[53] On the other, popular/commercial arts carrying out traditional social functions of historic arts, often more effectively than ever before, certainly indispensable to society; yet rarely rising in artistic expression much above crude and banal levels. Plainly, the imperative task for art schools of the early 1980s should be to put these sundered parts back together.[54] Architectural schools need to consider reintroducing an intelligent study of those eclectic styles with associative values which the Bauhaus blitz banished from them thirty-odd years ago, in the interests of their graduates' employment and a humane environment alike.[55]

Understand the social functions of popular/commercial arts, and the need for some revision of main-line art history will become obvious, too. A "History of Art from Cave-men to Picasso" makes little sense when you reflect that whatever function caves may have served in Palaeolithic or Neolithic life, art galleries for edifying leisured sensibilities surely was never one of them.[56]

Somewhere along the line this kind of survey—it's of course the aesthetic line-or-progress only slightly modified—starts talking about a different kind of activity altogether from the one it started with. Avant-garde arts of the 1970s descend from historic arts insofar as artistic expression is concerned; but that is only one of the traditional social functions of the activity historically called art. All the rest are carried on by popular/commercial arts, so that a "History of Art from Cave-Man to Photographer," or a "History of Architecture from Megaliths to Mobile Homes" would be more rational.

Most of all—once understand how popular/commercial arts function in response to social needs, and you also understand how historic acts were similarly created in response to the needs and demands of *their* societies. And once realize then, how they were not so much reflections of the spirit of their times as tools for sustaining and moulding that spirit, instruments for perpetuating and transmitting ideas and mental attitudes, and it must be self-evident that historic acts, properly so understood, embody the convictions and basic presuppositions of their times in forms which reveal the basic thinking processes involved. Arts so understood, so considered, are primary, crucial, essential data for historical study. There is nothing comparable to them for objectivity, because their evidence is inherent rather than surface. They are the record of what people *did* rather than what they dictated in documents; they are evidence for what they really believed, rather than what they wanted others to think.

This is the reply to one continuing suspicion of social-function methodology, common amongst historians trained to be suspicious of any theory not fully supported by written documents, who complain, rightly enough, that the motives attributed to commissioners and executors of artifacts can't always be proved. So Burckhardt asserts that Italian Renaissance art was made for propaganda purposes, to glorify political upstarts; where are the documents to prove that? Von Simson intimates that Gothic cathedrals and the *Chanson de Roland* alike owe their new "styles" (of architecture, of poetry) to an intent to promote certain socio-political interests of the Capetian monarchy; how do you document that? So it's been suggested that the Chateau Frontenac and Empress hotels were placed where they are in Quebec and Victoria respectively so that anyone approaching Canada, whether from east or west, would see first of all a statement of Anglophone capitalist supremacy in place of the French architectural symbols which stood on those sites before; can boardroom minutes of the Canadian Pacific Railway company, which built these hotels, be produced to show that they were sited for any such reason? Patently not. To all objections along these lines, one may confidently reply: throughout life and history, people don't always give the real reasons for their actions, much less write them down. Thus a big American corporation may say that it commissions a skyscraper by Mies van der Rohe because steel-and-glass-cage construction is more economical than masonry-sheathed structures with cornices and columns and other allusions to the official ideology of the American Republic, whereas in fact (a fact known to those giving such an explanation, before anyone else could be aware of it) Mies's insistence on having everything specially lathed to look simple makes his the most expensive kind of construction available. The real reason for its appeal is perhaps its more "scientific" look (not to mention subconscious attraction for images of Power, and the like). The great advantage of the social-function methodology is that evidence for motives is usually in the artifacts themselves. One is not arguing about the meanings of words in documents; one is simply pointing to the obvious explanation for what is *there*: it's *not* cheaper to build Miesian, therefore the proferred explanation *cannot* be true; it's not just happenstance that the chateau-style hotels stand where they do, because conspicuously better, more convenient sites were available; there is no liturgical reason for wanting higher and lighter cathedrals, therefore devising the Gothic style cannot have been in response to liturgical demands, and certainly not for structural reasons—Romanesque cathedrals rarely fell down, whereas Gothic ones did frequently; the Italian merchant-princes did not, after all, *need* new palaces and a different kind of art for any practical purpose, and to say their taste changed just begs the question—what made it change?

It's a matter of reading artifacts in terms of what they *did*; so read, they provide throughout history a basic record of developing thought and ideas, all the more revealing because it is integral, because it is unselfconscious, because it was in no sense intended as "art."

"Developing," indeed, is just what the record of thought and ideas presented in historic arts seems to be. For if you analyze historic arts in terms of social function, what seems to emerge is a pattern of successively appearing functions. To summarize the argument of the last section of this book: in the beginning, not all social functions are evident; they appear one after another, at least in demonstrable form.

Substitute imagery is the first distinctively human activity—something animals never do—to be provable in history. But substitute imagery is the only social function whose appearance is indubitable in prehistoric caves and earlier. There is no unequivocal evidence for illustration—the use of a base-line as an obviously deliberate device for relating substitute images, or for mimetic design deliberately relating a present form to a past one, until c4000. Beautification, in the historic sense of identifying use and humanizing artifacts, is not unequivocally demonstrable in arts before the first millennium B.C. And not until the first centuries A.D. can deliberate use of styles be demonstrated so as to promote abstract bodies of ideas or ideologies. What all this implies for human development is interesting, to say the least, particularly when you consider that for each social function a corresponding mental ability or level of creative growth is implied.

But there is even more: historically, these social functions seem to appear not only successively, but also everywhere simultaneously (i.e., everywhere that there is an economy and technology capable of sustaining arts at that level).[57] When the vast antiquity of prehistoric arts in the Pyrenees and southwest France was first confirmed, they were assumed to be unique. Now examples comparable in time and the social function of substitute imagery, demonstrating therefore a comparable level of conceptual thought, have been found elsewhere. When Susa A pottery showed that around 4000 unequivocal base-line painting and mimetic forms had been perfected, demonstrating the social function of illustration beyond all doubt, and hence of developed analogical thought, it was assumed to be unique, evidence perhaps for the Garden of Eden and the creation of Man as homo sapiens. Now comparable artifacts have been recognized from the same era everywhere, demonstrating that illustration was being done and human capacity for analogical thought being utilized at about the same time universally. So with beautification: Greek arts of the "Golden Age" (c600-400) are only the most effective examples of arts with this social function, not unique. Greek thought of the first millenium B.C. is only the best-known and most probing demonstration of a new level of analytical thinking that can be demonstrated in other developed civilizations of the age as well. Likewise, arts of conscious persuasion/conviction, which deliberately "style" artifacts so as to evoke associations with, or create metaphors of, ideological presuppositions, are not unequivocally demonstrable in arts before the early Christian era; but then the same social function, and the abstract causal thought necessary to accomplish it, is demonstrable throughout Buddhist realms as well.

The methodology of social function need not be followed to all or any such extremes. But it is the indispensable tool for making art history a significant historical discipline. And an understanding of popular/commercial arts is its indispensable beginning.

Notes to Section I:

[1] "The modern science of history," wrote Joseph Vogt in the opening chapter of *Wege zum historischen Universum* (Stuttgart, 1964, pp. 11-12, 18-19), "came out of a reaction against the Enlightenment kind of history. Chroniclers, philologists, researchers into law and linguistics, alike confronted mighty new territories of knowledge....The first attempts to recognize the framework of the total history of mankind and to grasp its significance were made in our century by philosophers and sociologists. New disciplines, like cultural morphology and cultural sociology, grew out of this undertaking...." Throughout Vogt's survey, one discipline is conspicuously missing. To this investigation art history appears to have contributed, for all intents and purposes, nothing. Not because it's too new; art history goes back at least to Winckelmann in the 18th century (1-12). Rather, because of a general assumption that art history is about aesthetic reactions to "art masterpieces," and has nothing to do with politics, religion, philosophy or economics. An assumption, I fear, all too often based upon observed practise. But far less often, let us hasten to add, than conventional historians often assume.

[2]A random example: Karl Löwith in *Meaning in History* (Chicago, 1949) treats Jacob Burckhardt's *Considerations on World History* as a milestone in intellectual history. But wasn't Burckhardt also an art historian—in fact, a founder of social function methodology? (q.v., fn. I-33). According to Löwith, art history was Burckhardt's "escape": "Disgusted by contemporary history, Burckhardt escaped to Italy to write his *Cicerone...*" (p. 23).

Second random example: Writing about Spengler, one historian who really does make considerable use of art (q.v. p.13), Harvard history professor H. Stuart Hughes says only, "Munich, where Spengler had chosen to live, was a recognized artistic and literary center. For Spengler's appreciation of painting, sculpture, and architecture, his trips to Italy, as in the case of so many young Germans, doubtless gave the decisive impetus..." (*Oswald Spengler*, New York, 1962, p. 57). Much of Professor Hughes' research concerns the literary sources of Spengler's historical and intellectual ideas; that his ideas about art might also have come from reading books (by art historians) simply doesn't seem to have occurred to him.

Third random sample: The introduction to *Man and God in Art and Ritual* by S.G.F. Brandon, distinguished professor of comparative religion at the University of Manchester (New York, 1975). "This is a pioneering essay in a field of study that has for too long been neglected by scholars," he begins. Noting, rightly enough, that historians of religion have generally been preoccupied with literary evidence, so that "too often it has been forgotten that man expressed his religious ideas in art and ritual long before he learned to write," he then concludes, "Help can be obtained from historians of art on styles, techniques, and art traditions; but the historian of religions is left to his own devices in evaluating the religious signficance of a cult image or a tomb-fresco." Well, up to a point, Lord Copper. Such colossal misunderstanding of a whole sister discipline has for consequence that ' Professor Brandon speculates, as if for the first time, on problems endlessly debated in journals of scholarly art history and long since solved.

[3]Lorenzo Ghiberti (1378-1455)'s *Commentarii* and Giorgio Vasari (1511-1574)'s *Lives of the Excellent Painters, Sculptors and Architects* (first edition 1550) are generally considered the beginnings of art history. Cf. Elizabeth Gilmore Holt, *Literary Sources of Art History* (Princeton, 1947), *loc. cit.*

[4] Wilhelm Bode (1845-1929, ennobled as "von Bode" in 1914) throughout his long career practised art dealing as well as connoisseurship. First appointed a curator at Berlin's Kaiser-Friedrich-Museum in 1872, he eventually became director-general and a kind of museum czar throughout Germany, renowned as creator of modern museum techniques and a condottiere among art collectors. His clockwork-like noon walks were one of the sights of Berlin in the 1920s.

Bernard Berenson (1865-1959), likewise a celebrity already in the 1920s, remained until his death a great American success story. His father was a Lithuanian Jewish immigrant who trundled a pushcart around Boston, scrimped to send Bernard to Harvard; there a studiously cultivated aesthetic personality made the contacts necessary to uncork Bostonian philanthropy. Commissions from Mrs. Jack Gardner laid the foundations of Berenson's fortune; expertise at a percentage for Joseph Duveen, premier dealer of the time, consolidated it, and established "B.B." 's villa of I Tatti outside Florence as a place of pilgrimage for Great Americans during his lifetime, and thereafter, a center for Renaissance art studies under Harvard's aegis.

The reverent *B.B. Treasury: a selection...from the most celebrated humanist and art historian of our times* (Hanna Kiel, ed. introduction by Berenson protégé John Walker, director of the National Gallery in Washington) conveys the tone of adulation surrounding Berenson very well (New York, 1964). The most objective biography seems to be Sylvia Sprigge's *Berenson* (London: 1962).

[5]*Historians' Fallacies* (New York, 1970), pp. 137-38.

[6]Janson's breadth of scholarship is demonstrated not only in his *Sixteen Studies* (New York, 1976) but even more in his slashing "Comments on Beardsley's 'The Aesthetic Point of View'," in *Metaphilosophy*, I, 1, January 1970; Gombrich's, in his two classics, *Art and Illusion (London, 1959)* and *In Search of Cultural History* (Oxford, 1969), in the latter of which he explicitly states that "*Kulturgeschichte* [read: historicism, aesthetic line-of-progress] has been built, knowingly and unknowingly, on Hegelian foundations which have crumbled." (p. 6)

[7]There is a brilliant essay on this subject by Fred E. H. Schroeder in *Outlaw Aesthetics* (Bowling Green: Popular Press, 1976).

30　Learning to See

[8]Sir Banister Flight Fletcher's preface to the original edition of *History of Architecture on the Comparative Method* is instructive. "My descriptions and criticisms are mainly from personal observations of the world's greatest monuments," it begins. How, precisely, the "greatest monuments" are defined is no concern of ours. Presumably it is by the same method Philip Johnson, years later in the *Inland Architect* for 1972, used in defining them: Great Architecture is architecture that gives Great Architects a thrill upon entering. Who are Great Architects? Great Architects are the builders of Great Architecture.... Or writers about it, in Banister Fletcher's case.

[9]Fischer, *Historians' Fallacies, op. cit.* The quote is from Berenson's *Aesthetics and History* (New York, 1949). Both he and his great admirer John Walker forgot he wrote this, apparently, when Walker reverently quoted as an example of Berenson's catholicity, a pronouncement from Vallombrosa on July 1, 1954: " 'So far as I can recollect it never occurred to me to make time or place, nation or period, a standard of value...'." (J. Walker, ed., *The Berenson Treasury*, p. 326).

[10]An amusing account of these and many other episodes can be found in the chapter "B.B." in S.N. Behrman's *Duveen*, New York, 1951, pp. 147-189. The reverential atmosphere so often misting accounts of Berenson is here dissipated. "Amico di Sandro" was a creation of Berenson's exquisite connoisseurship, to whom he attributed a mounting *oeuvre* over the years of work that did not quite fit his preconceived ideas of Botticelli's style; pictures were sold as by "Amico di Sandro" at mounting prices. Suddenly Berenson reversed himself, dismembered his creation, restored the pieces to various other painters. The Amico di Sandro market collapsed. Even more disastrous, from dealer Duveen's point of view, was Berenson's pronouncement that the Allendale Nativity (now in the National Gallery, Washington) which Duveen was trying to flog as Giorgione (rare, costly!) was Titian (plentiful, comparatively moderate): "Ten or twelve years ago the light dawned on me," Berenson wrote, "it must be Titian's... but only half out of the egg, the other half still in the Giorgione formula.... it is my deepest conviction that this attribution will ultimately win through." Some years later an article in *The Art Bulletin* published original drawings for the Allendale Nativity in Windsor Castle. They were by Giovanni Bellini.

[11]Variations on this theme are limitless. Leslie Fiedler, e.g.: "Literature is what is taught in classes of literature. What's taught in classes in literature? Literature. It's a perfectly circular definition." (*Firing Line* transcript taped at WJCT-TV, Jacksonville, Florida, 15 November 1974; host William F. Buckley, Jr.) How do you identify a great university? By the great professors who teach at it. How do you identify great professors? By the fact that they teach at our greatest universities. In this sense, what Harold Rosenberg was first to label "the great con game" of avant-garde Establishment is indeed, wittingly or not, a cultural expression of our age.

[12]Johann J. Winckelmann (1717-1768), for all practical purposes the first art historian who was not an artist, the first whose writings about art history were not fundamentally collections of anecdotes about artists' lives and opinions about taste. Holt, *op. cit.*, pp. 522 ff., gives a convenient excerpt from the work that made Winckelmann famous, *Gedanken über die Nachahmung der grieschischen Werke in Malerei* (Dresden, 1755). Rarely indeed has there been such an assemblage of falsehoods, deliberate and accidental; mispresentations; and general drivel, all deriving from the unchallenged axiom, "To take the ancients for models is our only way to become great...." A useful critical analysis is provided by Ludwig Curtius, *Johann Joachim Winckelmann*, Bad Godesberg, 1968.

[13]"Millenary Folly: The Failure of an Eschatology," in *On Art & Architecture in the Modern World*, American Life Foundation, Watkins Glen, N.Y. 1972.

[14]Letter to the author, 1 September 1978. Professor Ackerman's many constructive criticisms of social function methodology in general and this section of the present book in particular, are most gratefully acknowledged, especially since he is not, how shall we put it?, wholeheartedly in accord with either. I am all the more appreciative for his taking the time to comment at length on an earlier draft of this section.

[15]Heinrich Wölfflin (1864-1945)'s five principles, first published in 1915 (*Kuntsgeschchtliche Grundbegriffe*, Basel, 1915), went through many later editions and translations and made him one of the most, possibly *the* most influential art historian of his time. Yet he departed from his mentor Burckhardt's example, as Gregor Paulsson pointed out in his keen analysis (*Die Soziale Dimension der Kunst* [Bern, 1955, p. 12]): "Wölfflins Begriffe isolieren das Kunstwerk von den, mit ihm gleichzeitigen anderen geschichtlichen

Erscheinungen...." Fritz Strich, *Zu Heinrich Wölfflins Gedächtnis* (Bern, 1958) gives a powerful picture of Heinrich Wölfflin the seigneurial professor of *Kunstwissenschaft* at Munich.

[16]The current *Defensor Fidei* is Mark Roskill, a very good art historian who, it is to be hoped, will soon realize that his practise is far better than the principles he professes. His *What is Art History?* (London, 1976) is pure latter-day Berensoniana: "Art is luxury. It is not one of the basic needs of the human race," says he, for one instance. "The kind of paintings discussed in this book have always appealed to, and been appreciated by, a wealthy and privileged minority...if art is a luxury, art history must be a luxury of luxuries—the icing on the very top of the cake."

[17]"Wölfflin posited a law of development *within* the formative imagination, a cyclic theory to account for the parallelism to be discerned between the visual arts of any self-contained period, as well as for the alternation of certain generally distinctive characteristics from one period to another. He formulated five pairs of contrary concepts—the opposite poles, as it were, between which the artistic spirit oscillates: (1) From *linear* to *painterly*. (2) From *plane* to *recession*. (3) From *closed form* to *open form*. (4) From *multiplicity* to *unity*. (5) *Absolute clarity* and *relative clarity* of the subject." (Herbert Read, introduction of Peter and Linda Murray's translation of Wölfflin's *Classic Art*, New York, 1953, p. vi.)

So what? Why should such a change occur? How can you explain why it happens only in certain places and classes, and not elsewhere? Why was the north tower of Chartres and King's College Chapel in Cambridge being built in Flamboyant Gothic at the same moment that the High Renaissance was climaxing in Italy with Raphael's Stanze and Michelangelo's Sistine Ceiling? Following Wölfflin's principles through history is like travelling along a train-track so blinkered as to reveal only the track ahead, unaware whether you are travelling through forest or desert, winter or summer.

Consider patronage, and absurdities multiply. "See here, Watteau, I don't believe I much care for this last picture of yours. Too—what shall I say? fragile. Pastellish, Diaphanous. I like my Venuses solider. Brighter. Like Rubens's *Judgement of Paris,* say." "Most frightfully sorry, my dear Count, but you see, Rubens is out of fashion now." "Bosh! *I* set fashions here." "Well, my Lord, it can't be done anyway, because there's a law says I can't." "What law is that, Watteau?" "Professor Wölfflin's, my Lord. He has stated that art must progress from Baroque to Rococo. Rubens was Baroque. I'm Rococo. So you see, it's impossible for me to paint like Rubens." "And just who is this Professor Wölfflin?" "Well you see, my Lord, he's not born yet. He's due to be born a hundred and fifty years from now. And he—" "Watteau, if there's one thing I cawn't abide, it's a cheeky footman. Report to the rack ... ''

[18]Actually, Sir Kenneth is a comparative late-comer to this fold. Earlier books of his like *The Gothic Revival* (1935), *Rembrandt* (Wrightsman lectures, New York University, 1964) or *The Nude in Art* come close to typifying aesthetic line-of-progress. Only recently has he come out directly, as in a *New York Review of Books* article for 24 November 1977, to remind readers that

"Berenson and Bode never considered what contemporary patrons, guilds, princes, or ecclesiastical bodies wanted from their artists. And one reason for this was that Renaissance patrons of all sorts wanted something almost incredibly different from what we want today. Instead of an aesthetic specimen in a glass case they wanted a symbol, or complex of symbols, which should express their thoughts and aspirations. By the mid-19th century no one (except Ruskin) thought symbolically."

[19]*Kunstgeschichte als Geistesgeschichte* was published posthumously in Munich, 1924, as a collection of essays by Max Dvořák (1874-1921). Successor in 1905 to Franz Wickhoff and Alois Riegl in the chair of art history at Vienna, influenced also by Dilthey, Dvořak embarked around 1916 on a monumental study of universal history as a dialectal process manifested by interaction of naturalistic and idealistic styles in art. He was thinking, of course, of the seemingly inexorable "march of the Moderns" in his own time toward abstraction, and comparing it to the transformation of late Roman into Byzantine arts. He failed to see (it was too early!) that the "idealistic" abstract arts he perceived developing in "modern" circles were not so much different in form from traditional Western arts as different in essence—their social function was different; hence comparisons with early Byzantine arts are invalid.

Similar false analogies of historic with modern avant-garde flaw other early essays in art history as cultural expression from the 1920s: J. Huizinga's "The Task of Cultural History," of 1919, e.g. (reprinted: *Men and Ideas,* New York, 1959), or Erwin Panofsky's *Idea* (Leipzig/Berlin, 1929, reprinted Berlin 1960), not to mention later ones like Ernst Gombrich's *Art and Illusion* (New York/London, 1960).

[20]The central idea that made Vico's *Scienza Nuova* new, was not so much his cyclical view of history, all peoples going through stages of belief, imagination and reason, as that all aspects of their cultures during these stages will manifest which stage they are in. It is in this way that he anticipates not only Hegel and Spengler, but also Mommsen's intuitions about Roman history, Grimm's reconstruction of primitive life by etymology, or Marx and Sorel's idea of culture expressing an eternal class structure." Cf. Erich Auerbach, "Giambattista Vico und die Idee der Philologie," *Homentage a Antoni Rubio i Lluch,* Barcelona, 1936; (Auerbach, author of *Mimesis* and of a German translation of the *Scienza Nuova,* is particularly good in this point.); Löwith, *Meaning in History,* pp. 115 ff.; Joseph Vogt, *Wege zum Historischen Universum,* Stuttgart, 1963, p. 36 *et al.*

On Hegel, there is a masterly presentation of his use of art for cultural expression by Ernst Gombrich, *In Search of Cultural History* (London, 1969), pp. 5-13.

[21]The principle of cultural lag can also be used to date American architecture and furniture in the 18th century especially with extraordinary exactness. Cf. tables and point system from my *Images of American Living* (New York/Philadelphia, 1966; repr. New York, 1976), pp. 215, 222.

[22]Felix Gilbert in his chapter "Aby Warburg as a Historian," in *History,* Cambridge, Mass., 1977, declares (p. 431) that Warburg "rejected the view that art history ought to be chiefly concerned with the history of style. He regarded art history as an aspect of the history of civilization (*Kulturgeschichte*)." But this is still far from any conception of art as historical artifact, of arts as products of social function: "It ought to be added," Gilbert goes on, "that for Warburg it was almost a matter of course that the aspects of civilization in which a scholar interested himself were phenomena of high culture (the arts, literature, scholarship, and science..." See also Ernst Gombrich, *Aby Warburg* (London, 1970).

[23]Spengler moved to Munich in 1911 to read and study; the first volume of the *Untergang* appeared in 1917, so that he must have been writing it c1913-1916. In those years Wölfflin was at the height of his authority and Spengler would likely have attended his public lectures. Which of the other great German art historians active at this time Spengler might have read or known would be interesting to investigate (Cf. I-2).

[24]Citation from Spengler, *Untergang,* I, 188-190, by H. Stuart Hughes, *op. cit.,* p. 78.

[25]Spengler does not use this expression, but Lawrence Brown's *Might of the West* (New York, 1963), which is admittedly based upon Spengler, does, often and effectively, E.g. Prologue, p. 23:

"...artistic boundaries between the different nations of the same society are vague and often entirely arbitrary, but the artistic boundaries between different civilizations are so real and vivid that no aesthetic textbook is required to argue their existence....The rankest amateur can tell an Egyptian work of art and never confuse it with the art of any other culture, whether it was produced in 3000 B.C. or in the reign of Alexander....We talk of 'Oriental' art, but no one confuses Hindu work with Chinese or confuses either with Persian or Arabic....

So striking is the artistic integrity of each society that had Western historical writing originated in an aesthetic rather than a political or religious focus, the structure of history as the history of separate civilizations would long since have been accepted as an obvious fact of human life. But the history of the arts was undertaken long after the progress frame of political history had become rigid convention, so that instead of being the history of great self-contained aesthetic enterprises, it is a patchwork of assorted 'influence', all, of course, progressively leading to each author's favorite manifestation in the artistic life of the West."

[26]One possible reason for this blind spot in so many otherwise profound scholars may be that so many of them, for reasons beyond their control, were rootless, living in foreign lands, hence without abiding interest or stake in the State and its institutions. (Arthur Lower in *Canadians in the Making* tells of a president of Queens University in Ontario, an immigrant from Scotland, who was fond, on cold winter nights, of striding to his study window, pointing at snow-shovellers scraping away below, and saying, "Know the difference between me and them? Latin!") You can see this difference very strikingly if you compare Panofsky's *Gothic Architecture and Scholasticism* with Emile Mâle's *Religious Art in France of the 13th Century.* Both say the same things, essentially, but Mâle has a commitment to his subject—

i.e., to France, to French Culture, and to Catholicism—totally absent from Panofsky's coldly brilliant scientific documentations. Even more dramatic is the contrast between Mâle's books which were contemporary with Panofsky's on Suger and French cathedrals—i.e., in the late 1940s and 50s: *La Fin du Paganisme en Gaule* (Paris, 1949) or *Rome et ses Vieilles églises* (1953), where concern for the people and institutions on whose account these works were created is so evident. There is a comparable contrast in language: for Mâle, language is part of culture and should be written accordingly; his prose is itself a work of sparkling, limpidly flowing art. About Panofsky's style the most charitable thing ever said was that his English is lighter than his German—a 40-pound rather than a 60-pound sledgehammer for whacking nouns together.

  [27]Cf. Owen Barfield, *History in English Words*, London, 1953, pp 169-170.: "The consciousness of 'myself' and the distinction between 'my-self' and all other selves, the antithesis between 'myself', the observor, and the external world, the observed, is such an obvious and early fact of experience to every one of us, such a fundamental starting point of our life as conscious beings, that it really requires a sort of training of the imagination to be able to conceive of any different kind of consciousness. Yet we can see from the history of our words that this form of experience, so far from being eternal, is quite a recent achievement of the human spirit."

  [28]Thanks to James Ackerman for this point.

  [29]Cf. Michael Baxandall, *Painting and Experience in 15th-century Italy* (London, 1974). Ackerman points out that Michelangelo, at any rate, was hired by patrons because they wanted a "sample of his style" and Roman nobility were known to beg him for a "scratch from his hand."

  [30]The shift from "Beauty"—i.e., presenting things in their ideal aspects, the world as it ought to be—to "Reality"—i.e. presenting things naturally, the world as it is—is the central theme of my *Restless Art* (New York/Philadelphia, 1966). Linda Nochlin's *Realism* is the standard text on this subject (New York, 1970); she tends to take "realism" as the norm and any turning away from it, as in Courbet's later work, as some kind of inexplicable aberration. Cf. Norris K. Smith, "Ideas About Culture: Courbet and the Arts and Crafts," *On Arts and Architecture in the Modern World, op. cit.,* pp. 36, 39: "In an ironical or sardonic way, Manet declared (in his *Déjeuner sur l'herbe*), quite rightly, that poetic myth-making cannot be reconciled with 'the realities of our modern culture.' Indeed it cannot. But if Giotto or Masaccio or Titian had tried to base his art upon *appearances* he would have found himself in precisely Manet's predicament. All of them were concerned with ideas....There is no reason to suppose that it ever occurred to them that they should have been engaged in representing 'the life of their times' or any evidence that that is what they were doing without knowing it."

  Whenever and wherever you get sensitive and thoughtful people "expressing the realities" of their times, you get lamentations about dreariness and decadence. So in 1770, at the height of the power and glory of the First British Empire, we find Edmund Burke's *Thoughts on the Cause of Our Present Discontents* complaining that, "...hardly anything above or below, abroad or at home, is sound and entire....disconnection and confusion in parties, in offices, in families, in parliament, in the nation, prevail beyond the disorder of any former time.' But in 1145—a moment which for Toynbee and Spengler represented the vigorous youth of Western society—Otto of Freising's *Two Cities* ended with: "When I consider the miseries of the past, and the incomparably worse turmoil of the present, I cannot believe that the future could be better, and so must conclude that the end of the world is at hand." Truly, as Macaulay wrote in his 1848 *History of England*, "We are under a deception similar to that which misleads the traveller in the Arabian desert. Beneath the caravan all is dry and bare; but far in advance, and far in the rear, is the semblance of refreshing waters. The pilgrims hasten forward and find nothing but sand where, an hour before, they had seen a lake. They turn their eyes and see a lake where, an hour before, they were toiling through sand. A similar illusion seems to haunt the nations." Macaulay's own eyes were on the revolutions of 1848, of course, and he meant this passage for their zealots and visionaries to heed; but it applies just as well to all artists who undertake to "express the nature of their times."

  [32]No pejorative comparisons are involved, obviously. You don't criticize the design of a hoe because you can't hit golf-balls with it, nor damn your putter for being useless at weeding. Thus to say that avant-garde Establishment arts no longer perform traditional social functions, as argued in *The Unchanging Arts* (New York/Philadelphia, 1970) is not to "attack modern art" as some critics of that book suggested, only to contrast what it does with what historic arts did.

[33]Jacob Burckhardt (1818-1897) came of an old Swiss family of "intellectual aristocracy." He began his career as professor of art history at Zurich, 1855-58, related to which are the *Age of Constantine* (1848/9) in which he argues that that age is not a decline and fall, as Gibbon and Voltaire saw it, but a necessary transition from dying Antiquity to Christendom and medieval culture, *Cicerone* (1852), which is really the chapter on art for *Die Kultur der Renaissance in Italien, ein Versuch* (1860), and *Kunstgeschichte der Renaissance* (1867). His constant concern was with motivations for buildings and paintings, and their interrelations with prehistory, ethnography, geography, sociology, etc. In 1858 he moved to Basel to take the chair of History there, of which the great memorial is *Weltgeschichtliche Betrachtungen*, those pessimistic forecasts of deracinated masses manipulated by "terrible simplifiers" and military despots, for which he is best, albeit lugubriously, remembered. Cf. Karl Löwith, *Meaning in History*, which distills his earlier *Jacob Burckhardt, der mensch inmitten der Geschichte* (Luzern, 1936), and Arnoldo Momigliano, "Introduzione alla Grieschische Kulturgeschichte di Jacob Burckhardt," *Secondo Contributo alla Storia degli Studi Classici* (Rome, 1960, pp. 283-98, especially useful for the bibliography on Burckhardt's critics to 1959).

[34]One reason, Gombrich suggests, is the disguised and possibly unrecognized strain of Hegelian metaphysics in Burckhardt. Cf. *In Search of Cultural History*, pp. 14-25: "Not that we should reproach Burckhardt for having built his picture of the period around a preconceived idea. Without such an idea history could never be written at all...."

[35]Even such an admirer as Fritz Strich recognized this imperfection in his revered master: "Wölfflin in one way went past Jacob Burckhardt, in another not nearly so far. For Burckhardt always perceived the task of art history to include the collector, the patronage, the social status of the artist, what kind of commission it was, whether the artist had to paint for the church, the palace, the bourgeois house, whether his work was intended for sacred or profane usage, for public or private purposes. All that interested Wölfflin not at all." (*Zu Heinrich Wölfflins Gedächtnis*, p. 19)

[36]This book was still popular enough to be reprinted in translation three times, the latest in 1967: *Abstraction and Empathy, A Contribution to the Psychology of Style* (New York, International Universities Press). One reason for its original and continuing success is obvious enough: a powerful apologia for the "march of the Moderns." ("We may not be Michelangelos, or even Ingreses, but we're all you've got; and because of the 'impulse to abstraction' in our age, we're all you ever will get. So you better support us! We're your High Culture. Surely, Comrades, surely you wouldn't want Jones back—or Bourguereau, or Bud Fisher!")

[37](Bern, 1955). Paulsson's theory and approach are summarized on the last five pages; also in his inaugural lecture, "Konstvetenskap och Konstkultur," published in Gregor Paulsson, *Kritik och Program* (Stockholm 1949), pp. 134-145.

Third professor of art history at Uppsala (1934-1957), Paulsson gave that department its distinctive character (recently emphasized by a change of name from Konsthistoriska Institutionen—The Institute of Art History—to Konstvetenskapliga Institutionen—The Institute of Art Scholarship/Science). The best general summary of Paulsson's influence and place amongst the art historians of his time is to be found in the contribution by Allan Ellenius, the present (1978—) Konstvetenskapliga Professor at Uppsala, to a symposium of the Royal Scientific Society in Uppsala (1976-77 on "Men of Science in Society:" "Konstvetenskapens sociala dimension."

Alongside Paulsson should be mentioned Walter Benjamin, *Das Kunstwerk in Zeitalter seiner technischen Reproduzierbarkeit* (1936, repub. Frankfurt, 1970). An English version appears as Ch. 9, pp. 119-154) in H. Arendt, ed., Walter Benjamin, *Illuminations* (New York, 1968). Perhaps the most emphatic case for social function in recent times is the professorial address by Klaus Lankheit, *Kunstgeschichte under dem Primat der Technik* (Karlsruher Akademische Reden, Neue Folge Nr. 24, Karlsruhe, 1966).

[38](Stockholm, 1942/1963). Paulsson's writings are conveniently collected in his *Kritik och Program* (Stockholm, 1949). See especially "Samhällsform och Konstkultur" (1920) and "Konstvetenskap och Konstkultur" (1935), pp. 57-61, 135, 145).

[39]The classic treatment of the interaction of leftist political, social and artistic views is Donald D. Egbert, *Social Radicalism and the Arts in Western Europe* (New York, 1970; dist. American Life Foundation, Watkins Glen, N.Y.). Egbert's central focus is on contemporary arts (i.e. avant-garde arts) and how they got that way, rather than on art history; but he has perceptive and informative discussions of Klingender, Antal, Hauser, etc.

[40]"A building may be said to be a work of arcnitectural art, then, insofar as it serves as a visual metaphor, declaring in its own form something (though never everything) about the size, permanence, strength, protectiveness and organizational structure of the institution it stands for (but does not necessarily house)." *Frank Lloyd Wright, A Study in Architectural Content* (Englewood Cliffs, N.J., 1966), p. 10. (reprint, American Life Foundation, Watkins Glen, N.Y., 1979).

[41]Sweden provides a microscopic summary of European attitudes on this, as so many other historical matters; cf. the uses and discussions of art in Allan Ellenius, *De Arte Pingendi: Latin Art Literature in Seventeenth-Century Sweden and Its Background,* Uppsala/Stockholm, 1960. Also cf. I-29.

[42]As in all historical movements, there are presentiments of change long before the overt break. Thus Rembrandt's *Flayed Ox* can be viewed as an obvious presentiment of Courbet's *Head of a Pig* and Claes Oldenberg's cuts of meat on strings, etc. The difference, of course, is that Rembrandt's work was done in obscurity, seldom commissioned, and had no immediate issue, his pupils deserting him in droves; how altered was Courbet's case, how totally different Oldenberg's.

[43]Ad Reinhard, *Writings,* in *The New Art,* Gregory Battackock, ed., 1966.

[44]More than any other, it is this issue which characterizes art historians who use the methodology of social function effectively. Rhys Carpenter, for example, could write *The Architects of the Parthenon* (Baltimore, 1970) because already in the 1930s articles like "Spirit of Classic Art" (Oberlin College, Ohio, 1938) showed his understanding of how Greek pottery and sculpture were never Precious Objects but more akin to popular/commercial arts. E. Baldwin Smith could write *The Dome* (Princeton, 1950) because he was interested in how modern symbolism functions on the popular level. Later scholars write about popular/commercial arts as a matter of course, if they are seriously interested in social function.

Curiously enough, sociologists (of all people!) often fail to make this distinction. Thus, both Howard S. Becker's "Art as Collective Action," and Barbara Rosenblum's "Style as Social Process" (*American Sociological Review,* XXXIX, 1974, pp. 767-776 and XLIII, 1978, pp. 422-438 respectively) assume art historically to be the same as art now, and by "art" now they mean only avant-garde music, painting and architecture. Their historical insights suffer correspondingly.

[45]A number of theses and research projects have been conducted on these subjects at Uppsala University. Among them: Thomas Hörd af Segerstad, *Dagspressens bildbruk: En funktionsanalys av bildutbudet i svenska dagstidningar 1900-1970,* Uppsala, 1974 (with English summary: *Pictures in Newspapers);* Lena Johannesson, *Den Massproducerade Bilden,* Stockholm, 1978; Allan Ellenius, *Den Offentliga Konsten och Ideologierna,* Uppsala, 1971; Orjan Roth-Lindberg och Bjorn Norström, *Mysternas Marknad: Källor och motiv i Amerikansk Film,* Stockholm, 1975. Of course the *Journal of Popular Culture* has for years been the main English-language source for studies directly and indirectly related to this theme; thanks to its newly (1978) available *Index* these can now be conveniently used for the extensive research still waiting to be done in this vast new field of study.

[46]*Prints and Visual Communication,* Cambridge, Harvard University Press, 1953, p. 19.

[47]While writing this introduction, *Pakistan Today* for June 1978 comes across my desk. "Today's Karakoram Highway Follows Ancient Silk Route from China," it announces: "Throughout the centuries men have dreamed of a road between China and the fertile plains of the Indus River....This 500-mile long two-lane highway hacked out of the world's toughest mountains and glaciers...is the ancient Silk Route, over which history's fabled tourists once travelled, the Chinese Fa Hien in the fourth century, Huang Tsang in the seventh century, the Arab historian Al-Beruni in the eleventh century, and the Venetian trader Marco Polo in the thirteenth century...'."

[48]On popular/commercial arts generally being sources for avant-garde "innovations," see *The Unchanging Arts,* pp. 63-82. Further examples multiply constantly. American mass-produced mowers and reapers anticipated by sixty or seventy years certain Bauhaus futurist designs. Ferryboat seats in the 1870s anticipated avant-garde moulded plywood furniture, again by four or five decades. Not to mention the humble origins of brutalist styles in early 19th-century factories. In all cases an ideological shift is responsible, glorifying the proletariat, the factory system and Science.

36   Learning to See

[49]Cf. Robert L. Fishman, *Urban Utopias in the Twentieth Century,* New York, 1977, and my review thereof in *Inquiry,* I, 17, 10 July 1978.

[50]"A Defense of History in Architecture," RACAR (*Review de l'art canadienne/Canadian Art Review,* III, 1, 1976, pp. 51-59.

[51]This realization can be a veritable liberation of the spirit. Tom Wolfe's "Intelligent Co-Ed's Guide to America," for instance, in his *Mauve Gloves & Madmen, Clutter & Vine* collection of essays (Toronto/New York/London, 1976) wittily describes the Candides and Cunegondes in reverse, who are constantly being told that this is the worst of all possible worlds by modern Panglosses, who claim to express our culture—"and they know it must be true—and yet life keeps getting easier, sunnier, happier... Frisbee! How can such things be!" Or he satirizes the intellectuals who on the evidence of avant-garde arts talk about the "moral wasteland" against which they imagine themselves standing as saviours claim in "Stainless Steel Socialism."

[52]Jacques-Louis David, leading painter of Revolutionary France, still assumed his art would be a weapon to attack the old regime and support the new; since prints and posters and pageantry were proving more effective, he undertook to do some—even, indeed, some cartooning to counteract James Gillray's . Cf. James A. Leith, *The Idea of Art as Propaganda in France* (Toronto, 1965), Robert L. Herbert, *Brutus* (New York, 1973), pp. 108, 109) and Douglas Johnson (for illustrations) *The French Revolution* in Putnam's Pictorial Sources series). How the social functions of arts were still recalled in early America is evidenced by John Adams' famous letter to John Trumbull in 1817: "...the Burin and the Pencil, the Chisel and the Trowell, have in all ages and Countries of which we have any Information, been enlisted on the side of Despotism and Superstition.... Architecture, Sculpture, Painting, and Poetry have conspir'd against the Rights of Mankind."

By the end of the 19th century all that had been forgotten. In his *Menschen und Moden im 19. Jahrhundert* (Munich, 1919, Vol. IV, p. 97) Max von Boehn could note as a matter of course in his social history of the period 1878-1914 that,

"Since pictures, as Hausenstein so aptly noted, 'run around functionless in a dissolving world,' exhibitions were the chief organ of communication between art and the public.... Four-fifths of all paintings were made with no other intention than to be exhibited in an exhibition."

This, contrasted with, for all intents and purposes, none before c1750, and perhaps 98% by the 1970s.

[53]Which is what Alexander Rodtschenko meant by "There is no place for art in modern life"; what Duchamp meant by the urinal inscribed "R. Mutt" which he exhibited in a 1917 art show, etc., etc.

[54]Cf. "Art Schools Abroad," *College Art Journal,* XXIX, 2, 1968, pp. 209 ff.

[55]Cf. Dennis Alan Mann, *The Arts in a Democratic Society,* Bowling Green: Popular Press, 1977.

[56]From the first discovery of Altamira until quite recently, it was common to talk of painted caves as "Sistine Ceilings of Prehistoric Man." Those who did so, including the author of an anthropology text used at Harvard in my time there, of course did not imagine that these caves were Art Creations in the same sense the Sistine was. Unfortunately, this is precisely the meaning most freshmen there drew from this phrase.

[57]The relationship between studying arts with the methodology of social function and studying them universally; one leading directly to the other, is summarized in "Popular Arts and Historic Artifacts," *Popular Architecture* (Bowling Green, Ohio: Popular Press, 1973, pp. 87-103). An earlier example of it is how Dagobert Frey's interest in *Der Realitätscharakter des Kunstwerkes (Festschrift Wölfflin,* Dresden, 1935, pp. 30-67, expanded in Frey's *Kunstwissenschaftliche Grundfragen,* Vienna, 1946, pp. 107-150) led to his *Grundlegung zu einer vergleichenden Kunstwissenschaft* (Innsbruch/Vienna, 1949).

[58]See further Section VI. A preliminary statement of this general theme is contained in *On Parallels in Universal History* (Watkins Glen, 1974).

II

Traditional Forms and Functions of Substitute Imagery In Modern Popular/Commercial Arts

Definitions and Distinctions

Commemoration and reproduction of natural appearances, a primordial function of visual arts throughout history, is now done principally by arts of mass communication based on photography.

Nowhere, we fondly suppose, does the gulf between our Age of Science and all other ages that ever were, come into sharper focus than in the contrast between a snapshot and a cave-painting. Idle tourists, halting for a moment in some luxurious camper, take a quick picture they may not ever look at again. (3) Shaggy cavemen, laboriously scratching and smearing, leave images on rough rock surfaces of gloomy caves, for purposes unknown and unknowable. (4) Totally different techniques—sophisticated chemical and mechanical processes vs. smeared grease and earths. Totally different motivation. Totally different modes of vision: the modern picture, a record of something seen at one infinitesimal fraction of time, the cave painting, an assemblage of parts remembered from multiple observations, over many years and generations. But their primary *purpose* is not different. Fundamentally, tourists and cavemen are engaged in the same activity: preserving, commemorating, reproducing how something looked.

And in this fundamental respect, both photograph and cave-drawing are different kinds of activities from arts in the present-day avant-garde Establishment sense, made primarily to express personalities or explore form or capture the spirit of an age, only secondarily and incidentally—when at all—functioning to reproduce an image of something.

3. PHOTOGRAPH OF BISON. Representing one particular animal as it appeared in Elk Island National Park, Alberta, Canada, in the 1/250th of a second's time following 11:46 a.m. on June 1947.

4. DRAWING OF BISON on wall in deep recesses of Altamira cave, Spain, dated perhaps 8-10,000 B.C. A composite of parts each represented in most characteristist form—full-front hoofs with clefts, added to side-view hoofs with clefts, added to side-view legs, full-front eye added to side-view head and body, horns added outside head for distinctiveness.

5. ONE OF PICASSO'S LATE SCULPTURES, reproduced in M. Gieure, *Initiation d l'oeuvre de Picasso* (Paris, 1951). Undated; nor is date necessary. Identification of specific place or time would be as irrelevant as indicating any resemblance to prehistoric art, or indeed, to anything in particular—the primary purpose is to afford a vehicle for expression of the artist's personality, sensitivity to form, as role as "heraut [even more 'prophète'] de notre époque. All other considerations are secondary.

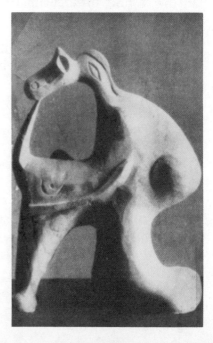

Conceptual thought and symbol-making, the basic operations in substitute imagery, are prerequisite for all human speech, thought, and art.

Arts of substitute imagery are among the earliest historical evidences for human as distinct from animal activity. Many sorts of animals, insects even, seem capable of recognizing and making symbols. Bees, it seems, can announce the location of flowers; dolphins can signal; dogs, of course, can recognize commands. And so on; but only humans seem aware of symbols *as* symbols— capable, that is, of reproducing mental concepts in some material (audible, visual) form, by a process of rudimentary analogical association—producing, i.e., substitute imagery.[1]

No animal evidences the ability of even very young children to invent original combinations of signs or to use symbols in new contexts, for purposes of their own. To associate collections of black marks on flat surfaces like the photo or bison-drawing here, with mental concepts of huge three-dimensional furry beasts— i.e., to relate two entities totally different in kind, texture, size, and material, is a distinctively human activity. It is because cave-drawings manifest this activity that we most easily think of their prehistoric makers as beings like ourselves.

Capacity to understand sounds or visual patterns as substitute images for mental concepts, and in turn refer them to physical objects or abstract forces, is the capacity required for all language: "without thought, no speech; without speech, no thought."[2] Likewise for all arts—that capacity is the primordial artistic skill. Need for recognizable symbols, and delight in creating and using them, is universal. What photography does so commonly and so matter-of-factly nowadays is something every society has required. Tourist snapshots, made simply to have a substitute of something seen, fill a need and produce a satisfaction felt by children everywhere, by artists throughout history, by cavemen. Differences in the images produced are of degree, not kind. Where a fundamental and essential difference occurs, is between their kind of substitute imagery and the motivations and satisfactions of 20th-century avant-garde Establishment art. Whatever the function of Picasso's sculptures (5), reproducing something seen or remembered was certainly not a primary or even important one. However many of his satisfactions in creating it, delight in transcribing images from nature was not among them.

Modern arts of substitute imagery differ in media from historic arts of substitute imagery, but not in social function; substitute imagery remains the foundation of all traditional artistic activity, High and Low arts alike.

6. One of 300 xerox copies of drawing made for course syllabus.

7. If broadcast on a television screen, millions of copies could be reproduced simultaneously.

So far from substitute imagery being a "delight" to the reigning art mentality nowadays, reproduction of natural appearances is at best suffered as a necessary evil. "Literal as a waxworks" and "photographic" are insults.

To account for this state of affairs, by the way of justifying and proselytizing for it, a popular 1940s theory—Frances B. Blashard's *Retreat From Likeness,* went so far as to put the blame on poor old Plato (once more into the breach, dear friends!).Plato, she claimed, banned artists from his Republic because "painting or drawing and imitation in general is remote from truth"; since when, "men who were outraged by his condemnation felt constrained to refute him on his own terms," to show that painting was *not* literal likeness. Thence began the March of the Moderns. "Abstraction" in the 1940s was thus made to seem the culmination of a line-of-progress, "a movement of thought...begun many centuries ago, a movement called here 'the retreat from likeness.' " Antagonism to abstract (i.e., non-substitute-imagery) painting was in effect attributed solely to ignorance and prejudice. Overlooked: the fact that Plato's antagonism was *not* to copying *per se* but to any art which cannot be measured or evaluated because it is "remote from reason." Overlooked, too: the difference between departing from the "copy theory" in the interests of an idealizing High Art, and abandoning substitute imagery altogether—in effect, embarking on a wholly different kind of activity. (3) Somehow the 20th century has come to take for granted that substitute imagery means literal counterfeiting of nature; that counterfeiting of nature is self-evidently not art; hence that art has nothing to do with substitute imagery.

So understanding substitute imagery, like understanding any social function in 20th-century arts, must begin by dealing with the but-is-it-*art*? syndrome—as William Ivins was perhaps first to realize in his pioneering study of *Prints and Visual Communication:*

My experience [in the department of prints of the Metropolitan Museum in New York, from 1916 on] led me to the belief that the principal function of the printed picture in western Europe and America has been obscured by the persistent habit of regarding prints as of interest and value only in so far as they can be regarded as works of art.... Prints (including photography) are the only methods by which exactly repeatable pictorial statements can be made about anything....

...this means that, far from being merely minor works of art, prints are among the most important and powerful tools of modern life and thought. Certainly we cannot hope to realize their actual role unless we get away from the snobbery of modern print collecting notions and definitions and begin to think of them as exactly repeatable pictorial statements or communications, without regard to the accident of rarity or what for the moment we may regard as aesthetic merit.

Is substitute imagery art? If you mean, is substitute imagery art in the 20th-century avant-garde Establishment sense of an activity concerned primarily with expression of personality, culture, material, or whatever, the answer must be No. But if you mean, is substitute imagery art in the sense that it does something, the doing of which has been characteristic of activities called arts from the beginning of human history—it is Yes. And insofar as that kind of activity is nowadays carried on by certain kinds of popular arts of mass communication, these are indubitably descendants of those historic arts.

Historic arts of substitute imagery were not necessarily limited to literal transcriptions of nature. Neither are their modern descendants in popular/commercial arts. Ancient and modern substitute imagery alike includes every kind of symbol, for every kind of concept, from waxworks to sign language.

Historically, substitute imagery could be done in any medium, in fact formed a foundation for all arts in all media. Nothing has changed in that respect. Now, as throughout history, substitute imagery forms the basis of illustration, calling to mind the necessary concepts for pictures to clarify stories and reinforce accounts of events. Now as ever, substitute imagery forms the basis of beautification, insofar as identifying use and relating objects to human experience necessarily involves reproducing natural shapes exactly or through abstracted symbols. And in its variant form of mimesis—reproducing in permanent and/or larger form shapes which have acquired meaningful associations in smaller and/or perishable materials—substitute imagery has demonstrably been the foundation for all those visual metaphors which have constituted the core of architectural art proper for thousands of years, and remains the essence of commercial, vernacular and popular architecture today.

Historically, arts in general functioned as prime cement for society, a principal means of transmitting values and traditions from one generation to another. Whence it follows that substitute imagery, being foundation for all of them, is a primary building block of human civilization at all times and places. If our civilization differs from others it is not because substitute imagery has become unimportant. Quite the reverse. It is unimportant only in the activity formally called art. In the daily operations of our civilization arts of substitute imagery (whatever names they go under) are as important as ever—differing only, perhaps, in being far more exact and far more efficient and far more numerous than ever before.

Ability to reproduce images exactly is the beginning and continuing foundation of all exact sciences. If you think of substitute imagery in terms of photography—snapshot, stroboscopic, interplanetary—rather than waxworks with their connotations of "bad art," its crucial importance in and to modern society becomes self-evident. Just as once humans were distinguished from animals primarily by ability to make images which would substitute for, function as symbols of, realities tangible and intangible, so now in the 20th century, photographic processes mechanically reproducing such images is an indispensable base of the technology on which modern civilization everywhere—for better or worse—has come to depend. In Ivins' words:

This exact repetition of pictorial statements has had incalculable effects upon knowledge and thought, upon science and technology, of every kind. It is hardly too much to say that since the invention of writing there has been no more important invention than that of the exactly repeatable pictorial statement.

It follows that substitute imagery has been throughout history the foundation not only for Low Arts but for High Arts as well; whence, that it can hardly be so inimical to "creative self-expression" as current avant-garde attitudes imply. The fact that every new photographic effect has been copied in avant-garde arts at a cultural lag of twenty years or so, regularly since the mid-19th century would be proof enough.[5] Even more dramatically the case is made by John Szarkowski's *The Photographer's Eye,* mounted and published by the Museum of Modern Art in 1966, as an "investigation of what photographs look like, and of why they look that way," which, in the words of Janet Malcolm's perceptive review in the *New Yorker,* resulted in "a shattering experience for the advocate of photography's claims as an art form:

...The accepted notion that in the hands of a great talent, and by dint of long study and extraordinary effort, photography can overcome its mechanical nature and ascend to the level of art is overturned by Szarkowski's anthology, whose every specimen is (or as the case may be, isn't) a work of art.[6]

Characteristically, avant-gardists copied this latest photographic discovery too, and began extolling bad snapshots as Art. The proper conclusion, of course, is: in photography as in all other arts, it's now time to go back to roots, to rethink the relationship of artistic expression to the other four social functions of the activity traditionally called art.

Substitute imagery is the matrix art—matrix of writing, matrix of money, matrix of art itself, through the sense of awe which it engendered, and which you can still see being experienced by small children in wax-works museums.

Substitute imagery of one kind or another—naturalistic reproduction or abstract symbol—is the foundation of all sorts of diverse modern activities.

It is the matrix of all writing, for instance.

8A. Descent of modern letter "A" from Phoenecian pictogram "aleph" (ox) c1100 B.C. via Greek form c800 B.C.
B. Descent of modern pictogram "chia" from 2nd-millennium pottery vessel called a *chia*, via bronze funeral *chia* c1000 and character meaning *chia* vessel-shape on Shang oracle bones, c1200 B.C.

Once upon a time all writing was by means of images— possibly, in the very beginning, by means of real images. It could be that the images of humans and animals from prehistoric sites (4) once functioned to communicate, like that "project" satirized in Swift's Laputa,

to abandon all words whatsoever... because it would be more convenient for all men to carry about them such things as were necessary to express the particular business they are to discourse on.... Many of the most learned and wise adhere to the new scheme of expressing themselves by things; *which hath only this inconvenience attending it,* that if a man's business be very great, and of various kinds, he must be obliged in proportion to carry a greater bundle of things upon his back....I have often seen two of these sages almost sinking under the weight of their packs, like pedlars amongs us....

Perhaps some atavistic memory of the delight of recognizing correspondences between sounds and pictures can explain not only the popularity of parlor games and newspaper puzzles of the "rebus" variety (Eye C Ewe) which survived through the 19th century,[7] but also those recurrent fits of enthusiasm amongst certain types of intellectuals for non-verbal communication, not only in Swift's time, but in our own. There is a Laputa-like quality about a 1972 issue of the *Smithsonian Magazine,* for example, where Margaret Mead describes and promotes a *Symbol Sourcebook* by Henry Dreyfuss with an introduction by Buckminster Fuller—octogenerians all, excited as ever over a "contribution to a new world technique of communication" expected "to catalyze a world preoccupation with its progressive evolution into a worldian language":

> We are living in a time of birth and growth of new kinds of language. . . the 'stop' and 'go' and 'curve' and 'crossing' signs on our highways, the blue and red dots for 'cold' and 'hot' water faucets, the skull and crossbones for poison or 'danger' on chemicals and medicines, and the circle with a cross on top which indicates church or government maps. . . .

Extraordinary, how it recalls Gulliver's

> Another great advantage proposed by this invention was, that it would serve as a universal language, to be understood in all civilized nations, whose goods and utensils are generally of the same kind.

In the real world, rebuses and hieroglyphics and other forms of picture-writing long ago were restricted to signs and symbols for simple single concepts, while out of them developed the infinitely faster and more flexible stylizations we call alphabetical letters, or characters. Release from precisely the kind of "inconvenience" Swift mocked, experienced by prehistoric man, may well have been a cause and effect of the great surge forward in civilization about 4000 B.C.—what immense energies were saved when picture-writing and pictorial symbols began replacing actual pictures and actual things! Only equally, perhaps, by the energies released when these ambiguous and complicated symbols were replaced by alphabets and characters capable of easily expressing precise meanings! How then explain perverse longings to restore all those inconveniences? In part by that obsession with Eden endemic in our age, perhaps, and already active in the 18th century; but also in part by the special disdain for substitute imagery peculiar in our artculture. Surely this is one reason why, whenever anyone notices the universal importance of substitute imagery, it's hailed as some great new discovery. Somehow we have been made to forget that our alphabet is substitute imagery just as much as red and blue dots, skulls and crossbones and stop signs are; that substitute imagery is, in sum, the foundation of all communication.

Substitute imagery is the matrix of money. Whether or not actual images ever served as words, they certainly did as money; in the beginning, all trade was barter—exchange of real goods. But very soon, the idea of a substitute image, easier to carry around, must have evolved. From that idea to paper money and compound economy is of course a long road, and we generally think of barter as a kind of economic life long gone. Yet in popular/commercial arts it still lives on vigorously. Usually in the form of coupons; but occasionally—oftener than imagined—actual substitute images still perform their immemorial function in trade.

9. Postcard with image of a "Big Mac Sandwich," redeemable at McDonald's fast food shops for a real version of same.

And substitute imagery is likewise the matrix of Art.

That substitute imagery is the beginning of certain branches of art seems self-evident enough. All that branch of art involved with preserving an appearance of the dead stems from primaeval substitute imagery, obviously. The painted skulls of Jericho 10,000-odd years ago, the death heads of Louis XVI and Marie Antoinette and wax images of Jack and Jackie (10 A, B, C) all belong in the same family, first cousins to photographic portraits by Steichen or Karsh, second cousins to State portraits by Reynolds, Velasquez and Raphael.

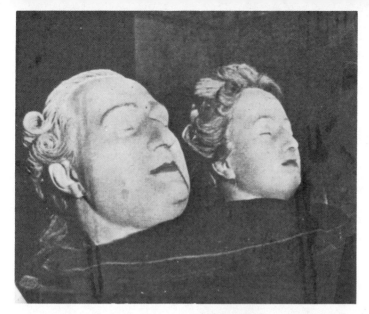

10A. The famous death heads of Louis XVI and Marie Antoinette made within minutes of their execution by Madame Tussaud, still preserved in her Paris waxworks.

10B. Skull, perhaps from the 7th millennium B.C., plastered and painted to produce a substitute image of a deceased person, of a sort found under door-sills in what archeologists categorize as the "B" phase of Jericho settlement.

10C. Wax figures of President and Mrs. Kennedy in the American Heritage Wax Museum of Scottsdale, Arizona, ©1970.

But I think there's more to it. According to Rudolf Otto, the great historian of religion, the root of all religious experience lies in the emotion of awe, aroused by awareness of the Numinous, a sense of "something other."[8] Perhaps Art began with the same emotion?—with the kind of emotion, that is, still to be seen when small children are taken to see that form of substitute imagery we call waxworks.

11. Image of a scribe, painted in lifelike colors with glass inset eyes. From the tomb of a nobleman near the Great Pyramid complex and Gizeh. Now exhibited as a work of art in the Louvre Museum. Paris, Limestone, 21 inches high. c.2500 B.C.

Waxworks are the very antithesis of art in the 20th-century sense [9]; and of traditional High Art too. Yet despite generations of disdain and ridicule, waxworks museums have not only survived into the 20th century, but flourish as never before! To understand why, ask what waxworks were made to do—and for whom? Then some of the ways substitute imagery functions in society will become clearer—and how even arts so elementary can be used for historical documentation.

Why do people visit wax muxeums? Watch the children there, and it's obvious—simple awe at things which look living, but aren't; things that look to be made of one material and turn out to be something else. A very humble emotion; but very real—and very ancient. Human beings have felt it from the moment they were capable of conceptual thought, apparently.

Sometime, somewhere, there must have been a moment when some creature first realized a connection between a thought and a sight or sound. At that moment the principle of symbol-making and symbol-using became operable. At that moment Man the rational being as distinct from Man the reactor to environments, emerged. Something of the awe and mystery and dumb exaltation of that first flash of association clung to symbols for a very long time, surely. Great substitute images of bison painted on the walls of Altamira and Lascaux (4) may well preserve its memory. In wax museums, children—and maybe more adults than care to admit—relive it.

The most famous historic examples of such efforts, perhaps, are the so-called *ka* figures from Old Kingdom Egypt.

Even now, they excite awe—Egyptians from the Old Kingdom who, with the slightest imaginative effort, spring to life before us—science fiction, "magic realism." How infinitely greater was their original effect, when (much evidence suggests) analytic faculties were not so keen as ours, and analogical thought correspondingly more compelling—when, in consequence, there was no effective distinction between "original" and "copy," so that a *ka* figure actually was an *alter ego* for a living person, preceding him/her into the tomb, preparing the way to another life![10] If this is art, it's not art in our modern sense of artistic expression; rather, it's art in the deep, primordial, awesome sense that fuelled Byzantium's bloody Iconoclasm, the kind of living "graven image" that Moses forbade his people from making unto themselves.[11]

To achieve such awesome effects did not always or necessarily require waxworks' literalism like the "Scribe." Mesopotamian cult images induced awe—to a degree still do!— without being particularly naturalistic.

12. Group of images found in ruins of the Abu Temple, Tell Asmar, Iraq. Usually interpreted as substitutes for worship—the two tallest being the vegetation god Abu and a mother goddess, the others being priests and worshippers who by means of these "living images" did constant service to the deities. Marble, tallest figure about 30″ high. From the Iraq Museum, Baghdad and the Oriental Institute of the University of Chicago.

12A. Detail of the god Abu's substitute image. The eyes are in colored inlay. Dated c2700-c2500 B.C.

The great Leo Oppenheimer once wrote that motivations and feelings of attendants at the great cult-idols of Mesopotamia[12] "remain removed from us as if pertaining to another dimension." But perhaps we can grasp something of their essence by observing small children at a wax museum by sensing the awe and mystery they feel face-to-face with a "living statue."

And on a more facetious level, we get some idea of the atmosphere surrounding the ritual feeding and clothing of god-images in Antiquity,[13] perhaps, by studying the rapt attention of tourists watching ritual garment-changings of idols in the Hollywood Wax Museum (13).

Perhaps the social function they share with ancient cult idols is responsible for much of the hostility to "wax works" in contemporary art theorizing; a subconscious or atavistic cultural conditioning rouses toward waxworks those feelings once evoked by idols. Oppenheimer thought[14] that the reason "the role and function of the divine image in Mesopotamian civilization have never been considered" was "a characteristic instance of the influence of subconscious associations on the selection of research topics:

The aversion to accepting images as genuine and adequate realizations of the divine presence, manifested in a traditional human form ('the Sun in human limb array'd') has played an important role in the religious development of the ancient world. The roots of the attitude of rejection stem not only from the Judeo-Christian heritage but existed, earlier and independently, in Greek thought. In fact, pro- and anti-iconic tendencies have often been instrumental in shaping trends and releasing events in the history of our culture. And they are far from dead now.

Could similar inverted "religious rage" lie behind much of the fulmination against naturalistic representation in avant-garde theory? Could it derive, like so much else in 20th-century thinking (Marx's proletarian apocalypse being the classic case) from an older religion, with all its characteristic attitudes and prejudices, "stood on its head"?[15]

However that may, there's no doubt that substitute imagery continues to have as lively and vital a function in and for our society as ever in the past. Nor is that function simple; in fact, four variant types can be distinguished.

Four Variants of Substitute Imagery

Within the general category of substitute imagery, four variant types can be distinguished—commemorative, didactic, hortatory, and mimetic—roughly corresponding to use of substitute imagery as an auxiliary to other social functions.

PRECISELY HOW SUBSTITUTE IMAGERY functions in modern society depends, in general, on whether it is used as substitute imagery proper—i.e., more or less simply to reproduce or perpetuate something—or in conjunction with some other social function—illustration, beautification, persuasion/conviction, as the case may be.

Used for its own sake, substitute imagery is essentially commemorative; such are all those images, from waxworks to snapshots, made simply or primarily to recall some original to mind.

Substitute imagery can also function as a kind of static illustration (for example, in two- or three-dimensional dioramas and museum exhibits), in which case it becomes didactic, the very existence of replicas of past events or present actualities serving to instruct beholders, usually with deliberate intent.

The most obvious example of hortatory substitute imagery is funerary sculpture and arts allied thereto: monuments to the deceased, whether simple grave markers or elaborate tomb buildings, presumably would not be erected to all unless beholding them served in some degree to exhort, to remind the living of their own end at the very least, at most inspiring them to emulate past generations' virtues, to carry on traditions, etc. Such a function necessarily involves some elements of beautification, in its traditional sense as the art of so presenting images to individual beholders as to make them more identifiable, more meaningful, more intelligible—i.e., more beautiful.

Finally, there is a whole category of substitute imagery best, perhaps, called compulsive. Particularly though not exclusively associated with architecture, its most representative form consists of those mimetic reproductions of revered architectural and sculptural shapes which constituted so much of historic architecture and still survive today in popular/commercial building. Insofar as this kind of substitute imagery helps to create symbolic metaphors of value and so transmit fundamental convictions from one generation to another, it involves persuasion/conviction, even though not primarily or consciously, as in arts of persuasion/conviction proper.

Substitute Imagery Proper: Commemorative

*Substitute imagery proper is concerned with "calling to mind"
material things and/or ideas associated with them. By their very
existence, substitute images constitute evidence for values held
by their makers; however this is something quite different from
deliberate persuasion/conviction.*

HOLLYWOOD
WAX MUSEUM

SEE THE SUPER-STARS
Relive the glory and excitement of Holl
wood's Golden Era as the movie capital
the world! Visit with the great ones fro
Clark Gable, Jean Harlow and Maril
Monroe to Raquel Welch, Paul Newma
Glen Campbell, and the blazing, smash-
brilliance of Barbra Streisand.

RELIVE GREAT MOMENTS
Turn the clock back to history-in-the-ma
ing at the Yalta Conference. Meet the gre
American Presidents from Washington
Eisenhower. Thrill to the likeness and t
actual words of the martyred J.F. Kenned
and that apostle of peaceful resistanc
Martin Luther King.

PAUSE WITH REVERENCE
—before the greatest wax masterpiece
all-time, the faithful, life-size recreation
Leonardo daVinci's immortal painting of t
The Last Supper of our Lord and his 12 d
ciples. One of the Wax Museum's impre
sive religious tableaux.

13. Excerpts from the Hollywood Wax Museum's descriptive folder, 1975.

TO MAKE AN IMAGE of something is to call it to mind—and by doing so, to fix it in mind. Waxworks, which excite that kind of awe which may well be the beginning of all art, also demonstrate very well substitute imagery's commemorative function (10A, 10B, 10C).

A great deal can be deduced about public ideals in England and America during the late 1960s from the fact that in that period Tussaud's most widely distributed figures, on the basis of mass appeal, were of Presidents Kennedy and F.D. Roosevelt, Einstein and Martin Luther King, others ranking comparably lower; Malcolm Muggeridge noted that

When I became a waxwork in Madame Tussaud's I was put in a room between Twiggy and the Burtons, with a massive DeGaulle staring down upon the four of us. Not a sparrow can fall to the ground, we are told, without concern in Heaven; so, likewise, the placement of waxworks.[16]

Bits and scraps from the past, preserved in waxworks by popular demand, reveal popular 20th-century line-of-progress conceptions of history. Disraeli, Queen Victoria, Lincoln, that's the 19th century. The Renaissance: Henry VIII and his wives. The French Revolution: "Lady Guillotine" and Napoleon. The Middle Ages here are still Dark, our last six generations of historians notwithstanding. Here Christianity is Leonardo's *Last Supper* and Bing Crosby's *Going My Way*.

Or in other words: commemoration involves a degree of immortalization. Waxworks freeze time where we want it. That is their great appeal; that is a perennial motivation for substitute imagery. Stop the world, we want to get off. Here, at this golden moment when Disraeli announces, once and forever, that Victoria Regina is Empress of India. Here, while Martin Luther King and the great FDR remain unflawed by frailties. Or here, in Hollywood soundtracks with Judy Garland's Yellow Brick Road still leading to an Emerald City, no Valley of the Dolls ahead; with Shirley Temple dancing, dimpled and seven. Stop the world here, while Jackie is still First Lady and Jack still the All-American Boy, Mrs. Onassis and seedy actresses alike inconceivable. Stop the world....

14. MODERN FOLK SCULPTURE: SYMBOLIC INDIAN, LACROSSE, WISCONSIN, made by Anthony Zimmerhakl, c1955. Accompanying inscription: "This Indian is symbolic of all the Indians of the area and is dedicated particularly to the braves of the Winnebago.... Lacrosse started as a trading post in Indian territory." Material: concrete, painted; the typical cheap, convenient, efficient material favored for popular/commercial sculpture until c1960, when fibreglass displaced it. If and when a history of popular sculpture in North America comes to be written, there will be hundreds, perhaps thousands of examples to illustrate it.

Folk sculpture and its twin, substitute-image advertising, likewise have power to evoke idyllic and stable worlds. Here Redmen are forever Noble and what's more, conveniently vanished (14)—never drunk, never demented, never discontented. Here auto tires are always new, the fair forever svelte; youth's forever young and cigarettes forever mild. Here the world smiles and you smile along. Incalculable, the net effect of the totality of such images on shaping public consciousness about the past. Incalculable therefore, the net effect on present policies. But obviously great; for what happened in history doesn't matter nearly as much as what people *think* happened. And what they think happened is what they make substitute images of.

The kinds of things commemorated by arts of substitute imagery not only indicate the values of a society, then, but also to some extent help to determine those values. History is shaped by their very existence. "The camera cannot lie," we say—and are the more deceived.

None of which necessarily demands literalness. So far from waxworks being typical of substitute imagery, numerically they represent the merest fraction of arts with this function. For anything requiring speed or multiplications, two-dimensional images are manifestly better.

Commemorative substitute images may be very permanent or very ephemeral, depending upon the social function their circumstances require.

15A. THE BEATLES: Reproduction from a card put in chewing-gum (c1963), of a photograph of four entertainment celebrities. Substitute images of these popular idols (significant term!) could also be obtained in plaster busts, ashtrays, posters, etc., all designed to familiarize the public with these shapes so as to transfer fame (and money) to the actual objects.

Images of celebrities whose fame may be fleeting must needs be produced fast, in overwhelming quantity (15A). Images of national heroes admired over generations and centuries can take longer (15B).

People having remembered Washington over a century and a half when the Mount Rushmore commemoration was begun, there's a good chance of his head still being recognized in another century—the sculptor could therefore work, as he said, "for the ages."[17] But with Beatle images, better get them out quick; already you can find their cards and plaster busts piled in junk shops, and within a few years it will be a matter of "whatever happened to...." The general principle has applied ever since mass production of substitute images on a theoretically unlimited scale became possible, that is, for about two hundred years or so now. In the same length of time required for Nelson's column to rise in Trafalgar Square or Napoleon's Arc de Triomphe next the Louvre, dozens of Beatle-type celebrities arose, spawned enormous shoals of fleeting memorabilia, and have been totally forgotten.

Ephemeral and permanent substitute images can complement each other in effective commemoration—the one, by force of numbers and ease of distribution, serving to establish the significance of the other. Such an activity obviously involves implicit persuasion, and thereby some forms of substitute imagery can become a kind of idolatry. A universal problem, shared even by avant-garde and popular Catholicism.

Of course, similar shoals of fleeing memorabilia were necessary to sustain all the lasting heroes of recent history too. Mount Rushmore and the Washington Momument are supported—metaphorically speaking—by hundreds and thousands of embroidered and block-printed and multi-copied portraits of the Hero; Chairman Mao's crystal casket, certifying him to have attained the immortal status of Shih-Huan-Ti, legendary First Emperor of all China, rests—again metaphorically speaking—on millions of portraits on banners and posters and little red books.

This is a kind of idolatry—worshipping a creation of one's own hands. All religions, ancient and modern, whatever their degrees of truth, have been prone to something like it on occasion.

15B. Heroic-size heads of four Presidents, carved on face of Mount Rushmore by Gutson Borglum, from 1927 onwards. A category of substitute imagery which includes colossal images of Stalin, Lenin, Mao and Castro as well as ancient gods and heroes.

16. Mel Ramsden, "Secret Painting," 1967-68. "The content of this painting is invisible; the character and dimensions of the content are to be kept permanently secret, known only to the artist." (from Ursula Meyer, *Conceptual Art*, p. 204)

In *The Painted Word,* Tom Wolfe mocked avant-garde painting for succumbing to just this kind of idolatry.[18] What started as a movement to restore art to its essentials, and to artists, by freeing it from Victorian literary baggage of content and commentary—i.e., to distinguish the creature from the creation—has ended with art more hopelessly mired in sophistries of content, artists more totally dependent on critics' opinions, than ever in history. The New York avant-garde art scene of the'60s and '70s is a counterpart to the despised (by it!) Mount Rushmore sculptures or Beatles playing cards, in its utter dependence upon mountains of supplementary ephemera to give its images whatever significance they may have.

Catholicism spread over the world, not by promising to bring heaven to earth here and now and to transform everything, but by accepting that the world of time and history cannot be changed until the Day of Judgement, hence that conversion means—and can only mean—turning in the sense of looking at this present world from a different viewpoint, seeing its ultimate meaning differently. Accordingly, wherever existing religious practises were not directly contrary to the Faith, the Church took them over and remoulded them. Thus, cult images like these Madonnas (17A, 17B) are directly descended from those of preceding religions. Still in the 18th century the image of Our Lady of Hope was being dressed and attended like images of Greek and Roman deities—like the image of Athena the Virgin in the Parthenon of Athens, for example, which every year received a new cloak and other necessities presented as the climax of a civic ritual procession (commemorated by the frieze carved onto the Parthenon's inner temple-house); indeed, as cult images had been for four millennia past (cf. fn. II-13). Likewise, the Virgin of the Plain (17B) probably owes its form to—and at its core may actually be—a *Matre,* one of those Teutonic or Celtic feminine fertility images which according to Emile Mâle were frequently found in fields, mistaken for early and miraculous Madonna images, and suitably enshrined as such.[19] The difference in both cases was, of course, that whereas in earlier millennia no hard-

17A. "Our Lady of Hope" (Nuestra Senora de la Esperanza). Image made c1700, in Seville Cathedral. Body of wood, painted and polished; crown gold; eyes glass; clothes real.

17B. "The virgin of the Plain" (La Virgen de la Vega), patroness of Salamanca. A wooden image overlaid with copper, jewels and enamels. Centerpiece of a complex painted reredos behind high altar of Old Cathedral of Salamanca. Early 13th century (?).

and-fast distinction was drawn between original and copy, between image and reality (q.v., 11, and fns. II-10, 11), here it was. These images were aids to devotion, no more. How was that difference of interpretation enforced? In both cases, by ephemeral arts, again. In contrast to the arts accompanying their predecessors and followers of the same type, those prayers, chants, ritual, shrine souvenirs or sermons which accompanied the Madonna images emphasized that image and reality were *not* one, that these were substitute images in the sense of bringing to mind and fixing in mind an object of devotion—nothing more. And in the case of the Virgin of the Plain, there was a further difference—the figure, while naturalistic enough to retain some of the power of magical realism—it has qualities somewhat like ancient Mesopotamian cult images (12)—nevertheless has been stylized by patterns of drapery and compositional lines so as to put that lifelikeness at one remove, and thereby heighten the effect, from simple magical realism to genuine awesomeness. To substitute imagery has been added artistic expression, in this case in the High Gothic style. The work thereby has become High Art.[20]

Deliberate stylization to make substitute images more and more awesomely persuasive can be identified long before this—and universally.

Awe, evoked by substitute imagery proper, is the basis for much of the world's great High Art. The social functions of beautification and persuasion/conviction are often, perhaps generally, effected by deliberate artistic expressions.

18. Comparison of typical Buddha figures from Gandhara (A) and Mathura (B) to show the typical stylization of Buddhist arts over the period 200-500 A.D.

During early centuries of the Christian era, in the northwest region of India called Gandhara, Buddhism spreading up out of its homeland met Greek culture, in the form of a huge colony established by migration eastwards from Greece in the 2nd and 1st centuries B.C. to the land then called Bactria, now Afghanistan. The result was a great outburst of Buddhist art, almost on a commercial scale, giving Greek visual form to the Buddha, his lives and his doctrines (18A). This art was literal, substitute imagery or illustration for the most part, far more like waxworks and comic-strips than modern taste cares to admit. But soon a change set in. Its center, apparently, was the city of Mathura, crossroads of commerce and seat of what can best be described as an art manufacturing business. The art produced there was distinctively styled. The first sculptures produced at Mathura, according to Herman Goetz,[21]

had followed the general course of early Indian art, from very clumsy to lively compositions....Thereafter, the figures are generally bigger, the scenes simpler. There is nothing of the naive freedom of the Andhra compositions. The positions as well as the anatomical details of the figures, the compositions of the groups, their balance, the mutual relations of all details are carefully studied....The whole change is intelligible only as a result of the contact with Hellenistic art [forms] *via* Gandhara....However, what we encounter here is not an imitation of the Hellenistic theory and canon, it is an Indian counter-theory and counter-canon with very different ideals...a really grand conception of the Enlightened One in which nothing of the Gandhara and, in the last instance, of the Hellenistic style, can be discovered....

That this styling is deliberate, there can be no question.[22] How it enhanced the power of substitute imagery to compel and persuade is demonstrated in the great Buddha figures of succeeding centuries, from Bamiyan to Lung-Men.

From comparable works (10B), it's not difficult to imagine what the effect of the two great Bamiyan Buddhas, visible for miles across the plain (18C), must originally have been.[23] Their significance (as with all such types of commemorative substitute imagery) was amplified in the multitudinous ephemeral arts—the ancient equivalent of popular/commercial arts, really—produced in the workshop/factories of Gandhara, Mathura and elsewhere so prolifically that even today fragments are picked up all over the Buddhist heartland (18D); there was also a wealth of

18D. Copper reliquary urn with Buddha and Boddhisattvas on lid, paradise images on sides, part substitute imagery and part illustration, for all intents and purposes mass-produced as souvenirs, but nevertheless with regional characteristics reminiscent of High Styles of the age in Andhran and Kushan India, as well as Greek Bactria. Found in Gandhara region, now in Peshawar Museum.

18C. Great Buddha of Bamiyan, made perhaps in the 4th or 5th century A.D., 175 feet (53 metres) high, originally brightly painted. This and the smaller seated Buddha (125 feet, 37 metres) are the climactic images among thousands made in this Buddhhist center at one of central Asia's greatest crossroads between c150 and c650 A.D.

paintings surrounding the figures themselves. But their primary effectiveness was a function of substitute imagery—the verisimilitude of figures painted and "dressed." The childlike awe evoked by waxworks was reinforced by size. These giant figures towered over viewers as adults tower over children—their effect, then, awful as the Old Kingdom Pyramids were aweful, as Stonehenge and Carnac and Ur were aweful.[24] But in addition they conveyed a sense of what is best called the Numinous, the sense of something Other, not fearful as physically dangerous things are fearful, but fearful as great spiritual experiences have been described—aweful. The effect was deliberately produced, by artistic expression operating to pattern the drapery and compose the forms hierarchically—a style worked out, as great High Art styles always have been, in the preceding "popular/commercial" workshops, responding to social function. The Bamiyan figures originally exemplified precisely what Rudolf Otto meant in "Means by which the Numinous is expressed in Art":

...We often say of a building, or indeed of a song, a formula, a succession of gestures or musical notes, and in particular of certain manifestations of ornamental and decorative art, that they make a 'downright magical' impression, and we feel we can detect the special characteristic of this 'magical' note in art with fair assurance even under the most varying conditions and in the most diverse relationships. The art of China, Japan, and Tibet, whose specific character has been determined by Taoism and Buddhism, surpasses all others in the unusual richness and depth of such impressions of the 'magical,' and even an inexpert observer responds to them readily....

Art here has a means of creating a unique impression—that of the magical—apart from and independent of reflection. Now the magical is nothing but a suppressed and dimmed form of the numinous, a crude form of it which great art purifies and ennobles. In great art the point is reached at which we may no longer speak of the 'magical,' but rather are confronted with the numinous itself, with all its impelling motive power, transcending reason, expressed in sweeping lines and rhythm.[25]

Above all, in our connection, exemplifying how simple commemorative substitute imagery becomes a powerful High Art of persuasive/conviction—not by abandoning its primary function, but by acquiring others.

Figures like these exemplify arts of beautification as much or better than substitute imagery proper. Yet it's important to introduce works like them here, to emphasize that they begin with the same social function as the Mount Rushmore heads, Beatle cards or Mao posters, that they belong indubitably to the same family—albeit relatives risen considerably in status.

When first found in 1863, the Prima Porta Augustus still bore traces of its original paint. So we should think of it, before we think of it as anything else—hair yellow, flesh reddish, eyes grey (the Julio-Claudian color!), cuirass gold, toga scarlet, skirt royal blue, looking in actuality considerably more like a cigar-store Indian than a Precious Museum Object in unsullied stone.

Elevating the statue's significance from the beginning, however, and contributing even more to its grand effect now that the lifelikeness has faded—were the kind of auxiliary arts that imparted meaning to commemorative substitute imagery everywhere. Appended to the statue itself were illustrations on the cuirass and a little putto, *genus* of the Augustan line, at the Imperator's feet; there were coins with inscriptions; there were paintings in wax, on boards; cameos and cheaper gems; small terracottas and metal images. Most effective of all was poetry— specifically the masterwork of Roman literature, Virgil's *Aeneid*. Oftentimes forgotten is the fact that *Aeneid* and Prima Porta Augustus were twins. Both appeared about the same moment in time.[26] Both served the same social function—to consolidate and stabilize the Roman realm after a half century of devastating civil war. The *Aeneid* told a story—so well that within months of its publication, verses from it were being chalked on walls, sung in taverns and quoted in salons as well as being set for memorization in schools—of how Rome had an eternal destiny to rule the world; how this destiny was to be fulfilled by a member of that *genus* symbolized by the Prima Porta putto, descended from noble Aeneas of Troy. It told how, once the rule of that Man of Destiny had been established, a new Golden Age of Saturn would dawn, with peace and power abundant forevermore—the very theme illustrated on the cuirass.

Grand epic art? Yes indeed, the more since the statue was composed according to the ideal canon devised by Polykleitos four hundred and fifty years earlier, exemplified in his statues of ideal athletes so well known and freely copied in Rome (19B). True, individual ethical virtue rewarded by triumph in ritual games was no longer being commemorated, but communal virtue incarnate in the Emperor's person—down which road lay much

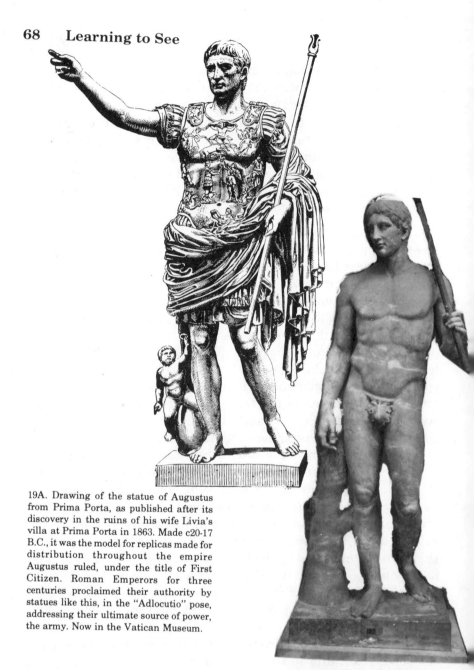

19A. Drawing of the statue of Augustus from Prima Porta, as published after its discovery in the ruins of his wife Livia's villa at Prima Porta in 1863. Made c20-17 B.C., it was the model for replicas made for distribution throughout the empire Augustus ruled, under the title of First Citizen. Roman Emperors for three centuries proclaimed their authority by statues like this, in the "Adlocutio" pose, addressing their ultimate source of power, the army. Now in the Vatican Museum.

19B. Also in the Vatican Museum is the marble copy of Polykleitos's bronze statue of a spear-throwing champion at the Olympic Games, c440 B.C. Admired by Roman critics as constituting a canon of ideal proportions, the visual counterpart of the sophist Protagoras' cliché "man is the measure of all things."

tyranny and disintegration. But it remains grand art. Or perhaps grand propaganda. For this was not a once-in-a-lifetime Work of Art made to record some master's sensitivities toward the theme of Augustus and his Empire; it was a master-model intended to be copied all over the new Empire which Augustus had established. Its purpose was to substitute for the Emperor's authority, to ensure that he would be present everywhere, always. A substitute image in the most literal sense of the word, then.[27]

Yet it is more; it is beautification too, in the sense of making the world more intelligible, fixing perceptions of reality, clarifying experience—as its formal inspiration, Polkleitos's "Spearbearer" had been in its time (q.v. VI). [28]But before any or all of these things, both were commemorative substitute images. Waxworks-like. Polykleitos's statue originally was in bronze, its surface polished and shining all too much (for our taste) like a sweating athlete fresh from a workout in the sun; its hair colored, its eyes glass and paste. Whenever we recover one of these Tussaud-like figures in anything like an original state, there's shock and aesthetic consternation; for the truth is, as F.P. Chambers pointed out fifty years ago,

...Aesthetic self-consciousness was born late into ancient Greek culture. The Greek knew not that he was an artist, till his arts were well past their prime. The Parthenon and the Propylaea were already built, and had become the accustomed sights of Athens, before it was dimly borne in upon the Athenians that they were works of Art. Prior to the fourth century B.C. there is no evidence that works of art were admired, except for their costliness and magnitude. In sculpture and painting, the first quality demanded was life and realism....[29]

What we do know is, in other words, that the Greeks liked and wanted their sculpture far more like waxworks than 20th-century taste does. Nobody has ever proved otherwise.[30] Why try to apologize for it? Why not try, instead, to ascertain the reason, and learn from it?

The reason that Polykleitos's "Spearbearer," the Charioteer of Delphi, even the Prima Porta Augustus, would strike us, could we see them in the forms Greeks and Romans made and loved, as by turns comical and obscene, childish and enchanting, garish and grand, is that they still prized and emphasized substitute imagery's power to evoke awe. Which means, really, that they still understood one of the basic roots of art as a humane activity.

They understood how without that awe for a base, arts of beautification are less effective, arts of persuasion/conviction less compelling. Mediaeval arts universally kept this base; so, in large part, arts of the Renaissance/Baroque ages. Our avant-gardists, great-great step-children of the Enlightenment and its prejudices against superstition, have lost it except for sporadic moments,[31] and been correspondingly enfeebled.

One great advantage of the methodology of social function is to fix upon essential beginnings, this power of substitute imagery to evoke awe being one of them. Substitute imagery is not the end or goal of artistic activity. But it surely is the beginning for much of it.

Substitute Imagery as Static Illustration: Didactic

Substitute imagery made for didactic purposes likewise exhibits a range from very literal to highly abstract, depending upon use, and hence revealing for cultural history. Its central type is the diorama or panorama.

DIDACTIC SUBSTITUTE IMAGES, reproductions made to teach, sometimes resemble illustration (21). But such exhibits tell no stories as such. Rather, they are *tableaux*—frozen moments in time and space, like waxworks, which instruct by their existence. And like waxworks, they are most effective on a low mental level, responding to simple wonder. So Russian or Chinese peasants, led from one tableau to another, get an impression of moving through time from darkness and suppression into Enlightenment, until Great Headmaster Lenin (as Edmund Wilson called him) or Chairman Mao is reached and no further revelation is to be expected.

To serve the purposes of this kind of substitute imagery, and for all its counterparts—panoramas, dioramas, movie spectaculars, TV documentaries of many types,—[32] high degrees of accuracy in transcribing natural appearances are requisite; —

21. Didactic substitute imagery at its most literal: three exhibits from the Museum of Religion and Atheism, in the Kazan Cathedral building, Leningrad. Savages grovel; Inquisitors torture; Lenin expounds new Marxist superstitions.

more, we might suppose, than possible in great art. Yet a close
counterpart in historic art, the allegory (especially allegorical
ceiling),standard in palaces of all kinds, was a commission the
greatest artists often coveted, with masterpieces by Rubens,
Pietro da Cortona, Andrea Mantegna, the Caraccis (to name only
a few!) resulting. And of course Raphael's four murals in the
Camera della Segnatura generally stand amongst the highest
peaks in aesthetic line-of-progress art history, on everybody's All-
Time Masterpiece list.

22. Didactic substitute imagery made into High Art: Raphael's "School of Athens"
commissioned by Pope Julius II, painted 1510-1511 on the wall of the Camera Della Segnatura
in the Vatican Stanze, to set forth in panoramic allegory the Catholic Church's claims to
reconcile all extremes in her central stream.

Every survey analyzes the *School of Athens*'s subtle interplay of primary colors, the compositional point-counterpoint of moving and static forms, the interwoven masses and voids that constitute and express High Renaissance perfection. Only recently has there been much serious discussion of its social function: why, precisely, did Julius II feel it worthwhile to commission so much art in so short a space of time—alongside this program for his Sealing Room was the ceiling of his Papal chapel, the Sistine, on which Michelangelo was working and from which Raphael borrowed an additional figure or two for his own "School of Athens," and the rebuilding of St. Peters, to cite only the most ambitious? Generous patron providing scope for genius's self-expression?

That will do no longer. This panorama, this static illustration—to identify it by social function—before it was anything else, before it was a Masterpiece or a Work of Art or an expression of High Renaissance Roman culture, was a propaganda picture, made to do something in and for society as specific as panoramas decorating stages and halls for Party congresses or veterans' reunions.

An interpretation so based[33] would thus begin with pre-existing political, social and religious factors: the complex of institutions in the Europe of 1510 being challenged by those interests and passions which, in the event, were to erupt in the Reformation of 1517:

In the Sealing Chamber, official Vatican documents were formally sealed with wax; there foreign emissaries and officials met the Pope, and Raphael was commissioned to cover its walls with images proclaiming the Papacy's pre-eminent qualifications for taking on the role of "godly prince," bringing happiness and security to men as organizer of an ideal State. What made the Pope's qualifications unique for such a role was his claim to combine both spiritual and temporal authority—the temporal authority consisting not merely of powers and privileges appropriated from the Holy Roman Emperor in the 13th and 14th centuries, but of actual political leadership over great territories (Alexander VI and Julius II both made it their business to cxpand actual and not theoretical rule of the Popes outside the traditional Papal States, and indeed hoped to unite all Italy into a kingdom under their command).

These factors determined the art forms: how literal, how idealistic, how abstract might be required:

Balance of spiritual and secular power is thus the main theme of all the Camera della Segnatura frescoes. Raphael, of course, did not invent those themes himself. Like all traditional High Artists, his commission was to give graphic form to ideas supplied him—in this case, by the Pope's official theologian, Marco Vigerio. What makes these frescoes Raphael's masterpieces was his skill at creating an image of balance through composition, color, etc.

Two major frescoes balance each other—the Disputa (Disquisition on the Sacrament) proclaiming the Pope's spiritual powers, and the School of Athens, proclaiming his powers as a peace-assuring prince who can reconcile warring factions. Within each fresco again there is a balance. The Disputa balances Heaven and Earth, shows how in the Host as consecrated by the Church whose head the Pope is, all powers of Heaven are concentrated. By a subtle composition of intersecting visual emphases, Raphael focussed all importance on the Host, related all human history to it through concave rows of human figures and saints, identified it with the Trinity through vertical alignments.

We can now then begin to talk in terms of a "cultural expression" of High Renaissance Rome:

The School of Athens likewise is focussed on a central point—in this case, the pair of figures ostensibly representing Plato and Aristotle, the two contrasting poles of philosophy in Antiquity ("universals" versus "particulars"; "idealist" versus "naturalist"; etc.), who are here represented conversing in amity beneath the vaults of the proposed new St. Peters. But these two figures also can be taken as representations of St. Peter and St. Paul, the two opposing parties within the early Church—St. Peter the evangelist to the Jews, St. Paul to the Gentiles (they closely resemble traditional characterizations of these persons); and of Leonardo da Vinci and Pope Julius II himself—Leonardo representing the Man of Theory, Julius the Man of Action. Beyond these triple symbols, the figures represent Active and Passive principles generally, in every case the contrast being between a standing motionless figure and one in twisting action; and this contrast is carried out throughout the composition in a complicated system of repeat motifs, including statues in the niches behind.

It is a great image of ideal society based on Order and controlled by Divine Reason.

And finally, then, about reactions to it in later times, whether or not intended or shared to the same degree by the makers and first beholders of the "School of Athens": 18th- and 19th-century aesthetic reactions; reactions by people trained in what Professor Rosenblum calls "the formalist experience of our century." These too are parts of the painting's history, and its continuing function in society. But everything begins as an allegorical panorama.

Other types of substitute imagery can be used for didactic purposes, as static illustration, as well. Dolls, for instance.

Doll-play with mass-produced accessories is a principal modern descendant of panorama arts of static illustration, which can be traced back to the beginnings of history.

23A. Three of the dozens of costumes and wigs for the "Barbie Doll," introduced in 1959 by Mattel, Inc., largest toymaker in the U.S. The doll is 11 1/2" high, 5 1/4" x 3" x 4 3/4" \ "vital statistics." By re-introducing the adult doll, Mattel discovered a best-selling device.

In modern society, dolls[34] may well be the most widespread and oftenest used form of didactic substitute imagery. Why didactic? Because in using dolls, children implicitly learn their society's conventions of dress and behavior. Relating to a doll by simple analogical thought—identifying something as similar to oneself—is well within even a small child's mental capapity; so is a mythopoeic relationship to the outside world (i.e., treating inanimate objects as if they were living, could think and talk, etc.). This usage explains why, until very recent times, dolls were invariably miniatures of adults (the baby doll only became popular c1850, possibly in response to some aspect of the Romantic movement); hence, why Mattel had such huge success re-introducing the adult doll, "Barbie," thus returning to the normal social function of this art form.

Dolls may well be the oldest form of didactic substitute imagery, also.

Through the ages dolls, it seems, have been played with as a sort of stage performance. They are made to form panoramas by standing up or sitting in settings (doll houses, e.g.). This sort of use reveals dolls' direct lines of ancestry from early puppets, marionettes and the like.

Druck u. Verlag v. C. Burckardt's Nachf. Weissenburg (Elsass)

23B. Detail from a page of printed cut-out dolls, made in Alsasce, c1880. These paper cut-outs are direct ancestors of paper comic pages of newspapers c1920-1950, descendants of marionnettes, shadow-figures, ultimately of idols clothed in processions.) From the collection of Klaus Lankheit, Karlsruhe).

How far marionnettes and puppet-shows can be traced back into history is hard to fix. One thing is sure—little girls dressing up dolls and arranging them in little domestic panoramas are carrying on one of the most ancient artistic activities of civilized human beings—and one, furthermore, responsible not only for quantitites of Low Art but some great High Art as well. Those Chinese shadow-figures which are now little more than an arty

24A. Chinese shadow figure from the collection of the Völkermuseum, Berlin. 19th century.

24B. Pottery figures of dramatic actors from Yüan tomb in Honan. 14th century. Some Yüan tombs had replicas of stages in brick built into their walls, indicating the enormous popularity of stage performances; their ritual character is suggested by the documented fact of their being accompanied by music, song, and dance—powerfully inculcating and transmitting lifestyles of that age and class. (Exhibition of Archaeological Finds of the People's Republic of China.)

variant of animated cartoons, descend from a major form of High Art in China, the great drama of Ming, Yuan and Sung periods— which, in turn, descended from ritual drama of T'ang and Wei times. Likewise in Japan, those masses of little dolls which you see crowding shelves of gift shops at every historical site and local markets, demonstrably descend on the folk level from the same early matrix of religious drama as the *No* plays. Whence the key: dolls are modern descendants, mass-produced and secularized, of historic ritual arts, universally. Among "Barbie's" collateral ancestors, then, may be numbered some of the most famous works of historical art: Klaus Sluter's Well of Moses in the Chartreuse at Dijon, which can be seen as a substitute image for a miracle play whose actors hold scrolls inscribed with their parts; coronations and festivals of every sort which artists were routinely called upon to design, from Charles V's entry into Antwerp to Washington's entry into New York; the Parthenon frieze, a substitute image of the panoramic procession of Athenian citizens to their Acropolis bearing their goddess's new cloak; rites of the dead in Egypt.[35] And perhaps the analogy with doll-play will help explain an otherwise puzzling practise, widespread in space and time, of burials with figures and furniture which appear to have no connection with or even reference to death or an afterlife.

Han tomb figurines and relief murals are a principal basis for the common assertion that the Han Empire was not "religious"; they involve

no special cult or worship; nor is there anything particularly appropriate to the tomb—no journey of the dead, no weighing of good and evil in the balance, no victory over the grave, no mourning for friends...[36]

Feasting, farming, sporting, shopping, playing—every sort of human activity, it almost seems, *but* what might be termed "religious." (25B, C.)

Nor are such practises limited to Han times; they continue for centuries, including the great T'ang era. Nor to China; parallels can be found in the Roman world also. (25A) To think of such tomb-making as an activity fundamentally similar in nature to arranging a doll's house may perhaps, and paradoxically, suggest that it is not as "secular" as supposed. Rather, they may have been didactic. Ritual acts, indoctrinating: "This is how We

25A. Roman sarcophagus from Simpelveld, Netherlands, c150 A.D., in the Rijksmuseum van Oudheden, Leiden.

25B. Rubbing from the Wu Tombs, c150 A.D., of relief carving on walls, indicating original arrangement of tomb figures and furniture of pottery.

25C. Pottery tower, from a burial of the later Han period, c150 A.D.

do things; this is how things ought to be done." Means of reinforcing awareness of the Nature of Things, *doctrina de rerum natura*. To understand death as part of the Nature of Things is profound wisdom, the kind of wisdom peculiarly associated with Chinese thought,[37] but of course hardly unique to China; *Ecclesiastes* belongs to the same age.

How effective such ritual acts might be depends, of course, on how closely ritual and "real" worlds are identified. In doll-play that is often very close indeed. *Winnie-the-Pooh* owed its success in part, surely, to how easily adults and children alike could accept the idea of Christopher Robin's stuffed animals being alive. And who has not seen little girls who talk constantly to their dolls, explain problems to them, seek advice from them, whose dolls in fact become a mythopoeic mode of thought (to use Frankfort's term from *The Intellectual Adventure of Early Man*)? Frankfort, among many others, suggested that indeed for early man there was a close identification—perhaps a total one—between original and copy (q.v.). To copy something was to re-create it. If so, if in fact these "doll-house" type of tomb furnishings are didactic substitute imagery, static illustrations of the Nature of Things, then we should expect to find the practise widespread in earlier millennia when the idea of Natural Law was powerfully expressed in the mimetic imagery of pyramids and ziggurats and megaliths. And so it may be.

As experts in the field readily admit (comparatively speaking), study of 3rd- and 2nd-millennium megalithic cultures of Western Europe and the Mediterranean is just beginning. About burial rituals involved in structures like Stonehenge, Los Millinares, Carnac, etc., little is known, unless Mycenaean practises be taken for typical of them, but the structures seem laid out for it. All the stranger, then, to find so much sculpture in the Aegean area that not only seems unritualistic (at least by our standards!) but unrelated to burials. The Vounous group, for example, seems positively informal, casual. It has been supposed to represent some ritual, possibly of fertility, associated with bulls and snakes; but that may not be so.[39]

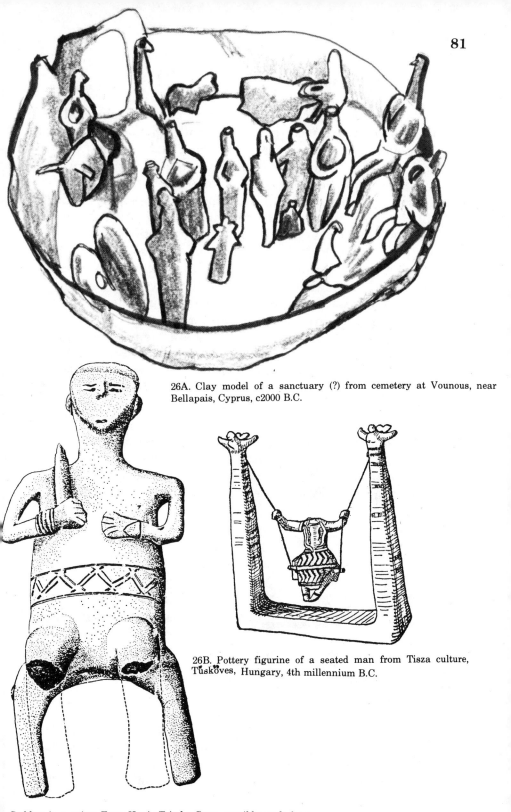

26A. Clay model of a sanctuary (?) from cemetery at Vounous, near Bellapais, Cyprus, c2000 B.C.

26B. Pottery figurine of a seated man from Tisza culture, Tüsköves, Hungary, 4th millennium B.C.

. Goddess in a swing. From Hagia Triada, Crete, possibly made for a sehold shrine. Late Minoan, c1400 B.C.

One guess that can be made with reasonable plausibility is that all the great structures of the 3rd millennium—Egypt's Great Pyramids, the ziggurats of Mesopotamia, the megaliths (which in their original form go back to around the same time) involved symbolic mimetic images of cosmic order—the cycle of the seasons, of birth and death, seedtime and harvest, the planets in their courses. A common denominator is the general principle of Natural Law, of the Way Things Are (q.v., Section VI). That the statuettes in such graves may have visually set forth the same principle in human life is not, then, inherently impossible. The idea that these were static illustration, by whose arranging cosmic order was somehow reassured or re-introduced, the way doll-play nowadays reassures and reinforces a comfortable security that "this is the way things are," is not incompatible with the idea that they may have also been literally substitute images in place of servants, consorts, etc., ritually killed for company in the next world, either. *Barbie redux!*

Another whole category of substitute imagery which can be traced from modern popular/commercial arts to ancient ritual origins consists of functional objects made into shapes of what appear to be totally unrelated natural forms.

27A. Bronze lamp from Roman Egypt, 2nd-3rd century A.D. Illustrated as No. 298 in catalogue of *Master Bronzes from the Classical World* (D.G. Mitten & S.F. Doeringer, eds.),. exhibition at Fogg (Harvard), City Art of St. Louis, and Los Angeles County museums, 1967-8. "H.O. 05, L:O. 32, L. of frog: 0.13: dark green patina.'

"Should the highest art serve for public admiration or private delight?" asks a foreword to the *Master Bronzes of the Classical World* exhibition, billed as the first such exhibition in world history—then typically proceeds, without attempting to define either "art," or "public," or "private," to dilate upon how "the ancients carried to unsurpassed levels of refinement such private (*sic?*) arts as vase painting, jewellery, and small sculpture in bronze...." From this one might gather that all such objects were made in exactly the same way and for the same purpose as, say, Brancusi's *Bird in Flight*. But the catalogue itself contradicts that idea. Introducing the Roman (surely the artiest!) section of that exhibition[40], Heinz Menzel describes how in buried Pompeii

splendid city dwellings of the prosperous citizenry were filled with decorative statues and statuettes; even the simplest implements, such as coal or fire pots, waterwarming vessels, fountain spouts, lamps and lamp stands, or legs of chairs and tables, were ornamented and formed as figures. This more or less rich heritage of bronzes is similarly found in villas of Morocco, cellars of destroyed English houses, fortresses along the German and Danubian *limes* (fortified zone) and in settlements through the entire Roman Empire....

—in fact, as close in spirit to mass-production as the technology allowed. (That molds have to be destroyed every time a bronze statuette was made does *not* mean each was individually conceived!) And what was the motive for making all this substitute imagery in the first place?

Viewed by itself, the bronze statuette is not only the transmitter of a meaning, that is, the bearer of a certain function, be it as a votive offering in a temple or decorative element in a house; it is also a work of art.

By "work of art" is meant here, apparently, simply that "the plainest and even most carelessly worked piece is still a link in a long chain which originated in and took as its model a statuary prototype."

With all this there can be no possible quarrel. Except, perhaps, over what modern representatives of such ancient arts may be. For it must be plain as it is unpalatable, that exactly similar observations could be made about popular culture today as about these ancient bronzes. Visit any five-and-dime store, any novelty counter, and you will find "pots...furniture...lamps" all "ornamented and formed as figures." And you will readily realize too that this popular/commercial art is likewise "transmitter of a meaning, that is, the bearer of a certain function, be it as a votive offering...or decorative element in a house." Just as these bronze statuettes can be read as documents to the interests and values of Graeco-Roman civilization, all the more revealing because not consciously made as such, so modern popular/commercial statuary and decorative arts have comparable documentary value for our own age. As for them being "also a work of art"—if by that is meant derivation from some prototype in High Art, that surely is quite as easily traceable, and to quite as convincing (or unconvincing) conclusions. Two can play at games like this caption[41] for the bronze lamp (27A):

The frog bites a shell; a water snake (ancient *hydra; tropidonotus natrix)* bites his l. hind leg. The shell was a nozzle for the lamp wick; oil was poured into an opening on the frog's back. The group illustrates the loves and hates of animals (Oppian, *Cynegetica,* 38). The water snake was a celebrated destroyer of frogs (*Batachromyomachy,* 82; Aelian, *De natura Animalium,* 9:15; Aesop, *Fabulae,* 76). O. Keller believes the frog-shaped lamps in Graeco-Roman Egypt continue an Egyptian belief in the frog as a symbol of resurrection because he was mistakenly thought to die in the winter, revive in the spring.

How about this caption for the "Firth of Forth Souvenir Cream Pitcher"? (27B)

The cow prances forward; obviously the Highland variety is intended (*bos cale-donius*). The open mouth was a spout; cream was poured into an opening in the cow's back; the curved tail (*queue courbée*) served as handle. The cow was celebrated in Scottish lore (Scott, *Marmion:* 118:472; Burns, *passim*; Ossian, I:14). I. MacTavish believes cow-shaped souvenirs continue a Highland belief in the cow as a symbol of wealth, hence a Celtic variant of the *cornucopia.*

Admittedly, exact prototypes in great High Art for this piece are not too easily come by (Paul Potter *via* Landseer?) But then, neither are they for classical bronzes. It appears that hinting at the existence of great prototypes to justify calling statuettes works of art is one thing, exact correspondences another: "Thus, our efforts must be directed towards finding these models and understanding the links of transmission whose modifications and reshaping determined the image we now encounter in the statues and statuettes which have come down to us...." Good luck. To find the great High Art masterpieces which inspired these little classical bronzes will take a while. For in fact great masterpieces of High Art and small bronzes alike come out of a common matrix—as do comparable pieces everywhere, from

27B. Mass-produced cream pitcher, imitation lustre ware, made in Japan c1935 for sale in Scotland, with stamped inscription "A PRESENT FROM FORTH BRIDGE" and picture of same. H. 4", W. 7", of image of bridge 1 ½".

every society and every community, universally; not least including modern mass-produced "decorative" objects. Nor was their original motivation "art." In only a few cases could the motive be categorized in any effective or conscious sense as the traditional art of beautification: identifying use and humanizing the artifact. In no case was the motive "art" in the avant-garde sense of self-expression. Almost all can be explained simply as didactic substitute imagery: responses to an atavistic need for, and delight in, recognition and reproduction of things seen and known; and thereby, inculcation of the values which they necessarily, by their very existence, stand for.

Didactic substitute imagery in the form of decorative statuary originates in sanctuary and tomb. Trace back the origins of a cheap lamp-stand, and you will find a chain of oil lamps and candlesticks, shrine and tomb furniture made in anthropomorphic and zoomorphic shapes which again leads back to the beginnings of civilization itself.

28A. Lamp base in form of a
Chinese woman's head, bulb
socket in skull. China, c1940, for
U.S. market. H. 8″.

28B. Anthropomorphic, pot
Tisza culture, Tuskoves,
Hungary. 4th millennum B.C. A
type of vessel presaging the
famous human-head vases of
5th-century Greece and 20th-
century mass-produced "Toby
jugs"—and much else.

Maps and their variants (diagrams, floor plans, etc.) are the most abstract form of didactic substitute imagery.

In direct contrast to panoramas, insofar as literal replication of natural appearances is concerned, are road maps. Here literalness just gets in the way. A birds-eye view of Black Forest roads with stylized peaks and greenery is attractive and might qualify for some "Maps-as-Art" show, but for a map that tells you where places are, how to plot routes, ascertain boundaries and generally get around the country, you don't want landscape, however stylized; you want a highly conventionalzed pattern of symbols by means of which you can get from here to there. You want simple abstracted substitute imagery.

It has always been so. "Maps-as-art," counterparts to the picturesque Black Forest postcard (29A) can be found at most times and places.

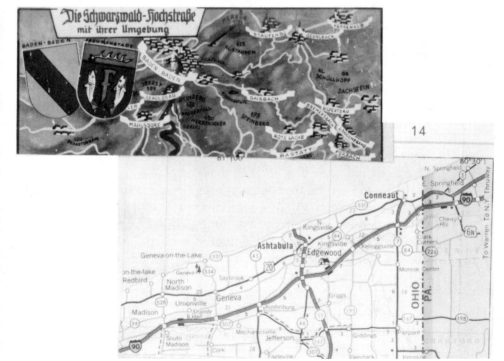

29A. Tourist postcard of Black Forest roads. 29B. Section of a map given out at service stations to m otorists.

30A. Panorama of the Italian coast south of Rome and the Via Appia, abstracted into the form of a relief map by Leonardo da Vinci, c1514. A pen, ink, and blue watercolor graphic in the Royal Library of Windsor Castle (No. 12684).

Hereford Cathedral has a late medieval map which is a fine example of beauty and symbolism at the expense of accuracy—it sets forth the Creator's glory in grand symbolic display, but implies that England and Scotland are separated by water, and has been duly derided on that account.[42]. Leonardo da Vinci's maps have been treated with greater respect. They are beautiful panoramas in pen, ink and blue watercolor, admired as evidence of the great artist's versatility. But like his flying machines that wouldn't fly and his war chariots that were useless in battle, they are not admired for their practical value; nobody ever used them to find the way to Rome.

Conversely, even in remotest Antiquity substitute imagery with the requisite total abstraction to serve for effective maps and plans can be found.

30B. Diorite statue of Gudea, Lord of Lagash (modern Telloh), in Mesopotamia, currently dated c2150. B.C., in the Louvre, Paris.

Of all the minor rulers of ancient Mesopotamia, statues of only one survived in fairly large numbers: Gudea of Lagash. There can be little doubt that all Mesopotamian rulers had quantities of statues made, not for aesthetic satisfaction or cultural expression, of course, but to serve like the votive images of Tell Asmar (cf. 12) for assurance of the lord's permanent presence at all his enterprises. Having a tablet on his knees with a ground plan of (presumably) the enclosing wall of his temple enabled him, we suppose, to be continuously present at its—or their[43]—continuous (i.e., timeless, eternally recurring, as the mythopoeic/analogical mind conceived it) dedication. Such plans being throughout Antiquity normally drawn on boards or on earth,[44] or on other perishable substances soon lost, this survival has peculiar interest as further proof that substitute imagery and architecture appeared in history together. (q.v.)

From didactic substitute imagery—arts whose existence implicitly teaches—it is a short and logical step to ancient and modern funerary arts, where the implicit purpose of substitute imagery is hortatory.

Funerary art by its very existence exhorts beholders. It urges them to ponder, to reflect—at the very least, upon their own end, functioning for a *memento mori:* "where they have gone, we must surely follow." Hopefully, too, inspiring emulation of the deceased's virtues: "learn from them, and be wise. Study their examples..." Obviously any such art involves an element of traditional beautification, though not necessarily as a conscious or primary goal: unless intelligible and hence attractive to beholders, the art will not "work" very well. But that is by no means to agree with those who say mere substitute imagery does not "work" at all.

Much of the world's greatest High Art at all times and places has been funerary. It's sometimes alleged that such times and places are all behind us. Erwin Panofsky, for instance, whose legendary erudition[45] became in later years all too reminiscent of Reginald Bunthorne's

Be eloquent in praise of the very dull old days which have long since passed away

And convince 'em, if you can, that the reign of good Queen Anne was Culture's palmiest day.

wrote in his fat volume *Tomb Sculpture* [46] that all was over by the early 17th century:

To end this hasty survey of funerary sculpture with Bernini is not entirely arbitrary. After him...the days of funerary sculpture, and of religious art in general, were numbered,. 'Modern tombs,' says Henry James, 'are a skeptical affair...the ancient sculptors have left us nothing to say in regard to the great, final, contrast.' ...He who attempts to write the history of eighteenth-, nineteenth-, and twentieth-century art must look for his material outside the churches and outside the cemeteries.

Well, up to a point, Lord Copper. What went outside churches and cemeteries was self-conscious artistic expression, on its way to becoming an end in itself. Funerary arts stayed there, serving their primordial social function. Only now they began reverting to type—popular/commercial type, that is, which is where Christian funerary arts (the subject here) first began, their first great examples being in fact products of "art industry,"

31A. DAVIS, TOMB, HIAWATHA, KANSAS. Commissioned by a wealthy neighborhood farmer, John Davis, to commemorate himself, his wife and their long marriage; executed over a twenty-year period c1940-1960 by a commercial tombstone-cutter. It consists of six pairs of statues of Davis and his wife and various stages of their life together (courtship, young marriage, old age, etc.) a sarcophagus with the wife's body, and a grieving Davis looking at it.

31B. In the most recent edition of Helen Gardner's pioneer (1926) *Art Through the Ages* the Taj Mahal in Agra is still described as built by Great Moghul Shah Jahan "as a memorial to his wife, Mumtaz Mahal." It was carried out by a corps of workmen from all over the Moghul Empire in a great variety of precious materials, 1630-1648.

commercial workshops in Antioch, Ephesos and other Levantine centers, shipped all over the late Roman Empire, as Riegl's classic long since demonstrated.[47] The split that resulted when artistic sensitivity went its own way and left popular/commercial arts to fulfil their functions unaided has been disastrous for modern funeral arts, as for all others in the 20th century. But it has not ended them. They still have a living relationship to society, which is more than can be said for artistic expression left on its own.

A case in point: the Davis tomb in Hiawatha, Kansas (31A). In the spring of 1973 a story about it was picked up and broadcast via Associated Press, to the effect that John Davis must have been a real mean man to squander all his substance on this lavish memorial to himself, his wife, their love and lifelong marriage, when he might have done something civic-minded with it. They had in mind, one supposes, a John Davis Public Park, an Amy Davis Municipal Sewage Treatment plant; maybe even a free abortion clinic (the couple had no children). That the Davis tomb might qualify as a work of art occurred, it seems, to nobody. Otherwise, its expenditure presumably would have been justified. Justified as are expenditures by the Guggenheim Foundation or Canada Council in aid of Artists. Justified, even, as modern opinion justifies the Taj Mahal (31B), perhaps. For surely this Davis tomb is art in the sense of fulfilling one of the fundamental social functions of the activity called art for thousands of years now, even if it doesn't fulfil artistic expression to meet modern taste.

Admittedly, its artistry leaves something to be desired compared to the Taj. But it performs exactly the same social function which is attributed to the Taj by guidebooks and art surveys alike: "If Shahjahan [so says the *Illustrated Guide to Agra*]—great king that he was—could not keep his peerless wife alive he had at any rate made up his mind to immortalize her memory..." John Davis wouldn't have said it differently. Furthermore, the pairs of statues at successive stages of life culminating in the old man with an empty chair beside him, then kneeling before the coffin, constitute a striking image of continuity. But an artless one, in the literal sense of that word. What differentiates the Davis tomb from the Taj (apart from grandeur of scale and cost, of course!) is that the Taj involves much more than a set of substitute images additively assembled. The Taj has to do not just with a personal feeling or with the marriage of one couple, or even with the institution of marriage (which the Davis tomb does, inherently), but with the endurance of a dynasty, with the preservation of a State.[48] Though it begins with substitute images—mimetic shapes (q.v. 40f) like domes and iwans and decoration which all had been meaningful to its historic community for aeons past—it composes them into an organically interrelated whole, analytically thought out. In short: the Davis tomb is a poor and mediocre specimen of the kind of hortatory substitute imagery represented at its most superb by the Taj. But it's the same kind of art,[49] and it's the best of that kind of art we have currently available.[50] What someone with Henry Moore's sensitivity to interplay of solids and voids could have done with a commission like this! Alas, it would have been beneath his dignity, irrelevant to his searchings in "the formalist experience of our century."

Most lavish and most famous example of hortatory substitute imagery in the modern world is Forest Lawn.

"Forest Lawn" has long been one of those names sure to draw ritual sniggers whenever two or three intellectuals are gathered together. Aldous Huxley, Evelyn Waugh, Jessica Mitford, these are only a few whose mockery of Forest Lawn made them a great deal of money.[51] It's easy; as social geographer Barbara Rubin so acutely observed, "Examined outside the historical and cultural context in which it evolved, Forest Lawn lends itself to parody and satire in much the same way that, viewed in isolation, any strikingly different complex of belief and behavior (and the forms they engender) tends to elicit contempt and derision. For example...the sculpture of Africa [routinely mocked by intellectuals until Cubist painters made it fashionable]...."[52] Avant-garde mockery of Forest Lawn, she argues, boils down mostly to this: "the wrong kind of art for the [sniff] wrong kind of people"—art described by the cemetery's founder, Hubert Eaton, as "narrative and emblematic...which will recall the population to virtue and honor," patronized by those Midwesteners who flocked into Southern California during the rich farming decades of the 1910s and 1920s anxious to find some substitute for the village churches and town halls which had given their earlier lives cohesion, i.e., precisely those "hicks" and "hayseeds" regularly the butt of Eastern intellectuals' knee-jerk derision.[53]

Not the least interesting aspect of Forest Lawn, objectively considered, is its fly-in-amber preservation of the outlook and

values of a white Protestant Anglo-Saxon America on the eve of
World War I, when its predominance in American culture still
seemed assured by Nature and Nature's God. According to the
official brochure, Forest Lawn was the product of Hubert Eaton's
vision on New Years Day 1917, of a cemetery filled with Art which
would exhort those visiting it to Higher Things—by which he
meant, apparently, notions of Eternity as a cross between
Jefferson's American Arcadia and the Land of Oz, a state
wherein everybody would be forgiven everything and realize all
their dreams, all without effort (Eaton and L. Frank Baum were
almost exact contemporaries); exhort them, too, to a romantic
patriotism idealizing the Founding Fathers as men above sin,
guileless and prayerful and pure; and to civic virtue as preached
from liberal Protestant pulpits and practised in Rotary and
Kiwanis. The result is Art conforming to popular demand;
democratically selected "for the people, of the people, by the
people." Here you can see how folk art comes into being out of
High Art: painterly forms in the *Signing of the Declaration of
Independence* being flattened out into a mosaic panorama where
additive and conceptual vision replaces the sophisticated
perceptions of late 18th-century painting so effectively that some
figures already have two left feet; or in the Lincoln panorama,
completed in 1976, where the Lincoln of liberal folklore, loving
every hair on l'il kinky black heads, frees the slaves within a
cosmic-present format reminiscent of Trecento "primitives."
Here too you can see perpetuated that integral conjunction, in
every culture at all times and places, of death and sex—for make
no mistake about it, in this setting the nude statuary (32A) with
which Forest Lawn abounds means "sex," idealized *via* Art into a
form acceptable for public display in this particular culture. Here,
finally (32B) you can see an environment shaped by the people's
wants, rather than people shaped into a mould devised by some
form-giver like Gropius or Corbusier or Wright: what Barbara
Rubin calls "a felt need for continuity in human existence
expressed through gestures of remembrance" overrode Hubert
Eaton's original idea that Forest Lawn should have only
communal sculpture and no individualistic markers, so that

...every year on major holidays—Christmas, Easter, Mother's Day, Memorial
Day—relatives and friends gather to refurbish and embellish the gravesite, and
'unsanctioned' ephemeral offerings appear on graves all over the park.
Personalized mementos...include papier mâché creches, pine-cone angels, gilded

32A."Maternal Tenderness," typical quasi-mass-produced sculpture of domestic virtues available at Forest Lawn Cemeteries, Los Angeles, California

32B. "Christmas Tribute:" quasi-mass-produced cardboard fireplace on a tomb in "Babyland," Forest Lawn, Glendale, Calif.

macaroni Christmas trees, a letter to Baby Bobby, a four foot high cardboard fireplace with felt stockings hanging from the mantel. In Babyland, where space for interment is no longer available and where the youngest occupant would be forty years old today and the oldest would be more than sixty, offerings still appear with regularity. These gestures seem as old as human culture.…

The gulf between the social function of modern popular/commercial arts and arts of the avant-garde Establishment, has nowhere been better summed up than in Rubin's concluding comparison of Forest Lawn with the Los Angeles County Art Museum's exhibitions:

As a phenomenon of Southern California, Forest Lawn draws more than a million visitors each year—school children, tourists, bereaved patrons. There is no admission charge. Indeed, as a business, Forest Lawn is a taxpaying member of the community, and its aesthetic landscape is now endowed by the purchases of art made by patrons. The landscape has become in effect a gift to the people. In contrast the 'culture industry' as typified by an institution such as the Los Angeles County Museum of Art, represents an expenditure of public monies averaging more than four dollars for every person entering the museum to see the 'free exhibits.'

Ironically, the derogation which the culture 'establishment' has engendered toward the perception of what art is and does in such a place as Forest Lawn, seems intrinsically linked to a perception of art as a vehicle for personal aggrandisement and economic investment rather than as experience or history. At Forest Lawn art is for appreciation—a posture as heretical as any which Forest Lawn has maintained over the past seventy years.[54]

To say that Forest Lawn is, like the Davis tomb at Hiawatha, Kansas, a modern representative of the ancient art of hortatory substitute imagery does not mean that it is necessarily equal in quality to great funerary arts of the past, any more than the Davis tomb is. Its differences are of another order, however. By the objective standards of judgment possible in traditional arts, the Davis tomb is a poor specimen of beautification. Forest Lawn's deficiences are, rather, in the area of content. It's about a theme that has given rise to great quantities of art in every medium through the ages. But what is said about Death at Forest Lawn is at best simplistic and at worst trivial—as can easily be seen by comparison with most historic arts, High or Low,[55] at almost all times and places—e.g. (33) and (34).

33. Gravestone made by local stonemason
in Forteviot, Perthshire, Scotland, 1729.
(Rubbing). The imagery is conventional
death symbolism: skull-and crossbones,
hourglass, *memento mori* emblem, angel of
death, and two figures too vestigial to be
plain: either a husband and wife, twins,
two children or a Dance-of-Death theme.

Death is inevitable. Death is natural. Death is the door to another life. Death comes to all; keep that in mind. Great arts can be and have been based on propositions like these; they lend dignity, even a sort of pathetic grandeur, to the crudest of Low funerary arts, like this (41) stereotyped yet powerful statement of the race's atavistic wisdom on Last Things. But Forest Lawn is dedicated to propositions like: Death can be Beautiful. Death can be ignored. Death doesn't happen. No great arts ever have been or ever can be based on banality and transparent fraud. If Forest Lawn deserves derision, this is the reason, and not because of it s popular/commercial art (let stone-casters beware their own glass houses!).

Forest Lawn's banality is painfully inescapable when set against traditional High funerary arts, not merely the great moments, but what might be described as standard funerary monuments of earlier times. For example, Gustavus Vasa's monument in Uppsala Cathedral. Willem Boy was not one of the great names in European sculpture; no Donatello, Sluter, Michelangelo or Bernini he, just one of those good competent Netherlandish craftsmen who had been coming up to Sweden to fulfil commissions for altarpieces and monuments for a couple of centuries. Boy's job: to reproduce as exactly as possible all the symbolic trappings devised for the funeral procession and bier to buttress the new monarchy which Gustavus Vasa (originally from lesser Swedish nobility) had founded, so that it might continue that function for later generations. How well he succeeded can be ascertained from the careful archaeological investigation of the actual coffins and corpses of Vasa and his two wives interred in a vault below the chapel, where costume ornaments and regalia corresponding exactly to Boy's sculpture were found. The result should, by modern standards, have been dull. It isn't; in fact the whole image of death as a link in the life of the State, is singularly moving; a *Denkmal* in the literal sense of an "occasion for thought." Hortatory substitute imagery can be art.[56]

That the art of costuming corpses, now practised exclusively by undertakers, was once a High Art (as it was here), and may furthermore have been one of the oldest of all the arts, is rarely suspected. Yet evidence suggests that this funerary art is a principal element, perhaps *the* root, of all the historic arts of costume and jewelry.

Origins of arts of costume and jewelry: funereal substitute imagery.

35. Drawings by Henri Breuil from the early 1900s of prehistoric figures wearing animal masks and caves. from the walls of Les Trois Frères cave, Ariège.

Ever since flakes of reddish paint were discovered on Mousterian cave levels, they have been linked to some "instinct for beauty" in prehistoric Man. But were historic arts of costuming ever beautification? Hardly. Throughout history, bodies have been painted and costumed for one of two reasons (sometimes both): either corpses were painted to preserve their lifelike appearance[57]; or, humans painted their own bodies and dressed them, to make them look like something or somebody else. Both practises persist into modern times on Low and popular/commercial art levels.

You can still see the first in any parlor of any funeral home, in any town, anywhere, all over the world: corpses "dressed" and painted for burial.[58]

Examples of the second too can be seen everywhere: children playing at "dress-up" in adult clothes; Hallowe'en costumes; festivals in native dress ("Highland games" for descendants of Scots immigrants who want to be Scots again for a brief period,

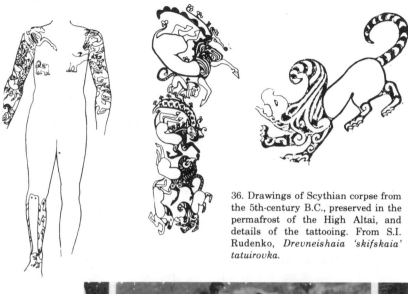

36. Drawings of Scythian corpse from the 5th-century B.C., preserved in the permafrost of the High Altai, and details of the tattooing. From S.I. Rudenko, *Drevneishaia 'skifskaia' tatuirovka*.

37. Postcard from Glasgow, 1969: clothes plaids, thistle brooch make the Scot.

e.g.); uniforms for soldiers or chorus girls (where costume minimizes individual differences, makes disparate individuals look like a single machine); personifications of the aged Old Year and the infant New Year.[59]

In all these cases what you have is not beautification, but substitute imagery. This painting or costuming or jewelry is put on in order to make a body look like something else. Or rather, to *be* something else, for this funerary art was obviously not meant to be seen—crowds at the Tutankhamen show notwithstanding (this exhibition's jewelry has usefully reminded us of the antiquity of gold as a symbol of changelessness in funerary art, and by extension, the original symbolism of gold halos and gold wedding rings). There is no reason to suppose funerary arts have changed their function since the beginning—why should they? Hence a suggestion for re-interpreting controversial cave paintings like those in Les Trois Frères (35) not "medicine men" on analogy with modern-day primitives, but simply substitute images—i.e., permanent impersonations of something or somebody else through costume and bodily adornment. And a further possibility: could caves in fact be thought of as a kind of substitute world, where the dead lived on in a "paradise" of game? (the painted bodies presumably having disintegrated with age, but the painted and carved animals on walls remaining?—the ritual touchings over years represented by "macaroni" being part of some ritual re-enactment functioning as "substitute living"?) Such a theory has at least this advantage, that no advanced kinds of mental configurations need be presupposed for prehistoric men to attribute such activities to them.

Arts of costuming, probably originating in funerary arts, in turn generate all sorts of images substituting in absentia: *seals, signatures, postmarks and stamps.*

38A. Roll-seal of aragonite, c2500 B.C British Museum, London. Often interpreted as depicting an episode from the Gilgamesh legend, but also (more plausibly, in some respects), as ritual dances of humans in animal costumes.

38B. Seal of Guy of Dampierre, Count of Flanders and Margrave of Namur, 1279 A.D. Both the costume and the seal are substitute images of the owner's authority.

38C. Abstract symbolic designs on 3rd-mellennium B.C. seals from Siyalk. (from Ghirshmann, Iran).

Just as early civilizations used substitute images to ensure continuous presence of worshippers at their shrines (12), so seals (38A) were used to ensure the continued presence of parties to legal transactions, [60] as "stand-ins" for the owners of property (e.g., merchants' goods), or the authorizers of actions, or granters of permissions. Implicitly exhortations to respect property and authority, they were in effect hortatory substitute imagery.

Costuming of images on seals varied according to what the seal was substituting for, just as costuming of corpses does (how the corpse is dressed depends upon what aspect of the deceased others are to be exhorted about; some are dressed in academic regalia, some in military uniform, some in business suits, evening dresses, etc.) (38B) Sometimes, for merely stylized "authority substitutes," abstract motifs would do (38C).

Use of seals as hortatory substitute imagery continued throughout Antiquity[61] and the Middle Ages. Only in Renaissance times, around the 16th century, did seals begin to be replaced by printed emblems. Why it took that long is an interesting and revealing question. At least five thousand years ago, exactly repeatable images of figures and symbols and writing were being made by means of seals. One might reasonably have supposed that printing with moveable type must inevitably follow soon. Yet in the event it developed only later— about four and a half millennia later! There are many possible reasons[62]; one is suggested by the way modern popular/commercial descendants of historic seals have developed in our own times.

Modern counterparts to ancient arts of substitute imagery via seals are manifold: ordinary written signatures; notary publics' paper-embosses; rubber stamps of immigration officers in passports; inspectors' stamps on meat and manufactures. Most of all in evidence are postage stamps, which historically replaced wax seals as guarantees of postage paid and protection by government authority.[63] Britain, being the first country to introduce postage stamps, enjoys the privilege of omitting words like "postage"; an image of the British monarch is all the authority needed, so that evolution and variation in that imagery is of special interest.

39. Authority seals for postage in Britain:

    A. Frank, 1978: authority represented by stylized abstract crown;

    B. Commemorative postage stamp, 1969: authority represented by a simplified royal head;

    C. Regular British postage stamp, five-pence denomination, 1969. Queen's head is naturalistic portrait bust, side view.

On ordinary British postage stamps, the monarch's image has from the beginning taken the form of a naturalistic rendering of statuary,[64] (39C)—appropriately enough, inasmuch as public statues of rulers are and always have been by far the most conspicuous of all authority symbols, from modern China and Russia to the days of the Caesars and Pharaohs. Authority images used by postage meter machines have always and everywhere been far more abstract. What you see in these British examples (39A) is typical. The more indirect, the more abstract— (i.e., mass- or junk-mailings are much less directly the monarch's concern and surveillance than first-class mail)—that seems the principle involved here, and probably determining abstraction vs. naturalism in ancient seals as well. Commemorative issues give this guess some support. For the social function of these special stamps (39B) involves persuasion/conviction to a far greater degree than ordinary stamps, and the hortatory substitute image of authority on them is correspondingly less direct—and correspondingly more abstract (but more naturalistic than mass- or junk-mail symbols).

Mimetic Substitute Imagery: Metaphors of Social Values

Substitute images of architectural or sculptural shapes function implicitly as visual metaphors of value and thus historically have provided one of the principal sources of meaning in the traditional art of architecture, both for architectural shapes, and decoration applied thereon.

"ARCHITECTURE," WROTE E. BALDWIN SMITH in his chapter on "The Formation of Ideas" in *Egyptian Architecture as Cultural Expression,*[65]

was on the way to becoming something more than mere construction when simple huts acquired in the imagination of men the significance of a type, an ideal, a concept, to which was associated meaning and importance. Once men began to value their structures, no matter how simple, and so formed the habit of thinking of them as something more than physical protection, the mere construction was elevated into art, even if there was no conscious enjoyment of the results as an aesthetic experience such as a modern man may experience in the presence of a work of art.

—When, in other words, shapes began to acquire associations and so began to function as metaphors of social values. You can see that process going on in the Ghana coffin-factory of Seth Kane Kwei.[66]

6'7"

40. Types of coffins made by Seth Kane Kwei of Teshi, near Accra, Ghana, in a business begun with custom orders, now with a "staff" producing a set of standard stereotyped items. The coffins are substitute images of objects having valuable associations for the deceased, such as a large house (symbol of prestige), coca-bean (wealth—cocoa being leading crop in the Ashanti region of Ghana),   Mercedes car.

This businessman is not some "primitive" nostalgically preserving some ancient custom. He is not a folk artist. He exemplifies modern popular/commercial arts carrying on the traditional functions of arts throughout history. In his case, the function being carried on is mimetic substitute imagery—the reproduction of a shape which has become revered and symbolic because of associations attached to it.

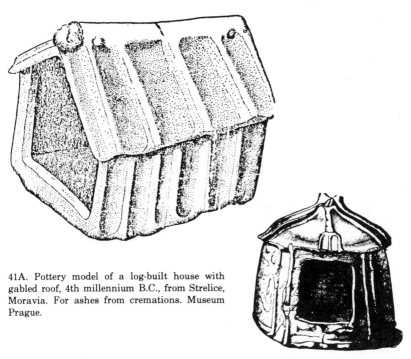

41A. Pottery model of a log-built house with gabled roof, 4th millennium B.C., from Strelice, Moravia. For ashes from cremations. Museum Prague.

41B. Bronze hut-urn for ashes, Villanovan culture, from Albano, north-central Italy, perhaps 9th century B.C. British Museum.

Seth Kane Kwei's productions are modern-day counterparts of the very ancient art of providing substitute homes for the dead, which goes back to the 4th-millennium beginnings of history, and is a principal source of the art of architecture through the ages. Although the great state of southern California offered a spectacular parallel to Ghana's best when a wealthy woman there was found to have specified in her will that she be buried in a Cadillac (or was it a Rolls-Royce?)—and a judge allowed it—

normally nowadays coffins don't take the form of houses or other revered objects. They are thought of more as reliquaries for precious objects—"casket," originally referring to jewelry, is now an undertakers' euphemism for coffin—and consequently take forms determined by popular/commercial arts of beautification more than substitute imagery (q.v., Sect. IV). Though house-forms as distinct from mausolea do often appear in our cemeteries (32B)—e.g., the cardboard fireplaces in Forest Lawn's "Babyland" (32B)—North American parallels to the mimetic substitute imagery of Kwei's coffins and those innumerable soul-houses, hut-urns, cinerary vases and the like from every early culture are to be looked for nowadays in non-funerary arts. And there they are found abundantly.

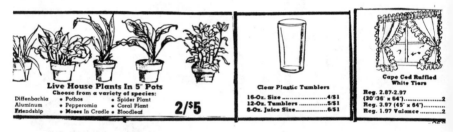

Live House Plants In 5" Pots
Choose from a variety of species:
Diffenbachia   • Pothos   • Spider Plant
Aluminum   • Pepperomia   • Coral Plant
Friendship   • Moses In Cradle   • Bloodleaf

2/$5

Clear Plastic Tumblers
16-Oz. Size ....4/$1
12-Oz. Tumblers ....5/$1
8-Oz. Juice Size................6/$1

Cape Cod Ruffled
White Tiers
Reg. 2.87-2.97
(30″-36″ x 64″)....................2
Reg. 3.97 (45″ x 64″)..........
Reg. 1.97 Valance 2

42. Items advertised in a Louisville, Kentucky, newspaper in February 1976. Some are made of traditional materials, some of plastics. From the shape alone it would be impossible to tell; in various cases this highly mouldable material has been treated exactly as if it were woven like cloth, baked like terracotta, fired like porcelain, or blown like glass, as need for identifiable shape dictated.

Historically, this human urge to provide substitute images of revered forms is the principal motivation for mimesis—that universal habit of mind whereby shapes originating in perishable materials and acquiring symbolic, sentimental, or associative social values therein, get perpetuated in new (and usually more permanent) materials when there is a technological change. Modern popular/commercial arts abound with examples.[67] Shapes originating in glass or ceramics and acquiring associations with gracious living, get perpetuated in plastic (42). Early automobiles perpetuated the shape of buggies and carriages (vehicles for the rich and socially elevated), even down to sockets for no-longer-existant horses (on auto design, see further under beautification, q.v. Sect. IV), with power-plant in front, all mechanical logic to the contrary. All-steel-bodied station wagons are shaped and painted to look like their wooden beach-wagon predecessors, for prestige reasons (43). All-steel

43. 1976 Dodge "Aspen" station wagon: steel-bodied, mass-produced, but painted to resemble custom-made wooden-bodied beach wagons of the 1920s—a characteristic piece of modern mimetic imagery. Standing beside it, one might observe facetiously, another perpetuation in permanent, indestructible materials of a extinct type—in this case, the strong silent Victorian Englishman exterminated in 1914-18.

golf-clubs perpetuate the appearance of earlier wooden-shafted steel-head types, presumably for associations with earlier, more rugged days of sport, "when shafts were wood and men were iron." Fibre Thatch's molded, fiber-glass reinforced polyester, will give you a thatched roof with chic lasting 1000 years. Plastic mullions can be inset over the broad panes made possible by modern glass technology to give your home that "colonial look"— assisted by aluminum shutters and clapboarding looking just like wood, etc., etc. A major means for humanizing 20th-century environments, in fact. (See further Sect. V).

Just so, ages ago, our ancestors perpetuated in newer, more permanent materials, shapes which had acquired some kind of revered associations in older, simpler, more perishable materials.

Mimesis in ancient times is most obviously to be seen in vessels (just as it is today [42]). In fact (q.v., Sect. VI) it appears at the very beginnings of civilization, along with writing[68] and history—not coincidentally, but rather because it manifests a stage beyond simple substitute imagery, which perhaps required

44. Hypothetical origin of mimetic forms in pottery: shapes and texture of a clay-smeared basket (A) imitated in the new techique of pottery, because of associations attached to them (B).

44C. A famous historical example of mimesis at the beginning of history: one of the cache of eggshell-thin funerary pottery discovered at Susa A, on the level c4000 B.C., which reproduced in "eternal" clay, for a tomb, the effects of painted leather bags. Compare also figure (8B), 3rd (?) millennium clay vessels mimetically reproduced in Shang and Chou bronzes, at the beginnings of civilization in China.

greater mental capacity, and certainly indicates a more complex social organization. Where substitute imagery necessarily manifests only conceptual and rudimentary analogical thought, mimesis requires mature analogical thought ("this new thing is like that old thing") and rudimentary analytical thought ("but it differs in certain respects"). Soon thereafter appears the first architecture in history, i.e., structures which are more than merely shelters, which involve visual metaphors. Again, no coincidence, but a consequence: mimesis was the process whereby early architectural forms were invested with those social meanings and values which made their perpetuation desirable, universally.

In one way or another, most of the great visual metaphors that we call the historic architecture of world civilizations are based upon substitute imagery—mimetic ornament being the commonest instance.

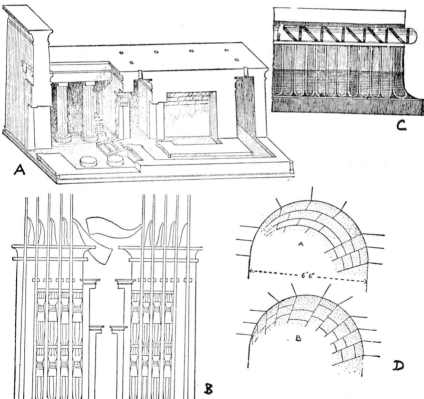

45. Mimetic forms in Egyptian architecture: (A) Mortu   temple of Amerirdis I, Medinet Habu, showing perpetuation of elements of predynastic chiefs' houses: entrance pylons, forecourt, hall of appearances, sanctuary, corresponding to progression from public to private ("harem") areas; (B) Pylon of temple of Aten as depicted in tombs at Tell el-Amarna, showing perpetuation of totemic poles and effect of bundled papyrus reeds; (C) Typical cornice perpetuating effect of bundled papyrus bent inwards over courtyard as fence for domestic fowl; (D) Cut-stone vaults in mortuary chapels, Medinet Habu, showing that Egyptians knew how to build keystone arches and vaults but did not do so in monumental architecture because there was no particularly revered shape whose perpetuation would have required them to use it. (from E. Baldwin Smith, *Egyptian Architecture as Cultural Expression*, Plate XVII.)

The principle of mimesis was first (to my knowledge) demonstrated to be the basis of Egyptian architecture—and thence, by extrapolation, of all ancient architecture and much building through all the ages thereafter—in Baldwin Smith's *Egyptian Architecture as Cultural Expression* (q.v., fns. I-65, 67) by arguing that, for instance, ancient Egyptians went on using post-and-lintel construction throughout their history not because they were unable to build any other way—they could do cut-stone vaults when they had to, for utilitarian purposes, perfectly adequately (45D)—and not because they were trying to "express their culture," but because their architecture remained in broad outlines based upon mimesis and little else. Their temples were not intended to produce aesthetic effects on spectators but to reproduce revered plans and forms of primaeval chiefs' houses (45A). Even as late as the XX Dynasty, Rameses III's great temple at Medinet Habu "was a veritable 'château dieu,' an enlarged but nonetheless literal survival of the primitive protected village with the dwelling of the god and the priest-chieftain at the center."[69] However vastly enlarged, temple pylons remained primitive gates in concept, carrying poles that proclaimed totemic affiliations for the clan (nation) and chief (god) (45B). The cavetto cornice of temples originated as "a parapet, or cornice, of reeds which bend forward over the walls. Such reed parapets, even to the curve and the vertical striations of the reeds, were stylized into the conventional cornice, used upon nearly all stone walls after the III Dynasty"[70] (45C).

But mimetic forms are by no means limited to Egypt. They are only more obvious there. They are the basis of all historic architecture (46, 47, 48).

Historic architecture—Maya temples in Yucatan, chaitya halls in India, Muromachi castles in Japan—begins with mimetic forms. To so perpetuate revered shapes was the motive for their creation. But that is not the whole of architecture. Mimesis is a beginning, a motive, a basis for the process of creating the High Art of architecture; it is not itself High Art. The difference is best demonstrated, perhaps, in the classic architecture of Greece. Greek architecture begins with the inheritance of a set of mimetic forms, common to all Aryan (Indo-European) peoples—first timber forms shaped like earlier, more pliant wood constructions, then stone forms shaped like the preceding wood, as Vitruvius's *De Architectura* had said already in the first century A.D.,[71] and

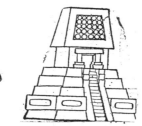

built from ancient times to the present in Yucatan and the
c reproduction in typical Maya or Aztec temples 700-1500

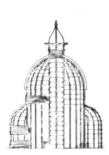

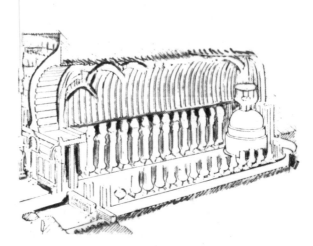

47. Bamboo tent/fire-temple of Vedic India, reconstructed from literary sources (L) and
reproduced mimetically in nave of chaitya hall, Karli, c150 A.D. (R). (Mimetic also is the
stone facade, reproducing ancestral Aryan forms of wood architecture, and the stupa,
revered round house associated with relics of the Great One.) The whole carved from
living rock—striking proof that its forms result not from structure, but as sculptural
shapes perpetuated in larger and more permanent form.

48. (L). Typical Japanese folk
building: farmhouse from Yoshiro
hamlet, in Toyonaka Farm
Museum, Osaka vicinity; and
mimetic reproductions of Japanese
folk forms in a typical castle of the
Japanese "Renaissance" period—
Matsumo in Shinano (1590) (R).

49. (A). Reconstruction of the Temple of Hera, Olympia, c700 B.C., by the German archaeologists excavating Olympia in the 1880s.

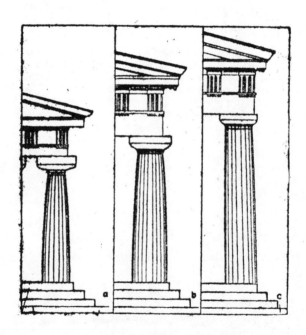

(B) Diagram of the evolution of proportions of Greek columns c550, c500, c450 B.C. (Q.v. Sec. VI)

the Temple of Hera at Olympia seemed to confirm, by being literally transformed from wood to stone over the centuries of its existence[72] (49A).

Mature Greek architecture demonstrably breaks away from any simple repetition of mimetic forms. What happens to the column typifies what happens to all. As early as 600 B.C. vigorously by 500, an experimentation with the proportions of columns and the entablatures they carry, begins to express relationships between load and support (49B). Such experimentation has nothing to do with the physical function of columns. Nor with social values and symbolism associated with them. Its concern is with how individual beholders perceive relationships between columns and the rest of the building—with making the interrelationship of all parts to the whole clear. This goes far beyond mimesis, far beyond substitute imagery; in it is manifest operations of analytical thought and arts of beautification (see further Sects. IV, VI). Its outcome is the classic art of Greece.

For two centuries now, the Parthenon has been a major peak in aesthetic line-of-progress art history. Its proportions, exquisitely adjusting load to support; its sculptures, so admirably related to each other and to the architecture, so perfectly incorporating naturalistic humanism and archaic dignity; its graceful lines, inspirited by an entasis that gives an optical illusion of elasticity—all such aesthetic qualities, and more, have been duly, justly, lavishly admired. As cultural expression, the Parthenon has been extolled as the mirror of Greek classical philosophy and rational *Weltanschauung,* reflecting how keen independent thought made its judgments by reasoned analysis of relationships between parts—whether architectural details or individual citizens—to wholes, architectural entities or bodies politic. In our own recent past the Parthenon has served important social functions, as prime visual metaphor for democratic liberties throughout much of the 19th century: the Valhalla monument at Regensburg, the Waterloo monument on Calton Hill in Edinburgh; in the Second Bank of the United States sturdily promoting freedom of business from government interference and in the United States Treasury asserting freedom of government from corruption by business interests; in the Oregon Centennial of 1915 recreated complete with pristine bark-covered log columns....[73] And in its own time, too, Rhys

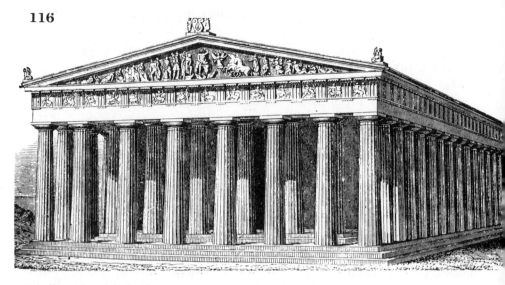

50A. Engraving of the Parthenon, conjecturally restored, from the 1880s. Wreckage of the actual mid 5th-century B.C. building was completed in 1687 when powder stored in it by the Turks was exploded by a Venetian shell.

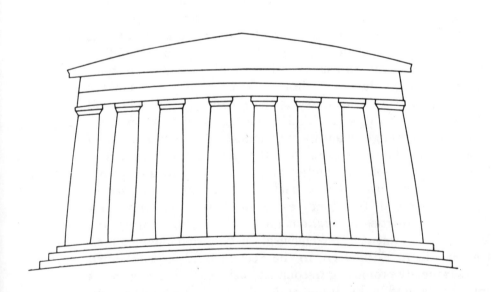

50B. Exaggerated diagram of the Parthenon's entasis.

Carpenter has argued, the Parthenon functioned to promote Pericles's type of democratic (demagogic?) government as opposed to Cimon's aristocratic conservatism.[74] But before all this—and the essential point in this context—the Parthenon was a collection of mimetic forms. Like all classical Greek architecture, like all architecture everywhere that functions meaningfully in and for its society as a whole, the Parthenon was founded on shapes having symbolic values imparted by mimesis.

Great architecture was created in Greece, as everywhere, by refining those shapes so as to provide, *in addition to* their meaning, aesthetic impact on individual eyes and minds. No great architecture ever resulted, or ever can result, from designing for aesthetic impact *instead* of meaning.

Perhaps the most classic example of mimesis in history is the dome, a shape found with symbolic value (and always more or less the same value) in every civilization. That being so, it was a logical step for Baldwin Smith from *Egyptian Architecture* to his classic *The Dome.*

Most dramatic of all historic examples of mimetic substitute imagery is the dome, evolving as a substitute image in large permanent form of the primaeval round house, because of early associations with the ancestral dwelling—i.e. perpetuated for its value as a shape, not merely as a structural device for roofing large open spaces.

Ever since the 19th century it has been generally believed that the dome, from its inception, was a functional means of vaulting which originated for environmental reasons either in the brick architecture of the Orient or in the masonry construction of the Romans....Actually, however, the dome was...a shape which, regardless of the materials used for its construction, had an antique sepulchral association with memorials to the dead and a long and highly complicated history in various parts of the ancient world....

So begins *The Dome: A Study in the History of Ideas.* "Behind the concepts involved in domical development," Smith continues, "was the natural and persistent primitive instinct to think in terms of customary memory images, and to attribute actual being and inner power to inanimate objects, such as the roof and other parts of the house. To the naive eye of men uninterested in construction, the dome, it must be realized, was first of all a shape and then an *idea.*

118

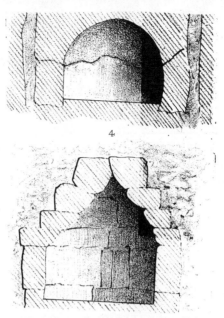

51A. Revered round shape carved from living rock
(above); reproduced by corbelling (below)—i.e.,
extending each successive level of stonecoursing.
Tombs from Cyprus, c1000 B.C.

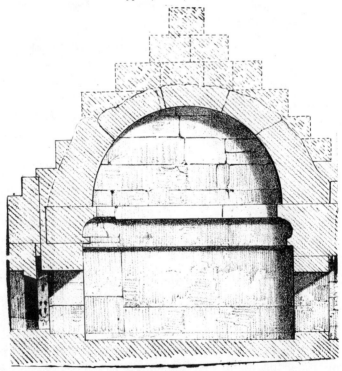

B. Revered shape reproduced by true or keystone arch
construction—i.e., shape not produced by
construction technique, but construction technique
invented as best means to reproduce the shape.

The domical shape must be distinguished from domical vaulting because the dome, both as idea and as method of roofing, originated in pliable materials upon a primitive shelter and was later preserved, venerated, and translated into more permanent materials, largely for symbolic and traditional reasons. . . .

"Moreover, the dome, like any other curvilinear form such as the horseshoe arch, could not have originated in cut stone, because rock is shapeless and the image has to exist in the mind of the stonecutter. Stone architecture the world over, from India to Stonehenge, began as an imitative and sculptural effort on the part of organized society to reproduce venerated forms which had formerly been constructed in more pliable materials. . . .

The basic theory of *The Dome* can be conveniently set out in a sequence of schematic drawings (52).

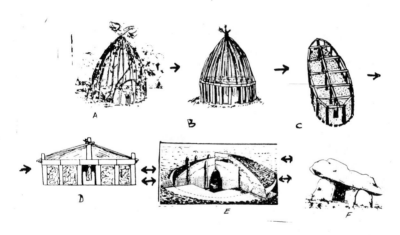

52. The dome is supposed to originate as a utilitarian shape, the simplest way of roofing a space with pliable materials, invented by savages—this drawing (A) is from E. Viollet-le-Duc's *Entretiens* of 1863. Improved tools able to cut heavier timbers produces the house with solid timbers set in a circle (B). Thence an oval shape becomes the best way to roof space (C), finally an entirely rectangular building (D) following the most natural shape of timber. But coexistent with the rectangular house the domical form persists, perpetuated now for associations acquired as a house-type—i.e., as a substitute image—in such examples as megalithic tomb from Holland of the 3rd millennium (E; illustration from Smith, *The Dome*) or dolmen from Savoy, c2000 (F; illustration from Bannister Fletcher, *History of Architecture*).

Possibly there was a time in history—so this theory goes— when utilitarian structures of the sort children make now, were the only kinds of building known. Given few or no tools, such structures would necessarily have been round in shape, round houses being easiest to make with pliable materials (e.g., modern teepees, grass huts, igloos, etc.). But once tools were invented to cut timber, hew stone and mold brick, this situation changed. Then the logical shape for houses became rectangular. Round houses became the most difficult and illogical shape to build. Logically they should have disappeared before history began. Quite the opposite happened, in fact. Everywhere at the beginning of civilization, in the 5th and 4th millennia B.C., round houses are to be found alongside rectangular ones, perpetuated for revered associations accumulated around them over the passage of countless earlier generations.

To continue: the domical shape became associated with authority and power because remote ancestors, source of the community's life, lived in round houses; with death, because there, those ancestors lay buried. Domical shapes were likewise associated with ideas of fertility and rebirth because grain had been stored in round houses; and with divinity, through associations with the round vault of sky-gods' homes.

> Because the conception and meanings of the domical shape were primarily derived from primitive habitations, many cultures had domical ideologies before they had domical vaults of masonry. Even after some cultures developed or acquired a monumental architecture with temples, palaces and churches of stone and brick, they religiously preserved the shape, and often the ancient construction, of ancestral and ritualistic shelters for their inner sanctuaries, tabernacles, aediculae, ciboria and baldachins.
>
> In those regions with an established domical tradition, where timber was at first plentiful or easily imported, wood carpentry, as in India and Syria, was an early and natural method of reproducing the symbolic shapes on an imposing and monumental architectural scale. Hence, in many widely separate cultures the wooden dome was an early form in the evolution of domical architecture. (Smith, *The Dome*, p. 9)

So domes can be found with approximately the same set of associational values in every society, every culture: Greece, India, Japan (53).

In the first millennium B.C., analytical thought refined and beautified the domical shape, as it did columns and brackets and all other mimetic forms—not only in Greece, incidentally; but demonstrably elsewhere also.[76]

In the first millennium A.D., abstract causal thought invested the domical shape with all sorts of associations from abstract systems of theology. It became as great and meaningful a symbol for the great world religions as it had been for the earliest river-valley cults of Egypt and Mesopotamia. Buddhism took over from Vedic building the dome as symbol of sacred presence, developing the pagoda out of stupa-and umbrella-dome

53B. STUPA FORM as typical of first millennium B.C. in Indian subcontinent: a primaeval round house form perpetuated on huge permanent scale for associations with authority and divinity. (Conjectural reconstruction of a stupa in time of King Ashoka, 4th-3rd century B.C.)

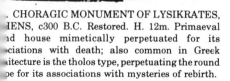

. CHORAGIC MONUMENT OF LYSIKRATES, IENS, c300 B.C. Restored. H. 12m. Primaeval ıd house mimetically perpetuated for its ›ciations with death; also common in Greek ᴀitecture is the tholos type, perpetuating the round ɔe for its associations with mysteries of rebirth.

53C. TOMB OF EMPEROR NINTOKU, near OSAKA, ground plan. 4th-5th century A.D. Covering around 80 acres in all, its principal features is a great tumulus—an earth mound reproducing on vast scale and in permanent form the primaeval round-house shape. Possibly a descendant of the famed burial mound of Ch'in Emperor Shih-Huang-Ti at Shansi, c200 B.C., first ruler of united China; certainly originating in world-wide mimetic domical symbolism.

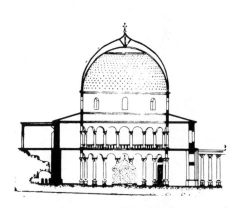

54A. Section through Church of the Holy Sepulchre, Jerusalem, c330 A.B. (reconstruction). Domical shape—death and rebirth, new life.

54B. Reliquary in terracotta from Gandhara. Stupa plus half-domes (umbrellas) equal sacred authority. 3rd-4th centuries A.D.

55. Medal struck in 1506 to commemorate destruction of Old St. Peter's and Bramante's plan for a new St. Peter's commissioned by Pope Julius II (seen here). Designed by Caradossa (?), now in British Museum.

54C. Pagoda represented in relief sculpture, cave of Tun-Huang, north-west China, 7th century A.D. Evolving from domical shapes of stupa/reliquaries symbolizing divine presence and authority.

shapes; Islam took over the Early Christian and Byzantine dome and made it into a great and continuing symbol of submission to the will of God (—Islam) for every mosque—both full domes on minarets and over mihrabs, but great half-domes, like Christian church apses, over *iwans* as well.

Well into our own era great domes continued to be built all over the world, with connotations, more or less conscious, of divinity and authority—i.e., sacred and royal symbols, broadly construed. The two best-known examples in the Western world— St. Peter's in Rome and the U.S. Capitol in Washington— demonstrate these connotations very well. But in both cases the choice was as much stylistic as for domical symbolism *per se.*

St. Peter's was originally designed in the early 1500s by Bramante on commission from Pope Julius II to make a statement—quite comparable in intent, then, to the frescoes he later commissioned from Raphael and Michelangelo (22)—of Papal powers and pretensions in the face of challenges to them: the dome of the Holy Wisdom in Constantinople, lost to Moslems in 1452; asserting the Church's willingness to move with the times, and build more correct Roman forms, just as intellectuals were urging Cicero's Latin instead of the "corrupt" Church Latin of Thomas Aquinas, for example; "correct" classical paintings following literary descriptions in ancient authors, in place of traditional renderings; and—most dangerously—primitive Church institutions in place of supposedly decadent and luxurious present-day ones.[77]

The U.S. Capitol dome in its present form was completed in 1863, at the height of the Civil War. President Lincoln ordered the work to go on, as a symbol of the authority of the Sacred Union.[78] So long, then, "sacred and royal" connotations of the dome were still remembered. This mid-19th-century work altered the dome's visual impression; made it higher, more overbearing, more Baroque, more like St. Peter's.[79] The original dome was lower, lighter, simpler, more like the Pantheon; but no less symbolic—in fact, more deliberately so. Originally the U.S. Capitol was a visual metaphor of the new revolutionary government's claim to authority based upon its being a reincarnation of that ancient

56. Popular print of the United States Capitol from
a tourist's guide to Washington, 1885. This shows
the building as completed in 1863, symbol of the
restored union.

Roman republic whose progress toward human perfection had so
unfortunately been interrupted by "the forces of barbarism and
religion" (as Gibbon, darling historian of the Founding Fathers,
had put it); now that the new United States was a reincarnation of
ancient Rome, complete with Senate and consuls and Cincinnatis
returning to ploughs, mankind's march toward Enlightenment *à
la Turgot*[80] would be resumed and never again stopped—in short,
the dome still signified a sacred and royal State, albeit now royal
in the sense that the People is King, now sacred in the sense that
government is an instrument of salvation.[81]

Almost all state capitols in the United States follow the form
of the U.S. Capitol in Washington.[82] Not exact imitations, but
recognizable adaptations—somewhat, one might say, like
medieval chapels copying the general formal idea of the Holy
Sepulchre in Jerusalem without its precise details.[83] But there is
an interesting difference between state capitols built before the
Civil War, and those built after it. Those before are usually by the
best-known architects in the country at that time—Strickland,
Bulfinch, Town & Davis, e.g. After, by bureaucratic appointees
(McKim Mead & White's Rhode Island capitol is an exception; but
Thomas Fuller's New York Capitol, which Richardson couldn't
rescue, is typical). The reason? Quite simply, that during the 19th
century, the whole idea of architecture as visual metaphor faded
away. Already in the 18th century the word "dome" was taking
on its present meaning of a constructional technique, losing its
earlier meanings of "sacred and royal house" and "building with

civic authority." By the end of the 19th, architects are building domes almost exclusively to create picturesque exterior forms and impressive interior spaces. They think of architecture as an exercise in personal expression, or at best, the art of creating complexes of forms with visual impact, which also assure optimum circulation, heat, light or whatever utilitarian else may be required. Copying an older building, or even adapting it, is a matter of good taste, not of meaning (another generation, and it will be a sign of corrupt unoriginality—unless of course it's an International Style building being copied).[84] Whence the road to our present situation, with on the one hand architectural schools turning out graduates inculcated with these attitudes and so unemployable, and on the other 80%-90% of all buildings being erected without benefit of architectural advice (see further Sect. V).

57. Popular/commercial postcard of the Iowa State Capitol, Des Moines. Date (omitted from card caption) 1872-1887. Designer (also omitted) J.C. Ferrand of Des Moines, erected by John C. Cochrane and Alfred Piquenard of Illinois, a firm also responsible for the Illinois State Capitol at Springfield.

More or less by default, then, designing of capitols over the last hundred years has been left to the equivalent of popular/commercial builders, generally speaking. For legislatures do represent the people, however inadequately sometimes; and populaces at large still do remember that buildings ought to stand for something, that a capitol ought to look different from a factory or a theatre no matter what be ordained by Monseigneur Corbu or the Venerable Gropius. Typical result: postcards of post-Civil-War capitols (57) with captions like: "Recognized as one of the most beautiful state capitol buildings in the nation. 29 kinds of marble were used in finishing this building." No mention of an architect—an omission not necessarily disqualifying a building for consideration as Architecture, since it could be made also about the Taj and Chartres, the Toshodaiji and San Vitale; and in Greece too, as Chambers noted, "prior to the fourth century B.C. there is no evidence that works of art were admired, except for their costliness and magnitude." To be called vaguely "beautiful" and praised for 29 different kinds of marble is not all one might hope for in a public building. But nowadays more can't reasonably be expected—and at least it represents a beginning on which something better might be built. For those few "modern" capitols designed by Architects in accordance with fashionable tenets of formalism (Oregon, Salem) or cultural expression (New Mexico, Santa Fe) are merely ridiculous; they don't even rise to the dignity of ineptitude like Nebraska's at Lincoln, where at least there was some dim understanding of architecture's function as visual metaphor of social institutions. If a State capitol doesn't signify association in the Union, then it's a poor piece of architecture no matter how thrilling Great Architects find it.

This by way of introduction to the present scene, where the ancient art of constructing visual metaphors by mimetic forms has been, with few exceptions, wholly confined to popular/commercial building.[85]

Although this typical popular/commercial hotel (58) can't be described as literally having a dome, either in form or utilitarian function, its rooftop restaurant in fact functions like a dome visually—or more precisely, like a crown, a variant of the same symbolic shape. No longer connoting "sacred" or "royal" but something like "special occasion," "significant building"; perhaps "people's palace" might be closest. The effective symbolism is of popular/commercial democracy: whereas in earlier ages only kings enjoyed such luxurious accommodations

58. Popular/commercial postcard distributed (free) to guests at the Holiday Inn, Hollywood, California.

and food, now anyone with a charge card can enjoy these and greater privileges—Fourier's and Saint-Simon's goal realized through liberal capitalism! Whence the entire appropriateness of this popular/commercial crown standing in direct line of succession from domed cathedrals, capitols and royal residences—in it as in them, the symbolism works at the popular, instinctive and illiterate level (as Baldwin Smith noted so aptly and so often). In modern popular/commercial arts, as in the U.S. Capitol and St. Peters, in the Holy Sepulchre and the Parthenon and the Pyramids, form follows *social* function; a crown-like effect is what the situation seemed to dictate. But once begin to consider how popular/commercial architecture works, and even more direct descendants of historic mimetic architecture than this can be found.

Forms and functions of mimetic substitute imagery are common in modern popular/commercial architecture

59. "The Chuck Wagon" diner on the Kirkwood Highway between Wilmington and Newark, Delaware, as originally built in 1958. The main door is of metal, shaped like a coffee pot. Half Wheels (windows) are about 5' high.

The "Chuck Wagon" diner (59) is always good for a laugh. Ask why, and the reply usually goes something like: "Buildings shouldn't look like anything else—and certainly not like a cook's wagon out of some TV Western. Buildings should look—well, like *buildings.*" Indeed the building is trivial. But the cause is not to be explained by third-hand Bauhauserei. For in fact all sorts of historic buildings have been this kind of mimetic substitute image. Entirely comparable to the "Chuck Wagon" insofar as origins of fundamental forms is concerned, are Indian temples like Konarak: Surya's sacred car hugely enlarged and transformed into a more permanent material (60). Other examples are plentiful.

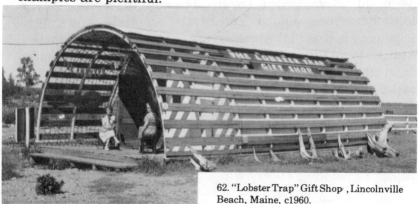

62. "Lobster Trap" Gift Shop, Lincolnville Beach, Maine, c1960.

60. Side view of the Black Pagoda of the Surya Temple, Konarak, built by the Chandella dynasty of Orissa in the 13th century as a stone replica of the chariot of Surya, the great Sun-God. (Drawing by Doris Kachanek).

What does the "Lobster Pot" giftshop (62) have in common with the "Piggy" bank building, and what do both have in common with Louis IX's Sainte Chapelle (61, 61A)?—sounds like some sort of riddle. No; the principle involved is the beginning of all architectural understanding. All of them, like the Surya Temple and the "Chuck Wagon" proclaim their social function by taking the form of some relevant object, vastly enlarged and made of some more permanent material. I.e., all of them are mimetic substitute imagery. Pyramids, mastabas, ziggurats and menhirs were the same.

61. Upper Chapel of the Sainte-Chapelle, Paris, built in the mid-13th century as a great reliquary or jewel-box to contain a relic of Christ's own crown of thorns, acquired by Saint Louis IX, King of France.

But—just as saying the Davis Tomb in Hiawatha, Kansas fulfills a similar social function to the Taj Mahal in Agra is not to say that they are of similar quality as works of art, so to say the "Chuck Wagon" or Lobster Pot or "Piggy" bank are substitute

61A. "Piggy" Savings Bank, Manchester, New
Hampshire, built 1968.

imagery of the same sort as the Surya Temple at Konarak or the
Sainte-Chapelle, is not to claim equally significant historical
status for them. They differ in two major respects (apart from size
and craftmanship). First, the 13th-century substitute mimetic
images in question (60, 61) have been systematically refined and
glorified following principles of traditional beautification (q.v.,
Sect. IV) and the popular/commercial ones minimally if at all.

More fundamentally, while these modern buildings are like
historic architecture in the sense they are *about* something (as the
13th-century ones were and as avant-garde Establishment
buildings are not) *what* these popular/commercial buildings are
about is trivial. "A bicycle shed," to quote Norris Smith's fine
definition again, "...may be designed so as to be aesthetically
appealing. But would this make it a work of architectural art? I
think not, because it would still be unrelated to...the
institutionalized patterns of human relatedness which make
possible the endurance of the city, or of society, or of the State."
Precisely. A temple, a shrine—such buildings are about
convictions central to the endurance of societies at given times
and places. A gift shop where you buy some trinket, a drive-in
where you stop off for a hamburger and fries—they are not.

Two points can be made in defense of modern popular/commercial architecture of substitute imagery. First, the idea of playfulness in architecture is not necessarily contemptible *per se*. It is at the very least a humanizing element in the built environment, infinitely preferable to that overbearing insistence on the Work Process which, as Adolf Max Vogt demonstrated, underlies so much 20th-century architecture.[86] "The cosmic is always in danger of turning into the comic," Vogt wrote. Indeed so—as "speaking architecture"—the "architecture parlante" of the French Revolutionary period—demonstrates all too well. Architects like Ledoux and Boullée, in efforts to break with what to them was a petrified Renaissance/Baroque vocabulary of aristocratic pretensions, and create an environment democratically intelligible to the whole populace, resorted to simple geometric forms with broad meanings, combined with mimetic sculptural forms. On a monumental scale the two combined effectively enough. In a great national cenotaph formed like a simplified and rounded Egyptian pyramid, an entrance formed like the half-section of a cannon ball, in allusion to ancient warriors, can be a meaningful element. For a monument to Newton shaped like a gigantic planetarium-sphere, a lower entrance calling to mind an open pipe can contribute to the total effect, alluding to the Biblical concept of the firmament and "the waters under the earth", because the grand scale can carry it off. A similar element in the lower storey of the Leningrad Bourse, to suggest riding on the bosom of the mighty Neva, is less effective, because on his scale it brings to mind other elements as well—an ancient sewer pipe discharge, for instance. On a still

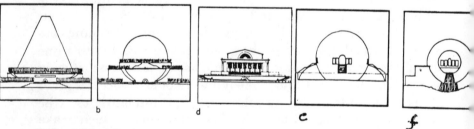

b   d   c   f

63. Examples of "architecture parlante" from Adolf Max Vogt, *Revolutionsarchitektur 1917/1789:* (a) Claude-Nicholas Ledoux, "design for a cenotaph" with the entrance formed of the section of a cannon-ball; (b,c) *ibid.,* "monument to Newton"; (d) Bourse, Leningrad, design by Ledoux's pupil Thomas de Thomon; (e) Guardsman's house, project for the new city of Chaux in 1775 by Ledoux, in the form of a cannon-ball; (f) Project for director of the river Loue near Chaux, in the form of a pipe. All from the 1770s and 1780s.

smaller scale, as in Ledoux's guardhouse shaped like a cannon ball, or his residence for a director of riverworks in the form of a pipe, too much Reality breaks in, and the effect is merely comical.

Such excesses and failures may have contributed to the steady abandonment of the whole symbolic point of view in architecture during the 19th century. But surely a proper solution was not to abandon the problem, and with it the whole idea of an architecture "speaking" democratically to the people, but to modify it suitably, according to scale and social function. A task impossible only if you imagine great art is easy.

Furthermore: if modern popular/commercial buildings are trivial, it's because of the triviality and commonplaceness of the actions and ideas associated with these shapes, and not because mimetic substitute imagery is in itself necessarily something trivial, unimportant or irrelevant to modern life and architecture. Quite the contrary. Mimetic substitute imagery for two thousand years now has provided a basic formal vocabulary for those architectural styles wherewith values have been transmitted from one generation to another.

Popular/commercial building in fact provides demonstrations of that age-old process still going on. The teepee, for instance (64-67).

64. "American Horse's Camp," hand-colored photograph from glass-place negative by L.A. Huffman, of part of the Cheyenne Reservation in southeastern Montana, 1889. On display at Coffrin's Old West Gallery in Miles City, Montana.

In origin the Western plains teepee, like all other architectural forms, was purely utilitarian—the sort of structure Viollet-le-Duc might have invented for his *Discourses* of the 1860s to demonstrate the primaeval human dwelling; archetype of the dome (52A). The difference is, that it originated late, almost within living memory. Teepees were part of a Plains culture based upon the technological revolution which followed introduction of horses to the Great Plains during the 16th century and only matured in the 18th. With horses, and sometimes also with guns— it was a culture strongly impregnated by European influences always—a new style of bison-hunting became possible. Leather became abundant. With leather, the conical tents called teepees, at first small and used only in hunting expeditions, became larger, more spacious, and still portable, so that they came to replace all other types of dwellings. Villages of teepees now developed, whose appearance was preserved by early photographers (64). In the villages, "laid out around three-quarters of a circle, open to the east. . . each sub-group had its own fixed and hereditary place. Sacred tents and council tents were found within the circle. . . ."[87] Just so, ages ago, had primitive conical shapes resulting naturally from pliable materials begun to acquire those symbolic values which would ultimately lead to their being perpetuated at enormous labor in permanent materials in historical architecture.

But time ran out. The teepee did indeed acquire permanent symbolic form, but not with sacred and royal connotations for Plains Indians. Its symbolic values derived from the white man's romanticism, ideals, utopian enthusiasms. The teepee became a famous image of the 18th-century philosophers' "Noble Savage," and as such passed into modern popular/commercial culture. Witness, e.g., the "Game of Nations."

"Nations" was a game invented for the white Protestant Evangelical middle class dominant in many areas of North America throughout Victorian times, who had scruples against playing cards because of their association with gambling, but nonetheless liked to while away long winter nights playing card games with the family. The solution: a game with suits exactly like traditional playing cards, except that instead of hearts, spades, diamonds and clubs there were four nations: Asia,

65. Lithographed playing card belonging to the "America" suit of the "Game of Nations." c1880, reprinted regularly until at least the 1950s.

66. Mass-produced "handicraft" souvenir teepee, made of sticks, leather and wood base, height c. 8″, bought as souvenir of Little Big Horn battlefield, Crow Station, Montana, for $10.

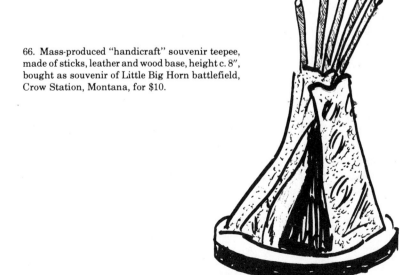

Europe, Africa, America; instead of Kings and Queens, fathers and mothers; for aces, maps; for number cards, characteristic dwellings. The stereotypes are fascinating. The European man (king) wears a top hat and cutaways, and lives in an Italianate Georgian villa as found in British suburbs c1820-1880. The Asian wears a coollee's hat and blue trousered suit; his "dwelling" is a pagoda. The African's dwelling is a round mud hut with palm trees above but—interesting switch!—the African man is in fact American, the contented darkey of Southern folklore. Grinning and dancing. Barefoot. Happy in old swallowtail coat and ragged pants. What represents America is a teepee decorated with celestial symbols, wherein lives a tall, dignified Indian chief wrapped in a toga-like mantle, immobile—the Noble Savage of the 18th century, an even more long-lived folklore stereotype. For whereas the plantation darkey is fading from the folk mind, the Noble Red Man flourishes there fresh and green to this day. Models of teepees are still for sale as images of the "free" and "natural" life, at every souvenir shop across the Great Plains (66).

The Noble Savage image has been fixed in avant-garde heads for a very long time. Paul Hazard describes an early case of possession by it—Baron de LaHontan's leaving French colonial service in 1715 to go and live among the "noble savages" (but of course, in the pattern followed by Gauguin and so many other later avant-garde types, never losing sight of Paris and its lucrative market for accounts of such experiences):

Never did anyone paint so dazzling a portrait, never had his friends the Savages been portrayed in livelier hues. They were handsome, active, strong and tireless; and happy, because they had loyally adhered to the habits and religion derived from Nature. They recognized neither *meum* nor *teum*, knew nought of money, that root of all evil, and cared not for arts or sciences. Then, by way of contrast, La Hontan drew a picture of civilized man, burlesquing his absurd blue coat, his red stockings, his black hat with its white tuft, and his green ribbons; mocking his fine airs, his polite greetings, his bowings and scrapings, his ceremonious obeisances, and his bombastic speech, his physique vitiated by drugs and sauces, and, worst of all, his mind poisoned by superstition. Foolish Frenchmen, who thought they were reviling a foe when they called him a savage! The Man of Nature was the personification of virtue, truth and happiness. It was not enough to praise the people of China or Siam; they had already fallen from their high estate, with their judges, their priests, and their mandarins. There was only one thing to do: say good-bye to the Old World and become a Huron!"[88]

The Noble Savage's irresistible attraction for the European mind corresponded directly to appeal of the idea of Mankind's Natural Goodness, and its concomitant: "We're all right; it's society that's wrong. Reform society back to its pure natural state! etc., etc., etc." And on that account the teepee form still appeals today. How strongly, is evidenced by the plethora of mimetic reproductions of teepees discoverable by anybody interested enough to look for them (67).[89]

67. "Sleepee Teepee" Motel, Blairmore, Alberta. Built c1955.

The "Sleepee Teepee Motel" (67) is simple mimetic substitute imagery: an originally utilitarian teepee shape reproduced in large permanent (i.e., non-dismantable) form because of associations attaching thereto: of free untrammelled natural life on the great plains, once found among the Noble Savages who roamed Alberta, still vicariously available, via Sleepee Teepee, to latterday motoring wanderers in these parts. How partly or wholly mythical such associations may be, whether Indian life was freer than European or only ruled by taboos instead of laws, superstition instead of custom, are matters irrelevant to the point here: buildings like these repeat the process whereby mankind first began creating intelligible environments. The mimesis which determined these forms determined the first forms of the architecture everywhere.

True, there is in this modern popular/commercial art an element of deliberate choice among alternatives absent from the earliest architecture. In theory, this motel could have taken other forms. But in practise there was no real choice—if you want a motel called "Sleepee Teepee," your shapes are as immutably determined by their social function as any Egyptian pylon or porch. That is to say, these mimetic forms are not used stylistically—not handled so as to make a deliberate contrast with some preceding style, as mimetic forms in Gothic style contrasted with similar forms in the preceding Romanesque, as Renaissance forms in their turn were deliberately styled to contrast to Gothic, and so on. Rather they are handled as in Egyptian architecture, where mimetic substitute imagery derived from primaeval times remained the *only* way to build "meaningfully" throughout history. The "Sleepee Teepee motel" represents simple substitute imagery, with persuasion/conviction inherent only.

68. Postcard of the Immaculate Heart of Mary Church on Isutlin Bay, Teslin, Yukon, built in 1960. The long poles were transported for miles (local trees being stunted, so far north) to simulate effects of a teepee, but they are essentially decorative stylistic elements; the building is not structurally dependent upon them.
"Teepee style" is intended to make a statement to residents and visitors alike about the motives and attitudes of this mission.

A contrasting example, where teepee forms *are* used as a stylistic element, may clarify this point (68).
Why is this a church in "teepee style," rather than being a

mimetic substitute image of a teepee? Because references to a teepee shape are only one element in its design. The building's shape is by no means derived entirely from a teepee. Those references only give it some "character"—to be exact, some persuasive character. They help make the building into a visual metaphor of those "patterns of human interrelatedness" by which this community lives. They help make a statement about the values of those who built the church. In a word, they give it style. They thereby make it High Architecture. Not great High Architecture, perhaps—not of the same quality as Frank Lloyd Wright's proposed Arizona State Capital in vaguely teepee form, for instance; or his Temple Beth-El in Elkins Park, Pennsylvania, shaped like the Ark of the Covenant; or his Orthodox Church in Milwaukee so dramatically refining traditional Byzantine church shapes. But architecture of the same class, consciously choosing forms which have originated in mimetic substitute imagery, and still retain meanings therefrom for the community using them, as the basis for more advanced symbolism creating a visual metaphor for some social ideology. How precisely this ideology is to be understood—as an attempt to imply a logical connection between Christian ideals and the idea of the Noble Savage; as an appropriation of an earlier culture's forms by a later one, like the incorporation of Mixtec walls or classical columns into Christian churches of earlier ages; or whatever else—is irrelevant here. How far such ideologies may be valid is not at issue either, insofar as this architecture's social function is concerned. Nor aesthetic evaluations. For like it or not, popular arts are pretty much all we have currently available to carry on the great historic tradition of architecture eclectically styled to make statements of persuasion/conviction.

What do arts like a souvenir ashtray of New York City (69A) and a decal for Oaxaca (69B) have in common? Both manifest that persistent habit of thinking of architecture in terms of space—as a kind of sculpture, if you like—which attended the birth of architecture six thousand years ago. It is, if you like, a low level of thought, requiring no more than simple analogy—this architectural shape is like that symbol and so means something the same. Elementary? Indeed. But fundamental—the basis of all architecture in the traditional sense of constructing visual metaphors of community values and convictions. At this point architecture in the aesthetic sense can begin. Styles can begin.

But discussion of the survival and flourishing of traditional eclectic styles in popular/commercial architecture belongs in Section V.

69A. Souvenir of New York City, in the form of a chrome ashtray made in Japan c1960, representing the Empire State and U.N. Buildings, Statue of Liberty, Brooklyn Bridge, etc.

69B. Decal sold in Oaxaca for affixing to car windows, in aid of campaign to restore Dominican church, Oaxaca (Mexico).

Notes to Section II: Substitute Imagery

[1] It is far from my intention to make light of the complications and philosophical problems of symbolism and language; I am aware of studies like David M. Rasmussen's *Symbol and Interpretation* (The Hague, 1974), and the legendary feats of Washoe, Lucy, Lana and the rest in Ameslan and Yerkish. But to delve into them at this point would mean proceeding no further. For our present purposes it is apposite merely to recall that we use words, and art, for two quite different purposes: to communicate necessary information via some commonly understood code; and to think, then express, our thoughts. Most speech involves elements of both, except for end extremes, like tourists' foreign phrase-books (entirely communication) or solipsistic avant-garde poetry (entirely personal thoughts). So, of course, does art, with again two extremes, one being arts with nothing but social function, the other being avant-garde conceptualism; art likewise, until modern times, usually had elements of both, but now can be found either limited entirely to social function or entirely to personal expression. See further Section VI.

[2] Quote from G. Revesz, *Origins and Prehistory of Language* (New York/London, 1956). Revesz's summary of the relationship between thought and language (p. 102):

(1) Human thought presupposes speech. It follows that children in the prelinguistic state, to the extent that they are unable to understand the language of their environment, and the mentally ill who are completely lacking in the function of speech, are incapable of thought. (2) Speech is introduced by thought. The content of speech and its representative and explanatory power is governed and controlled by thought. (3) Through speech, thought is accompanied by the words and sentences required for the development of ideas. (4) Thought and speech are inseparably associated with each other despite their disparity in fuction, intention and structure. The existence of the one presupposes the other. *Speech does not exist without thought, nor thought without speech.*

[3] Quote and reference from Frances B. Blanshard, *Retreat from Likeness.* New York, 1949, p. 32. The crucial passage in Plato's criticism comes from *The Republic,* VI, 510:

"Painting or drawing and imitation in general is remote from truth, and is the companion and friend and associate of a principle which is remote from reason, and has no true or healthy aim."

[4] *Prints and Visual Communicaton,* Cambridge, Harvard University Press, 1953, pp. 1-4, 128-29.

[5] The process is documented in detail in *The Unchanging Arts,* pp. 65-82. My favorite demonstration of it is the comparison made on p. 469 of John Canaday's *Mainstreams of Modern Art* (New York, 1959) between Marcel Duchamp's *Nude descending a Staircase (No. 2)* of 1912 and Burne-Jones's *Golden Stair Stairs* of 1880. Canaday talks about the great superiority of Duchamp's "reassembling" of a "shattered figure," whereby was created "a pattern of great order and vivacity, more expressive of bright descending movement than an imitative painting of a nude descending a staircase could be" and far more visually exciting than "eighteen young women in pretty costumes descending a stair in graceful attitudes." Most teachers using his text took (and take) the comparison to be between "photographic naturalism" (Burne-Jones's) and modern art's "retreat from likeness" into non-photographic abstraction. In fact the comparison is the other way round. Duchamp retreats *into* photography—the kind of multiple-image scientific photography common since the 1880s, well-known from reproductions (e.g., Charles Marey's "successive images recorded on a single plate," from *La Nature* 29 September 1883, cited in Beaumont Newhall's *History of Photography,* p. 109.) Burne-Jones carries on High Art traditions of abstraction from natural appearances.

[6] Janet Malcolm, "Diana and Nikon," *The New Yorker,* 26 April 1976: "Szarkowski cites John A. Kouwenhoven's seminal study 'Made in America' (1948) in which vernacular forms of

design, architecture, painting, writing and music are resuscitated from neglect, held up as expressions of our most vital national energies, and contrasted with the less vigorous fine-art forms derived from aristocratic European sources—as the inspiration for his approach in 'The Photographic Eye.' But there is a significant difference between the two studies. For where Kouwenhoven's examples underscore the contrast between the 'fine art' and the 'functional' traditions, Szarkowski's create the opposite impression—one of their *sameness.*"

A very useful reprint of early documents and summary of the "art photography" question by contemporaries is found in Beaumond Newhall (ed.), *A Source Book of Photography in Facsimile* (Watkins Glen, N.Y., 1956). For another discussion of the question, Heinz Buddemeier, "Die theoretische Ausenandersetzung mit der Photographie," in *Panorama, Diorama, Photographie* (Munich, 1970), p. 89f. The whole discussion seems to have got off on the wrong foot—forms, rather than function—because the earliest discussants were all aestheticians of one sort or another, beginning with Rudolphe Töpffer, professor of aesthetics at the University of Geneva, whose *A Propos des Excursions Daguerriennes* in 1841 lists the three main sorts of argument ever since: (1) [traditional] painting is simply imitation of nature, therefore photography puts an end to [traditional] painting (i.e., the simple-minded retreat-from-likeness approach; (2) painting is something commissioned by wealthy patrons for delectation of a small elite, whereas photography is available to everybody, so in the coming democratic era photography must invariably supersede painting (i.e., the simple-minded populist approach); (3) through an "exploitation daguerrienne gigantesque et incessante" the world will be filled with beautiful pictures which will raise the level of mass appreciation (the simple-minded "salvation through design, education through Art" avant-garde photography approach).

[7]A comprehensive scholarly summary of the rebus is provided by Eva-Maria Schenk, *Das Bilderratsel*, Hildesheim, 1973.

[8]Rudolf Otto, *The Idea of the Holy* (Oxford, 1923), esp. Ch. IV.

[9]The vogue for "pop sculpture" (Oldenberg's giant hamburgers, etc.) and "realism" (lifesize statues of corpses, fish, whatnot) in the later '60s and '70s is not waxworks, but another example of how avant-garde arts have consistently, over a century now, taken ideas and forms from popular/commercial arts and made Precious Objects of them via metaphysical apologia—in this instance, a kind of image originally made for informative purposes. Replicas of food available inside Japanese restaurants can be seen in glass cases outside, to this day, for instance. Or you can see them in giant size on billboards; or in drooly color on TV screens.

Some appropriate readings: Lester Gaba, *On Soap Sculpture* (New York, 1935); Richard McDermott Miller, *Figure Sculpture in Wax and Plaster* (New York, 1971); J.T. Tussaud, *The Romance of Madam Tussaud's* (New York, 1920). And on elevation of such works to Precious Objects for museum display, Harold Rosenburg, *The De-Definition of Art* (New York, 1972), especially Ch. 4, 5. Example:

"With Pop, the tribe of the art galleries and museums acculturates the artifacts of the supermarkets, billboards, and women's magazines by passing them through an art-historical filter. The tool is the pedagogy of the picture plane, today in full swing in assimilating, by reinterpretation and trimming, all art into what Professor Rosenblum calls 'the formalist experience of our century'—surely one of the emptiest and most contrived modes of 'experience' ever conceived by the academic brain." ("Marilyn Mondrian: Roy Lichtenstein," pp. 109, 110)

[10]Cf. Henri Frankfort, etc. *Before Philosophy* (Chicago, 1946), p. 93; and further, Section VI on creative and mental growth in history.

[12]Forbidden in three books of Moses (*Exodus, Leviticus, Deuteronomy*), graven images of cherubim, fruits, etc., are in fact made by specific order for the tabernacle and the art. (*Exodus* 26, etc.) There is a similar dichotomy in Islam, where tradition but not the Koran itself forbids substitute imagery. What's forbidden is substitute imagery in this primordial sense, not imagery *per se.*

[12]A. Leo Oppenheimer. *Ancient Mesopotamia: Portrait of a Dead Civilization*, Chicago, 1972, p. 173.   "The monuments of a cult we know only through a few written documents can reveal, even if perfectly preserved, only a fraction, a dim reflection, of the cultic activities which they served. Their mechanics and functioning, and the meanings which motivated the enactments of the cult, remain removed from us as if pertaining to another dimension."

[13]E.g., Oppenheimer, *op. cit.,* p. 186, describes how "images were fashioned in special workshops in the temple; they had to undergo an elaborate and highly secret ritual of consecration to transform the lifeless matter into a receptacle of the divine presence. During these nocturnal ceremonies they were endowed with 'life,' their eyes and mouths were 'opened' so that the images could see and eat. . . . " All these ceremonies would be worthless without the initial "lifelikeness" of substitute imagery. And substitute imagery retained this power for a long time in many parts of the world. Still in 13th-century Japan, Buddhist cult images were being consecrated by "eye-opening" ceremonies (cf. John Rosenfield, on the Hachinan shrine in the Todai-ji, for Kai Kei's statue, in 1201. *Proceedings* of the 1977 ISUH Institute in Cross-Cultural Studies, p. 27). Anthropologists report comparable ceremonies yet to be seen nowadays in rural parts of Africa.

[14]*Ibid.,* p. 184.

[15]And thus suggest yet another in Karl Löwith's series of movements deriving their impetus from "ghostly origins" in traditional Christianity (*Meanings in History,* Chicago, 1949, *et al.*)!

[16]Malcolm Muggeridge, *The Infernal Grove* (London, 1973), p. 214.

[17]On the technical problems and history of the Mount Rushmore project there is an interesting study by Gilbert C. Fite, published by the University of Oklahoma Press in 1952. The statues were in the last, Academic phrase of the Roman Revival tradition, official style of the American republic, and as such, recalled the legendary project of Dinocrates, Alexander the Great's official architect, to carve the whole of Mount Athos into a bust of Alexander (c330 B.C.)

[18]Tom Wolfe, *The Painted Word* (New York, 1975).

[19]Emile Mâle, *La Fin du Paganisme en Gaule* (Paris, 1950), p. 319 f.

[20]A simplistic statement, admittedly; we touch here on one of the perennial aspects of the "what is art?" question—as whenever "artistic expression" has to be defined in other than the most general terms. This is the point of departure for Wilhelm Worringer's aesthetics, for example; cf. Chapter II of *Abstraction and Empathy* or his discussion in *Probleme der Gotik* of a strain of "primitive magic" adding to the powerful effect of Gothic architecture and sculpture.

[21]Herman Goetz, *Art of India* (Baden-Baden, 1970), pp. 94-75.

[22]Cf. John Rosenfield, *Dynastic Arts of the Kushans* (Berkeley, 1966), pp. 76-77. "The first unmistakable image of the Buddha on coins [of the Kushan ruler Kanishka, found in a reliquary deposit at the stupa of Ahin-Posh near Jelalabad, in ancient Gandhara] is aesthetically a positive and coherent statement. Although it would be hazardous to establish parallels in monumental sculpture of the time for such a unique and tiny icon, nevertheless this image has certain distinct qualities which could only have been derived from large-scale sculpture—it was not the invention of a mint master. The figure shows none of the contrapposto which can be found on other Kanishkan coin reverses; the garment folds obscure the sense of the underlying forms of the body and are symmetrically arranged along the center axis of the body; the ushnisha is prominent and wide; the sanghati folds about the neck in a heavy, collarlike fashion."

[23]Nancy Hatch Dupree, *Historical Guide to Afghanistan,* Ch. 7 (Kabul, 1971), "Buddhist Complex, Bamiyan Valley: To imagine the scene as it was during its moment of greatest splendor, one must close one's eyes and mind to the crumbling, pockmarked, monotone cliffs which stand before you today. Instead one must see the facade decorated with realistic representations of wooden structures such as jutting roof beams, and curved doorways and windows, each painted in rich polychromatic hues. In the niches of the colossal Buddhas, the smaller stood resplendent in a blue cloak, the larger in red, their faces and hands shining with gilt unrivaled by the glitter of countless ornaments festooned upon them. At the foot of the cliffs tall pennants fluttered above monasteries filled with myriads of yellow-robed monks, and pilgrims dressed in exotic costumes of far off lands, roamed about the entire complex."

[24]See further, section VI. This is the quality Walter Benjamin called "aura." *Op. cit.* I-37.

[25]Rudolf Otto, *Idea of the Holy* (Oxford, 1929), p. 69. A footnote quotes Oswald Siren's description of the great Buddha from the Lung-Men Caves in *Chinese Sculpture* (London, 1925), I, p. 20: "Anyone who approaches this figure will realize that it has a religious significance without knowing anything about its motif. . .the religious element of such a figure is immanent; it is 'a presence' or an atmosphere rather than a formulated idea. . . .It cannot be described in words, because it lies beyond intellectual definition." Far beyond waxworks, yet just so would small children describe one of those, were they able.

144   Learning to See

[26]The *Aeneid* was written in 29-19 B.C. and released in 17 B.C. The gens *Iulia* claimed descent from Aeneas's son Ascanius, called Iulus.

[27]Cornelius C. Vermeule, *Roman Imperial Art in Greece and Asia Minor,* Cambridge, Mass., 1968, p. 200, describes how imperial images were distributed:
"...in workshops in Athens or Corinth the master image from Rome was copied mechanically and faithfully by some, and with various degrees of creative freedom by others. Often the master images were merely faces, accounting for the variations in hair. In most instances something indelibly Greek was stamped on these likenesses. The Greek creations were then dispatched throughout Greece, to the islands, and to Asia Minor. At the same time Roman workshops bypassed Athens and exported portraits directly to such islands as Crete, to centers such as Byzantium, and especially to the imperial province of Egypt. The Athenian portraits were used as the basis for groups of portraits in the third stage from the Roman model....heads modelled and carved in the great cities of western Asia Minor—at Smyrna, Ephesos or at Miletus...."

[28]Polykleitus' great achievement seems to have been organic composition corresponding to the effort in architecture to fix regular orders—i.e., to create an environment where parts relate intelligibly to wholes. It is a typical goal and accomplishment of the analytical thought which constituted "the glory that was Greece." It goes without saying that this quality is what keeps the figure from being just a waxworks. Cf. Rhys Carpenter, *Greek Sculpture* (Chicago, 1960), esp. p. 107, and S. Ferri, "Nuovi Contributi Esegetici al 'Canon' della Scultura Greca," *Revista del R. Instituto d'Archaeologia e Storia dell' Arte,* 7 (1940), pp. 117-152.

[29]*Cycles of Taste* (Cambridge, Mass., 1928), p. 15.

[30]J.J. Pollitt, introducing *The Art of Greece, Sources and Documents* (Englewood Cliffs, 1968), which is adapted from Overbeck's *Die Antiken Schriftquellen zur Geschichte der Bildenden Kunste bei den Griechen,* Leipzig, 1968, pp. ix, x:
"With the exception of Vitruvius's *De Architectura,* and the rhetorical descriptions of works of art which became fashionable in late antiquity, there are no writings which deal intentionally, directly and exclusively with art as such. Many of the passages which will be found in this volume are in the nature of parenthetical remarks made by writers like Herodotus or Aristotle. Even the all-important sections on art given in books XXXIII-XXXVI of Pliny's Natural History are really digressions from more basic subjects. Nor can Pausanias' meticulous and invaluable description of Greece in the second century, A.D., be said to deal primarily with art...."

[31]Recent enthusiasm for "magic realism" suggests some renewed awareness of how substitute imagery works; but, being still unattached to anything consequential, any potential in the movement thus far has been dissipated.

[32]The name and principle of the panorama (ancestor of the diorama, museum exhibit, etc.) was patented in 1787 by Robert Barker, a Scottish portrait painter, whose demonstration piece was a semi-circular view of Edinburgh from Calton Hill. First panorama proper was a view of the Russian fleet off Spithead, exhibited in its own building 1793/94—a round structure with the painting done all round the walls, and spectators occupying a place in the center fitted up to imitate the deck of a frigate. The need for correct perspective (criticized by Sir Joshua Reynolds when he saw Barker's first effort in 1787) was one factor in research on photography generally in the early 19th century, and photography was extensively used by panoramists and their successors. A good scholarly discussion of the whole subject is Heinz Buddemeir, *Panorama, Diorama, Photographie* (Munich, 1970), volume 7 in Wilhelm Fink Verlag's *Theorie & Geschichte der Literatur und der schönen Kunste* series.

[33]The field of Renaissance studies is so vast, any general presentation of it must be simplistic. But without a general theory to hang history upon, no history would get written at all. Among the many, almost innumerable works on the subject, I am most partial to Frederick Hartt's *History of Italian Renaissance Art* (Englewood Cliffs, 1970). The quotations following are from an unpublished work of my own.

[34]The best-known of the many studies of dolls is perhaps Max von Boehn's 1926 *Dolls and Puppets* (trans. Jos. Nicoll, New York, 1966). It grows naturally out of his pioneer studies of Costume *Die Mode: Menschen und Moden im 17., 18., and 19 Jahrhundert nach Bilden und Kupfern der Zeit* (6 vols., Munich, 1908-1919), which, along with Edouard Fuchs's *Karikatur*

der Europäischer Völker (1901) and *Sittengeschichte* (1905-6) marked a major expansion of German art-historical horizons in the early 20th century, anticipating *Kunstgeschichte als Geistesgeschichte*. (The 1932 edition, including Ancient, Medieval, Renaissance and 16th century material was republished in a translation by Joan Joshua, New York, 1971; a supplemental volume on ornaments (1929) was also republished in translation, New York, 1970). In recent years there has been a spate of books on dolls and toys, mostly mirroring fashionable anthropological views to some degree: e.g., Antonia Fraser, *A History of Toys* (London, 1966); K.E. Fritzsch, M.Bachmann, *An Illustrated History of Toys* (London, 1971); Gwen White, *Antique Toys* (London, 1971) etc.

[35]Cult and ritual is another vast subject, of course. I am concerned here, I hope self-evidently, only with the general principle, what the arts were made to *do*, not with detailed examinations of variations amongst specific cases, which are great. An extensive bibliography and useful illustrations on this theme may be found in S.G.F.Brandon, *Man and God in Art and Ritual* (New York, 1975), a book otherwise, alas! not the definitive work its publishers deserved. Cf. Fn. I-1).

[36]F.S. Drake, "Sculptured Stones of the Han Dynasty," *Monumenta Serica*, VIII, 1943, p. 287.

[37]Cf. H.G. Creel, *Chinese Thought from Confucius to Mao Tse-Tung* (Chicago, 1953).

[38]Glyn Daniel, *Megalith Builders of Western Europe* (Harmondsworth, 1962), esp. pp. 49-53.

[39]V. Karazeorghis, *Treasures of the Cyprus Museum* (1965), pp. 11-12.

[40]*Master Bronzes of the Classical World* (Cambridge [Fogg Art Museum], Mass., 1967), p. 228.

[41]*Ibid.*, 299.

[42]The Hereford map is mentioned in the discussion of how medieval arts and scientific knowledge relate to theological/poetical world-views by C.S. Lewis, *The Discarded Image* (Cambridge, 1961.)

[43]According to inscriptions, he built or restored fifteen temples. Cf. Georges Roux, *Ancient Iraq* (Harmondsworth, 1966), pp. 153-156. Cuneiform writing all over the statue assisted it in this function.

[44]Cf. W.B. Dinsmoor, *The Architecture of Ancient Greece* (New York, 3rd ed., 1950), intro.

[45]Cf.Fn. I-19, I-26.

[46](New York, 1964), p. 96.

[47]Alois Riegl, *Spätromische Kunstindustrie* (Vienna, 1901), reimpression (Wissenschaftl.Buchgesellschaft), Darmstadt, 1973.

The commercial character of these sarcophagi, first recognized by Riegl, is now generally admitted; for a summary of the question, see Gloria Ferrari, *Il Commercio dei Sarcofagi Asiatici* (Rome, 1966); Antonioi Giuliano, *Il Commercio dei Sarcofagi Attici* (Roma, 1962); Nikolas Himmelmann, *Romische Sarcophagreliefs des 3. u. 4 Jh. nach Chr.* (Mainz, 1973); and still insightful, K. Lehmann-Hartleben & E.C. Olsen, *Dionysiac Sarcophagi in Baltimore* (Baltimore, 1942).

[48]The story about the Taj being solely a monument to love cannot, of course, be true. The Great Moghuls didn't indulge in affairs like Segal's *Love Story*. Dynastic tombs have a long and central function in Islam (as in most cultures); there are many precedents for the Taj. Wayne Begley of the University of Iowa proposes a theory (in a public lecture which I had the privilege of hearing) that the Taj actually was a gigantic image of the throne of heaven, as indicated from the inscription from Sura 89 (apocalyptic terror).

[49]Truly, "things hidden from the learned have been revealed unto babes!" Shelved alongside Panofsky's lavishly illustrated well-subsidized *Tomb Sculpture* (Library of Congress NB 1800/Pa) is a poor little volume by a lesser-known (to put it mildly!) author: *Memorial Arts, Ancient and Modern, Illustrations and Descriptions of the World's Most Notable Examples of Cemetery Memorials, Arranged and Published by Henry A. Bliss, Monument Photographer* (Buffalo, New York, 1912, Library of Congress NB 1800/B5). He reveals, as Panofsky did not, that the death rate remains 100%, that people still have memorials on their graves (even Dr. Panofsky got one), that these memorials still have a social function, namely hortatory substitute imagery ("Monuments photography," says Bliss—setting the social function at one remove—"has been the means of a general advancement, furnishing an exchange of ideas and inspirations to the designer and educating the public to higher ideals") which they share with earlier ones....

[50]Over the past two decades books about funerary art have been multiplying mightily. To discuss them all would require a volume in itself. Here it's much to the point to notice the trend, however: conclusions to these histories come ever nearer the present.

Three outstanding books on funerary arts were published in the 1960s—Erwin Panofsky's *Tomb Sculpture* in 1964, Alan I. Ludwig's *Graven Images* in 1966, and Barbara Jones's *Design for Death* in 1967. Of these only   Jones's touched on the Victorian period. Three on Victorian funerary arts appeared in quick succession in the early 1970s—John Morley's *Death, Heaven, and the Victorians* (Pittsburgh, 1971), James Stevens Curl, *The Victorian Celebration of Death* (Detroit, 1972), and Edmund V. Gillon, Jr., *Victorian Cemetery Art* (1972, New York). To this list should be added a masterful review of the last three by John Maass in *Journal of the Society of Architectural Historians*, XXXII, 1973, pp. 78-79, and an essay by Klaus Lankheit in *Bibliographie zur Kunstgeschichte des 19. Jahrhunderts* (1968). Maass observes:

"Victorian cemeteries survive as fine and unspoiled examples of 19th-century architecture and town planning. The Victorian necropolis had its public buildings (gateways, chapels, offices) on squares and boulevards, its mansions (mausoleums) on large lots with a view along fashionable drives, its middle-class homes (tombs) on winding urban and suburban streets (walks); some cemeteries also boasted apartment buildings (catacombs, columbariums) and transient accommodations (mausoleums for rent). The Victorian cemetery was also the people's museum which had few other specimens of the art."

In the later 1970s books on Victorian funerary arts, especially in England, were becoming something of a minor industry.

Aldous Huxley's *After Many a Summer Dies the Swan* (1939), Evelyn Waugh's *The Loved One* (1948) and Jessica Mitford's *The American Way of Death* (1963) were all best-sellers in their time.

[52]"The Forest Lawn Aesthetic," Journal of the Los Angeles Institute of Contemporary Art, IX, 1975, pp. 10, 16. Expanded and emended, this essay was published as a small book by the author (Los Angeles, 1980).

[53]One might say Forest Lawn is the diametric opposite of the *New Yorker's* art of the '20s and '30s, about which Thomas Craven wrote perceptively in *Cartoon Cavalcade* (New York, 1943), pp. 102-3, that its audience was

". . . a set of metropolitans, New Yorkers to be specific, the bright boys and girls about town—and they were anything but lost. They knew all the answers and loved nothing so much as a well-turned crack against the yokels; they were the 'sophisticates' of society, to use a noun which must have been coined by. . . Warren G. Harding. . . provincials who had just come to town, and had to prove their urbanity by outshining the true children of the pavements in the fripperies of elegance and mode. The great dudes of the world, it seems, like Balzac's Lucien de Rubempre, have been provincials suspicious of their origins, and thus constrained to disguise the fact that their fathers were country-town apothecaries or keepers of livery stables. . . . It is characteristic of provincials trading on sophistication to be on the defensive, and to be constantly assertive of their rights as arbiters of smartness and wit. . . ."

[54]*Op. cit.,* p. 16. To substantiate the "four dollars for every person entering the L.A. Museum," Rubin footnotes the following: "This sum is only approximate, based on fiscal year 1974-75 attendance at 'free' shows (827, 369) and the 1974-75 operating budget of $3,762,600. Of this sum, Los Angeles County provides $2,762,600 while the museum's 'Associates' raise some one million dollars through tax-deductible donations from their members."

[55]The definition underlying the following observations is that in *The Unchanging Arts*, pp. 12-20, "Low Arts, High Arts, Fine Arts: Some Critical Definitions and Relationships."

[56]The basic documentation is found in Martin Olsson (ed.) *Vasagraven i Uppsala Domkyrka*, Stockholm, 1956: a series of essays describing the historical background and exhaustive medical and archaeological investigations; it is therefore an invaluable record showing that a royal funeral was in 16th-century Europe, as among first-millennium Scythians, in Ch'in China and in 3rd-millenium Ur of the Chaldees (not to mention Mao's China or Stalin's Russia!) one of the great "art works" of its time. Willem Boy was of course not an "Artist" in the modern sense; nobody in the 17th century was (cf. the very intelligent chapter on "The Function of the Work of Art," by Judith Hook, *The Baroque Age in England,*

London, 1976, pp. 134 ff: "The autonomy of the work of art, art largely for art's sake, the heroic artist-individual alienated from society;..in Europe in the 17th century they would not have been understood. Then the arts were seen in highly functional terms...) Boy (Guillaume Boyen, c1520-1592) came from Flanders to Gustavus Vasa's court in the late 1550s to do royal family portraits in sculpture and painting, and generally arrange spectacles and everything else a court artist was expected to do. That he would have a large part in arranging the funeral procession, and that his commission would be, as Olsson says, "to record it" were matters of course. He also worked for two of Gustavus's sons and successors, Eric XIV and Johan III, for the latter doing the poignant tomb effigy of his little daughter in Strängnäs Cathedral c1590, as well as his first queen, Katherina Jagellonica, in Uppsala. Occasionally too he did architectural and goldsmithing commissions. A typical "renaissance artist," i.e.—not temperamental genius, but all-round a-political executor of necessary work—in contrast to the "divino" Michelangelo.

[57]Cf. Alexander Marshack, *Roots of Civilization,* New York, 1972, p. 288, *a propos* of a female figurine from Brassempouy: "The statue was not marked, but it had been painted with red ochre, a symbolic and storied gesture comparable perhaps to marking. The red apparently signified, somewhat broadly, the blood color of life and vitality...."

[58]Hairdressers are hired to beautify the corpse and corpses are frequently buried in favorite outfits or new, very expensive clothing.

[59]One of the many perpetuations in Popular/Commercial arts which Enlightenment philosophers began stamping out of High Culture in the 18th century, was this New Year's personification. Already on High Gothic cathedrals it was represented by Janus "closing a door through which an old man was disappearing, and opening another to admit a youth," according to Emile Mâle, *Religious Art in France of the Thirteenth Century* (New York, 1963/70), p. 70.

[60]Cf. Leo Oppenheim, *Ancient Mesopotamia* (Chicago, 1964), p. 281: "As indispensable as the presence of witnesses was the practise of having the person who assumes [legal] obligation indicate this responsibility on the tablet by rolling his cylinder seal over the soft clay, or by impressing the seal of his ring, or—at certain periods in certain regions—making an impression with his fingernails in a prescribed way, or even by pressing to the clay the hem of his garment. The purpose in all these instances is to indicate his presence, and thus his consent, during the transaction. It was not a method of identification...."

[61]"Seals...in ancient life took the place of the modern signature on documents and, to some extent, of locks and keys." *Oxford Classical Dictionary* (Oxford, 1949), p. 821.

[62]Curiously, William Ivins' *Prints & Visual Communication* does not address itself to this subject. The answer is obviously complex. But the social function of seals is a key factor. For as long as the seal is thought of primarily as a substitute image it isn't thought of as a tool, a symbol used to do something else (as moveable type is). Then, why wasn't it thought of, earlier? I suggest, because the whole principle of an image deriving meaning from a body of abstract belief outside itself is quite foreign to the thought process of earlier times; it is a form of abstract causal thought that doesn't begin demonstrable operations much before the Christian era. (Cf. section on abstract causality in *On Parallels in Universal History*, pp. 74 ff.)

[63]On the social function of the postage stamp, especially noteworthy is the Karslruhe doctoral dissertation of Kurt Asche, *Das Europäische Postwertzeichen als Kunstwerk, 1840-1954,* 1977. Useful also are the observations by Lena Johannesen in *Den Massproducerade Bilden,* Uppsala, 1978, pp. 127-34 on "Frimarker och andra vardetryck."

[64]Robson Lowe, *Masterpieces of Engraving on Postage Stamps 1840-1940*, London, 1943, gives the history of the British "one-penny black."

[65]On the pioneering nature of E. Baldwin Smith's *Egyptian Architecture As Cultural Expression* (Boston, 1938/Watkins Glen 1968) a noted Egyptologist commented: "...his analysis agrees very much with what is now fairly well *communis opinio.* This is at least in part due to Herbert Ricke's *Bemerkungen zur ägyptischen Baukunst des Alten Reiches,* which pursues very much the same ideas, sometimes with almost the same words. He does not seem to know Smith's book, which was first published on the eve of World War II (Ricke's book was completed in the Forties, and published in Zürich 1950). Since then, he and

his disciples have continued along these lines, and I have the impression that Smith would have been very pleased with their work.... What truly distinguishes the book is the fact that Smith saw as early as 1938 what others proved much later and on the basis of much material: the imitative character of Egyptian architecture...." (Dieter Muller, letter to the author, 26 January 1975).

[66]Non-scholarly articles on Kwei's coffins and pictures of them can be found in Adolphus Patterson, "In a Spotted Whale, R.I.P.," *London Daily Telegraph*, 28 June 1974, also Vivian Burns in *African Arts*, winter 1974. From these we learn that Kwei is a carpenter who makes furniture and roofs houses as well as providing litters, staffs, and other badges of local authority, and whose business is consequently expanding; he hopes to install electricity and increase exports of his products. They already go to neighboring Togo and to Afro-oriented blacks in Britain and America. About half his production, however, consists of a type of stool, ancestral symbol of authority among Ghana's bigwigs. Kwei's is, in short, a popular/commercial art of substitute imagery.

[67]The term "mimesis" to describe this process was invented (to my knowledge) by E. Baldwin Smith in *Egyptian Architecture as Cultural Expression* (q.v.). It's unfortunate that the same word was used in another great book to describe a similar though not identical process in another field: Erich Auerbach's *Mimesis: The Representation of Reality in Western Literature* (Bern, 1946/Princeton, 1953).

Similarities to mimesis in avant-garde building, such as reproduction in concrete of the texture of rough form-boards, might seem a further complication. Actually, the distinction is easy: avant-garde building does not induce these effects from any desire to preserve an earlier revered shape or texture as a metaphor of traditional values, but for sensual visual effects or/and a general taste for rawness originating in metaphysical convictions about Natural Human Goodness.

·[68]In fact it was writing, not "decoration" in the sense of beautification, as was convincingly established by the discoverer of Susa A pottery, Edmond Pottier, "Notes sur les vases peintes de l'acropole de Suse," *Mémoires de la Délégation en Perse*, 1912: "Was the true primitive (prehistoric Man) aware of what we call the delights of beauty? An unsolvable question, since we can never get into the mind of humans who created the arts of prehistoric ages.... Writing and ceremic ornament had the same origin and derive from the same source...in function, symbols are words..."

[69]E.B. Smith, *op. cit.*, p. 145.

[70]*Op cit.*, p. 69.

[71]Book IV, chapter 2, section 6: "The ancients held that what could not happen in the original [i.e. wood] should not happen in the copy [i.e., stone]. For in all their works they [the ancients] proceeded on definite principles of fitness and in ways derived from the truth of Nature." Progressive architects in the age of the French Revolution, filled with enthusiasm for Natural Human Goodness and thence for naturalness in general, seized upon this passage to justify "pure" and "primitive" Greek architecture as a revolutionary symbol: so you find, for example, a "rustic temple" designed by architectural professor Olof Tempelman c1790-1800 on the grounds of Forsmark model manor and factory in Sweden's Upland province—its sides slabs of sheered off logs with the bark still on, its columns rough poles, its timbers unevenly axe-marked.

The German excavation of the 1880s seemed to confirm the *Description of Greece* by Pausanias (c150 A.D.) who said one column was still of oak, the rest had been gradually replaced over the centuries; the Heraion's Columns showed great differences of proportion and detail. The rest of the building was always sun-dried brick and wood, apparently. Mimetic origins of Greek architecture having thus been proved, progressive architects of the 1890s and onwards drew the opposite conclusion from their predecessors and began denouncing it as not "in the nature of materials" and therefore corrupt and worthless (!).

[73]Cf. *Images of American Living* (New York/Philadelphia, 1966), "The Classical Revivals," pp. 243-284.

[74]Cf. *The Architects of the Parthenon* (Harmondsworth, 1970). Summary of the argument, p. 67; bibliography pp. 184-6.

[75](Princeton, 1950). Thence Smith went on to his last, almost posthumous book, *Architectural Symbolism of Imperial Rome and the Middle Ages* (Princeton, 1956). Baldwin Smith's pre-eminent place among historians of ideas has not yet been properly recognized. He, like so many others, was caught in the "Bauhaus Blitz" (look at the dates of his books!) whose enthusiasts dismissed all "meaning" from architecture as irrelevant to their mission of world salvation through design (theirs).

I attempted to pay some tribute to this great man in introducing the American Life Foundation reprint of *Egyptian Architecture* (Watkins Glen, New York, 1968).

[76]Cf. *Proceedings of the 1977 Institute in Cross-Cultural Studies*, ISUH, Watkins Glen, N.Y., 1978: Parallels and contrasts in civilizations c600-c400 B.C.: Greece, Etruria, Late Vedic India, Late Chou China, Scythia and Urartu, Chavin Peru and Olmec Mesomerica. J.P. Oleson, Partha Mitter, David Waterhouse, Boris Piotrovsky, C.R. Wicke, A. Gowans (ed.).

[77]The general assumption is that St. Peter's dome, like Brunellesco's for the Cathedral of Florence earlier, took the Pantheon as its model. But in Renaissance/Baroque times, unlike the 19th century, classical buildings were seldom if ever copied exactly, a general allusion to the authority of classical Antiquity on behalf of desired goals being enough for purposes of persuasion/conviction. Carodossa's medal suggests that some inspiration may have been taken also from the Castel S.Angelo, once Hadrian's tomb. Not only was this suitable as an ancient domical symbol of a dynastic family, thus proclaiming Julius II's goal of combining in his own person the spiritual powers of the Papacy with those of an Italian dynastic prince and so rivalling the Catholic kings of Spain or the Valois in France in the Tudors of England as leader and organizers of an ideal class-structured State (a goal which fired the enthusiasm of Michelangelo, among others!) but it also got around the awkward difference that the Papacy, unlike the Valois or Hapsburg or Tudor kingship, could not legitimately be a hereditary dynasty; for Hadrian was not a natural son of the preceding emperor, Trajan, but adopted, and in turn adopted *his* heir. The dome thus makes an admirable symbol of the endurance and continuity of the institution of Papacy and the Church Militant in the face of its critics (whence its relationship to other commissions from Julius II becomes comprehensible—Raphael's Stanze, Michelangelo's Sistine Ceiling, etc.)

The vast bibliography on this subject is not pertinent here; in another book, d.v., I will hope to go into such questions in detail.

[78]There is a mass of bibliography on the U.S. Capitol, as befits its status as one of the most symbolically significant, certainly one of the best-known buildings in Western civilization (though not yet symbolically significant or well-known enough to crack the aesthetic line-of-progress, apparently, since it appears in neither of the two leading art-history "surveys.") For a short general account of the building's history, cf. *Images of American Living* (New York/Philadelphia, 1964), pp. 256 ff.

[79]Designer of the present dome was engineer Montgomery Meigs in the 1850s, and there is some evidence that his basic idea came from St. Isaac's Cathedral in Leningrad. If so, an appropriate enough inspiration, for this was the great monument to Russian victory in the Napoleon Wars—i.e., a symbol of irredentist nationalism.

[80]"The progress of history toward perfection is a most glorious spectacle, revealing a presiding wisdom. We see the establishment of societies and the formation of nations which one after another dominate other nations or obey them. Empires rise and fall; the laws and forms of government succeed one another; the arts and sciences are discovered and made more perfect. Sometimes arrested, sometimes accelerated in their progress, they pass through different climates. Interest, ambition, and vainglory perpetually change the scene of the world, inundating the earth with blood. But in the midst of these ravages man's mores become sweeter, the human mind becomes enlightened, and the isolated nations come closer to each other. Commerce and politics reunite finally all the parts of the globe and the whole mass of the humankind, alternating between calm and agitation, good and bad, marches constantly, though slowly, toward greater perfection."

This passage, from Turgot's essays on universal history of 1750 (*Oeuvres de Turgot*, Paris 1844, II, 598), mixing Voltaire's and Bossuet's views of history, epitomizes the Founding Fathers' understanding of the French Enlightenment, and describes admirably what the

Capitol dome meant to them.

Inverted religious values are seldom acknowledged by either French or the American philosophers in the 18th century, yet in retrospect they are obvious—this perfection to which "the whole mass of the humankind" marches is an apocalyptic end to history, an *eschaton.* The dome thus retains its ancient symbolism, inverted.

[81]Other ideological inferences could easily be read into the Capitol dome, and undoubtedly were. So strongly does the general feel of the Capitol rotunda recall St. Paul's under the dome, or General Washington's crypt recall Admiral Nelson's, that some intentional allusion to St. Paul's seems probable—the more since it was the cathedral church of that First British Empire which the American Revolution destroyed (Westminster Abbey being the cathedral church of the Second British [Waterloo to Ypres] Empire). As newly republican Rome expelled the corrupt Etruscan kings, so the new republic has expelled modern Tarquin George. Likewise present in many minds must have been a comparison with St. Peter's dome in Rome, and with Versailles (in L'Enfant's street layout: another symbol of victory) transforming The People into secular pontiff and popular sun-kings.

[82]A most useful reference is *Temples of Democracy,* by Henry-Russell Hitchcock and William Seale, New York, n.d. (c. 1976), giving statistics on all the capitols. The book's value is marred somewhat by an outdated attitude dictating that the latest capitols, which did not follow the model of the National Capitol in Washington, be considered moves toward "freedom." Failure to find documented references to domes symbolizing national unity by no means constitutes proof, as these authors seem to assume̦that no such symbolism existed. Indeed, this is a classic instance of Baldwin Smith's premise:

"...Without any intention of begging the issue with scholarly critics who are historically trained to be suspicious of any interpretations of the past which are not fully substantiated by documentary evidence, it must be pointed out that symbolism in an art as abstract as architecture was always most effective on a popular, instinctive, and illiterate level." (*Architectural Symbolism of Imperial Rome & The Middle Ages,* p. 3).

And the truth is (as the authors frankly report) that designs departing from the National model were always strongly resisted by a majority of the population.

[83]Re copying, Richard Krautheimer has written ("Introduction to an 'Iconography of Medieval Architecture'," *Journal of the Warburg and Courtauld Institutes,* V, 1942, pp. 1-32) that the medieval mind had "a quite different approach as compared with that of the modern mind to the whole question of copying....In the Middle Ages it would seem as though a given shape were imitated not so much for its own sake as for something else it implied." Noting that some "copies" of the Holy Sepulchre had (to our eyes) nothing in common with the original but the name,

"The common element between a church which shared with its prototype only the name or the particular manner of its dedication, and an architectural copy proper, was evidently the fact that both were mementoes of a venerated site. The difference is rather between a more or less elaborate reproduction; and one might say that the more elaborate one only adds some visual elements to the 'immaterial' features, that is to the name and dedication. Both immaterial and visual elements are intended to be an echo of the original capable of reminding the faithful of the venerated site, of evoking his devotion, and of giving him a share at least in the reflections of the blessings which he would have enjoyed had he been able to visit the Holy Site in reality." (p. 16)

Yet in fact the relationship between State and U.S Capitols could hardly be phrased better!

[84]Cf. Norris K. Smith, "Frank Lloyd Wright and the Problem of Historical Perspective," *Journal of the Society of Architectural Historians,* XXVI, 1, 1967, pp. 234-237, regarding Wright's unsolicited Arizona State Capitol Project.

[85]Cf. the *Popular Architecture* issue of the *Journal of Popular Culture,* VII, 2, 1973. Other examples keep appearing: *Architecture Plus* for October 1973 presented the Bavarian Motor Works Administration Building in Munich as

"...a sort of four-cylinder engine, cast in aluminum...the new administration building for BMW, one of the world's great manufacturers of automobiles, motorcycles, and other related bits of hardware. And the BMW tower, with its four clusters of pistons...is a worthy symbol of what its owner is trying to sell...

In the days, long ago, when sacred and profane architecture were practised separately, the BMW four-cylinder tower would have been ruled *hors de concours;* but ever since pop started to shack up with MOMA, there has been a relaxation of tensions, and a new infusion of imagination; any Work of Architecture that also advertises its owners' products is no more an anomaly than the Statue of Liberty (which advertises Democracy, American-Style); and so this four-cylinder piece of hot-rod hardware, 19 stories tall, is entitled to serious, critical evaluation...."

[86]Adolf Max Vogt, *Revolutionsarchitektur 1789/1917,* Cologne, 1974, pp. 50-51 (my translation):
"the central importance of work as Marx represented it ['one of the social forms which above all proclaims the distinctive existence and life-form of Man,' Marx said of work in the first volume of *Capital* in 1867] has been questioned by modern anthropology. With good reason anthropologists ask, on ethnological and psychological grounds, 'Are human communication, erotic love, discussion, play, gestures, dreams, contemplation—are desk work, administration, buying and selling, hobbies, etc.—in short is everything that belongs to human character to be described as "Work"? In other words: don't the field researches of ethnologists, and likewise the psychologists' investigations of human relationships, indicate that humans, whether primitive or highly civilized, by no means find self-realization only in work, but fulfil themselves equally if not more and display distinctive character by their need for play...."

[87]Wolfgang Haberland, *The Art of North America* (Baden-Baden, 1914), pp. 153, 156.

[88]Paul Hazard, *European Thought in the Eighteenth Century.* New Haven, 1956, pp. 365-366.

[88]A particularly striking example of a teepee shape reproduced by white builders for associations with Indian life could still be seen in 1972 in the hamlet of Busby, Montana (founded 1927). It was about sixty feet high, visible for miles across the plains, a very complicated piece of wood construction. From local people I was able to ascertain that the carpenter's name was Fred Rich (Indian? white? nobody knew, or cared much, it seemed), but that the moving spirit in the enterprise was W.P. Moncure, an Indian trader who "loved the Indians" and chose this shape for a restaurant and community center to honor them, and symbolize free life on the great plains. Moncure also erected a substantial stone monument to honor Chief Two Moon "who led his people in battle against Custer at Little Big Horn"; it is still there, but relics picked up by Indians from that battlefield once encased in it were "stolen four or five years ago"—i.e. about 1968, and "are now in Washington [D.C.]." Why? How? again nobody seemed to know or care much. Such are the delights of research in the popular/commercial field; such the frustrations, that if anybody has published the facts about this extraordinary place, nothing was available at the place itself nor did anybody there seem to feel it worth saving.

III

Traditional Forms and Functions of Illustration in Modern Popular/Commercial Arts

Definitions and Distinctions

Relating images coherently and so relating (i.e. telling) a story has been a function of activities called art since the 4th millennium B.C. Since the early twentieth-century, that function has been fulfilled normally, and almost exclusively, by popular/commercial arts.

70. Two boxes from a 1904 comic-strip by George McManus. *The Newlyweds* in the *New York Evening Journal* (ancestors to *Rosie's Beau* and *Bringing Up Father*). The same figures (wife, parrot, husband) appear in each box, the story being told by mentally recognizing similarities from one box to the next. The second box contains a multiple image of the husband's head, a sequence which to the eye suggests rapid movement—basic principle of movie film strips, developed contemporaneously in both comics and films c1890-1900.

71. Fourth-millennium B.C. illustration on an alabaster vase from Warka, Mesopotamia (ancient Erech/Uruk). Substitute images of offering-bearers, sacrificial animals, goddess and totemic emblems related to one another by means of a base-line, thus "relating" (i.e., telling the story of) their participation in a ceremonial ritual.

IN ESSENCE, ILLUSTRATION is the art of telling stories or recording events by means of pictures—visual symbols, more precisely. Technically, an illustration consists of substitute images (forms understood to symbolize some material actuality or mental concept, whether literal as snapshots or figures on a stage, abstract as pictographs or spoken sounds) related in some coherent sequence by analogical thought—i.e., by a process of recalling similarities. Comic strips, in which the eye remembers images from one frame to the next, are the most obvious example; film strips represent the same process, but so quickened as to be involuntary (70).[1]

Illustration is an art that goes at least as far back into Antiquity as the fourth millennium B.C. (71). It includes forms as diverse as modern television and Egyptian tomb-painting, sculptural friezes and comic mime.[2] The media of most modern illustrative arts—comics, movies, television, animated cartoons—are less than a hundred years old.

Common to all forms of illustration through the ages, however, has been one operative principle: clarification. As indicated in its root "lux" ("light"), the fundamental concern of illustrative arts must be to make things clearer, to reinforce meanings of words by pictures, and vice-versa. This function has made them vital to civilization at all times and places. That unequivocally illustrative arts and writing appear together in history is no coincidence, one being a form of the other.[3] Nor that at the moment they appear, around 4000 B.C., civilization begins too.

For arts of illustration in the historic sense have nothing to do with idle prettifications of books to make them salable. Still less are they optional means of self-expression. Illustration proper has always been a device essential for the transmission of ideas, values and traditions of all sorts, not to mention the simple reporting of information. Thence it follows that the great distinguishing mark of historic arts of illustration was and is: primacy of the text.

By this principle historic illustration can be distinguished from avant-garde use of an illustration format for expressions of medium or texture or aesthetic sensibility. Unlike Blake's drawings on *Paradise Lost* themes which claimed to correct Milton's misunderstandings of his own text, or Picasso's perennial self-expression, or the modern cinema maker's use of filmed images to mean what he chooses, historic illustrative arts made fidelity to text their first concern, artistic expression (if any) being always secondary to and supportive of the text[4]—as continues to be the operative principle in comics and television to this day. In so doing, popular/commercial illustrative arts stand in a long line of counterparts and ancestors defined as art because of what their forms *did* in and for society. And this was and is the main line: insistence on social function as the foundation of anything called "art" has been typical of all societies, at all times, at all places, until ours. It is *our* concept of "art" as an exclusively expressive activity without objectively evaluatable social functions that is unique. Herbert Read once observed that "The idea of a society without art, or of art divorced from society, was unknown until modern times." True enough, though many nowadays would draw from this observation a conclusion opposite to his. Read meant to criticize society [bourgeois, capitalist society, it goes without saying] for failing to appreciate

72. Woodcut accompanying André Saurès's *Hélène chez Archimède,* by Picasso, c1934. Here the multiple image is used as a device for its own sake rather than to tell a story or make anything clear—in fact it has a reverse effect. Although referred to as an "illustration," plainly has nothing to do with the traditional art of illustrating—neither clarifying nor relating, but principally intended to express the artist's aesthetic theories and sensibilities (whence likewise the woodcut technique, by the 1930s an entirely archaic way of doing illustrations, abandoned by serious illustrators for five generations past).

that they do their work more clearly, faster, more convincingly, with greater movement than any arts in history is beyond question.

art, with a corollary that society ought to be changed until it better suited and furthered avant-garde perceptions. In our post-modern era avant-garde art theory appears at least equally at fault, and there is increasing realization that arts like comic-strips are a kind of illustrative activity called "art" by every other civilization and in every other time until our own.[5]

Our popular/commercial illustrative arts are modern forms of historic illustrative arts, but vastly superior technically to their predecessors, so that they are capable of much greater complexity of illustrative function.

Most illustration in modern times is done by photographic processes (e.g.,half-tones), in comics, movies, animated cartoons or television. All five of these arts have come into existence within the last hundred years; television, indeed, well within living memory. All are partly product and partly agent of mass education on an unparalleled scale coinciding with equally unparalleled advances in applied science (rotogravure presses, electricity and electronics, celluloid and plastics, etc.). By reason of this superiority, our popular/commercial illustrative arts have almost entirely displaced the 19th century's narrative easel painting, book illustration, legitimate theatre, opera, popular stage—and reduced them to Fine Art. No need to weep, for these had with comparable thoroughness displaced earlier illustrative arts. Narrative easel painting had displaced the great Renaissance and Baroque tradition of murals, book illustrations had supplanted the great medieval art of manuscript painting; theatre had supplanted court dances and masques, popular stage had subsumed all sorts of earlier folk culture—all of which arts had in their turn been transformed into Fine Art for sophisticated 19th-century connoisseurs. The operative principle here, whereby arts technically more competent to carry out social functions invariably displace arts less competent to do so, and reduce them to Fine Art, is in fact observable at all times and places in history, as *The Unchanging Arts* undertook to demonstrate in some detail. Here that process is worth briefly recapitulating insofar as it helps explain more precisely how illustrative arts work in society, particularly the complexity of their functions.

In one respect the shift from 19th to 20th century forms of illustrative arts has been unique: unlike 19th-century arts, each of which took over the functions of some predecessor more or less directly, no 20th-century illustrative art derives directly from one particular 19th-century art. The reason is that our illustrative arts are so much more versatile—or, to put it in plainer words, so vastly superior to anything before them, at least in technique. The superiority of *what* our arts illustrate may be questioned.

Once the importance of photographic processes for making exactly repeatable pictorial statements had been pointed out (by William C. Ivins, *Prints and Visual Communication,*   in particular: how man thereby "had at last achieved a way of making visual reports that had no interfering symbolical syntax of their own"), excellent studies of photographic illustration have proliferated. Typical of their range are Peter C. Marzio's catalogue for the 1973 *Men and Machines of American Journalism* exhibited at the Smithsonian's Museum of Science and Technology, profusely illustrated with concise captions and a brief introduction carrying the text, and the detailed statistical study of how pictures functioned to illustrate news in Swedish newspapers from 1900-1970, *Dagspressens Bildbruk,* by Thomas Hård af Segerstad in Uppsala's Konstvetenskapliga Institution's series.[6] From the historic 1880 halftone of "Shantytown" in the *New York Daily Graphic* through rotogravures, picture tabloids, newsreels and television transmissions from the moon,[7] it is a record of such rapid and ceaseless improvement over anything preceding as to make specific comparisons with woodcuts in broadsheets or handbills almost a mockery.

Try Cream-Indigo-Blue.
Will not streak the Clothes.
Sample Bottle will last 3 months.

74A. Lithographed trade card, c1880, representing a burlesque-stage-type scene (as is common, the illustration bears no relationship to the function of the card and only a tenuous relationship to the product being advertised: washing blue): "Sudden start and a stare / on his Coat sees a Hair."

SUDDEN START AND A STARE,
ON HIS COAT SEES A HAIR

73A. The first illustration of an event to appear in an American newspaper—in James Rivington's *New York Gazetteer* for 20 April 1775, used the same sort of woodcut introduced in Gutenberg's time, three centuries earlier. It illustrated the following:
"Last Thursday was hung up by some of the lower class of inhabitants, at New Brunswick, an effigy, representing the person of Mr. Rivington, the printer at New York: merely for acting consistent with his profession as as free printer...
"Lest this piece of heroism should not be sufficiently known, he has thought proper to exhibit a Representation of the scene in which he was thus offered up a Victim, that the fame of the exploit may spread from 'Pole to Pole'..."
(Smithsonian Collections, from Peter Marzio, *Men & Machines of American Journalism.*)

Gross On Namath: P. 68	**New York Post Sports**	Rudy On Racing: P. 64
72	NEW YORK, MOONDAY, JULY 21, 1969	

'.. In Peace for All Mankind'

NASA via Associated Press Wirephoto

Astronaut Neil Armstrong dangles left foot—the one that first touched lunar soil—as he stands on Eagle's ladder a moment before becoming the first man to walk on the moon. Buzz Aldrin came out of the module 20 minutes later.

73B. Front page illustration of Moon landing by Neil Armstrong and Buzz Aldrin reproduced in halftone by wirephoto a television picture sent from the surface of the moon a few hours before—at 2:12 A.M., Eastern Daylight Time, to be exact, 21 July 1969, same day as the tabloid. (from Marzio, *Men & Marchines*)

Comparable superiority is self-evident in comics, next of the modern forms of illustration to appear.

74B. Last three boxes of a *Mutt and Jeff* comic-strip of 1908, reproduced from Budd Fischer's *Mutt & Jeff Cartoon Book,* first comic book ever published, typifying the original format of this comic classic, which was Mutt's misadventures as a compulsive race-track gambler, and revealing its close ties with the popular stage—Mutt was in effect a standup comedian translated into another medium, complete with foil when Jeff appeared in 1909.

We call them "comics" or "funnies" first because of what Fred Schroeder so shrewdly identifies as the persistent tendency of North American critics to think primarily or only of the "entertainment" side of popular culture,[8] but also because the first strips to appear were in fact intended to be comedy. In style they descended from a tradition of grotesque drawing which goes far back into Antiquity, more immediately from the *caricatura* which appeared in the 17th century (reputedly the invention of renowned sculptor and architect Bernini), most immediately from 19th-century proto-comics with strong affinities to the popular stage—Gustave Doré's *Histoire de la Sainte Russie,* Rodolphe Toepffer's *Histoire de M. Vieux Bois,* Wilhelm Busch's *Max und Moritz,* and—earliest of all—Thomas Rowlandson's *Doctor Syntax* series consisting of pictures obviously composed like domestic comedies of the period, expressly "texted" by William Combe.[9] They also had a direct descent from the popular stage, demonstrable in the first two comic classics to appear.

Mutt and Jeff (begun 1907) was for the first decade of its existence hardly more than a series of old burlesque or vaudeville routines illustrated, and tidied up for family consumption. Quarrelling couples, the race-track addict, the drunk, the comic darkey, the Jew; stage falls and stage violence (characters whopped, punched and pounded mercilessly, leaping up fresh for the next performance—a practise brought to perfection by animated cartoons; stage props (lamppost, hydrant, potted fern, one stuffed chair)—in early strips (74B) appear all the stock paraphernalia of that vaudeville burlesque stage then in full vigor (74A), now chiefly remembered as the matrix whence came the classic stars of radio and TV, Burns and Allen, Hope, Benny, Crosby, etc.

75B. Illustration of the famous suicide scene, where Bill Sikes hangs himself, from John Moore's 1874 production of Dickens's *Oliver Twist.* "The pictorial cutting technique employed here effectively anticipated the work of both Porter and Griffith," according to Vardac (*Stage to Screen*, p. 36). Other companies were less professional. Twain satirized them with his Duke and Dauphin's "Shakespeare" performance in *Huckleberry Finn.* But from experience in popular stage and burlesque companies grew almost all the best performers of 20th-century radio, movies and television.

The earliest comics also descended from that second branch of the popular stage called melodrama. Webster defines "melodrama" as "a romantic play, generally of a serious character, in which effect is sought by startling incidents, striking situations, and exaggerated sentiments, aided by splendid decoration and music." How early the "serious character" altered is indicated by Webster's meaning for the

75A. Three boxes from a *Thimble Theatre* comic-strip of Feb. 1935, reproduced from *Two Classics of Modern American Art.* Here this comic's origins as a spoof of melodrama are very obvious. Unlike *Mutt & Jeff,* this is a suspense strip, so that the full sequence needs to be read to grasp the many layers of meaning and symbolism Segar built onto this traditional foundation. Cf. 110.

adverb "melodramatically": "in an affected and exaggerated manner." Obviously it is from this aspect of melodrama that the second comic classic, *Thimble Theatre,* descends.[10] Originally *Thimble Theatre* was a gag-a-day parody on Ed Whelan's *Minute Movies;* it took on a suspense-sequence format and melodramatic character, significantly enough, just in 1929—the year when the Great Depression began, and people began looking for some means cheaper than theatre tickets to satisfy their taste for melodramatic entertainment.

Thimble Theatre's great suspense sequences of the 1930s were by no means the only response to this social need, of course. There was radio, and there were all sorts of other suspense-sequence comics. *Tarzan* too began its comic-strip life in 1929.

The French "bande dessinée" is really a much better word for comics. For by no means are all of them comic, descendants of burlesque, melodrama, caricature and the grotesque. A whole branch descended from popular 19th-century book illustration, for example, which is not and never was "funnies," and furthermore is and always was easily distinguishable from descendants of burlesque, vaudeville and grotesquerie, by style.

76. Part of the cover of a 1974 *Tarzan* comic book. Illustration by Joe Kubert, successor to Russ Manning, Burne Hogarth and the original *Tarzan* strip illustrator, Harold foster, who in 1937 began his *Prince Valiant* strip, which still contines (cf. 98).

To this day, a glance over the comic section of any newspaper will reveal two distinct strip styles. One—comics proper—has caricatural and quasi-abstracted forms; the other, narratives drawn in naturalistic forms often reminiscent of old commercial art schools, with chiaroscuro, cross-hatching, anatomical niceties, and the like. The one is represented by Budd Fisher's *Mutt & Jeff* or Segar's *Thimble Theatre;* archetype of the other is *Tarzan,* claimed to be the first comic-strip proper (as distinct from a collection of gag-a-day strips), which first appeared in 1929 with Harold Foster's illustrations.[11] Here descent from 19th-century book illustration—as well as illustrated versions of *Tarzan* itself, of course—is patent.

 Tarzan perpetuates a pen-and-ink technique similar to Kemble's (or Tenniel's; cf. 95A-B); similar balanced formal compositions; above all, similar traditional attitudes to and concepts of what illustration involves: artists first and foremost

77. The typical format of 19th-century book illustration, exemplified by Edward Winslow Kemble here illustrating *Huckelberry Finn,* is a small stage set, drawn naturalistically with simplified conventions of academic composition, shading, etc. Add balloon speech, and it becomes the 20th century's narrative "comic" strip.

following the text, confining personal aesthetic expression (of which Foster especially had a good deal) within that text's bounds, thus clarifying, in the original sense of "illustrating," Burroughs's word pictures.[12] Other traditions persist in illustrations like most recent *Tarzan* also—Man against beast in the St. George-and-Dragon sense. Man *as* beast in the ancient shamanistic sense. Noble Savage. And others.

Along with tricks from the melodramatic popular stage and 19th-century book illustration, suspense-sequence strips of the 1930s also borrowed, so heavily as to be considered in some degree descendants, from the movies. Movies had of course been "illustrating" books from their beginnings. *Wash Tubbs, Prince Valiant, Buck Rogers* are typical of 1930s strips that borrowed heavily from movie techniques, *Mary Worth* and *Apartment 3-G* of later strips borrowing indirectly from movies via television— but in all cases the influence is obvious in the alternation of long-shots, close-ups, angle-shots and air views in succeeding boxes. Ability so to alternate viewpoints was one of the movies' most obvious points of superiority over the conventional stage; in taking it over, comics comparably improved upon conventional 19th-century illustration. Once get used to the strip style of

78. Characteristic of narrative comic strips after the 1920s is alternation of viewpoints, as in this typical example syndicated in May 1975. Immediate inspiration is the movies; but the trick (it avoids monotony, enhances dramatic effect) is not uncommon already in proto-comic-strips of the 19th century by Busch, Doré and others.

narration, and those 19th-century miniature stage sets, so little changed from the 18th-century formula used alike by Hogarth and chap-book block-prints, seem dull indeed.

Yet another distinct strip style identifies the "underground" genre[13]—making a first appearance with the so-called eight-pagers of the 1930s wherein popular comic-strip characters enjoyed an explicit sex life denied them in mass circulation; further developing in arty circumventions of the comic industry's code of ethics adopted in the mid-50s; maturing in the late 1960s and early '70s as part of the New Left movement (and in consequence becoming about as underground as whiskey ads and porn shops on Times Square). The style of underground comics is quite consciously and plainly related to avant-garde Establishment arts of their same period, not so much in forms—actually, Picassoid heads, surrealistic backgrounds, and cubistic conventions in comics *preceded* their appearance in avant-garde arts, as Alexander Dorner noted in *Way Beyond Art* as far back as 1942—as in attitudes. Underground comics of the late '60s and '70s used forms self-consciously, in a Fine Art way—not as the best tools for the job in hand (often indeed they got in the way), but for extrinsic, Fine Art reasons, as expressions of faith in naivete's rejuvenating grace, the virtue of existentialist ugliness, or inverted power-worship. Just as avant-garde movie-makers used 1915-type camera techniques, and treated film as an end rather than a means, so Shelton, Crumb, Jay Lynch and the rest took earlier comics for their models, not only the eight-pagers' plainly incompetent drawing, but *The Gumps*'s feeble caricature style, and the *Yellow Kid*'s confusing *horror vacui* (Cf. 109). Result: a contradiction in terms, testifying at once to comics having such a tenacious hold on the masses that would-be reformers and revolutionaries everywhere would descend to using such a medium; and to the marvellous ability of avant-garde art forms to deflect protest harmlessly into self-expression that affects nobody not already persuaded.

As for movies, their most immediate ancestor is of course the popular stage. That Chaplin and Keaton, Laurel and Hardy and all the rest are in fact counterparts of the comics, like *Mutt and Jeff* comedy acts transplanted from vaudeville and burlesque to another and superior medium, is self-evident. Almost as plain is movie derivation from melodrama, documented so convincingly by Nicholas Vardac: not only sets and atmosphere, but even music—in early movie houses the music component of melodrama was supplied by a piano player, whose presence there might otherwise be inexplicable. To these popular stage origins early American movies, especially, owed their primordial orientation toward mass entertainment and their penchant for exaggerated effects and sensationalism.

But movies by no means derived exclusively from the popular stage. Back of the popular stage itself was the popular novel, and while many early movies derived from popular novels *via* the popular stage (*Uncle Tom's Cabin* being the classic example), others soon appeared which were taken from popular novels direct (75B). How much of the social function of 19th-century illustrated books was fulfilled by movies was much more obvious during their silent era, when movies literally were pictures with written captions.

Back of 19th-century book illustration, again, was that narrative easel painting whose persistent influence remains traceable in the style of narrative comic-strips right into our own

Uncle Tom's Cabin, the play produced by William Brady (1901).

Uncle Tom's Cabin, the film directed by Edwin S. Porter (1903).

79. Comparative stage sets from the popular stage and an early film, from A. Nicholas Vardac, *Stage to Screen* (Cambridge, Mass., 1946).

times (76B). It likewise passed into movies, both indirectly via the intermediary of book illustration, and directly: what 19th-century academic painters called "machines" often became *tableaux-vivants* for early movies. (The Paul Delaroche series of paintings on the theme of Queen Elizabeth I of England providing compositions and inspiration for Zukor's early *Queen Elizabeth* movie, and other examples, are given in *The Unchanging Arts*).

Consider these complex functions of modern movies, and it must be obvious how very much better they perform the traditional functions of illustration than any or all of those earlier arts which they replaced. One medium does, and does better, what earlier required three or four. Edwin S. Porter's lasting accomplishment was to perceive these possibilities, and to perfect the movie as an illustrative art almost from its outset. Porter was first, perhaps, to comprehend fully what it meant to have a *moving* medium. Vastly improved simulation of movement, compared to 19th-century and all earlier illustrative arts, is the common denominator of all modern illustrative arts.

Seen simply as a still, this frame from Porter's *Rescued from an Eagle's Nest* can be compared with many other similar pictures (80), for this is a theme which for some reason interesting to analyze has delighted and awed human beings of all diverse ages, civilizations, epochs and regions: a gigantic bird carrying some human off to a lair. Greeks and Romans pictured Ganymede carried off by Zeus in the form of an eagle, and so did Corregio and Rembrandt (among others). Moslem folktales told how Sinbad the Sailor was carried off by a ferocious Roc, and Germanic folktales, of Tom Thumb; Swift's Gulliver suffers this among other misfortunes. But none of these are really comparable to the Porter still, because it was never seen as a still at all. It moved. This image only stood on the screen for a twentieth of a second, then flashed off to be replaced by another, slightly variant. Furthermore, Porter dubbed in backgrounds that moved; he had the camera move to different angles; he cut the finished film to direct and speed its action still more—and all without violating the illustrator's central function to clarify, to illuminate the old stories. Consequently, there really is no comparison between Porter's illustration and any others earlier. For better or worse, movies could tell stories, disseminate information and entertain on a scale with an efficiency undreamt-of before.

80. Still from Edwin S. Porter's *Rescued from an Eagle's Nest* (Edison, 1907), with (inset) cut from an 18th-century chapbook illustrating the story of Tom Thumb, for comparison. (Museum of Modern Art, New York.)

"George! George! Drop the keys!"

81. Cartoon by Charles Addams from "The Late Forties" in *The New Yorker Twenty-fifth Anniversary Album*, New York, 1951. Fundamentally a spoof on horror movies, which derived from technical possibilities and example of pioneers like *Rescued from an Eagle's Nest.*

Even arts where movement is not necessarily inherent were affected by the movies' success at putting stories into motion. Social cartoons, for example.

One word sums up any comparison of Charles Addams's early *New Yorker* cartoons with his later ones,[14] and the evolution of cartoons over the 1900-1970 period generally: faster. They *move*. Maybe not literally, but visually and psychologically. Lines are quicker, more nervous. Brushwork is sketchier and lighter. Captions are brisker. The shift from older *Punch*-like social cartoons with quite long descriptive captions and elaborately composed pictures can be attributed to many causes, and no doubt *New Yorker* editor Harold Ross's editorial policy did have a lot to do with it.[15] But explanations overlook the movies' pervasive impetus toward putting illustration into motion. For the fact is that all modern illustrative arts are interrelated (as all traditional illustrative arts were). That comics and movies have a common matrix is made almost self-evident by the similarity between a roll of movie film and a comic strip, each box or still being in effect a little stage, comic strips being film strips with intervening boxes omitted—or however you want to phrase it. That social cartooning and other variants of book illustration are likewise affected by this matrix should be self-evident also, once the catalyst is recognized: animated cartoons.

Talk about illustrations put into motion in the most literal sense—all sorts of illustrations—and you're talking about animated cartoons. Comics are the best-known art to be animated by this medium: Felix the Cat, Mickey Mouse, Popeye, Betty Boop, etc., etc. Book illustrations likewise, especially by Disney: Snow White, Bambi, Pinocchio, Ichabod Crane, not to mention Ernest Sheppard's illustrations to *Pooh*. Movies themselves: the Three Stooges, Marx Brothers, later the Beatles, etc., etc. Topical prints of the Currier & Ives variety (what the Germans call *Bilderbogen*)—their descendants too can be recognized in animation. And when you find even *New Yorker* cartoon characters being brought to animated cartoon life, you know you're dealing with a truly eclectic medium! Social cartooning had affected movies in the 1920s, to be sure; styles and mores set by Charles Dana Gibson's 1880s drawings were recognizable in them (85). But Gibson's was a far more mass-oriented art than the

New Yorker's self-consciously urbane sophistication,[16] exemplified by Addams's arcane, if not tortured, spoof of that whole genre of the horror story, descended from 18th-century Gothic novels *via* 19th-century popular novels and melodrama.

Such versatility could not retard development of the animated cartoon *sui generis*.

Animated cartoons did not become a true mass medium until put on televison, one fact which helps explain the otherwise puzzling hiatus between their early invention (devices for projecting animated drawings were available as early as the 17th century, and innumerable means of doing so by the 19th) and general recognition of the essential difference between a movie and an animated cartoon, which did not in fact occur until the late 1950s.[17] In contrast to comic strips, whose format was perfected during the decade 1910-1920, animated cartoons of the early 1930s were hardly different in technique from the very earliest animations, like *Gertie the Dinosaur* (1906).[18] Disney's persistent efforts to elevate the medium—meaning to make it more like a "good movie"—didn't help matters at all. Chuck Jones showed the way with little gems like *Road Runner* and *Froggy Night*;[19] but in animated cartooning as in so many other popular/commercial arts, the most recent is the most effective—work like Hanna-Barbera Studios', which fully understands what the medium can and cannot do.[20]

All these arts—comics, movies, animated cartoons—have been subsumed to some degree into television.

Oldest and newest, simplest and most complex, television does every kind of illustrative art. Oldest and simplest of illustrative arts, for example, is the reporting of events. Current-event cartoons of the sort Dahl did so well for so many years in Boston are an amusing version of it, and furthermore stand well within the traditions of history painting and ritual commemoration in all epochs and cultures. But in the 1970s, any and all kinds of reporting "by hand" were something of a luxury, a frill—like having your portrait painted instead of photographed. The normal way events are recorded in our culture is by television—as indeed this caption (83) plainly demonstrates: "a film of this ceremony will be shown on television...." Usually,

83. Drawing by Frank Dahl and caption from the *Boston Globe*, 15 May 1973.

FAVORITE "GROUP"— THE GRAND BOSTONIANS.

SEVEN GRAND BOSTONIANS—Mayor Kevin White asked the late Frank Dahl to join in honoring seven venerable Bostonians in a ceremony at the Parkman House on April 30. This drawing, one of the last by the Globe cartoonist before his death on May 6, was the result. The illustration, copies of which were presented to the Seven, is included in a Grand Bostonian exhibit at City Hall which opens to the public today and continues Monday-Friday through June 1. The exhibit of biographical material, works, prizes and assorted memorabilia honors, from left, impresario Arthur Fiedler, poet David Mc-

Cord, historian Samuel Eliot Morison, poet Archibald Mac-Leish, former US Speaker of the House John McCormack, heart specialist Dr. Paul Dudley White and civic leader-philanthropist Ralph Lowell. Also represented at the exhibit will be Walter Muir Whitehill, retired head of the Boston Athenaeum, who was master of ceremonies at the Parkman event. A 30-minute film of the April 30 ceremony will be shown Monday, May 21, at 9:30 p.m. on Channel 2, and repeated Saturday, May 26, at 9:30 p.m. on Channels 2, 44 and 57, and on Sunday, May 27, at 5 and 10:30 p.m. on Channel 2.

173

nowadays, that means clips on news broadcasts, which have steadily expanded from ten minutes or so into full-fledged programs in prime half-hour slots. One-hour documentaries have become commonplace, two-hour documentaries not unusual. Yet the essential social function being served is the same one served by illustrative arts of the 4th millennium (cf. 82). Whence an inescapable conclusion: television is the most immediate, the most comprehensive, the most comprehensible illustrative art the world has ever seen.[21] And not necessarily more deceitful than its predecessors (cameras don't lie; people do.)

Newest and most complex of illustrative arts is the motion picture—and television, so far from putting an end to movies, has taken them over. Or more exactly, vitality in movies has migrated to television, just as, half a century before, vitality had migrated to movies from 19th-century narrative easel paintings and the popular stage. Insofar as movies can still be called a mass art— and it's questionable—they remain so only *via* television, as is strikingly demonstrated by the contrast between movies made for television and those not. Without discipline imposed by the social functions of a mass market, non-TV movies have tended to become Cinema, vehicles for artistic self-expression, creative in their own way but not illustrative arts in the original sense, or indeed socially responsible arts in the traditional sense at all.

Television is the last and finest representative of traditional melodrama. In television, the novel as an art capable of holding and swaying mass audiences still survives and flourishes in a manner gratifying, I imagine, to Dickens or Mark Twain[22] (can you imagine what either would have said about Literary Artists who sniff at the *Forsyte Saga*?) In it, plays Shakespearean in the sense of offering something for everyone, learned and groundlings alike, survive and flourish also, in the form of situation comedy, skits and soap opera. TV drama does not, however, descend direct from movies. Inbetween came radio.

Radio, though not visual and hence not an illustrative art of the sort properly under consideration here, nevertheless had catalytic importance in the transition from 19th-to 20th-century popular/commercial arts generally, and arts of illustration most especially. From the mid-1920s to around 1948 radio perfected a distinctive art of story-telling which prepared the way for, conditioned, and to a considerable extent determined, television's mass audience. Surprisingly much of this art was related directly or indirectly to popular graphic illustration. *Little Orphan Annie,* for example, was adapted from Harold Gray's arch-conservative comic strip, whose popularity was a cross left-liberal types had to bear even then. *Vic and Sade* was a counterpart of Norman Rockwell's kind of anecdotal back-home-by-the-ol'-general-store-stove painting. *Amos 'n' Andy* in part represented the old "darktown" comic print in new radio form. But of course radio's most immediate source was the popular stage; Amos 'n' Andy were essentially old blackface comedians of 18th-century origin. The walk-on joke routines, stock props and stage violence of burlesque and vaudeville (cf. 74) were all translated into appropriate radio forms, so that in Jack Benny and Mary Livingston, Fibber McGee and Molly, Fred Allen and Portland Hoffa, George Burns and Gracie Allen, you can easily recognize radio counterparts to Mr. and Mrs. Augustus Mutt, Andy and Min Gump, Blondie and Dagwood, Toots and Casper—as well as forerunners of Sid Caesar and Imogene Coca, George Gobel and Alice, Carol Burnett's skits with Harvey Korman, Johnny Carson's routines with Ed McMahon, etc., etc.

"Westerns" and soap operas likewise went from the popular stage to radio and then, with the advent of television, got translated back into their originally visual medium, beginning with Irna Phillips's *Guiding Light* in 1953 (but never including "Oxydol's own *Ma Perkins,"* which lived and died as the greatest of radio soaps—demonstrating thereby, perhaps, the dinosaur principle of too much adaptation to environment).

And I think it would be no more than fair—indeed, self-evident—to say that all of these arts improved vastly in the new medium. For television is a far more flexible medium than the legitimate stage, affording long shots, close-ups, all sorts of stage changes, sound effects far beyond conventional possibility. It will never replace books, for books offer an active learning experience and pause for reflection no mass medium can match. But it certainly can and has largely replaced movies and in many ways gone beyond them in quality. Of which the *Mary Tyler Moore Show* offers as good an example as any.

84. Still from a 1973 episode in the *Mary Tyler Moore* show (1970-1977) with the four principal characters: Mary (Mary Tyler Moore), Lou (Edward Asner), Ted (Ted Knight) and Murray (Gavin MacLeod). (From *Journal of Popular Culture* VII, 1974).

The *Mary Tyler Moore Show* is as typical of TV situation comedies in the 1960s and 1970s as *The Pursuit of Polly* was of movie comedies of the 1910-'30 period. Both observe traditional canons of illustrative arts throughout history: telling a story effectively, rather than expressing artistic personalities of actors or writers, is what dictates evolution of plots and characters. Shakespeare's plots and characters evolved in the same spontaneous way, from play to play, in response to audience reaction;[23] by, as Carol Traynor Williams observed in her study of the *Mary Tyler Moore Show,* "accident rather than design..., the normal, proper way of creating *for a company.*"[24] And in television, such traditional evolution finds fuller scope than ever before, because of its format, calling for one show a week for month after month, over years, rather than a single two- or three-hour performance every new season.

But is it *art*? Surely "spontaneous" in this context means "manipulation of stereotypes *d'occasion*"? Indeed so. All comedy relies heavily on stereotypes. We can go further: all illustrative arts rely heavily on stereotypes. Stereotypes are like words; they are necessary vehicles of communication, even for avant-garde playwrights—the difference between them and traditional drama

85. Still from *The Pursuit of Polly*, a Paramount film of 1918. Billy Burke here plays a stock role of sheltered female, taken over directly from domestic comedies on the 19th-century popular stage, with perhaps a dash of styling from popular turn-of-the-century cartoonist Charles Dana Gibson. (Museum of Modern Art collection, New York).

being that they invent their own stereotypes, with their own Humpty-Dumpty meanings. The difference between *Romeo & Juliet* and *Polly* and the *Mary Tyler Moore Show* is not in using stereotypes, recognizable in the still (85) even if you've never seen the movie: stern but (we know) soft-headed and soft-hearted papa; slick villain (you can tell *him* by the moustache, of course!); dumb but honest joe; earnest, hopeful, virtuous youth who'll certainly get the girl at last. The result is nothing like a High Art of drama, but a marionette show, wherein each figure does no more and no less than it is typed to do. In the *Mary Tyler Moore Show,* by contrast, the stereotypes grow. They have more than one dimension, too, so that the plays are understandable on more than one level, appeal to diverse audiences, emotions and reactions:

All in all, though, it is a pretty special sitcom, and mainly because of its humanistic values. They transform Georgette's 'dumbness' and Ted's; they give rise to Lou's refusal to hurt someone else in order to save face. . . .It is critical to humanism that its values shape Mary. . . .Love, *companionship,* shapes every MTM episode; it makes us believe when real conflicts are resolved in friendship. Only a company can make that dull virtue, companionship, a value of power and promise at this point in time. The values underlying MTM are all like companionship—specifically unexciting, banal, 'old fashioned' (in fact conservative), and humanistic. . . .They achieve their aim, I think, because the complex, sometimes apparently contradictory human characteristics MTM portrays are real human characteristics, and the complex values of human dignity and companionship that underlie and shape the series are real human values that we cherish—perhaps wistfully—beyond all militant fads in 'values.'[25]

Of soap operas the same can be said; they too expand past stereotypes:

As any watcher in the evening can attest, most of the women on TV have all the depth, subtlety and sensitivity of the Doublemint Twins. Only on the daytime soaps—the most slighted genre in the whole entertainment field—are women the true equals of men. On some soaps this may mean they're as dull as the men; but at their dreariest they still have real, often complex, motivations. Men on soaps also seem three-dimensional, in part because they do consult, as well as consort, with women.

And because the story is continued from day to day, characters are able to change. . . .[26]

Of Shakespeare's, Molière's, Lope da Vega's plays you could say the same. It's an attribute of High Art.

With which introduction, let's consider in detail how popular/commercial arts of illustration worked in society, past and present.

Four Variants of Illustration

Like substitute imagery, illustration can function as an auxiliary to other arts, so that four variant types can be distinguished: illustration used as substitute imagery, illustration proper, illustration used as beautification, and illustration used for persuasion/conviction. This last type of illustration is so frequently confused with arts of persuasion/conviction proper that understanding the functions of illustration in society must begin by elucidating this point.

FIGUR VI, 14: *Utopiens resultat* (71, 20e, »Skillinger fra skyerne«. Genoptryk fra 51, 9b).

Utopiens globale realisation medfører generel arbejdsvægring og mangel på varer. Pengene mister deres magiske værdi, som netop er inkarnationen af det samfundsmæssige arbejde.

FIGUR VI. 15 *Den puritanske kapitalist* (Ekstrahæfte nr. 7, 1971).

86. Two illustrations from *Tegneserier, en ekspansions historie,* published by Aarhus University, Denmark, 1974, explaining how Walt Disney Productions function as a running-dog lackey of capitalist imperialism. To the machinations of wicked Scrooge McDuck there is truly no end; he even manages to become the only Anglo-Saxon capable of scheming in fluent Danish.

ILLUSTRATION MORE than other popular/commercial arts has suffered from the recent (last couple of decades, in acute form) intellectual fashion of attributing subtle motives, unrecognized even by those accused of them, to the most obvious activities—a version of what Tom Wolfe tagged "the Great Adjectival Catch-Up" of leftish American intellectuals:

The Europeans have a real wasteland? Well, we have a psychological wasteland. They have real fascism? Well, we have social fascism (a favorite phrase of the 1930s, amended to liberal fascism in the 1960s). They have real poverty? Well, we have relative poverty (Michael Harrington's Great Adjectival Catch-Up of 1963). They have real genocide? Well, we have cultural genocide (i.e., what universities were guilty of in the late 1960s if they didn't have open-admissions policies for minority groups).[27]

The Chinese and Russians rigidly control the content and thrust of comic strips and movies, and use them for obvious propaganda? Well, the United States invented those comics for the sinister purpose of spreading capitalist imperialism across the world, the more cunningly because disguised as mere entertainment. Walt Disney's Scrooge McDuck[28] a mere figure of fun, a satire even (as the name from Dickens' *Christmas Carol* character epitomizing the greedy capitalist might imply to the naïve)? Don't you believe it! He's an insidious tool of capitalist imperialism, subtly and secretly inculcating a Puritan work ethic so the proletariat will the more willingly accept its exploitation!

A recurring favorite for demonstration and denunciation purposes is a 1951 comic-book story about Uncle Scrooge's entire fortune, stored in a gigantic corn-crib, blowing away in a tornado and being distributed all over the country; how, when everybody gets a million dollars fallen from the sky, nobody works except Scrooge, who with his nephews goes on cultivating his farm; how as a result money is so inflated as to be worthless, and Scrooge gets his fortune back. "A fable about capitalism," according to Les Daniels, whose *Comix*[29] reproduces the entire comic-book episode:

...explicitly a lesson for the children about the disaster of daydreaming or loafing. But more serious than the overt content are the implications about the impossibility of equal distribution of wealth and about Marx's contention that he who controls the means of production controls—fill in the blanks....

Lots of people have rushed to fill the blanks in. A fat volume of studies compiled by a GMT group at Aarhus University, for example, examines McDuck's significance in what can only be described as exhausting detail.[30] Others see Disney's insidious power in the Chile coup against Allende, although without explaining why it had no similar effect in Cuba, Angola, Mozambique, Iraq, etc. That the original strip was satire seems never to have entered such critics' heads. "What is disturbing" to Daniels "is that

the economic balance is here made to look like a natural balance. It is a system that justifies Donald and the kids working in the fields at such wages that Scrooge can feel magnanimous at considering a ten-cent raise; it is a system that mocks the middle class dreams of instant wealth as surely as it subverts the notion of public reponsibility. The only redeeming quality here that relieves Scrooge's smugness at having money and knowing he will always have it is the injection of his childlike fascination with the feel and smell of it. . . . Donald has in fact the last word: 'Disgusting.'

But it's Donald who says this; no shrewd scholar had to ferret the moral out! Only a slight acquaintance with American humor is needed to recognize in Scrooge McDuck's top hat and striped trousers the stock uniform of wicked capitalists in cartoons from the 1880s to the present, from the *Judge* to *Krokodil.* Uncle Scrooge wallowing in his vat of money ("I love money! I love to dive around in it, like a porpoise!") is an obvious satire on the pre-1914 state of affairs when, as Orwell put it, "the sheer vulgar fatness of wealth, without any kind of aristocratic elegance to redeem it, was so obtrusive. . . ."[31] Maybe Scrooge McDuck's contemplating a ten-cent-a-day raise for his faithfully toiling nephews, while everybody else in the world is off trying to spend their newfound millions, incites love for The System amongst the gullible young, instead of mirth. If you can believe that, you can also believe that all comics and all popular/commercial arts in the world ought to be put in the category of propaganda,their only social function being to persuade and convince on behalf of some Establishment. And of course, the element of truth in such a contention is that people can and do read anything into anything, and what they so read can be, and often is , managed. But to study history in art, motive must be read from the art itself. For example (87).

87. "The Red Army captures Berlin," from a 1974 booklet distributed in Soviet airports free to tourists: *History of the Soviet Union in Artists' Drawings.*

Circumstances suggest a propaganda element in such a booklet as *The History of the Soviet Union in Artists Drawings* (87): its free distribution to tourists, the fact that in tracing World War II from Hitler's invasion of Russia to the capitulation of Japan, allies are only once mentioned. But you could not prove propaganda intent from the picture itself. Overtly, it is just what 'it purports to be: an illustration of events. And as such we should categorize it.[32]

In sum: lacking internal evidences of deliberately persuasive intent (for examples, see Section V), if an art relates, if it tells a story, it's illustrative. Within illustrative arts, however, as in other modern popular/commercial arts generally, variants can be identified by the degrees to which they are auxiliary to arts with other social functions:

(1) There is a kind of "static illustration" which essentially functions as didactic substitute imagery and was discussed in that category (21-30). But conversely there is a kind of substitute imagery which essentially functions as ritual illustration; pornography is the best-known example.

(2) Most illustrative arts do illustration proper—their main and only overt concern, that is, being the relating of stories or recording of events (disregarding, for reasons just set out, whatever beyond that may be read into them!).

(3) Insofar as illustrations adorn architecture or artifacts so as to identify their function and relate them to human experience, illustration can be a means of beautification.

(4) And insofar as illustrations are attached or related to other artifacts explicitly concerned with persuasion/conviction-i.e., architecture, usually—illustration can function implicitly as an adjunct to those social functions too.

Once recognize these variant functions and they can be identified in historic arts of illustration as well.

Ritual Illustration Functioning as Substitute Imagery: Pornography

There is a kind of "static illustration" which essentially functions as didactic substitute imagery and was discussed in that category (q.v.). But conversely, there is a kind of substitute imagery which essentially functions as ritual illustration: pornography. Two basic kinds of pornographic illustration are identifiable: the same figure in a variety of poses going through some action; and illustrations of two or more figures in sexual activity.

NO CULTURES PAST or present, and few individuals within any one culture, have ever agreed entirely on a definition of pornography.[33] But the core of it, in all times and places, is the art of exciting sexual desire. As such, it is an art almost as primaeval as that symbol-making and using which sets humans off from animals (q.v., 3, 4). For just as no animal both makes and uses substitute images as symbols, so no animals artificially excite sexual desire; in their kingdom, sexual relations are so physiologically fixed and predetermined that no such art is requisite.

The basis for all pornography is substitute imagery;[34] insofar as painted or photographed or carved bodies serve the purposes of the real thing *in absentia*. But pornography is effectual only insofar as those substitute images are involved in some kind of action—i.e., the illustration of a sequence or process. In theory, a nude body or bodies alone might have the desired effect, as Praxiteles's Cnidian Aphrodite (to give the kind of chaste classic example professors are supposed to) was reported to have so inflamed youths visiting the shrine that they attempted to violate the statue.[35] In practise such an account merely arouses derision—and laughter of any kind, even derisive laughter, is the death of pornography. Some kind of sequence is required. Modern popular/commercial arts provide two sorts: one, a single figure in some kind of provocative action (88) and the other representations of sex acts going on. Both sorts have abundant ancestry in historic arts and reveal a good deal about the past.

That our popular/commercial single-figure pornography is more illustration than substitute imagery becomes self-evident when you realize that even a single picture is always thought of as in some kind of action, a frame on a film-roll, if you like; and that it is in the form of movies that pornographic arts have flourished most abundantly and abandonedly in modern times. Whence, possibly, insight into the social function of the many historical arts with comparable social functions.

88. Sura-sundari figures from Khajuraho. A, Kandariya-Mahadeva temple: Apsaras removing thorn: B, Kandariya-Mahadeva temple: Apsaras standing: C, Visvahatha temple: Apsaras playing on flut. Usually dated 10th and 11th centuries. Found at all periods in Indian art history, such figures attain a prolific and refined climax on High Medieval temples like this and Konarak. (72)

"Ancient erotic arts" used to mean Pompeii. Now Khajuraho and Konarak and Elephanta come oftener to mind—blessings of jet travel! In all "enlightened" discussions since the 18th century, however, much is always made of an alledged contrast between repressed cultures like ours which keep pornography underground (however ineffectually), and those healthier and opener psychic times to which Indian and Roman brothels seem such enviable testaments.[36] An official (and very sober, very factual, very good) guide to Khajuraho is typical. There we read,[37]

As the sculptures mirror their times, it is evident that the age which produced them had none of the taboos or inhibitions against sex as we have now. The people of that age took a healthy integrated view of life and gave sex its due place in the scheme of things. . . . The representation of erotic scenes, therefore, was not taken as banal or abnormal or unnatural.

Admittedly, the description goes on, "Behind the familiar human facade of the *sura-sundaris* is hidden a deeper meaning and symbolism." This is no place to venture a toe into that turgid sea of controversy over what metaphysical, mythological, spiritual or other symbolism Indian erotic imagery may involve. But it is worthwhile to explore the neglected possibility that modern popular/commercial arts might be fundamentally similar to traditional historic arts of pornographic illustration.

For it does seem that, however different their outward forms and media, there is an identity of social function between what the Germans so precisely call our *Einhändigliteratur* and those decorative sculptures for which Indian temples have become so well-known.

"*Apsarases* or *sura-sundaris,*" the guide goes on, "who account for the finest and most numerous sculptures at Khajuraho,

are usually represented as handsome and youthful nymphs, attired in the choicest gems and garments and full of winsome grace and charm. As heavenly dancers (*apsareses*) they are shown as dancing in various postures. . . . But more frequently the *sura-sundaris* are portrayed to express common human moods, emotions, and activities and are often difficult to distinguish from conventional *nayikas,* such as those *apsareses* shown as disrobing, yawning, scratching the back, touching the breasts, rinsing water from the wet plaits of hair. . . . writing a letter, playing on a flute. . . painting designs on the wall or bedecking themselves in various ways by painting the feet, applying collrium, etc.

So could be described, with hardly a word changed, typical layouts in any monthly issue of *Playboy, Penthouse, Gallery, Hustler, Cheri,* etc., etc. But in these modern cases the social function is plainly establishable: not simply illustration of events, but a special kind of *tableau* (as the term "lay-out" implies) where the substitute image has a special function and greater importance than in most illustrations. Establishable with like ease, thanks to photography's ability to produce exactly repeatable images, is that these layouts represent the same figure in different poses. Could these temple sculptures (89) not be seen the same way? Not as all different figures, but as successive images of one, then another, each thus illustrating in proto-movie style (88) a provocative routine? Some are indeed already so identified as successive poses in erotic dance.

So seen, figures like the Khajuraho *sura-sundaris* and all comparable Indian temple sculptures function as strip-tease preliminaries to the main exterior scenes of sexual ecstasy, (91) which in turn are carnal counterparts to and hence preparation for the inner cult images (the difference being manifested by contrast of severe vs. luxuriant style, rigidly canonical vs. lissom poses). The whole architectural, sculptural and painted complex of a Khajuraho temple would then appear unified in a grand integrated scheme. High medieval Indian architecture and arts generally then would be understandable no longer as additive compositions, mimetic shapes plus garish miscellaneous illustration (as Indian arts were in fact interpreted by Fergusson, by Toynbee, even by Baldwin Smith), but in the way Gothic cathedrals are understood, all the exterior sculpture interrelated, and in turn complimented by interior arts whose style only seems different (solid, material stone sculptures on the outside, etherial glass and canonically-dictated crucifixes and reliquaries within). So understood in terms of social function, high medieval Indian temples thus afford parallels to the West's abbeys and cathedrals of this same time stratum—and to the age's great Buddhist temples in China and India, Islam's most impressive mosques.... All have to do with creating a visual metaphor of the promises of their several religions, to bring heaven to earth.[38] What constitutes "heaven" obviously diverges from one belief-system to another. Detailed discussion of the differences would be irrelevant here, however rewarding; to the present point is simply: the concept of a heaven which consists of endless sex play is by no means unusual. Acknowledged or not, it is a utopian element in our society quite as much as in earlier ones.

Observing how such arts as the Khajuraho sculptures functioned comparably to our popular/commercial arts of strip-tease dance, magazine and movie pornography thus leads to contemplation of one of the mysterious parallels in universal history. But that's only a beginning.

The kind of dance nowadays called strip-tease originates far back in time. Already in the first century A.D. a Latin verse describes

The Syrian cabaret-hostess, whose hair is bound back by a Grecian headband/ whose quivering thighs sway to the rhythm of castanets/ dances intoxicated, voluptuous, in the smoky tavern....[39]

And already in those times this dance was being called a secularized, lascivious variant of primitive fertility rites. Discussing such rites and fertility cults, underdocumented and overdisputed as they are, is well beyond our present purposes— even if displacement of primaeval female deities by Aryan male-dominated cults and social outlook, or the relative importance of male vs. female fetiches, were not so tediously and tendentiously bound up with prejudices pro and con contemporary feminism, church canons, Lenin's views on public morality, and whether children corrupt our comics. Only a speculation, again: could the strip tease, practised by every known people in one form or another today,[40] derive from some equally universal origin in some primaeval ritual of fertility? Considering its social function—exciting of sexual desire—it's by no means impossible.

Religion in its broadest sense is both a system of belief and a means of clarifying relationships which defy rational explanation. For the latter purpose it has always made great use of tableaux and rituals which illustrate the ineffable: Man and God, Earth and Heaven, Birth and Death. Among the most mysterious of these has always been sex and the sexual instinct. It's so inexplicable as to be often classed among forms of madness. Violence and frenzy, love and voluptuousness were joint attributes of Ishtar of Erech, of Cybele, of Dionysius. Nor do we explain sex any better; we have a choice, as a wise contemporary once put it, of the language of the nursery, or of the gutter, or of science—and all are equally unsatisfactory. Our current real religion, Science, explains what things are made of and how they work, but not what they are or what starts them working. To this day the interaction of male and female remains a profound mystery. That is why nobody to this day can define pornography, why you must start with a non-definition. That is fundamentally (obviously there could be many reasons) why in all cultures sex has been something hidden. Cybele was to be found deep in a cave. Dionysius and the Maenads held their rites in wild fastnesses. *Naturvölker* in the South Seas and Africa make puberty initiations dark tabus. According to *Genesis* secrecy and sex came into Eden together. 3rd- and 2nd-millenium

cult images of the Great Mother, Earth Goddess, ritual
attendants, etc., were secreted in graves.

What form of ritual illustration was used for these mysteries?
About what has always been secret, posterity can expect to learn
little. But there are indications. The power and madness of erotic
love is made demonstrable by some ritual which excites it. What
sort of ritual was involved is suggested by Ishtar's attempt to
rescue Tammuz from the underworld. The "courtesan of the gods"
undertook

'to journey towards that land without return, towards that house from which he
who enters does not come out again,' she had the gates opened and penetrated the
seven precincts, at each gate stripping off one by one a piece of ornament or dress:
the great crown from her head, pendants from her ears, the necklace from her
throat, the jewels from her breast, her girdle adorned with birthstones, the
bracelets from her hands and from her feet; and finally the garment which covered
her nakedness....[41]

Likening such a myth to strip-tease would be facetious in terms of
quality or profundity. But both represent ritual illustration, with
similar physiological social function: to induce a desired mood
amongst spectators.

Ishtar, so associated alike with the underworld, the dead and
erotic passion, has often been suggested as the Mesopotamian
counterpart to the central cult figure of that megalithic culture
discovered by archaeology over the last half-century[42] to have
extended all round the Mediterranean littoral from the Cyclades
to the Orkneys. That such megalithic building functioned as
ceremonial centers, with rites of some kind at burials and
regularly thereafter, has long been suggested also. That such
rites could have been something like Ishtar's performance is by
no means impossible. The figures being in sequential groups
supports such a speculation; their not "looking sexy" to us, as art-
history surveys sometimes take unnecessary pains to point out,
does not imply that they had no such significance for their
makers either. That grave images functioned like dolls for role-
playing is long established fact (q.v., 23f).

Logically, linking sex and death accords with human
instincts and practises at all times and places. In our culture that
connection has been pushed underground, not by Christianity
which in fact recognizes the connection in many ways
throughout the centuries, so much as by our present religion,
which considers death along with sin and poverty and war as
something to be abolished in due course by Science, and in the
interval between now and the coming utopia to be thought of

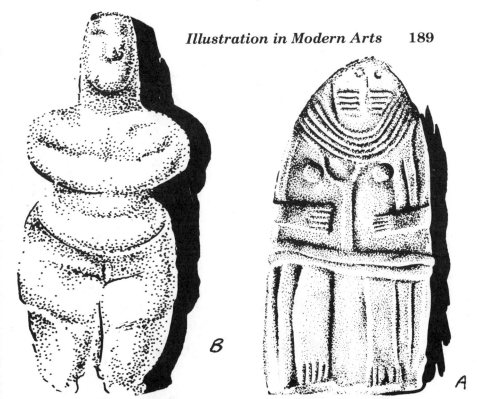

89. Megalith from St-Sernin, Brittany (A) and figure from the Aegean Cyclades (B), Ashmolean, Oxford, variously described as images of the Earth Goddess, the Great Mother, fertility fetishes. Third millennium B.C. Though the megalith is over life-size and the Cycladic figurine a few inches high, size in that age did not change social function but only made more potent its efficacy in relation to a ritual of fertility and death, earth and sky, described (insofar as known, which is not far, in Robert Graves' 1955 *Greek Myths*, introduction.)

seldom by people of sophistication, and mentioned never except in jest. Nevertheless the connection is real and remains in our underground in the truest sense. It bubbles up whenever and wherever pressures force up our protective scientific/utopian lid to reveal the actual continuing state of our affairs. One instance was the Dionysiac celebrations marking the end of World War I, when rioting crowds, berzerk with relief that the Great Slaughter had ended, copulated in public places while officially mourning the dead.[43] Another, public ritual sites like Forest Lawn, where symbols of sex and death mingle in defiance of science and utopia alike, in ago-old interaction (32).

Like all popular/commercial arts, then, strip-tease and associated pornography respond to deep-seated individual and social needs. Energies expended fulminating against them might more constructively be channelled into ways of realizing their potential for promoting more humanely and metaphysically meaningful environment.

90. Group sex illustration from the Kandariya-Mahadeva-temple in Khajuracho, c1000 A.D. Techn[?] known as *mithunas* (loving couples), such scences can be found in almost all periods of Indian art his[?] But only in high medieval temples like Khajuraho is their contribution to a complex image of heave[?] earth unmistakable.

Contemporary theory makes much of a fine distinction between hard-core pornography, which seems to be actual depiction of sexual intercourse, and soft-core, depiction of preliminaries thereto. Pretentious and pedantic apparently, since in life one presupposes the other and likewise in historic arts: on the Khajuraho temples, *sura-sundaris* and *mithuna* couplings are interrelated logically, visually and conceptually (91).

Nevertheless, studying these arts' social function reveals a subtle difference. At Khajuraho, the group sex scenes make plain what the *sura-sundaris* only implies: how the temple functions as a metaphor of heaven-on-earth (q.v., fn. 38). It doesn't matter precisely how this kind of heaven was understood, whether only symbolically, as is so often claimed[44] or literally, as promised faithful Moslems in the Koran, "with ever-youthful companions, the black-eyed houris, and the *ghilman*, lovely boys."[45] The point is that it illustrates a ritual which is the justification and symbol of a new state of society still to be attained rather than actually existing in the world of time and history, a fore-taste of joys forever in some future time. Utopian scenes, in fact, to be understood in some context like:

"In a royal temple the idol was of gold, set with diamonds, rubies and emeralds, hung with crowns, necklaces, bracelets, anklets, studded with costly stones, and beneath it untold treasures filled a cellar in the substructure. When His Majesty the Paramarabhattaraka Maharajatadhiraja attended the service accompanied by his queens, ministers, and other relatives and friends all in fashionable, costly attire, when a choir sang accompanied by a great number of instruments when beautiful dancing girls displayed their art before the idol, furtively throwing amorous glances at the visitors, it must have indeed have been a magnificent spectacle, a masterpiece of refined showmanship built up around the divine presence in the idol. What it was worth in genuine religiousness is another matter. But official religion in an aristocratic society always tends to develop in this direction and did the same in Medieval Europe, China, and Japan."[46]

—symbol and justification of a new state of society far different from any heretofore known in time and history.

Just so, can our own "hard core pornography" be explained— not so much popular/commercial as the reverse or underside of our avant-garde Establishment High Culture.

91. "Strip-tease" type of pornography: first three of a series of pictures made from a 1970s swingers' magazine, purporting to show how the wife of a swinging pair starts the action.

Balanced minds find hard-core acrobatics more ludicrous than exciting; but then, this is no art for balanced minds (as ancient mythology recognized by invariably coupling erotic love with madness and folly). Hard-core pornography has nothing to do, really, with any sober, factual, existing world, as may easily be discovered from a few captions in sex magazines, a few lines of dialogue from sex films, a few pages of pontificating by any modern sex guru. It's ritual illustration of our 20th-century religion's ecstatic visions of future social bliss, times when all humanity will be liberated as only those gurus are now, when pleasure will be unalloyed by responsibility, all life as uninhibited as—I was about to say, Eden before the Fall, but remember where you are!—in that prehistoric Age of Natural Man. Mythologic, to be sure; for of that idyllic time when mankind lived free of all restraint and peacefully browsed on fruits and berries, the most diligent researchings have as yet produced no proof. But fervently believed as an article of faith nonetheless. Faith is what hard-core pornography demands if it is to carry any conviction. Faith that dirt, smells, impotence, disease, all are abolished and need no longer be taken into any account. Faith even more that Natural Man (Redux) can continue indefinite co-existence with all the benefits of high and highly-disciplined technology (central heating, no goosebumps; chemical hairsets and shampoos, no dishevellment; deodorants; nylons that don't run—and, of course, contraceptives and prophylactics that work infallibly), as our avant-garde creed has held lo these long years.

For the orgy is in fact one image of what our 20th-century religion promises its faithful (or at least, its docile), just as Khajuraho's art is one image of Candella dynasty promisings. Or perhaps only an updated version of one continuing fantasy, for counterparts inbetween abound. Lucas Cranach, recorder of Luther's Reformation, painted a *Golden Age* to come when godly princes would be firmly in control of State churches and a contented peasantry, so that lords and ladies could disport themselves in palace gardens, naked and unashamed;[47] in that same century Rabelais gave literary form to something similar in his Abbey of Thémèle. Our hedonistic utopia already found literary form in H.G. Wells's 1896 *Time Machine* with its Eloi dancing through sunlit gardens free of science, free of learning, free of thought, free of responsibility—Wynwood Read realized.

Zamiatin's *We* described that vision too. So did Huxley's *Brave New World*. All ignoring the Morlocks also found by that *Time Machine;* the regimentation of *We;* the nihilism of *BNW*. Most of all ignoring those overtones of *Nineteen Eighty Four* where pornography was calculatedly used to divert potential protest into safe (from the Party's viewpoint) channels—add the fact that pornography may well have been used for such a purpose often before; John Rosenfield asserts that Japanese 18th-century pornography had this kind of State use[48].

A case, in short, of historic arts telling us something about popular/commercial, rather than the other way round.

Illustration Proper: Stories Related

What is chosen to be illustrated constitutes an assertion of values. Example: perception of incongruities as humor.

ONLY INSOFAR AS the study of art is not about art but about what art does can it qualify as a humanity. Assume, as we must (q.v.) that there is such thing as illustration proper which is not consciously telling stories for propaganda, still, as in the case of substitute imagery so in illustration, *what* is chosen to be illustrated necessarily constitutes an assertion of value priorities.

Fred Schroeder in his introduction to *Popular Culture Before Printing*[49] has usefully observed that "following the Gutenburg revolution...the almost exclusive religious, political, economic and military dimensions of [early and historic] popular culture have given way to entertainment popular culture":

If you mention popular culture to a typical person today, the immediate associations are with mass entertainment: comic books, television comedies, movie westerns, paperback mysteries, junk foods, and the like. In large part this is due to the popular definition of culture, which does not include such anthropologically significant elements as banks, supermarkets, schools, churches, and the army.

It's also due to the avant-garde Establishment definition of culture as Fine Art, an expressive end in itself, I think; but perhaps most of all to the fact that for a variety or reasons, which would be interesting indeed to explore, while modern popular/commercial arts like illustration are just as concerned as any historic and traditional arts with "religious, political, economic and military dimensions of culture," they subsume those concerns in entertainment forms. Analysis of comedy, most prolific category of popular/commercial entertainment arts, easily proves the point.

Entertainment, especially comedy, constitutes so large a proportion of illustration proper because it affords a vehicle for presenting and transmitting traditional convictions and attitudes, safe from censorship by current intellectual fashions. For such purposes talking animals are especially good, and have long so functioned in our society; possibly in other societies also.

Humor, we're told, results from perception of incongruities. Runty sailors are not supposed to beat up 300-pound brutes; when they do, it's humorous (93A).[50] Psychiatrists and airline pilots and Men of Medicine are supposed to be masterfully in charge of all our destinies; when they're victims of every hapless circumstance, bossed by wives and secretaries, forever fuzzy with jet-lag, more devoted to golf and bedgames than to patients, it's humorous (93B).

No great acumen is required to realize that humor reveals society's basic convictions in reverse. Only because our society holds for more or less self-evident truths that we have counterparts to the saints and heroes and lords of times past, i.e., professions which by natural right command respect and carry authority and status, can presenting them as buffoons be funny; otherwise, it would be not only unfunny, but subversive, even sacrilegious.

More significant is the question, why do basic convictions in our society—whose widespread acceptance is attested by the popularity of mass entertainment thus built upon them—have to be presented in so oblique a way? Once upon a time they were not. Once, great pageants and communal drama and stately ritual set forth those fundamental beliefs on which the stability of all societies depends. Why should our age's counterpart to miracle plays and Sophocles and Ise dances be Popeye, the Bob Newhart Show and John Wayne westerns dubbed in Japanese? Most probable answer: because the beliefs sanctioned by our society do not correspond to the beliefs on which people actually operate and by which they live their daily lives.

Our society is officially committed to the proposition that total equality of all human things is not only desirable but possible; to attain it all we need do is keep manipulating our

. Still from animated *Popeye* cartoon by Max Fleischer, whose first
mation of E.C. Segar's *Thimble Theatre* strip appeared in 1933, four years
er it began achieving national popularity. By 1938 a poll of children
icated preference for *Popeye* over *Mickey Mouse* animated cartoons, despite
ious impoverishment of content and technique compared either to Segar or
Disney. And Fleischer cartoons were still being run on TV in the 1950s and
0s.

. "The Cast of the 'Bob Newhart Show'," cover from
Guide for July, 1978. The series relied for its humor
n a reversal of stereotypes.

institutions until we get the right combinations. Nobody commands respect or wields authority by natural right. A good majority of our people would maintain, if questioned, that they do indeed believe such things. But their practise is something else— necessarily, since total equality is and always has been an article of faith, never a state of affairs. From this embarrassment several escapes are possible. One is *via* avant-garde arts, which implicitly take total equality for granted (the anti-hero in literature; automatic music; found art, etc.), but deny it in fact— all human beings are equally artists, so discipline or severe technical training is dispensable; but some artists are more equal than others, namely Us, the Ins. Another is by popular historicism, retreating into some past age whose hierarchical societies and high heroics can safely be admired: hence the huge popularity of historical novels, mounting steadily and inversely with the progress of official equality, 1689, 1776, 1789, 1832, 1917; thence passing into movies; thence TV, unabated Scott, Hugo, Henty. Ben-Hur and Scarlett O'Hara. Far better a retreat into humor, contemporarily set. There platitudes and fortitude can be honored in and by jest, safe alike from censorship of fashion or fist.

Humor mouthed by animals is the safest way to assert values.

Any time truth as perceived cannot be openly spoken, any time people are forced to profess that two and two make five, humor has provided relief, if not escape. We make jokes of what we are embarrassed to put plainly; hence cute animals declare our deepest loves and longings via greeting cards. But it's for those truths that fear of persecution or slander or unpopularity keep us from saying in the open, that animals speak best and oftenest; hence it is that their proliferation in popular/commercial arts has accompanied the march of the moderns to avant-garde Establishment status, jump by jump.

The more that official dogma conformed to Wonderland's "*Everybody* has won and *all* must have prizes," (95A), the more traditional wisdom found refuge amongst funny animals. In their animated cartoon world, as in *Ecclesiastes,* all things are governed by time and chance, so that races are not always won by the swift, nor battles by the strong, nor does bread always come to the wise, nor wealth to the intelligent, or recognition to the

94A. Frame from a *Road Runner* animated cartoon made for showing in movie-houses, by Charles M. Jones, director of Warner Brothers' animation unit 1938-1962. Like Disney, Jones insisted on each frame being a separately painted picture.

94B Frame from a *Rocky & Bulwinkle* cartoon, made for showing on television, by Hanna/Barbera Productions 1964. In these TV animations, long sequences may consist of identical backgrounds and bodies, only mouths, hands, and other details being overlaid in each fram to simulate movement.

gifted;[51] but courage, loyalty, wisdom, shrewdness win out often enough, stupidity and wastefulness and folly regularly enough get their just rewards, for songs and stories about funny animals to display a sanity conspicuously missing from the 20th century's controlling ideology. Such illustration therefore does for our society what illustrative arts throughout history have done—keep before populations those values and attitudes necessary and unavoidable if society is to survive, however unspeakable they may temporarily be. All official doctrine to the contrary, dentist and patients are not equals, nor airline pilot and passenger; and there are times when one individual is right and the majority is wrong; a David carrying only pebbles of fact must have courage to confront Goliaths however thickly sheathed in public opinion.

Popular/commercial entertainment like Popeye cartoons and TV sitcoms which speak such necessary truths hardly endear themselves thereby to official tastemakers. Vulgar they get tagged and for vulgar they will continue to be taken as long as they go on projecting values so subversive of established dogmas. But penitents are always welcome to the fold; hence the curious cycle in humorous animal art over past decades: in turn we see Disney in the '20s and '30s, Chuck Jones of Warner Brothers in the '40s and early '50s beginning with violent, rude, loyal, courageous animal characters that spoke for the old virtues, becoming progressively more respectable, liberal, arty, and flaccid. Perhaps the same thing is happening to Hanna-Barbera's work between the late '50s and now. Disney begins with a doughty, brash Mickey Mouse who holds his own against the villanous cat Pegleg Pete to claim the affections of a languishing Minnie, St.-George-and-Dragon, Perseus-and-Andromeda style; he ends with the saccarine inanities of *Pinocchio* and *Bambi*.[52] Jones' Coyote and Roadrunner were violent, crude, exaggerated and real; his *Froggy Evening* has justly been called "a morality play in cameo"; then he became infatuated with the medium as an end in itself, locked himself into archaic technique and senseless sound effects in the interests of "creating pure cinema"; and like Disney, refused to accept the limited animation forced on the medium by television.[53] Hanna-Barbera, originally *Tom and Jerry* animators for MGM, took over with half-hour TV cartoons requiring eight weeks to make compared to seventeen weeks for a six-minute MGM cartoon, thus restoring animation's central technique[54]; restored, too, were characters with guts and loyalty (Rocket J. Squirrel and Bulwinkel the Moose) and parodies much in Lewis Carroll's *Alice* vein. Too violent! Child-corrupting! clamored Cultured Opinion, and Hanna-Barbera bowed, hopefully only for the moment—without reflection on either side, perhaps, that whereas the essence of pornography (which this same Cultured Opinion usually defends on grounds of artistic freedom) is imitation—monkey see, monkey do—nobody watching cartoon animals annihilate each other is ever physiologically moved to go out and do likewise. . . .

A variant of this phenomenon (you might call it the Law of Progressive Disintegration, Low-Real to Genteel to Futeel) seems to occur when one generation's humor gets recognized by the next as a classic and put into some other medium for the edification of some other people (children being the usual victims). Disney showed the way with his version of *Three Little Pigs* as a welfare-state morality play; from such cues, no doubt, sprang inspiration for the Judy Garland movie version of *The Wizard of Oz,* a panegyric on optimism in tough times and faith in absolutely everything. Surely the most fearsome instance was what happened when *The Story of Doctor Doolittle* and *The Voyages of Doctor Doolittle,* written and illustrated by Hugh Lofting in 1920 and 1922, became a movie in the 1960s. However could the original Doolittle, stolid and unprepossessing spokesman of the British Empire-Builder's total superiority in all phases of life whatever to all people whomever but most especially to natives, a humorous personification of all the implicit attitudes of Macaulay's 1832 Report on Education in India, get bowdlerized into a string of liberal platitudes drivelled out by Rex Harrison, Mr. Suavity Himself, like a slug crossing a lawn? Rock bottom, though, was the 1933 Paramount movie of *Alice in Wonderland* and Disney's animated version of same a few years later. How fortunate it is that the originals have survived, are still being read, and still fulfilling their function of preserving sanity for those disposed toward it.

So understanding the function of entertainment via illustration of talking animals in our society, we can begin to recognize how similar arts may have had similar functions historically. The *Alice* fantasies, for example, have long been recognized as hardly limited to children's edification.[55] "*Everybody* has won and all shall have prizes...and *she* shall give them...." spoken by a Dodo, perfectly satirizes the "to-each-according-to-need-from-each-according-to-ability" doctrine which so captivated the more simple-minded sort of 19th-century socialist. Or more exactly, it is sanity presented in reverse, by jest—just what our own talking animals do for us.

A story of all revolutions, recollected in tranquility—after the upset, only the Mad Hatter is ahead. Heads the politicians win, tails we lose.

95A. Illustration by John Tenniel to *Alice in Wonde*
Ch. III: "At last the Dodo said '*Everybody* has w
all shall have prizes.' 'But who is to give the prizes?'
a chorus of voices asked. 'Why, *she*, of course,' sa
Dodo. Alice...in despair put her hand in her pock
pulled out a box of comfits...and handed them ro
prizes."

95B. Tenniel's illustration of the Mad Tea-Party, *Alice*,
Ch. VII: "'I want a clean cup,' said the Hatter, 'let's all
move one place on'."

"I want a clean cup," interrupted the Hatter: "let's all move one place on."

He moved on as he spoke, and the Dormouse followed him: the March Hare moved into the Dormouse's place, and Alice rather unwillingly took the place of the March Hare. The Hatter was the only one who got any advantage from the change; and Alice was a good deal worse off than before, as the March Hare had just upset the milk-jug into his plate.

Grimms' fairy tales—

Such violence! Whatever could parents in earlier ages have been thinking of, to let their kiddies hear such tales? There are, of course, lots of theories about the function of folklore.[56] But primarily, these tales were told for their morals, to inculcate commonsense precepts: don't wander off alone into unfamiliar places; don't confide in strangers, weapons aren't necessarily bad things to have around. In the original, these precepts were reinforced by repetition: "It happened that Red Riding Hood was sent out to her Grandma again. *This* time..." But why were they cast in talking-animal format? Nowadays that kind of covert

Darauf ging es zum Bett und zog die Vorhänge zurück.

Da lag die Großmutter und hatte die Haube tief ins Gesicht gesetzt und sah so wunderlich aus. „Ei, Großmutter, was hast du für große Ohren!" „Daß ich dich besser hören kann."

96. Illustration to a 1961 printing of *Grimms' Fairy Tales*. Like *Alice*, these famous stories have had many illustrators over the years, but the perennial favorite is Tenniel's contemporary Ludwig Richter, here, set into the text as in the original, giving visual form to the famous Red Riding Hood dialogue: "She[das Madchen] went to tHe bed and drew back the curtains. There lay Grandmother.... 'O, Grandmother, what big ears you have!' 'The better to hear you, my dear.'...."

approach might be understandable, for the precepts of *Little Red Riding Hood* are not what is taught on *Sesame Street*—and, since they are nonetheless imperative precepts for life on the streets of Roxbury or South Boston or anywhere else outside PBS's Boston studios, they have to be taught circumlocutiously. But the tales collected by the brothers Grimm are residue of Old Germany, from the 15th, 16th and 17th centuries mainly.[57] Why humorous talking-animal tales, village buffoonery, tavern jokes and nursery rhymes to insinuate truths then? Because these too were centuries when German lands, and all of Europe—perhaps all the civilized world—was committed to the controlling vision of a hereditary class-structured state, pyramidally built, with a dynastic godly prince at its apex, as a panacea for all human ills. Divine Reason, they held, had ordained that society consist of king and nobles, priests, townsmen, peasants, each born to a place, each assured of happiness if content with "that station in life to which it hath pleased Providence to call me," as Prayerbooks from that age put it—if nobles fight and rule, priests pray and teach, townsmen trade and tinker, peasants till and toil, all doing their part for no other motive than to assure each other peace in this world and life eternal in the next. A grand vision, set out in many a work of art from those times—14th and 15th-century books of hours and frescoes (*Très Belles Heures,* Shifanoia), 16th and 17th-century architecture and pageants and panoramas,—and by no means in the West alone.[58]

Perfection of this vision lacked only one thing: some solid contact with reality. Some cognizance of actual life. A situation not unlike our own, indeed; its talking animal art should not, in consequence, be too hard for us to understand. Then as now an Establishment imposed its way of seeing reality so that reality as actually perceived had to be presented via other vehicles, couched in safely allusive, diffuse, humorously ambiguous forms. Then as now, the reigning Establishment itself had once been revolutionary. And humorous animals had been a resort for reason under its predecessor too.

Before there were illustrated books, and block prints, and chapbooks with stories of talking animals, there were manuscripts, illuminated—and oftentimes provided with extra illustrations in the margins of folk tales, including many of talking animals.

It can be no accident that marginal illustrations of animal stories, especially that *Roman de Renard* which was so popular in the Middle Ages that the old French word for fox, *goupil,* was everywhere replaced by *renard* (as if we all took to talking about mickeys when we meant mice) began to appear in the 12th century, and were at their most prolific from 1300 to 1325.[59] For that was the age of what Friedrich Heer called the "Revolution from Rome," opened by the *Dictatus Papae* of 1075: "The Pope alone can wear Imperial insignia. All princes should kiss the Pope's food....He can depose kings....No one can judge him....He is the sole representative of God on earth; he holds the keys to heaven and hell...."[60] In such an atmosphere, these marginal illustrations, made as most were directly under ecclesiastical commission, are not necessarily revolutionary in our sense. They're just illustrations of sanity. Randall is surely right in citing satire of the rich and powerful (i.e., lords and ecclesiastics, often identical), and use as preaching aids, to explain what these illustrations were for. But what is satirized tells us, as in the *Bob Newhart Show,* what is believed. Officially it may be proclaimed that the world has now been transformed by a Church whose power, greater than the State's by the differential of Sun to Moon (7,644½ times greater to be exact, according to later canonist Hugo Hostiensis, calculating by Ptolemy's estimate of sun-to-moon ratio), enforces love and mercy and charity as the laws of Christendom; but you better not count on that.

203

96. Stories of Reynard the Fox, from 13th century manuscript margins: A. The Fox plays dead in order to catch birds. B. Reynard confesses his sins to Chantecler the Rooster. (C) Reynard tricks Ysengrim the Wolf into a bucket so that the wolf is beaten instead of him. (From Lilian Randall, "Exampla As a Source of Gothic Marginal Illumination," *The Art Bulletin,* XXXIX, 1957.

97. *Chogu Giga* handscroll of animal caricatures, ink on paper, about 33 cm. high. In the Kosan-ji, Kyoto.

The world still abounds in foxy rascals who'll eat you alive if you take their professions for fact; who'll pretend to help you as Reynard helps Ysengrim, only so you'll be caught and take his rap; who'll profess all manner of piety like Reynaud confessing his sins to Chantecleer the Cock, if piety will fill their stewpot.

In a word: the world goes on. No matter what the Great Ones do, generation after generation, the ordinary person's round of life remains much the same—and whoever forgets it will be sorry! In that sense, these talking animal illustrations are counterparts to the labors of the months on Gothic cathedral facades, or the lower band of the Bayeux tapestry with its scenes of harvest and sowing, death and sex—this round of ordinary tasks is the foundation, the substratum, of all ideologies, the ultimate ground of sanity on which survival depends. By putting such truths in a humorous way, illustration of talking animals was not different, only more effective.

Coincident with the appearance of talking animals in Western medieval manuscript illustration, something very similar seems to appear in Japan: scrolls of animal caricatures. These have hitherto been analyzed, like most other Japanese arts, mainly from aesthetic and technical points of view.

Thus Elise Grilli's book on scrolls admirably explains how they should be read as story-telling devices,[61] what types there are (text and image parallel; ditto alternating; occasional text at beginning or end but main story told by continuous pictorial unrolling; interspersed or talking style with captions or bits of information above speakers as in modern cartoons); analogies with "unfolding stage drama"; even

an analogy with cinematic structure, with its more flexible juggling of time, speed, and motion. In the course of this evolution, the Japanese scroll painters have, in fact, made many discoveries in the arts of time and space, such as the Occident learned some seven hundred years later through the cinematic genius of D.W. Griffith and his followers.

But not much about content. What actually is the story being told? Why is it told by means of talking animals? This we don't get answered, except obliquely: "ribald fables which manage to mock all classes." But speculations based upon social function of comparable modern popular/commercial arts, may offer ideas.

Many aspects of Japanese civilization in the period 1000-1300 suggest at least superficial parallels with Europe's in the same age: institutions and movements rooted in a fundamental assumption that the model on which earthly affairs should be structured was a supernatural Order revealed to and best understood by saints, mystics, and priests—Buddhists primarily, in this case; corollary to that, a pre-eminent role for ecclesiastical bodies in the theory and oftentimes the practise of government.[62] An age and culture, then, beset by the fatuities inherent in all visionary enterprises; needing, then, compensating assertions of ongoing common sense. No reason why humorous talking animals could not have maintained sanity in that time and place as they do in ours.

Have talking animals always seemed humorous? Or does their effectiveness have yet another, deeper explanation? I think so. I think that there wasn't always incongruity about animals who talked like men, hence that talking animals weren't always vehicles for humor. Once upon a time there was a deep sense of identity between mankind and the animal kingdom, and it's in part due to atavistic memories from this age that talking animals speak so effectively to our needs.

Talking animals in ancient arts are not necessarily humorous; they could have originated in shamanism.

Humor in another language than one's own, let along humor in another culture, is always tricky to grasp. Not merely do things incongruous within one culture seem perfectly normal in another—and so what's funny to one is serious to another; but what seems funny can come to seem unfunny, even highly offensive, quite suddenly. Historians two thousand years hence might well not realize that the "comic darkey" humor, for example, which flourished so exuberantly throughout the United States during the 19th century and was still accepted as funny during the first decade of the 20th in a nationally syndicated form like *Mutt & Jeff,* was considered tasteless already in the 1920s and by the 1960s actually reprehensible, banished from all except the lowest common denominator locker-room humor.

Conversely, they might in all logic suppose that Tarzan the Ape-Man must have been a hilariously comic figure. Imagine, a human baby found and raised entirely by great apes, who talks ape language, thinks he's an ape, has an ape's strength and skills, yet at an early age finds books in his parents' abandoned cabin and teaches himself to read, eventually to talk perfect English; the first white woman he ever meets, he treats with perfect bourgeois chivalry—but enough, who could take such nonsense seriously? "A thousand million" 20th-century people, that's who.[63] They made *Tarzan* book after *Tarzan* book best-sellers, *Tarzan* movies into consistent money-makers. Historians could guess it only if they realized that Tarzan was actually an archetype of the 20th century's religion of Natural Human Goodness, Greatness, Creativity, cast into an archetypal image of man's relationship to the animal creation, at once one with it and its master.

In Antiquity the hero Herakles was often represented on stages and in sculpture of Hellenistic times as a comic buffoon, but in earlier times—7th through the 5th centuries B.C. roughly—the stories told of his feats illustrated (in the root sense of explained, cast light upon) complex interrelationships within the natural and supernatural worlds. Son of Zeus and an earthly mother, Herakles was a natural mediator between gods and men. So in the twelve metopes of the Temple of Zeus at Olympia the hero is depicted, possibly for the first time in Greek (or any) art, as totally intelligible on a human plane. His labors shift in logical geographic sequence from local to ever more remote arenas. His interpersonal relations become ever more complicated as he moves on in life—like ours! His physique, like ours, goes from the slimness of beardless youth to the chunky stiffness of old age. His mentor and patronness, the goddess Athena, is depicted conversely and contrastingly. She appears in some metopes as his guide and stay, but not in all, and her appearances are dictated by no rule; she is not bound by human time and space. Nor does she age. So far from humorous, Herakles is here presented as symbol of relationships between god and man worthy of the greatest tragedian.[64]

98. Drawing by Harold Foster illustrating Chapter 25 of the first modern comic book, a version of Edgar Rich Burroughs' *Tarzan of the Apes*. Here the "apeman" (for Tarzan is both a talking animal and a human with animal abilities), "leaping upon the great back, plunged his long thin blade a dozen times into the fierce heart." (Cf. 76).

99. Black-figured Athenian vase-painting, representing the story of Herakles shooting the carnivorous birds of the Valley of Stymphalia. On the Temple of Zeus at Olympia, the metope depicting this scene is second in the series of Herakles' twelve labours; it follows directly his killing of the Nemean Lion, after which he puts on the lion-skin so that his head seems to come out of the lion's open mouth; and this "lion's-head" becomes Herakles' identifying sing ever thereafter. (c500 B.C.)

But Herakles also is a mediator between mankind and the natural world. His early feats all have to do with lions, boars, birds of prey, wild horses, hinds with brazen hoofs, snakes with seven heads. He is sign and symbol of man's dominion over nature. "Dominion over Nature" admittedly sounds ominous in modern ears; hard things are said of alleged sanctions in *Genesis* for ravaging Nature to suit filthy capitalism. Not so; dominion over nature means that, being part animal as well as part angel, we must live in harmony with nature as well as with gods. Herakles kills creatures that run amok, who are *un*-natural. Man disciplines Nature, as God disciplines man. In sign of which, Herakles wears the lion's head as his own; in this guise he in a very real sense asserts his one-ness with the animal kingdom, man's proper leadership of it. And this is not humorous either, but a variant image of one of the ancient world's greatest and most universal religions.

Nowadays the notion of man/beast fusion survives amongst us only in realm of fairytale (Beauty and the Beast, perennial favorite for kiddies' theatre; enchanted Frog/Prince, on which there must be a hundred parodies in the *Wizard of Id* alone), and amongst primitive peoples in the form of a kind of magic generally going under the name of Shamanism. Precisely what a modern Shaman is and does has long been the object of intense research, and subject of vigorous controversy among anthropologists, historians of religion, and students of myth.[65] But about Shaminism's origins there can be little doubt. It represents the vestiges of a cult once universal, at its height perhaps in the second millenium B.C., possibly contemporaneous with the Great Mother or earth goddesses. Its universality is evidenced in motifs like the human head in a great cat's (lion, tiger, jaguar) jaws, found not only across Eurasia (Herakles; Scythian animal-style metalwork; a variant in the Mesopotamian hybrid-animal seals, cf. 38A) but also in the Americas—something so unusual as hardly to have occurred spontaneously. Absorbing to pursue though the subject is, [66] our point here is simply: about these anthropomorphic animals there is no question of humor. That animals should talk like man and man impersonate animals is funny only when the idea is considered to be incongruous or grotesque; so far from either, images of man and animals being one flesh originally constituted

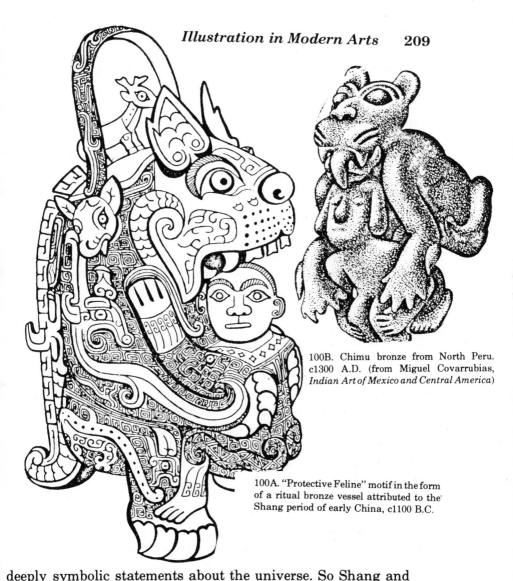

100B. Chimu bronze from North Peru. c1300 A.D. (from Miguel Covarrubias, *Indian Art of Mexico and Central America*)

100A. "Protective Feline" motif in the form of a ritual bronze vessel attributed to the Shang period of early China, c1100 B.C.

deeply symbolic statements about the universe. So Shang and Chimu animal vessels (100) were made (at great labor in difficult bronze technique) to serve purposes of that animal worship which for millenia was (and to some extent still is) the most typically Chinese perception of cosmic harmony—each generation fulfilling ordained obligations under Natural Law. In the 3rd and 2nd millennia such images were (there is good reason to believe) all the more powerful because analogical modes of thought were less trammelled by analytical reservations than later (q.v., VI). To dress in an animal skin was, by a mode of perception imaginable but not real to us, to become that animal; an animal depicted as upright and talking was in some sense stronger than impersonation, to be a kind of human.[67] Later times and modes of metaphor undermined the effectiveness of this kind of image and left it to degenerate into primitive shamanism—perhaps the Chimu image (100B) had already so lost its original meaning.

But it may well be that the persistence of talking animals in our civilization and their pervasiveness throughout our popular/commercial arts owes something to these roots deep in our past: "mankind is not like a train passing through stations; whatever we have been, in some sense we are still."

With such examples before us, we should be all the more cautious about accepting as humorous any ancient arts which represent anthropomorphic animals, no matter how much they seem to resemble ours.

What is grotesque, like what is beautiful, all too often has been in the eye of an ignorant beholder. So until well on in the 19th century, any extreme deviations from Renaissance norms were assumed to have been intended as gross, grotesque, or humorous. So Malcolm in 1813, Thomas Wright in 1864, Parton in 1878 all lumped examples of Hindu, Chinese, South Seas, Romanesque and Egyptian together in books about caricature, the grotesque and comic art.[68] They took the simple view that what looked funny or grotesque to them had always looked funny or grotesque, to everybody.[69] It would be nice to report that, with mounting evidence of all kinds showing that ancient man's perception of the world was radically different from ours, not to mention that the activity nowadays called "art" does different

101. So-called "comic" scroll assigned to 20th-22nd Dynasties, c900 B.C., during years of Egyptian decline. Often taken to be a burlesque of older traditional ritual scenes.

things in and for society from what we call "art" historically, such automatic assumptions occur no more. Alas, that would hardly be true. In the volume on Ancient Egypt of the *Time/Life* series on "Great Ages of Man" we find a scroll of talking animals (101) captioned:

Comic-strip art was popular in the New Kingdom and included this whimsical papyrus, intended as a humorous commentary on the breakdown of the old social order. It shows ancient enemies stepping out of their accustomed roles. . . . In the nation's declining years, art, once reserved mainly for religious purposes, came to be used also as an instrument of social protest.[70]

Leaving aside such questions, not only unanswered but unasked, as, to whom was this protest addressed? how circulated? or, what precisely is the story being told?—which need to be put prior to any assumptions about "humorous commentaries" and "instruments of social protest," it's apparent that this is hardly more informed than writings about alleged humor in Egypt a century before.

John A. Wilson (in whose *Burden of Egypt* the *Time/Life* interpretation may in fact originate) was never so naive. "A sense of humor is highly individual to a culture and we can rarely be absolutely sure whether the passage was deliberately humorous and so appealed to the ancient, or whether we moderns find some of the solemnities of the ancient amusingly peculiar and thus read humor into them," he wrote there, introducing several pages of discussion about Egyptian humor.[71] Most of it he assigned to the latest Egyptian period, called it "mordant," and attributed it to pessimism and disillusionment once "Egypt as a great power was finished":

there appears a broad streak of irreverence directed against things once held sacred. The period provides us with caricatures in which the proud figure of a pharaoh charging against the enemy is degraded into a battle between cats and mice. The gods did not escape such burlesquing. . . .
The treatment of the gods as subject to human foibles and weaknesses was not new in Egypt but the broadness of this treatment in the late Empire suggests that the sacred was no longer held in the same reverence. The supporting post of Egyptian culture was showing visible cracks. If nothing could be taken with complete seriousness, what would hold society together?

Were such an interpretation literally true, this art could hardly be called comic. Tragic might be the better word—sardonic, surely. But a case could surely be made, especially in a situation where no hard evidence at all has ever been adduced (even the story this "comic scroll" may tell has never been conjectured), that Egyptian animal art was never humorous, early or late; that in fact humor in our sense was impossible in old Egypt because its mental set from beginning to end did not perceive our kind of incongruities.

To the uninitiated, it's not easy to perceive precisely why the famous harp inlay from Ur with its parading animals has never been classified as funny or an evidence of decadence like the Turin comic scroll (cf. 101, 102B), nor why jackals weighing souls of the dead, with haunches of beef on offering tables nearby (102A) should be solemn and jackals herding goats (101) should be taken for sardonic, let alone mirthful. Nor, apparently, do the initiated find it much easier. Wilson's last chapter, for example, explains how Egypt as known to the Greeks was a fossilized, degenerate, perverted version of a once-great civilization. Its animal worship, which so amazed and disgusted them, was typical:

> The term 'worship' should not properly be applied before the first millennium B.C., by which time the characteristic faith had perished, leaving only its empty shell. In earlier Egypt...the animal devoted to a god was to be cherished and respected just as much as the physical structure of a temple and no more. Later Egypt confused the form with the substance and began so strict and so detailed a cult of the sacred animal that the term 'animal worship' was then justified and in its generalities, was correctly reported by the Greeks.[72]

Comparably, then, where once anthropomorphic animals and men in animal guise had signified the whole cosmos's deep underlying unity, now rank superstition reigned; and animals were worshipped as people. In such circumstances, scrolls like the late "comic strips" (101) would be simply illustrations of such sacred beasts, and no more. If cats and mice are sacred, what would be funny about using them to represent pharaohs and their enemies?

In sum: even such seemingly trivial popular/commercial arts of illustration as humorous talking animals reach far back into, and cast new light upon, human culture at all times and places. How much more, those that touch upon war and government, life and love.

102A. Judgment scene from *Book of the Dead* (Turin), assigned to 18th Dynasty, first and most imperialistic of New Kingdom eras, c1400. Jackal-headed Anubis weighs heart of priestess against Truth; on cross-bar, baboon-headed god Thoth records result.

102B Inlay on the second box of a harp found in Ur, assigned to c2600 B.C. (University Museum, Philadelphia).

Traditional attitudes and values are preserved also in popular/commercial illustrations related to war and government. Battle scenes, for example.

103B. Illustration of an episode from the Franco-Prussian war: *Champigny, 30 Novembre 1870,* by Etienne Beaumetz, exhibited at the Salon of 1884 with an official commentary extolling its presentation of "true heroism" "looking death in the face, ready to submit to it for fatherland and duty! These are the sentiments M. Beaumetz has inspired in his painting of Champigny, a beautiful military episode full of vigor and truth, which permits his name to be inscribed in the golden book of battle painters alongside those of Neuville and Détaille."

103A. Stele erected by Naram-Sin of Akkad, c2300-2200, whose Mesopotamian domains may have been the first self-proclaimed empire, commemorating an expedition against mountaineers and presumably teaching the futility of resistance. Found by the French expedition to Susa and now in the Louvre.

Through all the history of art, no subject is more consistently illustrated than battles. They have been commissioned by every culture, everywhere, from early Antiquity to the early 20th century (q.v. 124). Battle scenes must have been among the first kinds of art to be truly public—made to be on continuous view, unlike tomb images or ritual objects. Over the millennia they changed only slightly. Individual episodes and individual soldiers were more emphasized in the 19th century than formerly, but glorifications of leaders like those thousands of years before remained common—Meissonier's paintings of Napoleon's battles, for instance. Battle scenes, like all illustrative arts, gave better illusions of movement the nearer modern times were approached.

But no art has been so widely denounced in our own time. Battle painting, already rare by 1914-18 except when officially sponsored by governments, went into museum basements and stayed there. Movies like *What Price Glory? All Quiet on the Western Front* and *For Whom the Bell Tolls* ostensibly replaced them, the novels' pessimism, cynicism and pacifism being altered in tone to suit continuing public taste for more patriotic inspiration; but after 1945 progressives managed to impose their views on movie makers to such an extent that pacifism, direct or indirect, (e.g. impugning motives of heroism, etc.) became and remained almost mandatory in all avant-garde arts—novel, theatre, even movies.

In dramatic—and, it would seem, unfavorable—contrast to progressive arts and attitudes has been the massive proliferation of war illustration in popular/commercial arts.

104. Street battle in South America—or is it Africa? Southeast Asia? Lebanon? Radiophoto—or is it a movie still? or a TV kineoscope? What and which hardly matter anymore—there is so incredibly much illustration of war in all popular/commercial media. All of it fast, all of it accurate—that captions so often misrepresent facts is not so much a reflection on the accuracy of the illustration as on the veracity of those using it.

Easel paintings of war may be extinct since the last commissions of World War II, but that's only because they have been so redundant. For reasons which might prove rewarding to research, at the very moment when High Culture was being totally and finally taken over by the avant-garde Establishment—i.e. between 1945 and 1955—a flood of war art of every description burst over the Western world and has never abated since.[73] Attendance at places like the Imperial War Museum in London, where people thronged to look at posters, uniforms and other paraphernalia and propaganda from World War I, began to surpass other galleries. Magazine racks in stores began to overflow with war books of every description, from comic-book tales of World War II to official and unofficial histories of the Civil War. Novels about war multiplied; so did movies—whoever saw fewer than three or four reruns of *The Desert Fox* was lucky. Nowadays hardly a television newscast can be switched on without actual clips of battle to be seen— government troops, terrorists, guerillas. Hardly a newspaper or newsmagazine without regular illustrated stories about non-peace. Arts so vivid, so immediate, that even the most prejudiced had to admit, they illustrate better, faster, in every way more accurately than any predecessors. But do they also illustrate, perhaps, the inherent and inescapable brutality, violence,

105. Still from the 1927 movie *Ten Days That Shock the World,* one of the long series of patriotic Russian war movies by Sergei Eisenstein, which includes *Alexander Nevsky* and *The Battleship Potemkin* and the 1953 *Ivan Grodny.*

vulgarity and intellectual poverty of popular/commercial arts generally? Indeed that was said often enough.[74]

But the gulf between popular/commercial and avant-garde arts and attitudes about war is not as wide as it seems. All too often progressives' aversion to war and war art plainly varied according to who fought whom for what. There was enthusiasm enough for war when Ho Chi Minh was waging it. Admiring books on Sergei Eisenstein's cinema art abound[75]—and he never made a film that was not about war, revolution and bloodshed, pacifism in the Soviet Union having been from the beginning strictly an export commodity. To date, Eisenstein has been the Beaumetz, Neuville and Détaille of our century all rolled into one; but he may find a Chinese rival sooner or later, since Iliad-like epics of Mao's Great War of Liberation proliferate steadily, all duly adulated by many whose contempt for southeast-Asian-set movies about Flying Tigers or comics like *Terry* and *Steve Canyon* knows no bounds. (Readers may recall that war movies glorifying the ongoing war of liberation were still the most popular form of entertainment in Orwell's *Nineteen Eighty-Four*). It's as short a hop from pot-and-flower-children to porn/violence in underground comics,[76] as from academic classrooms where pacificism is urged on all and sundry to academic politics where rivals are murdered in all but the most literal senses. Malcolm Muggeridge, whose autobiography provides rich fare in this field, attributed such inconsistencies to secret, often unrecognized power-worship, like Beatrice Webb's showing him

a portrait of Lenin, presented to her by the Soviet Government; as stylized and cheap, artistically speaking, as any print of a Saint of the Church or Blessed Martyr offered for sale in Lourdes. She had set the picture up as though it were a Velasquez, with special lighting coming up from below, and a fine vista for looking at it....For her, I realized, the place was a shrine; she looked positively exalted there, uplifted, worshipful, in an almost frightening way,like someone possessed. A frail, aged, bourgeois lady, wearing, as she usually did, a grey silk dress and pretty lace cap on her head, prostrating herself, metaphorically speaking, before the founding father of the twentieth-century totalitarian state, the arch-terrorist of our time! It was extraordinary and rather horrifying. Afterwards I reflected that the two scenes I had witnessed—the Webbs at work, and Mrs. Webb at prayer before her Lenin picture—embodied the whole spirit of the age, showing her to be a true priestess and prophetess; pursuing truth through facts and arriving at fancy, seeking deliverance through power and arriving at servitude.[77]

There are hopeful signs of an end in sight to such hypocrisies. "It is obvious," Duncan Williams wrote (for one example),

That one cannot be in favor of total, unbridled freedom and at the same time support the necessity for strict regulations to ensure clean air, pure water, and an environment fit for human life. It is equally illogical to clamour for 'justice' while at the same time engaging in a doctrinaire repudiation and denigration of authority, symbolized by the police, the sole guardians of anyone's rights and the only bulwark against the *bellum omnium contra omnes.*" [78]

One can at least hope that it is obvious. ("Next time you're mugged, call a hippie," as bumperstickers of the late '60s— reputedly some on police cars in certain districts of San Francisco—used to display). Certainly it has always been obvious in the popular arts, past and present.

Fashionable intellectuals of the 1920s and 1930s in France found one of their favorite anti-war targets, their most useful examples of banal literature and art corrupting youthful minds, in Bruno's *Tour de France,* widely used in the French school system from the 1880s through 1918, and also as a textbook for French-language courses in North American universities and high schools in the same years (whence the picture here—106A— comes). Its text, written just six years after France's humiliating capitulation to the new German Empire of 1871, admittedly contains rich material for satire. Julien (one of the "deux enfants"), reading to the child Jean-Joseph, describes how the patriot Vercingetorix organized resistance to the foreign invaders of France, was captured, then strangled after six years imprisonment, by Caesar:

"Alas!" cried Jean-Joseph with emotion, "That Caesar was very cruel!" · It's not over, Jean-Joseph; listen: "Children, reflect within you, and ask yourselves which of these two men, in this war, was the greater? Which would you rather have within you, the heroic soul of the young Gaul defending the soil of his ancestors, or the ambitious and insensitive soul of the conquering Roman?" "O!'" cried Julien quite carried away with his reading, "I would not hesitate..." "Nor I," cried Jean-Joseph.

Astérix ostensibly burlesques Vercingetorix, and all such patriotic sentiment as the *Tour de France.* But in another, it really performs the same function in visual and textual language suitable to more sophisticated times—or at least, times sophisticated in other ways. He is a small star (Astérix—asterisk) n ludicrous contrast to Vercingetorix, as Obelix is a burlesqued Gargantua; but essentially he performs the same role, humbling the mighty Caesar, showing the old French individualistic resistance to bureaucratic authority.[79] All the more significant, then, that this comic should be an intellectual fad in France, a major factor in making the *bande dessinée* an object of serious study, more so perhaps than in its native American habitat. To become interested in comics like this is to begin regaining a saner and balanced approach to the facts of life after war.

Vercingetorix, de la tribu des Arvernes (habitants de l'Auvergne), vivait au dernier siècle avant J.C.

106A. Woodcut illustration from a 1904 edition of *Le Tour de France par deux enfants,* by G. Bruno (pseudonym of the wife of philosopher Alfred Fouillé). The statue of Vercingetorix illustrates a story of this Celtic hero's resistance to Roman invaders.

106B. Astérix, anti-hero of the comic strip drawn by Albert Uderzo and scripted by René Goscinny since 1959, from an episode in the *Tour de Gaul* sequence which plainly burlesques Bruno's *Tour de France.*

Awareness that popular/commercial arts offer a civilized substitute to war is becoming more general, too.

Popular/Commercial arts offer a civilized substitute for war in (e.g.) sports, superheroes figures, detective stories.

Were Fred Schroeder's admirable *Outlaw Aesthetics*[80] being published today, a different title might well be chosen for it. Football and wrestling, detective stories, superheroes and other subjects he there analyzes as art, are rapidly becoming respectable for cultural historians generally to talk about.

When you put weed-killer on a lawn, the change is imperceptible at first. Then quite suddenly you become aware that weeds are shrivelling and fresh grass is growing up through. Something of the sort has been happening in cultural studies generally during the '70s, I think. It would go too far, perhaps, to claim that professional sports have become entirely respectable. But at least they are getting something better than routine, ritual contempt, as in the past. Maybe a straw indicating that the wind which has been dissolving the 1950s and '60s utopian fog in architectural thinking[81] continues to spread. That ever more people are abandoning attempts to improve the world based on ideas of what it ought, or should, or might desirably be, in favor of trying to improve what is there. And what is there, is a lot of people with aggressive instincts better satisfied vicariously by professional sports than by assault and battery.

Baseball was early promoted as fulfilling that role;[82] but the best-known attempt to put that theory into practise came back in the 1890s when founders of the modern Olympic games argued that nations might compete in amateur athletics as a substitute for war, following classic Greek precedent (also a theory, one might add). The idea got massive governmental support. To this day huge sums of public money are laid out on Olympics, not only for stadia and expenses but for the most comprehensive sort of TV and radio coverage. The problem is, somebody forgot the fundamental idea of games being a war substitute. Running, jumping, swimming, discus-throwing may have kept the ancients on the edge of their chairs, but for most moderns these are sports only a shade more interesting than championship fishing or the

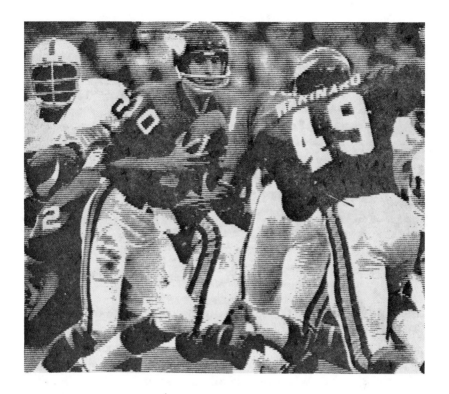

107. Weekend football telecast—the most popular single programming on TV, according to some surveys. Partly, of course, because like all modern popular/commercial arts, it illustrates so much better than any other medium (including direct onlooking!). But why look on in the first place? Ultimately, as a war substitute.

Great Fertilizer Contest, Sit and See Whose Grass Grows Fastest. The Olympics in consequence could be described as possessing literary authenticity (though somebody might have recalled that in fact chariot races were the most popular Ancient Olympics event)—or more exactly, as a kind of Fine Art, arts done for other artists to criticize, and the public be damned.

Only recently has there come to be some awareness that what the Olympics are supposed to do and manifestly don't, is in fact being done admirably by newer kinds of sports. International soccer performs the ancient Olympics' professed role best, perhaps (even to involving mini-wars among national spectator delegations). Auto racing is for us what chariot racing must

108. Advertisement heading, for the introduction of the *Superheroes* comic strip to a newspaper in Victoria, British Columbia, April 1978.

anciently have been! Wrestling and boxing have hardly changed at all. But it's football, perhaps, that functions for a war substitute most effectively today. Whatever—society is surely better off when people with aggressive instincts sublimate them vicariously by watching rival monsters bash each other according to ritual rules—just as unruly populaces of the Middle Ages lined up on the tournament grounds to watch their favorite jousters carried insensible off the field, bleeding on their behalf.

Superheroes have comparable social uses. If we must have religious fantasies of men as Gods waging war on lesser beings possessed of lesser truths, then let's indulge them by the creation and promotion of comic-book, film and television characters than by trying to make superheroes out of Kennedys, Hitlers, Lenins and Maos.

One hopes that this may be happening, on hearing of new synthetic comic-strips, pastiches of Superman, Wonder Woman, the Flash, Batman, Aquaman and others, which seem capable of attracting mass followings even on the tip of Vancouver Island. Encouraging indeed, because——

——There is no real counterpart in earlier arts to our popular/commercial substitutes for war because earlier cultures had no real substitutes for war.[83] Think that over....

Not so long ago, illustrations of violence seemed a black-and-white, wrong-and-right, matter. Everybody could see through the pretensions of detective "heroes" like *Dick Tracy*. Only finks and stooges would believe that

The real-life inspiration for Dick Tracy was the state of law and order in America, especially in the big cities....A tidal wave of crime and corruption had all but submerged the big cities of this country...Chester Gould, concerned citizen and artist, did something about it. And inevitably what he did reflected the hard, rough times that had America in its gangster grip. Chester Gould produced a contemporary knight in shining armour who was ready, willing and able to fight the criminal with, if necessary, the criminal's own weapons....Dick Tracy's job was to regain the almost vanished respect for the law and to be the instrument of its enforcement. As Chester Gould once said in an interview, 'I decided that if the police couldn't catch the gangsters, I'd create a fellow who would.'[84]

Anybody who could pronounce the word sociology knew that "law and order" was a cover for "institutionalized violence to minority groups." The underground comics certainly knew it (e.g., the "Crimestoppers" tip, 109B)—knew that calling Tracy "the first procedural detective in the modern sense" was no compliment; that that famous lab of his was an instrument of oppression, something the rich could afford and the poor couldn't. Kids like Junior and Nellie were suckers being moulded to the System. Violence won't solve evil; goodwill is the answer to every problem. If anything, detectives and police are what cause evil, their hasseling innocent citizens *is* the problem. And even those goodthinkers who couldn't pronounce sociology were horrified by the violence of crime shows, TV's counterpart to detective novels and comics. They were easily persuaded that if you didn't have all that violence on TV you wouldn't have violence in the world; that kids went out and copied whatever they saw on the tube.

In all of which there was much sense. You don't need vast experience with police to disbelieve stories picturing all officers as tender-hearted blue knights singlemindedly devoted to the care of children, pets, old folks and flowerbeds. You don't need great insight to see that comics and television which give detailed instructions on how to plan and commit crimes, how to manufacture bombs, how to poison people, are unarguably public menaces, no more protected by the First Amendment than people crying fire in crowded theatres.

109A. Boxes from *Dick Tracy* strips of the early 1940s, by Chester Gould. Popularity of Gould's creation is indicated by its many parodies both by the Right (e.g. Feerless Fosdick in *L'il Abner* and the Left [109B]). The drawing style—solid black areas with quasi-abstracted props—was distinctive, but the strip's appeal lay far deeper, in an atavistic concept of the world as an arena where Good forever struggles with Evil.

109B. One of the numerous *Tracy* parodies on the Left: "The Fabulous Furry Break Brothers Favorite Law Enforcement Officer, Tricky Prickears," by Gilbert Shelton, c1969.

But the nonsense was greater. TV didn't create violence. Violence was in the world long before television was. In *Romeo and Juliet* or *Hamlet*—which could hold their own for gore and mayhem with TV scripts any day. In classical Japanese theatre. In Javanese puppetry. In waxworks and dioramas. In classic Greek theatre. In a word—in the human heart. Violence is a constant of human nature, part of the human psyche. Calling police the cause of crime is like calling umbrellas the cause of rain, armies the cause of war, spectacles the cause of myopia. Total confusion of cause and effect.

Far better than futile campaigns to get rid of something so persistent and so perennial in everyone—quite as much in those viewing with alarm as those so viewed—would be an understanding of what it is about illustration of violence that seems to have so tenacious an appeal. That could be ascertained from most of the great arts of the past—which all have to do with violence in one way or another—were we to study them more for what they do and less for what forms they take. But it's ascertainable just as well from *Dick Tracy*'s persistent appeal over almost three generations.

Popular/Commercial Arts respond to a historic understanding of the world by peoples and societies, as a place of struggle between good and evil.

No art can live, in the sense of establishing and maintaining a continuing and meaningful communication with its audience— the only kind of life that matters in any art—unless it corresponds to something in its audiences' experience, unless it somehow touches reality as they have understood it. Throughout history one image of life that has consistently carried this kind of conviction to human beings has been a battlefield, whereon Good (however variously understood) battles evil (ditto). Us versus them. Creation versus Destruction. God versus Devil. Progressive readers of the *Manchester Guardian* and *Washington Post* versus reactionary non-readers thereof.

All civilizations have developed vehicles appropriate to their backgrounds and need for imagining this dualism in perceptive allegorical form: prophecies, epic poetry, stately ritualistic dance, monumental reliefs and mighty dramas, amongst them some of the greatest High Arts of all time. Our High Arts unfortunately having been preoccupied for the last few generations with problems of formal and personal expression, we have had to develop our allegories on media like comic-strips and television. Hence it is not facetious, merely apposite, to describe what comic strips like *Dick Tracy* or a Western like *High Noon* or a TV series like *Hawaii Five-O* are fundamentally *about*, by likening their scripts to the series of cosmic duels between Ormazd (Ahura Mazda, the forces of Light) and Ahriman (Angra Mainyu, agent of Darkness) which constitutes the *Zend Avesta*'s drama of creation:

> Thus spoke Ahura Mazda to the holy Zarathustra: "I have created a world where none existed....In opposition to this world, where all is life, Angra Mainyu created another where all is death....
>
> "I created Ghaon, the abode of Sughdra, the most delightful place on earth. It is sown with roses; there birds with ruby plumage are born. Angra Mainyu then ‣ created the insects which are noxious to plants and animals.
>
> "Then I founded the holy and sublime city of Muru, and into it Angra Mainyu introduced lies and evil counsel.
>
> "Then I created Bashdi the enchanting, where surrounded by lush pastures a hundred thousand banners fly. Angra Mainyu sent wild beasts there and animals to devour the cattle that serve for man's use.
>
> "Afterward I created Nissa, the city of prayer; and into it Angra Mainyu insinuated the doubt which gnaws at faith.
>
> "I created Haroju, the city of rich palaces. Angra Mainyu caused sloth to be born there and soon the city was poverty-stricken..."

Summon the hero—Ormazd, Tracy, Superman, as the age dictates. For of course Ormazd must win in the end; Angra Mainyu's victories are transitory and self-destructive, since he is a parasite, always preying on what Ormazd created. The myth would offer nothing, were Angra Mainyu's triumphs to be represented as final and forever. Good triumphing in the end is what makes the stories meaningful and comforting (as Bruno Bettelheim observed about fairy tales). Just so, in those ritual enactments of the same myth that we call cops-and-robbers games, the cops catch the robbers in the end and put them in jail. Just so, the deep appeal of *Tracy* and its counterparts, and the transitory self-destructiveness of attempts to produce something more "realistic," where the villains win and the forces of virtue are laid low. For one of the great functions of historic arts—a reason people have made arts and cherished them for so many generations—has been to keep the world humane by keeping it intelligible. Comforting, not by pretending evil doesn't exist, but by assurance that it can be resisted. *Tracy* fulfills this function as Truman Capote's *In Cold Blood,* for instance, does not. For in Chester Gould's strip, violence always has a function. "Redeeming social value," they'd call it, were pornography the issue.

On this theme two writers in the 1930s and '40s made more sense than most. One was George Orwell (1903-1950), fundamentally a journalist whose many books and essays culminated in *Nineteen Eighty-Four.* The other was E.C. Segar (1894-1938), whose two longest *Thimble Theatre* suspense sequences, *The Pool of Youth* and *Popeye's Ark,* count among the most effective utopian allegories of the times and strikingly counterpoint Orwell's writings. This is worth presenting at some length because, as has been so justly said,[85] the strip since Segar's untimely death from cancer has undergone such an "extreme simplification and demeaning over the past thirty years in comic books, newspaper strips, and movie-TV cartoons, that

> ...readers under 40 have no choice but to turn to the actual Segar strip if they wish to see *why* it was the most popular strip of its time and...very possibly one of the three greatest achievements in the art of the comic strip....
>
> Here, unfortunately, a particularly absurd situation exists. Unlike virtually any book of popular or academic interest, the run of a comic strip cannot simply be plucked off a library shelf or ordered at a book store; nor, like most widely appreciated pieces of graphic art, can it be looked at in a gallery or found reasonably well reproduced in a number of accessible forms....But since—of course—*all* comic strips have long been condemned out of hand by educators and academics as trash, individual work in the field has never had the critical attention and study individual works of prose fiction have received without question....

The '20s and '30s were times of utopias abounding. Thousand Year Reichs and Workers' Paradises, Wright's Broadacres and Corbu's Radiant Cities, the Webbs' plans to end poverty (and much else) in Britain and Upton Sinclair's ditto in California; Social Credit, Fascisti, Huey Long....One difference: these movements were supposed to be serious, *Thimble Theatre* was a comic strip. Another: *Thimble Theatre* was based on sober realities of time and history, starting where the others concluded, with an awareness that perfectibility of mankind and of society is *a priori* risible, a crazy quest.[86]

On board the Sea Hag's ship (allegorically, the U.S., founded by revolutionaries, now run by "old pirates"), an expedition led by Popeye and detective Castor Oyl (funded, in good dime-novel tradition, by an eccentric millionaire out to better the world by bettering himself) searching for the Pool of Youth (immortality, human perfectibility), makes an unpleasant discovery: also on board is a "new pirate," the Sea Hag's Sister. And she has with her, to guard herself and the Pool of Youth which she (the new revolutionary) alone can find, a fearsome monster preserved from prehistoric times by the pool: Toar. Almost an illustration of Orwell's article in *Time and Tide* for 6 April 1940:

There was a long period during which nearly every thinking man was in some sense a rebel, and usually a quite irresponsible rebel. Literature was largely the literature of revolt or of disintegration. Gibbon, Voltaire, Rousseau, Shelley, Byron, Dickens, Stendhal, Samuel Butler, Ibsen, Zola, Flaubert, Shaw, Joyce—in one way or another they are all of them destroyers, wreckers, saboteurs. For two hundred years we had sawed and sawed and sawed at the branch we were sitting on. And in the end, much more suddenly than anyone had foreseen, our efforts were rewarded and down we came. But unfortunately there had been a little mistake. The thing at the bottom was not a bed of roses after all, it was a cesspool full of barbed wire.

It is as though in the space of ten years we had slid back into the Stone Age. Human types supposedly extinct for centuries, the dancing dervish, the robber chieftain, the Grand Inquisitor, have suddenly reappeared, not as inmates of lunatic asylums, but as the masters of the world.

In *Thimble Theatre*'s allegorical apparatus, Wimpy functions as the representative intellectual ("the trouble with Wimpy is," Popeye once confided to Olive Oyl, "he went to collich onc't an' never got over it.") He simply ignores the facts, refuses to credit what was before his eyes. For Orwell, H.G. Wells was the representative intellectual: "I doubt," he wrote in "Wells, Hitler, and the World State," a 1941 essay included in *Dickens, Dali & Others* (1946), "whether anyone who was writing books between 1900 and 1920, at any rate in the English language, influenced the young so much." Wells recognized realities no more than Wimpy. Having spent a lifetime identifying science with progress and agitating against patriotism in sure confidence that reasoned socialism must everywhere prevail and induce a new enlightened age, he would not admit that in Germany science was on fanaticism's side and at the service of a criminal lunatic:

Hitler is all the war-lords and witch-doctors in history rolled into one. Therefore, argues Wells, he is an absurdity, a ghost from the past, a creature doomed to disappear almost immediately.

110A. Boxes from *Thimble Theatre*, 6 and 7 February 1935. Castor Oyl, one of the oldest characters in the strip, going back to the early 1920s, meets the newest character, Toar, prehistoric monster preserved for 20 million years by the Pool of Youth.

110B. Boxes from *Thimble Theatre*, 10 and 11 February 1935. J. Wellington Wimpy (who appeared in the strip in 1931 as a dishonest prizefight referee and functioned as Popeye's opposite in a Sancho Panza/Don Quixote, Weller/Pickwick, Fool/Lear, Body/Soul duo, discovers Toar.

110C. Composite boxes from *Thimble Theatre*, 11 March and 1 April, 1935. In our time the great Popeye-Toar fight took over two weeks, on and off. In strip time, several days.

Of course Wells was far from unique. Alongside great orators and statesmen in the United States Capitol's Statuary Hall there was erected about this same time a monument to Will Rogers, cowboy entertainer (d. 1935) revered for declaring "I never met a man I didn't like." Over at the White House was Franklin D. Roosevelt. He never met a man he didn't like either—even at Yalta.[87]

Hitler eventually did disappear—but no thanks to enlightened intellectuals, pacifists, pragmatists or old revolutionaries. All of them were sent flying (like their representatives in *Thimble Theatre* here) in a true allegory of things to come. Resolute force alone laid the monster low. Orwell, writing *Nineteen Eighty-Four* amidst the devastation of a totally unnecessary six-year war, had only had minimum political common sense been exercised, was moved to reflect,

In past ages...war was one of the main instruments by which human societies were kept in touch with physical reality. All rulers in all ages have tried to impose a false view of the world upon their followers, but they could not afford to encourage any illusion that tended to impair military efficiency. So long as defeat meant the loss of independence, or some other result generally held to be undesirable, the precautions against defeat had to be serious. Physical facts could not be ignored. In philosophy, or religion, or ethics, or politics, two and two might make five, but when one was designing a gun or an airplane they had to make four....War was a sure safeguard of sanity.

A truth new to his colleagues, perhaps; hardly new to populaces at large. They had always known it. Always, too, they had responded to arts which embodied it. Once those had been the High Arts of great civilizations. Now they were arts like comic strips. No matter; some arts had to do it. Some arts every society must have, which defend that right to life which the Founding Fathers wrote into the Declaration of Independence, which function as vehicles for visualizing and recording that axiom of practical reason discovered by analogical thought at the dawn of recorded history and maintained throughout all civilized societies since: that humans as rational beings distinct from unreasoning animals have a basic right to self-preservation; a right to life while they live. It is a truth beyond all argument—indeed, the foundation of all possible argument, one of those principles without which no argument can proceed. From it derives by logical extension the rightness of self-defense, the rightness of defending one's family, kith and kin, race, nation, society—incidentally the rightness of defending intellectually elite causes too.

Popular/commercial arts have likewise had to be our vehicles for fundamental truths about government.

DEAR LANDLUBBERS— YER DICTIPATOR SPEAKS— JUS' AHEAD IS A UNKNOWN CONTINENT, YER NEW HOME— I NAMES IT "SPINACHOVA"— I ALSO NAMES MESELF ABSOLUKE DICTIPATOR—WE ARE MAKIN' HISKORY ON ACCOUNT OF A NEW NATION IS GETTIN' BORNDED—IT WILL BE A LAND OF LIBERKY AN' JUSTISS! FOR THEM WICH OBEYS ME—AN' THEM WICH DON'T WILL GET BLOW'D DOWN LIKE NOBODY'S BIZNESS! I HAVE SPOKIN!

111. Concluding box of a *Thimble Theatre* strip for 11 July 1935. Popeye the Sailor addresses colonists on "Popeye's Ark," on the occasion of the founding of Spinachova, the new "land of liberty and justice."

"Popeye's Ark," E.C. Segar's longest utopian satire, ran from 22 April 1935 to 19 April 1936. It told of Popeye's moving with the times—the 1930s, but it could have been the 1960s just as well—to create (in his own image, of course!) the perfect land: Spinachova, flowing with spinach and anchovies and good health (you are what you eat!), free of all vexation (including, at first, women!). An ark is built (financed by another millionaire, of course, who stands behind Popeye in the box, cf. 111), settlers recruited (with some difficulties, owing to the original clause that they had to be perfect in every respect[88]), and after due vicissitudes, a new continent found. It's American history relived, with Popeye playing the part of John Winthrop addressing his Pilgrims on the *Arabella* (my translation),

Just ahead is an unknown continent, your new home.... We are making history, because a new nation is being born. It will be a land of liberty and justice for those who obey me—and anybody who doesn't will be put into line, fast!

The only difference between Winthrop putting his pilgrims into line, or Lenin on the locomotive in Finland Station: "All power to the Soviets, namely me!" or the New Left at Chicago in 1968: "All power to the people who yell 'all power to the people'." is that Popeye tells it like it is.

Like old Samuel Johnson, chiding American malcontents in *Taxation No Tyranny,* 1775:

All government is ultimately and essentially absolute....
In sovereignty there are no gradations. There may be limited royalty, there may be limited consulship; but there can be no limited government. There must in every society be some power or other from which there is no appeal....

Or like Orwell, ruminating on revolutions in an essay on Arthur Koestler in *Dickens, Dali & Others:*

Revolution, Koestler seems to say [in *Darkness at Noon*] is a corrupting process....It is not merely that 'power corrupts'; so also do the ways of attaining power. Therefore, all efforts to regenerate society by violent means lead to the cellars of the OGPU. Lenin leads to Stalin, and would have come to resemble Stalin, if he had happened to survive.

How could a comic-strip artist born in rural Illinois, trained in cartooning by a correspondence course, hired to do hack work for a minor Chicago newspaper on Richard Felton Outcault's recommendation, moving slowly up from obscurity to insignificance through the 1920s, have come to know and put into graphic form truths seemingly hidden from the greatest political pundits of his time? Why was *Thimble Theatre* so much closer to real political and social life in the 1930s, '40s and '50s (for implications of its utopian satires projected for decades) than what social progressives were prophesying? Because, in order to provide amusement for its mass audience, *Thimble Theatre*'s stories had to be based upon principles of unchanging human nature which its audience took for self-evident truths (in contrast to the theories about possible perfectibility of mankind on which contemporary leaders were all too often acting). Verisimilitude demanded that these principles bring appropriate results and endings to the fables Thimble Theatre presented; if indeed valid, they must unfailingly produce comparable results in the "real world." Given human failings and foibles, similar actions have similar outcomes whether they take place on Main Street or Downing Street, Wilhemstrasse or Red Square, or the Sea Hag's ship, or Popeye's Ark.

If *Thimble Theatre* seems to predict the course of national and international events during the 1930s and '40s so remarkably, that is simply because this comic-strip world was in a curious way more real than what Schwarzschild called the "World in Trance" which politicians and dreamers of the '30s were living in.[89]

Illustration of life and love, the private side of human lives, complements illustration of war and government, the public side. Here again, in arts like television situation comedies and "soap operas," and "domestic idyll" comic strips, modern popular/commercial arts carry on the social function of earlier High Arts, unifying society, making life meaningful for the average non—New-Elite human being.

112. Scene from *The Edge of Night:* a familial and romantic crisis, stock-in-trade of the "soap operas." Protagonists: Donald May and Maeve McGuire (1972).

Of all popular/commercial illustrative arts, dramas of love and life—soap operas, love novels, love comics, and the like— seem the most hopelessly (and therefore vulgarly) modern. Both content and media look quintessentially 20th century—in the bad sense. Suburban problems, suburban minds, suburban attitudes. Serious criticism (if any, when any), concentrates not on lack of psychological or dramatic depth, but allegedly shallow concern for modern problems. Defense (if any, when any) takes similar grounds—yes we are up-to-date! So Agnes Nixon, veteran soap-opera script-writer, creator of *One Life to Live* and *All My Children:*

A Drexel University researcher has written recently that daytime serials devote 84 per cent of their time to familiar and romantic entanglements rather than to substantive social issues. Mrs. Nixon...questions the glib use of terms like 'educational' and 'social issues.' When Kitty [on *All My Children*] undergoes analysis and comes to realize that she has never been visible to herself except in the company of a man, *that*, asserts Mrs. Nixon, is education. 'But it's the kind of education I don't think this researcher understands when she compiles her 84 per cent. She would think it's just dialogue. When she looks for educational elements, she probably asks, 'Are they doing something on VD? Are they doing something on drugs? But education is sometimes very subtle.[90]

On all sides the assumption is that TV drama portrays love and life-styles which are typically, and uniquely, modern. Superficially, it does seem so. Genre- and love-stories from other times and ages pivot on different motivations: class barriers, courtly conventions, erotic disguises,[91] in vehicles like ballads, epics and folk songs with a subtlety and beauty of language beyond anything attainable nowadays. No wonder the soap opera and its kin are so routinely despised, despite—indeed, because of—the huge mass audiences they command.

Yet, huge mass audiences do not necessarily indicate vulgarity or banality. Epics, ballads, dances of love and life in earlier times had mass followings, too, and their language was not always as richly archaic and evocative as time has made it seem.

These were arts speaking for the populace at large, "the voice of the people," in a very real sense. So Friedrich Heer in the first volume of his intellectual history of Europe, talks about how the great ideas and concepts that bound European civilization together were understood and communicated on two quite different levels, indeed in two quite different languages. The upper level, that interlocking system of "leading families" who gave Europe its bishops and kings, its philosophers and lords and lawyers for a thousand years, verbalized ideas and values in Latin treatises—theology, philosophy, history. The other—"the people"—verbalized them in vernacular "sagas, legends, ballads, epics":

Heaven and Earth; Mind and Matter; Natural and Supernatural; God and Man; Fate and Free Will; Sense and Reason; Life and Death; Soul and Body;...all these form "dialectical entities," i.e., unities and combinations, which for the populace's simple comprehension had continually to be reiterated, reinforced, renewed through cult rhythms of feasts and festivals, celebrations, rites of work and death. For European folk speech possessed not a single word for these dualities and components of mind and spirit. It lacked any because it dealt with such problems and concepts on another level, in another dimension. Only much later, sometime between the 15th and 19th century, did vernacular expressions develop for such theological and philosophical concepts. For long, poetry (sagas, legends, ballads, epics) in conjunction with a distinctive ethical stance, was the only vehicle for this folk wisdom and its concepts of cosmos and chaos.

"Any effective and comprehensive history of the European mind," Heer wrote, "has to take into account the interaction of these two worlds:

Alcuin's half-Pelagian court philosophy and the ballads of Hildebrand and Hadubrand; the ostentatious humanism of Lupus of Ferrières and Godescalc's teachings on grace; Hugh of St. Victor's humanistic cosmos and the Niebelung lied; the 18th century's fairy-tales and moral philosophy....

I submit, any effective and comprehensive history of the European mind—at home and overseas—has likewise to take into account those arts which today perform the functions of "sagas, legends, ballads, epics" and today carry on a distinctive ethical stance. That means, popular/commercial arts generally, and in particular broadly comprehensive illustrative arts like the television situation comedy and soap opera.[93]

Ron McAdow, writing on "Experience of Soap Opera" in the *Journal of Popular Culture,* described it as a celebration of the "flow of life"

...all more or less inevitably. Characters in soap opera do not escape from one another except to die. They do not fall, they are not Reborn, they do not conquer; they flow—day after day, month after month, actor after actor, the characters flow through complex, cluttered, non-progressing situations...

and he correctly emphasizes the very traditional, ritualistic character of the soap opera which evidences its ultimate derivation from medieval miracle plays, and long before that, from the religious drama of earliest human societies:

Soap opera has some appeal which gives it a large and devoted following of ladies. Usually these women are shy about their devotion—they don't really understand what soap opera holds for them, and are defenseless against its many slanderers. I suggest that the message which is the core of the experience of soap opera is the reaffirmation, the litany, of their view of existence: all of us are part of a turbulent, passionate, interconnected flow of life in which our purposes and efforts have only a minor importance.[94]

This "reaffirmation," this "litany" of a "view of existence" is our modern counterpart to that "cycle of festivals" Heer describes as unifying Old Europe:

...participated in by households, clans, villages, families, the cycle which unified folk culture with court and urban High Culture.... The cycle of festivals celebrated the interdependence...of humans, things, animals.... All have their part to play in this right ordering, all have responsibilities to others...in this sacred and saving bond which united everyone in work and duty, technics and cultural patterns.[95]

Some such sense of the vital unity of all Creation has helped make the world bearable in all societies, in all times and places. It has comforted all sorts and conditions of people in the face of calamities, wars, pestilences; it has inspired socio-religious systems of thought in Christendom, Buddhist and Hindu worlds alike; it underlies the idealistic harmonies propounded by Newton and Leibnitz, and the romantic vistas of brotherhood proclaimed by Hegel and Marx. That it should find 20th-century manifestation in the popular mass arts is no surprise; that is where all traditional stabilizing forces are found. Thence it comes as no surprise, either, to learn that recent research reveals the idea of soap operas commanding only audiences of women to be just one more hardy but quite unfounded myth. Given any chance, men are just as avid viewers of daytime television—i.e., the life-and-love dramas, as women:

There simply was no doubt about it—the soap opera is a male phenomenon too. But *why?* I decided to conduct a few in-depth interviews.... Then... an astonishing hypothesis hit me. Was it possible that men watch the soaps for exactly the same reasons that women watch soaps? .... 'Of course,' said [producer] Joe Stuart, 'men like the dramatic story as much as women do. If these shows were on at night, you'd get the same number of men as women.' 'Obviously,' said Agnes Nixon, 'if not for the hour of the day, the male and female audience would be the same. Look at the popularity of *Upstairs, Downstairs* and *The Forsyte Saga* on PBS...' "[96]

'What kind of men watch soaps?' 'All kinds watch.'

113. Illustrations to article by Edith Efron, "Only His Buddies at the Garage Know for Sure: But the Great Male Secret May be Out," *TV Guide*, 10 May, 1975.

What's the appeal? Vulgarity, banality only? Only rankest prejudice would say so, or deny excellence in the traditional sense to *Upstairs, Downstairs* and *The Forsyte Saga* and even dramas not on PBS—someday *All in the Family* may be recognized as a great American dramatic creation of our age. Nor is it capitalist mental conditioning, either—the appeal of these life-and-love dramas is truly universal.

Blondie is found all over the world, from Japan, where the strip is used to teach conversation, to Sweden, where socialists are entertained by Dagobert Krikelin and his boss Herr Dittling (though "Blondie" never changes). Television life-and-love dramas are just as universal. First programming to crack the Soviet "blue-screen"? *The Forsyte Saga!*[97] How is it that such apparently trivial art speaks to so many diverse people? Just because it is trivial? I think, because it is *not*. Because under the trivial surface, this is an art deeply concerned with the human condition, with what used to be called "the human comedy." *Blondie* is a real love story, not like Segal's novel of the same name—now that really was something trivial!—but in the deep sense. It was one of those strips whose characters lived in real time. Blondie first appeared as a flapper, Dagwood as a rich

- ・ユウウツだな…何もかもきょう
  はうまくいかなかった

- ・でもあなた、シアワセの条件が
  そろってるじゃないの…健康と
  ちゃんとした仕事、幸福な家庭

※ Everything went wrong

- • Everything goes well （すべてうまくいく）
- • Everything goes wrong （すべてダメだ）
- • Everything goes just so and so （すべてまあまあだ）

- ・そして、あなたを愛してるカワ
  イイおくさん

- ・ダグウッド、あなたハゲてきた
  わよ！

- ・少し気分がよくなってきたよ

※ cheering me up

アメリカン・フットボールなんかのとき，かわいい女の
コが超ミニで応援団の前でガンバッてるの，みたことあ
るでしょ。あれが*Cheer leader*。学生服のヒゲの団長と
は，だいぶムードがちがうね。いったい，どっちが本当
に元気が出るんだろう。〈元気だせよ！〉っていうのは，

- • Cheer up !
- • Be of good cheer !

といえばいいのだ。→★

114. Excerpts from *Blondie's English
Conversation School*, Tokyo, 1971, Tsuru
Comic Sha.
Idiomatic speech explained; but no need,
apparently, to explain the plot or the jokes.

playboy (a little bit like Segal's stereotyped opening) who was disinherited for marrying her.[98] They settled in as young marrieds, Dagwood toiling in an office under the eccentric Julius Dithers, Blondie raising a family (first a boy, Baby Dumpling, who later got his name changed to Alexander; then Cookie); they partied and quarreled with their neighbors the Woodleys; the children grew into teenage problems....They ate and slept, made love, got sick and got better, fretted some, laughed some, got older. All very dull, if you like; but all very much like life. Like life, not just in American suburbs, but life in Osaka, in Örebrö, in Tobolsk.

Like life in Renaissance Florence, in Benin, in Babylon, too. For when all is said and done, the family is the fundamental unit of civilization. Conventions as to what comprise the family change from time to time; some societies' ethics allow several wives or husbands, some only one. But the idea of children being given to the State like eggs dropped from hen roosts onto a conveyor belt is and has always been nightmarish to all but fanatics. Arts like *Blondie* or the *Forsyte Saga* speak to people about things *they* care about (instead of what artists care about!). That is why life-and-love drama in popular/commercial arts have a role in modern times comparable to those Dickens novels for whose successive chapters crowds in New York awaited boats from England a century ago. And to those entertainers whose arrival was awaited with comparable eagerness by courtiers and kettlemaids and counsellors in medieval castles, centuries before.[9] And to the classic role of poets in Homeric Greece and Biblical Israel. That role is, in a word, to tell people who they are. To reassure people stumbling along the small ups and downs of life that their fates are not unusual, that they are not lonely failures or fools, but just living—for this is the nature of human life. This is what it means to be human. Samuel Johnson, as usual, said it all:

The main of life is, indeed, composed of small incidents and petty occurrences; of wishes for objects not remote, and grief for disappointments of not fatal consequence; of insect vexations which sting us and fly away, impertinencies which buzz a while and are heard no more; of meteorous pleasures which dance before us and are dissipated; of compliments which glide off the soul like other musick, and are forgotten by him that gave and him that received them. Such is the general heap out of which every man is to cull his own condition; for, as the chemists tell us...that the boundless variety of things arises from the different proportions of a very few ingredients; so a few pains, and a few pleasures are all the materials of human life.... As these are well or ill disposed, man is for the most part happy or miserable.

For very few are involved in great events, or have the thread of life entwisted with the chain of causes on which armies or nations are suspended...[100]

It's to this human condition that the life-and-love dramas of popular/commercial illustrative arts speak. It's to this condition, and not to the condition of Great Artists Expressing Themselves, that great arts of the past spoke also.

That modern popular/commercial illustration of history carries on a principal social function of traditional illustrative arts seems at first to be self-evident. But on examination, it turns out that popular/commercial arts break with traditional illustration (e.g., Masaccio's life of St. Peter, Shakespeare's English kings, Rubens's religious and historical allegories) in a crucial respect: no real continuity is perceived between past and present. They share the "historicist" attitude which came in during the 1700s— and the resulting alienation of our culture from its past.

Illustrations, like such substitute imagery as waxworks and panoramas (q.v.) are by their nature didactic. They instruct by existing. And they are in fact the principal way populaces now learn about the past, about history.

There are books aplenty about World War I (q.v.). But how people lived through it, you get from arts like *Upstairs Downstairs* sequences of hospital trains dumping their dead and dying onto station platforms, footmen enlisting in frenzies of patriotism, then trying to hide out to escape the horrors of the front, casuality lists in the newspapers, dread cablegrams to next-of-kin (115). Here, vividly portrayed, is the pre-war class structure which had survived two English, an American and a French revolution, master born to an appointed place upstairs and servants down. Here, vividly portrayed, is its breakdown at last, climaxed in the final episode with the heir dead—a war casualty *de facto* though not *de jure*—, the great house sold to be split into flats.

When we lived a year in Edinburgh we inhabited the servants' quarters of just such a great house on Buckingham Terrace, downstairs, complete to the chairs, cracked, glued, but still recognizably the same as on *Upstairs Downstairs*—we knew them the minute we saw them on the screen, and through that series got to understand how our Edinburgh flat came to be available for rent to visiting Edinburgh University faculty. The series taught us a bit of our own history, that is to say. I think it taught everyone history— real history.[101]

115. Still from "Upstairs Downstairs": Hudson the butler (Gordon Jackson) and Mrs. Bridges the cook (Angela Baddeley) comfort Rose the housemaid (Jean Marsh) who has just learned of her fiancee's death in the trenches of World War I—a scene which, historically, occurred about a million times in Britain between 1914 and 1918. (Halftone from newspaper syndication).

In one way, it's almost platitudinous to say that such a modern popular/commercial art carries on the social functions of historic arts. Compared to the productions of Beckett or Artaud or Anouilh, *Upstairs Downstairs* obviously is the modern counterpart to historical dramas, from medieval miracle plays to Shakespeare's series on British royalty and Addison's *Cato.*

But there is one big difference. Those earlier arts, up into the mid-18th-century, were costumed contemporaneously: Rubens in the 1600s, Masaccio in the 1400s, medieval manuscript illuminators, mosaicists of Ravenna, Greek vase-painters, to none of them did it occur to attempt any exact reconstruction of the past. A few touches here and there, perhaps; otherwise the costumes and the architectural background were those of the audiences. Between those early illustrations of history and a modern counterpart like *Upstairs Downstairs* comes 18th-century and early 19th-century romantic historicism.

Few intellectual movements have ever triumphed so swiftly and so completely. Nowadays the smallest child learns that earlier ages were different from his/her own, in costume, clothes, manners, speech, customs—every way; and takes that fact for granted throughout life thereafter. *Upstairs Downstairs* follows that convention. The series ends in 1930, which for most of its audiences was a very long time ago. Back in those times people wore funny clothes and talked funny. They were not like us. Any illustration which suggests that they were, is *ipso facto* humorous—indeed, modern people in costumes of another era has become a stock recipe for popular/commercial comedy.

Fred Flintstone and Barney Rubble are as modern suburban Americans as Dagwood Bumstead and Herb Woodley, as Archie Bunker and Stretch Cunningham. Putting them and their activities into a prehistoric setting—clothes, car, everything of primitive stone, fur, bark is a comedy gimmick. An inversion of the *Jetsons,* the same studio's suburban couple who lived in the 21st century on a space satellite. The implications are significant. For what such arts really teach is that the past can teach us nothing—the very opposite of traditional historical illustration.

In traditional illustrative arts, people were represented as in costumes and buildings contemporary with their audiences', but of nobler purpose, loftier ideals. The past provided models for us to follow—including useful examplars of vice and folly to be avoided. Their being costumed similarly to their audiences told those audiences: you could be like these people. Our arts tell them the opposite: those people were just like us. Only more primitive. Without the Advantages of Science. Whence we get cut off from the past by monstrous misconceptions.

Nowadays, what can most charitably be called a half-baked skepticism about history is all too common. Misunderstanding of scholarly caution about sources spawns assumptions that nothing is really known about the past at all.

Mohammed, Aristotle, Napoleon, Queen Elizabeth are not "real people" but something made up from untrustworthy books. Cave men, by contrast, are real. They were discovered by "science," which is infallible. Corollary: equally widespread assumptions that nothing before the age of science—i.e., the present—is important anyway. For millennia mankind's greatest sages and scholars languished in childish errors correctable in any modern grade-school science course. Correspondingly, historic arts are taken to be self-justifying expressive activities of the same sort that arts are now; since nothing can be learned from arts so conceived, we are thereby cut off from our past. We learn nothing from it; where once history was studied to avoid its mistakes and so improve it—"we see further than our ancestors because we are dwarfs standing on the shoulders of giants"—our intellectual enterprises all must start from the very ground—every past mistake repeated. In consequence our society more and more comes to be a collection of atoms drifting about rootlessly without determination or destination. Needless to say, a state of affairs no government of any kind is predisposed to discourage. For alienated atoms must sooner or later look to governments for security and protection; sooner or later surrender to them their fortunes, their honor and their powers.

It's in reaction to this situation, perhaps, that the popularity of *Roots* is to be explained. The book and the television series, which commanded huge mass audiences for consecutive nights, is essentially traditional historical illustration. While there is of course the historicism pervasive in our time—the past is the past, in its own costumes and its own settings, the actors who move through it are manifestly the same people, contemporaries of the audience. Perhaps part of the success of this series is attributable to an atavistic sense that here is really meaningful historical illustration—the traditional sort.

Historicism, not kitsch, is what distinguishes 20th-century popular/commercial religious illustration from traditional.

117A. *Flevit super Illam:* Christ weeps over the city of Jerusalem. A typical late 19th-century conventional religious history painting, by Enrique Simonet of Malaga and now in the Museo Provincial de Bellas Artes there, where the young Picasso, who grew up in this town, probably saw it.

Religious art *qua* religious art nowadays is simply historical illustration. Uncouth characters in striped dressing-gowns go through theatrical gestures in a strange land, long ago and far away. In arts of earlier times—Baroque, Renaissance, medieval, universally—you would have had at least the crowd in such scenes wearing whatever costume was contemporary (127B). Nowadays, the thought never even occurs. A crowd of ladies in shorts and halter tops and sandals? Men in business suits? in a *religious* movie, or painting, or play?

That attitude, taken so unthinkingly, so matter-of-factly, tells everything. "Religious art" deals with lives and times which have nothing in common with us. Something we just look at, if and when we pay any attention at all. It's been so for a long time—beginning back in the 17th century, with Rembrandt van Rijn.

Rembrandt's illustration of Christ preaching "seems to take place," according to H.W. Janson's standard *History of Art* survey, "in some corner of an Amsterdam ghetto." Indeed so. Interesting to us on that account, it is evidence also of Rembrandt's similar interest in authentic settings for Christian

117B. Still from *From The Manger to The Cross*, one of the many early (and late) movies based upon The Greatest Story Ever Told—a blurb coming frequently to the pens of movie-promoters during the 20th century. Despite technical improvements, this concept of "religious illustration" was still unchallenged in TV of the 1970s, like NBC's *Stories from the Bible*.

117C. *Christ Preaching.* Etching by Rembrandt, c1652, in the Metropolitan Museum of Art, New York (Bequest of Mrs. H.O. Havemeyer, 1929).

events. That we and he should unquestioningly approach religious art this way is part cause, part effect, and dramatic reflection of a theological disintegration spreading within Christianity ever more widely since the 17th century.

As Rembrandt's plate was etched in acid, so traditional Christian *a priori* assumptions have been steadily eaten away by a belief in Natural Human Goodness. First explicitly surfacing in Europe during and just after the Thirty Years' War, it succeeded, like all beliefs that gain general acceptance, in capturing minds because Europe was ready to believe it. For that, there were many reasons; perhaps the most cogent was the solution it seemed to offer to endless cycles of bloody wars waged in the name of traditional Christianity. Those wars, it seemed to promise, would end once people came to realize how traditional Christianity was not worth fighting over; and that could come about once Christianity's basic premises were shown to be false. Man is not weak, sinful, in need of a savior and damned if he chooses the wrong one, as that religion had taught. *Au contraire!* Man is strong, pure, noble. He needs no savior at all; all he needs is social institutions changed, so that this natural strength, natural purity, natural nobility will no longer be corrupted by the present corrupt institutions. Whence many corollaries—the artist as leader of Mankind, for one. The artist as free spirit, showing Mankind the way to his new human condition by defying authority and convention in the name of innate, untaught creativity—all Mankind being equal in natural creativity, but some more equal than others. In the steady march of this doctrine across Europe, Rembrandt and the legend attached to him played a mighty role, hence his place as a culture hero amongst the founding fathers of the avant-garde Establishment, today's New Elite.[101]

Bound up inextricably with this role is Rembrandt the initiator of "realistic" religious painting. Initiator of a new image of Christ—no longer the symbolic sacrifice, the Son of Man, but a tragically dramatic historical figure. Deluded, no doubt, given to outlandishly pessimistic evaluations of mankind's immediate future; but showing a tasteful modesty in denying claims to kingship here and now, while in fact the very image of Natural Human Goodness incarnate, noble and pure and strong as all humans might one day be in a different kind of Kingdom. Why wasn't this plain all along? Christ the culture hero, artist even, martyred to bigotry, victim of unprogressive attitudes in high places; but overcoming all at last. Maybe not quite how the Church traditionally pictured its Founder, but certainly the view to take if you wanted to be thought fashionable and enlightened henceforth. So 19th-century avant-garde (Preraphaelites, Nazarenes, Arts-and-Crafts, Beaux-Arts narrative painters) portrayed Christ as a carpenter, as an egalitarian foot-washer, as a preacher of social reform to underpriviliged and laboring classes. So Marx and Engels portrayed Christianity in their *Communist Manifesto* of 1848 as leader of a revolutionary movement from the first expressly committed to world conquest— "all power to the Son of Masses!" So nowadays under the name of "religion" we get movies like *Manger to Cross* reworked; we get *O God!* rehashing the Turgot-Voltaire sublimated heaven; we get—oh, God, what we get!

Where secularization of religion generally led is the theme of Löwith's great survey of escatology inverted: *Meaning in History.*[103] Where secularization of religious art led, has been nowhere more dramatically set forth than in James Billington's account of how the Preraphaelites' Russian contemporary Alexander Ivanof put his art at the service of a "messianic patriotism" based on "a general assumption that Russia was to provide spiritual salvation for all mankind...a kind of fantastic eschatological chauvinism.

Ivanof set forth on a frenzied secret project to found a new academy for a consecrated army of 'public artists.' Their shrine was to be a temple to the 'golden age of all humanity'...dominated by a vast fresco....The thinking elite of Russia sought with increasing intensity to find a prophetic message in history and art....They seemed almost to be feeling their way back to the dimly perceived, half-remembered world of Muscovy where belief was unquestioning and where truth was pronounced by the original prophetic historian and artist: the monastic chronicler and iconographer.

Ivanov's vision of universal Russian rule aided by 'public artists' and adorned with 'temples of humanity' seems at times like an anticipation of Soviet ideology.[103]

Or, Billington would probably agree, an anticipation of the peasant painters of Huhsien County.

118B. Li Feng-Lan's painting of *Spring Hoing*. "In the early spring of 1973, when the willow tree were turning green, the peach flowers blossoming pink, and the swallows flying low in the sky, th women members of our production brigade enthusiastically plunged into the movement of graspin revolution and promoting production. Joyously, we marched into the fields and started the sprin hoeing in high spirits.... We went to the fields against the cold in in the early morning and got hom under the evening mists, working overtime for days on end." From the exhibition of the Peasan Paintings from Huhsien County of China. The artists, according to the accompanying catalogue were peasants trained in an art class set up by the county Party committee in 1958.

Robert Hughes, *Time*'s art editor was (as so often) more perceptive than most when he called the peasant paintings of Huhsien County "in essence religious art, full...of salvation through works."[105] He was thinking primarily of such efforts as *Announcement of the Two Great Happy Events in October 1976* (one being Chairman Hua's accession to power), so like some illustration of the Gospel ("good news") brought to a Chinese Home from an old missionary magazine, or *Tree Painting* with its Sermon on the Mount setting, its symbols of salvation (flowering twigs, electricity carriers and pageantry so reminiscent of the old parade rituals of state Confucianism. Its social function is of course identical to Russian social realism except that the peasants here smile and strain instead of sweat and strain.

But this is superficial religiosity; the real conversion experience—the actual subject here—is on deeper level.

This illustration of a specific event, described at length by the artist in a caption, is much closer to the heart of all religions: a conversion experience. For are these peasants actually doing anything Chinese peasants have not been doing for four or five thousand years at least? Generation after generation they have had to rise in red dawns and work in cold winds and trudge muddily home in evening mists, "working overtime for days on end." The difference is in the attitude to it attributed to them by this painting. They do it now in a transformed spirit, which transforms the work.

About the same time as these women were doing their same old work in a new spirit of paradisal dalliance, another set of women on the other side of the world were having an experience of similar religious nature, however different its other circumstances: the Manson "family," whose story is detailed and documented in several books on the trial of Charles Manson, a sensation of the early 1970s. Charles Manson was one of numerous petty thugs, thieves and con men to see rich opportunities in the late 1960s jejeune utopian enthusiasms. Concocting a cult of his own, he set about with extraordinary success to recruit female adherents, all of the same type; girls educated above their intelligence, professing a half-baked kind of feminism which justified (in their own minds) running away from home, breaking with their mothers, refusing to be "sexual objects," abhorrence at the idea of "obedience," assertions of sexual freedom *a l'homme,* and the usual litany of petty gripes and grievances against life. Once having swallowed Manson's crazy religion, however, their whole attitude changed. Everything looked different. What they hated and defied before, they now did gladly. Joyously they functioned as Manson's sexual slaves, in high spirits they bore his children and washed his dishes and obeyed orders to satisfy his friends, robot-like they hacked random victims to death at his whim. Their experience too was conversion in the literal sense of "turning around," seeing life from a new angle, another perspective. It is one of the main axes of all religious life, whether the religion be satanic, moronic, maniacal, politically utopian, romantic materialism, or supernatural. And painting recording that conversion (the beginning of all religious experience) is true religious illustration.

True religious illustration has to do with fundamental beliefs:
for example, illustration of Religion of Science in our own times

Once recognize the fundamental nature of religious
illustration, and other examples abound. Comics, for instance.
Peanuts' religious message has been too ably documented in
Robert Short's two books to justify recapping here;[106] nor need
analyses of religious utopianism in *L'il Abner* and the like from
The Unchanging Arts be repeated. Let's do another: *The Wizard
of Id,* created in the early 1960s by Brant Parker and Johnny Hart
of Endicott, New York.

The strip takes its name, plainly enough, from L. Frank
Baum's perennially popular children's story *The Wizard of Oz,*
which appeared in 1900.[107] The two wizards have much in
common. Both are humbugs. Both are really embodiments of
Science. In Chapter 16 the Wizard of Oz soliloquizes:

How can I help being a humbug, when all these people make me do
things that everybody knows can't be done? It was easy to make the
Scarecrow and the Lion and the Woodman happy, because they imagined I
could do anything. . . .

The Wizard of Id, too, is Science the miracle-worker, believed in by
the masses as priests, we are told, were believed in in the Middle
Ages—capable of any wonder, of solving every problem, salving
every pain. "O Great Wizard," cries the frog in the name of so
many in the late 1960s, "I have become an adult. I don't want to
grow up to be thirty, when nobody will trust me. I want to be
forever Peter Pan, forever Elvis, forever a flower-child!"
"Certainly," says the Wizard of Id. "Just a moment, please. This
may take a little time. . . ." The Kingdom of Id in fact satirizes that
kind of State which can be called in German a *Heilsreich:* a state
which offers its members salvation, holiness, wholeness and
integration.[108] The Holy Roman Empire of Old Europe was such a
Heilsreich. Lenin's Soviet State was another. Chairman Mao's
China is a third example.

119A. 1966 *Wizard of Id* strip reproduced by Tsuru Comic Sha, Tokyo, 1970. The theme is constantly recurring in this strip: endless variations are played on the prince transformed into a frog by an enchantment, who is freed from the spell by the kiss of a princess (here, the Wizard, as embodiment of Science, who undertakes the task).

No matter what its superficial jokes and allusions, then, the *Wizard of Id*'s real concern is religion—and specifically the real religion of our times, as distinct from any formal professions. *Id*'s humor, like all humor, depends upon incongruity; it creates situations different from what the audience expected, given the common assumptions of our age. The Wizard of Id is funny because he's a humbug—that is, the strip's audience expects wizards who have test-tubes and laboratories to be omniscient and superlatively honest (witness the furore of disillusionment over continuing Piltdown Man revelations—how *could* scientists deliberately deceive the public? they're not like politicians!).

No problem identifying what the King of Id stands for in this allegory. He is the Establishment—not a Right or a Left, but any and all Establishments, everywhere. "The object of power is power"—this sum of Bertrand de Jouvenel's wisdom *On Power,* of O'Brien's solipsisms to Winton Smith in the torture chambers of *Nineteen Eighty-Four,* is likewise the burden of the King of Id's symbolism. Most of the jokes about Power in which the King of Id functions as the vehicle have to do with mass-suffrage democratic power—the King beguiling "voters" from his balcony with preposterous electioneering promises, the king stuffing ballot-boxes, gerrymandering constituencies, silencing opponents (plenty of free speech as long as you talk right), and the like. Given the strip's audience, that's only to be expected. But there are plenty of implications for other power-structures. For all Establishments of all persuasions are committed to a phantasmagoria of progress (symbolized by the King's constant self-viewing in trick mirrors and other devices to increase his height). All essentially demonstrate the truth of Malcolm Muggeridge's axiom from *The Thirties in Britain,*

> The logical end...of romantic materialism is some form of utopia. If heaven is transferred from Eternity to Time, from beyond the skies to earth, then it must come to pass; and if it refuses to come to pass, then what has come to pass must be called heaven, and woe unto those who question its celestial pretensions.

Consequently, central joke-themes—the King's relationship to the Wizard (science), to Rodney (military/industrial complex) and the Spook (deluded masses) all turn on maintenance of the facade of Progress.

119B. An endless source of jokes in the *Wizard of Id* is the King's short stature, and the strategems he employs to compensate for it. Shades of Louis XIV, perhaps (who wore high-heeled shoes and had trick mirrors), but also perhaps a reminiscence of Popeye (the King of Id speaks from a balcony just as Popeye did in "Popeye's Ark")—symbolic statements about the nature of Power.

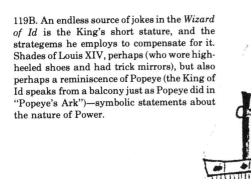

For illusions of progress the King of Id is dependent upon his wizard—i.e., technological advance, Science's real or pretended accomplishments at Making a Better World. In turn, the Wizard is always expected to do *something*. He can make tides recede—twice a day. Sooner or later he can always make it rain, though not necessarily make it stop on command. Sometimes his magic is downright disastrous, as when he changes Rodney into a stone statue or the King into a rooster, by mistakes. In one Sunday page, he solves the problem of frogs whose croaking from the royal moat disturbed his Monarch's sleep, by changing them into dogs, cows and cats, with tenfold worse racket than before—like Science called upon by popular clamor to abolish death and provide all mankind with abundance of goods, creating infinitely more insolvable problems of overpopulation and world pollution. [109] First and continuing victim of the Wizard's phoney promises, however, is the *Wizard of Id*'s most striking character, the Spook.

It's never made entirely clear why Spook is imprisoned; at some time long ago he called the King names, apparently. He doesn't remember exactly himself. All he knows is that he wants to escape, and tries over and over again—sometimes tunnelling, sometimes pushing out blocks, sometimes tricking his jailor. Always he finds himself back in cramped cell living on swill. If the Wizard represents Science, and the King Establishments generally, who can Spook be? Sequences like this earthquake make that clear,

119C. The actual relationship between King (Establishment) and Wizard (Science) in Id is not what first appears. All sorts of jokes turn on the Wizard's incompetence and failures rousing the King's wrath; but, like scientists serving a New Order in Russia or China, the Wizard's magic is so important to the regime that he can get away (as in this strip of 2 August 1972) with talk that would land most other denizens of Id in the King's dungeon for keeps.

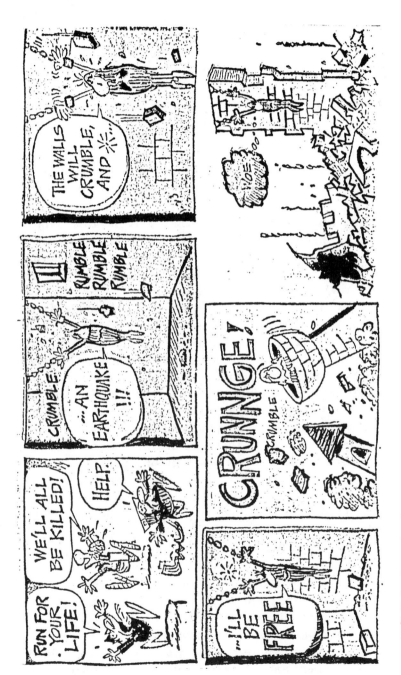

119D. To free the spooks takes more than an earthquake. *Wizard* Sunday page for 22 November 1969, less first two boxes.

In the Spook is epitomized populaces so moulded by generations of liberalism as to be unable to see the world as it really is, and hence to understand their own miserable condition: only as something to be escaped from rather than dealt with. For what manacles the spook is only the dark little prison of his own ego. For "earthquake" read here "revolution"—modern man's substitute for his ancestors' faith and hope in miracles. The Spook lives in an illusion that he is naturally good and happy. Whence he asks, parroting Rousseau, why it is that he finds himself miserable and in chains? And he gets the only possible answer—It must be wicked institutions which corrupt him and prevent his natural goodness from developing to fuller and fuller perfection. Only abolish these corrupting institutions, and Humanity will immediately and effortlessly rise to a plane with angels. So here. For "walls" read "institutions," and you understand the Spook's joyous cry: "the walls will crumble and'I'll be FREE." But comes the revolution, when the walls do crash down, and nothing at all happens. The Spook remains where he was, hanging miserably as before. Because, of course, the walls never did his prison make. He made that prison himself.

Herein is revealed the ruling religion of our age. Ask, what is this comic strip *about,* and the answer must be: "Heaven on Earth." A commentary, that is to say, on the vision of, or obsession with (depending on one's point of view), an ideal society, endemic in our times. At the back of almost every literary 20th-century person's mind, subtly influencing decisions of all kinds in every area of life, there is a picture—often enough quite unrecognized—of a future whence all sin, all pain, all toil, all trouble (i.e., whatever the dreamer so labels) has been done away with. All vexing responsibilities cease; poverty disappears, climates alter—whatever ills may plague us now in that day will vanish like puffs of smoke. Precisely how or by what agency all these miracles come about varies, naturally enough—some looking to technology, some to drugs, some to psychotherapy. But however accomplished, the end result is similar: what anciently was taught in all the great world religions as a state of being to be consummated after death, in another dimension of existence, is to be experienced here and now. The world of time and history as known for the past umpteen millennia is to dissolve. In its place timeless, limitless happiness and immortality forever is to come upon earth....

The *Wizard of Id* is *about* this vision in the sense that it is fully intelligible only against that background and in that context. Id, like Oz, is a fairytale kingdom. But Id, unlike Oz, mocks the vision of heaven on earth. The King's, the Establishment's pretensions are absurd. There is no good Glinda to come, *deus ex machina,* and set all to rights. The Wizard—Science—is no loveable humbug, but a nasty one. The Spook—humanity in the mass—will never escape his cell and swill as long as he refuses to accept the truth about himself, prisoner of his own dark resentments.

To realize how far opposed a comic like *The Wizard of Id* is from any utopian visions compare it to Bacon's *New Atlantis* or Wells' *Open Conspiracy;* contrariwise, see how close it comes in spirit to Erasmus's *In Praise of Folly,* how similar is its view of this world as a vale of tears to Dante's or Samuel Johnson's, or Solzhenitsyn's.[110] In a word, how traditional. Traditional religious art, like all traditional arts, survives in popular/commercial form.

Illustration for Beautifying
And Some Observations about *Kitsch*

BEAUTIFICATION PROPER, unlike substitute imagery or illustration, does not involve the actual making of objects. It means a process, a way of deliberately shaping artifacts so as to make their function(s) plain to individual beholders, and thence to communities at large (i.e., the more intelligible, the more beautiful). In addition to shaping objects, beautification involves adding substitute images, symbols, or illustrations to artifacts so as deliberately to link them to beholders' experience and to the historical experience of communities. Again, the key word is *deliberate.*

In distinction to beautification proper, illustration for beautifying simply involves adding pictorial illustration to artifacts more or less indiscriminately. Insofar as such additions make an object look more attractive, such illustrations could be considered a means of "glorifying" objects, and thus a kind of beautification (q.v. 132F). But oftener than not the illustration has manifestly nothing whatsoever to do with the actual object. Then such beautifying lies open to charges of *kitsch* (129C).

Kitsch can most succinctly be defined—when anybody bothers to define it at all, which is not often[111]—as art for art's sake which happens to be out of avant-garde fashion. It calls to mind descriptions of the late Victorian art world, like Adolf Loos's oft-quoted diatribe against what constituted "good taste" in Vienna *circa* 1890:[112]

A craze for totally meaningless articles of decoration...a craze for satin-like surfaces: for silk satin, and shining leather...as also for totally meaningless articles of decoration.... Everything was mixed too, without rhyme or reason: in the boudoir a set of Buhl, in the drawing-room an Empire suit, next door a cinquecento dining-room...through it all a flavor of polychrome.... In this connection too there was a conspicuous absence of any idea of usefulness or purpose; it was all purely for show....

Thanks to the post-World War I climate of suspicion, even paranoia, about anything smacking of "secrecy," "hypocrisy" and "empty formulas," an extraordinary solution to the problem gained fanatic ascendancy for several decades: abolish all ornament. Instead of objects buried under profusions of meaningless decoration, objects with no decoration at all—stark, machined, monastic.[113] Now that the reinforcing wave of World War II fanaticism seems to be receding, both problem and solution need re-examination. Is it necessarily such a wicked thing to apply substitute images or illustrations to walls or vessels or artifacts? Is it necessarily true that "well designed" objects must always and only express the nature of their structure and materials? Perhaps, instead of going on ranting about "kitschmen" and the depravity of mass taste, it might be more constructive to try and understand what social function applied images on artifacts might have.

The old practise of applying substitute images and illustrations more or less indiscriminately to artifacts of all sorts survives, like all traditional arts, in modern popular/commercial form. And, as in traditional arts, different principles and practises can easily be discerned.

The first obvious function of applied images and illustrations is simply to label things. If avant-garde design had its way, we would be surrounded by tasteful glassware exquisitely showing off the nature of glass and the process of glass-blowing,

120A. Wine-bottle label, 1978.

120C. Enamelled glass beaker, made in Germany 1585. Metropolitan Museum of Art, New York.

120B. Part of cardboard milk container distributed by Arla-Fakta dairy, Stockholm and Uppsala, 1978. "Do You Know the Runic Alphabet?" it asks, and proceeds to give one, along with information about rune-stones and Viking Scandinavia generally.

moulding, and cutting—but only with difficulty (if at all) could we ascertain what might be contained therein. In some utopian future labelling might be unnecessary. All citizens would live on milk and honey, wine and rosewater, and you could easily tell which bottle contained which. But in these as yet unregenerate times, it's important to know what's in what. Labels have that function.

But why such kitschy labels as this mass of medals and flags and architecturally outdated factories—even angels bestowing laurel crowns? (120A). Surely a simple tasteful "martini wine," perhaps moulded in glass, would be enough? Enough, indeed, if only one kind of martini wine were available, at only one price (like Sidney Webb's accolade for Stalin's Soviet Union—"only one kind of pen available! no dickering! no decisions!"). But as long as some freedom of choice is available, you need ways of advertising what your choice is. Applied images like this help keep that freedom open, in some small way humanizing environments thereby.

To breakfast is to learn, it seems—not only in the U.S., but in Sweden; indeed, everywhere. Everywhere, i.e., that some freedom of packaging is permitted. And is it necessarily so bad to have bread wrappers and all the rest covered with illustrations of kiddies petting calves, flowers and cows and champion skaters and games and informative snippets? Would the world be a better place to live in, were beautifying illustration banned, leaving nothing except, perhaps, vestiges of creative self-expression by Artists Approved by the State? Hard to believe. Maybe such packaging adds little to life. But little is better than nothing. In which sentiment, five millennia of human history concur. From the time human beings first could do illustrations, they have been putting them on artifacts of daily use. Older ones get put in museums (120C).

A major function of beautifying by illustration on historic arts has always been to create souvenirs. Matchbook covers demonstrate the modern form. It's rare to find an unadorned matchbook cover or box. Almost every conceivable kind of image appears on them from views of mountains to softcore porn.[114] But the commonest sort of image relates to where the matchbook was picked up. And thereby make it serve as a reminder of an event (advertising, of course; but incidental, not direct) (121B). Historic counterparts are legion.

263

121B. Matchbook cover distributed by Silja Line, between Stockholm and Helsinki, 1978.

121A. Matchbook cover distributed by the Henry Ford Museum and Greenfield Village, Dearborn, MI in 1976.

122A. Silver phial to contain holy-water or oil gathered on pilgrimages to sites in the Holy Land, from a collection in Monza cathedral near Milan, mostly 6th-7th century.

At all sorts of times and places human beings have desired to recall moving experiences (or even experiences of passing interest) by means of artifacts brought back from wherever they occurred, and suitably "illustrated." We have already noted how substitute imagery has traditionally helped to fulfill this need (27B, 69); objects with applied illustration do it better. Examples are literally innumerable: cheap sou venir pins handed out at Soviet shrines, souvenirs of funerals from 18th-century New England, commemorative medals from Renaissance times (55). Of particular significance in historic arts was the practise of beautifying objects from shrines of great religions, with illustrations associated with various buildings there. Thus from illustrations on phials once containing holy oil from the great pilgrimage sites of early Byzantine Jerusalem, something can be reconstructed of the mosaics once designed to proclaim truths of the Christian religion from its holiest places: originals carefully composed in collaboration with theologians to serve as approved models for sequential illustrations—rescensions—of sacred stories, bringing out correct doctrinal significance of the events, especially the doctrine of Christ's human and divine natures co-existing at all times (122A).[115] Comparably, terracotta and metal objects from Buddhist monastic sites like Bamiyan, Taxila, or Sarnath (18C, 18D), may well preserve some idea of lost works of major arts illustrating, in the fundamental sense of "clarifying," the Buddhist faith for its believers.[116]

How far back does this use of illustration for "beautifying" (as distinct from "beautification" proper) go? Almost to the beginning; the famous Warka vase (71) is surely an example of it—that is to say, there is no internal evidence, as in Greek vases, for the shape of the vessel having been refined in order to make its use clearer to an individual looking at it; the illustrations of ritual events are applied to an object as unrelated to them as a match-book cover usually is to what happens upon *it*. But this is where we came in—and whence we shall take off for a discussion of beautification itself.

Illustration for Persuasion/Conviction

123. Illustration of a child's bedroom from Sears catalogue, 1978. Also, perhaps, an illustration of Muggeridge's observation that *Winnie the Pooh* books enchanted adults, as realizing their picture of childhood, but rarely pleased children themselves though sometimes they pretended otherwise to ingratiate themselves with adults..." (*The Green Stick*, p.163).

IT'S OFTEN BEEN SAID that we treat children nowadays more humanely than we do adults. Perhaps that has always been so. Certainly we provide them more humane environments—in the old sense of organized by and for human comfort in conformity with human values—than for ourselves, oftentimes. Nowadays the use of illustration applied to architecture, in order to help create more meaningful environments is found outside children's rooms only in trivial, banal and ephemeral ways.

Commonest, perhaps, is adolescent decoration of walls with posters and banners to make statements of value: hero-worship, exotica, erotica, whatever. (An activity easily distinguishable from the use of posters for advertising; adolescents are convincing themselves—one of the ancient functions of this art [q.v. 125]—not being "sold" in an advertising sense).

One can also think of such things as pick-up trucks with painted blinds in back windows; farming scenes ornamenting produce counters in supermarkets, and the like—not much to show for a great tradition. Fine and avant-garde arts have little more to offer. A flurry of WPA murals in the 1930s (with an occasional masterpiece like Thomas Hart Benton's murals for the Missouri State Capitol in Jefferson City, but mostly hacked-out fiascos, including those by Jackson Pollock which prompted his teacher, Benton, to suggest he take up some other line of work requiring less talent); turn-of-the-century Arts-and-Crafts efforts to revive the practise of painting walls and doors, from William Morris's furniture to Carl Larsson's house at Sundborn in Darlana; the prominent use of lettering urged by *De Stijl,* Bauhaus and Constructivist designers.

How definitely the great tradition of illustrative murals in Western arts had expired by the mid-19th century is indicated by the origin of our word "cartoon" in the sense of "funny drawing"—from *Punch's* ridicule of "cartoons" (in the old sense of preparatory sketches) for the new Houses of Parliament in London in the 1850s. What killed it, technically, was wallpaper— why pay artists extravagant fees to decorate walls when wallpaper will do the same at a fraction of the cost, in a fraction of the time? But it was not only for technological reasons that illustrative murals became obsolete. Even more, it was because their social function had been forgotten and lost. As long as it was remembered, the tradition remained. For example, in the decoration of the United States Capitol by John Trumbull.

Asked to support John Trumbull's (1756-1843) proposal of 1816 to embellish the United States capitol with four large scenes of the American Revolution, beginning with a larger version of his painting of the Declaration of Independence, old John Adams wrote on 1 January 1817 that he doubted Congress would be amenable: "The Burin and the Pencil, the Chisel and the Trowell, have in all ages and Countries...been enlisted on the side of Despotism and Superstition," he wrote. "Characters and Counsels and Action merely Social, merely civil, merely political, merely moral are always neglected and forgotten."[117] But two months later Trumbull was able to tell Adams of an "unexpected Success"—Congress' authorization to the President to order four

124. The Declaration of Independence painted in 1817-18 by John Trumbull on commission from the United States Congress for $32,000. It is a larger version, painted specifically for the United States Capitol rotunda (where it was installed in 1824) of a record for p osterity of what Trumbull regarded as a sacramental event, painted 1786-1797.

paintings with "figures as large as life." The United States thus continued a long tradition of using illustrative history painting to help make visual metaphors of its convictions in architectural form—the United States capitol building being, of course, the country's great example of this traditional kind of architecture (q.v., 56).

Just as the great Capitol dome was the secularized version of an ancient symbol of divine and royal presence, so Trumbull understood that his painting of Jefferson's committee presenting its draft of the declaration to John Hancock, president of the Second Continental Congress (28 June 1776) was a sacramental event. John Maass thought he could detect many elements from earlier religious illustration in it—from Leonardo's *Last Supper* to Poussin's *Sacrament of the Eucharist,* among others. However that may be, in Trumbull's *Autobiography* his "militant Christianity" was revealed:

Trumbull contrasts the 'calm splendor' of the American Revolution with the atheistic horrors of the French; he sees the American Revolution as a sacred cause. In the entire *Autobiography* Trumbull quotes from the New Testament only once: his own paintings of the Revolution bring to Trumbull's mind the words spoken by Christ to John at the Last Supper: 'greater love hath no man than this, that a man lay down his life for his friends.' The sentiment is echoed in the last sentence of the Declaration of Independence: '...we mutually pledge to each other our Lives...' Thus are linked John Trumbull, the Declaration of Independence, and the Sacrament of the Last Supper.[118]

This was a good instance of illustration's traditional social function in conjunction with architecture: to support, defend, persuade, promote truths professed by an Establishment. Its success is evidenced in the way successful accomplishment of social function has always been evidenced: by imitation. Trumbull's *Declaration* was not only copied innumerable times in the United States, not least in a curious quasi-folk mosaic mural in Forest Lawn Cemetery, Glendale, but adapted for other uses: by Charles Huot, for example in a 1910 mural for the Quebec Provincial Parliament Building depicting the successful fight for recognition of the French language in 1791.[119]

125. *Justin of Nassau surrendering the city of Breda to the Marquis of Spinola,* painted in oil on canvas by Diego Velasquez in 1633-35, but as one of thirteen murals for the palace of Buen Retiro. Now in the Prado, Madrid.

The farther back into Renaissance/Baroque centuries we go, the more powerful do examples of this kind of art become.

Velasquez's *Surrender of Breda* is one of those paintings so famous in art history as to have a nickname: "The Lances," referring to the orderly massed weapons of the Spanish army in its middleground. It is also used in every survey of Renaissance/Baroque art in contrast to paintings like Uccello's *Battle of San Romano* or Leonardo's Battle of Anghiari to demonstrate Baroque as contrasted to Renaissance *Fundamental Principles of Art History* as defined by Wölfflin (q.v., I-15): painterly vs. linear, deep space vs. planarity, and the rest. Rarely is it contrasted to other paintings of its own time with similar social functions—a pity, for that contrast effectively brings out its greatness as an instrument for *doing* something in and for society, rather than merely a link in some line of stylistic progress. Since Velasquez could not, after all, help having been born in the 17th instead of the 15th century, his being a Baroque painter instead of a Renaissance one was no remarkable accomplishment. What is remarkable is how he took a standard commission of his times and made this kind of masterpiece out of it. For the *Surrender of Breda* was in no way a unique or out-of-the-ordinary commission. There were twelve others even in the palace where Velasquex painted this one. Every palace with any pretensions at all in this age had huge battle galleries, from Drottningholm to the Escorial. Their function was to help make palaces into visual metaphors of the class-structured state in general; and in particular, to validate the nobles' place in it as hereditary fighters and rulers. Comparing Velasquez's battle scene with others demonstrates why he is *the* great master of Spanish painting: while his art performs the same social functions as others, it also makes what was, after all, a somewhat insignificant military episode into a comprehensive statement of the whole chivalric code of war: magnanimous victor in polished aristocratic armor backed by a forest of well-disciplined lances shows the proper way to treat a defeated foe, even if the foe is a republican in loutish clothes commanding a disorderly rabble of pikemen. Who was supposed to be moved, persuaded, convinced by such a picture? Primarily, its commissioner, the Marquis of Spinola, and his class. Art reinforcing an Establishment always has this primary purpose: to persuade the commissioners themselves.[120] For the fall of any social order most often begins when its leaders lose faith in their own mission and right to rule; once they come to regard themselves as unjust possessors of power (no matter how long ago inherited), the end of their power is in sight. Something of the sort was happening throughout 17th-century Baroque Europe. Republican rebels were triumphing in the Netherlands (*Breda* depicts about the last Spanish victory in that war!), in England (where they executed Charles the First) and elsewhere not alone by their own valor but by their aristocratic enemies' will to fight being undermined by uneasiness about the justice of their cause—republicanism was "in the air" and the European mind would soon cross what Hazard describes as its "watershed" between Old and Modern Europe.[121] In this context Baroque arts can be seen as desperate rearguard actions defending an endangered institution—the more endangered, the more extravagantly defended by a style becoming ever more dramatic, ever more adept at drawing spectators in to participate in demonstrations of aristocratic virtue. Baroque principles come into being not because some evolutionary law required them but because they were required by a particular social function. The Baroque style, like every other major stylistic development in Western art, is to be explained by persuasive/convincing function.

Since its completion in 1512 after a four-year program, Michelangelo's series of illustrations on the ceiling of the Pope's private chapel in the Vatican has been considered *the* consummate work of Western painting, one of those cultural achievements constantly cited to justify continuing quest of and support for contemporary High Culture. Yet what kind of art is it, exactly? It's illustration—and illustration done, no matter how camouflaged by Renaissance Italian flattery—under conditions uncomfortably close to hired commercial illustration today.

That however highly regarded "the divine Michelangelo" may have been by connoisseurs, this commission was no outburst of genius given scope for expression by enlightened patronage, dozens of documents attest. The artist was in fact forced to execute the commission against his will, by strategem; Pope Julius II delle Rovere in fact so contrived things that Michelangeo had to paint his way out of debt. Instead of proceeding with sculptures commissioned from Michelangelo for

6. Interior view of the Sistine Ceiling in the Vatican, looking toward the altar, and a schematic diagram of that
rtion of the ceiling painting which can be seen in the photo. On the end wall: The Last Judgement, painted by
chelangelo in the 1530s.

the mausoleum which, in the manner of a "godly prince" of the age, he planned to install in his "State church," St. Peter's (55), the great Pope decided to order from his "staff artists," Michelangelo and Raphael, some powerful visual metaphors of his claims to authority—to reinforce his belief first, perhaps; thence to rebut sedition and heresy generally. From Raphael he demanded static illustrations, for didactic purposes, in the Vatican Stanze (22). Michelangelo's was more conventional: a series of illustrations of *Genesis* from the creation of the world to the Fall of Noah. A common enough commission; churches of all kinds had been so decorated throughout the Middle Ages (there are many rural churches with similar vault paintings all over Sweden, for example), and there was even plenty of precedent for painting scenes from *Genesis* on vaulted ceilings (Saint-Savin-sur-Gartempe from the 12th century is often cited in surveys). Almost, one might say, a utilitarian job, like painting insignia on an airplane—without such paintings, the chapel would not "function" properly, hence they can hardly be called "decoration" in the sense of something you could add or remove at will. Furthermore, the job was paid for almost like "piece work"— whenever the Pope stopped paying, Michelangelo stopped painting.[122] The artist's creative agony and ecstasy is a legend deriving from artistic life and outlook of later times; Michelangelo did not even have to invent the iconography.[123]

That is not to deny great artistic qualities to the Sistine Ceiling. It is simply to say that before talking about monumentally scaled forms, rich color harmonies, exquisite line, bold dramatic effects, subtle interrelationships of major and minor themes, the function of the Sistine Ceiling needs to be remembered and kept in mind. It was illustration—the ancient art of telling stories and clarifying events by means of pictures. And illustration attached to architecture for a persuasive/convincing purpose: to recall how the world had been created good but how Man had fallen—not once, but twice, the second time with Noah; to show, therefore, how hopelessly sinful was the nature of Man, and his consequent need for a Redeemer; and by such a theme in such a place, to establish by association how the role of that Redeemer on earth was being carried out by the institution of the Papacy[124]—to make, in short, of an architecturally undistinguished structure a powerful art of persuasion/conviction.

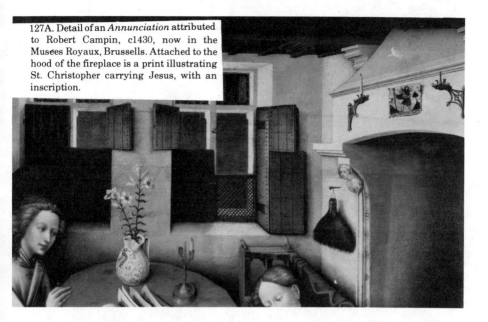

127A. Detail of an *Annunciation* attributed to Robert Campin, c1430, now in the Musees Royaux, Brussells. Attached to the hood of the fireplace is a print illustrating St. Christopher carrying Jesus, with an inscription.

It's normal to trace posters back to block-prints of the late Middle Ages, as David Kunzle does, for instance, in *The Early Comic Strip;* and quite correct too. What should not be lost sight of, however, is that such prints were merely cheap versions of the same kind of art—i.e., art with the same social function, that covered walls in fresco and constituted major painting programs of the age.

Harkeberga is a typical, though better preserved, example of many small Swedish churches vaulted at the end of the Middle Ages and completely painted with Biblical scenes[125] taken from some popular printed source—in this case the "Bible of the Poor," a preaching manual with early block-printed illustrations.[126] One could without being facetious at all call it a permanent poster-display. Certainly when the colors were fresh, the effect must have been as garish as any teenager's room; even now the effect is curiously similar: like walking into a particular mental world. In this case, the world of those decades just before the Protestant Reformation, when all sorts of covert and open opposition to the old Latin church was boiling through every European nation; when, in consequence, just as in the Papal capital Julius II assigned Raphael and Michelangelo to help combat the threat with compelling images of Papal powers and authority, so compelling arts of every sort with similar functions were being commissioned throughout late Medieval Europe: Chartres' flamboyant north tower (1503), Kings College

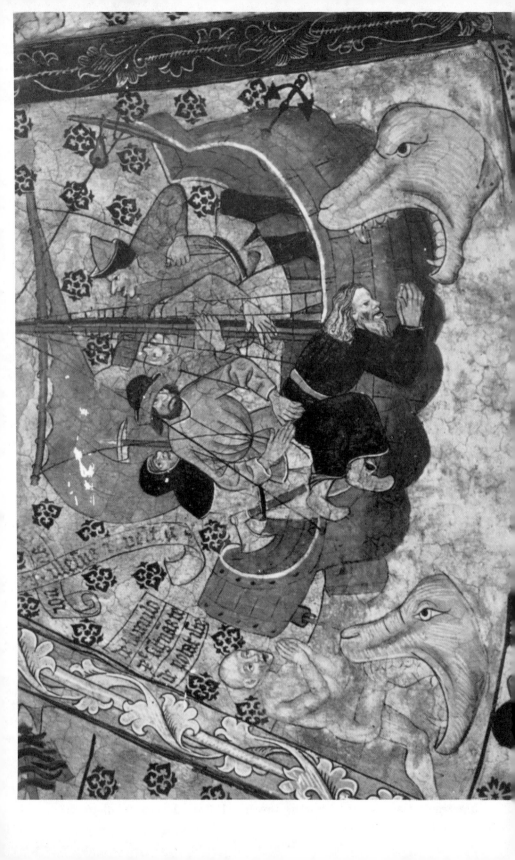

Cambridge's fan-vaulted chapel (1508-1512), fabulously detailed altarpieces from workshops in the Netherlands; and, in country parishes all over remote Sweden, new vaultings for country churches with ambitious decorative programs which are really comic-books writ large—Hakeberga is typical. And make no mistake; this *is* popular art. Its primary purpose was not aesthetic satisfaction (any more than Raphael's or Michelangelo's art had that primary purpose!). Its primary purpose was to keep before the eyes of the population basic tenets of faith: how Man was created and fell and needs redeeming; how through all ages the purpose of God was effected by saints and prophets and priests; and how this process is still ongoing.

The social function of this art is to convince and persuade. It tells the story of Jonah in a cosmic present—in one part of the picture we see Jonah cast overboard because the sailors believe themselves imperilled by a great storm aimed at forcing Jonah to return to his preaching duties, and in another we see him cast ashore, having lost his clothes, but repentant—this is how God sees time, with past and present and future all one and the same, rather than how we see it. But the scene is still more believable than our religious art, cast in our time-space perception as it is, for these historical personages, unlike the actors in ours (117), are dressed not in attire from some dim distant era, but in constumes of their own day. They are people you could meet anytime in "real life." Which means, they *are* real life! Sailors you could meet any day on Swedish or German ships of the 1480s; Jonah dressed like a typical wandering friar; peasant-soldiers with bills and pikes— believable all. And coming from a believable source, images comprehended of the people—a mass-produced block-print book. It's as if we were to decorate church walls with blown-up "Classic Comics," Great Tales From the Bible series. Only we wouldn't call that art—forgetting or ignoring that, just as Michelangelo made High Art out of dictated iconography and a piece-work commission, so did Master Albert (their commissions were in fact identical in kind, if not in degree!). Forgetting or ignoring also that Velasquez and Michelangelo are no extreme, unusually, carefully culled instances of artists beautifying architecture by illustration to create metaphors of persuasion/conviction, but examples of normal practise, typical ways for works of historic art to begin, standard foundations for creation, at all times and places until our own.

128A. Reconstruction of the first, third and last (twelfth) metopes from the inner cella of the Temple of Zeus at Olympia, set in place c460 B.C. Represented here were the earliest labor of Herakles (defeat of the Nemean Lion) shown here as accomplished by a youth, with assistance of patrons Athena and Hermes); Herakles brings dead Stymphalian birds to Athena as trophies, in first vigor of manhood; Athena guides the aged Herakles in cleaning the Augean stables, back in Elis region after feats of superhuman and supernatural strength all over the world. These reconstructions were made by the 1878 German archaeological expedition to Olympia: the originals were painted, with details (like the birds, e.g.) in metal or consisting of actual objects.

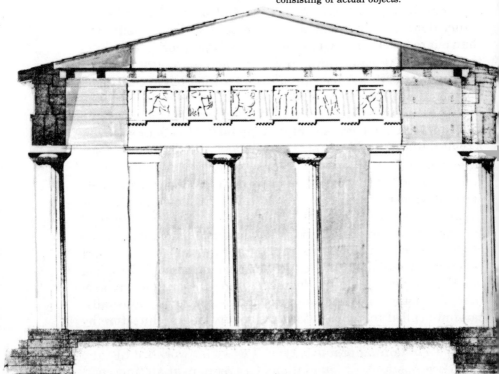

128B. Section through the Temple of Zeus at Olympia, erected 468-475, showing how the metopes illustrating the twelve labors of Herakles were related to the architecture, six on either end of the inner temple-house.

Founded on the site of a much older Mycenaean sanctuary associated with a cult of the Earth and the dead, and therefore a natural site for ritual funeral games, Olympia was the site of those games from whose establishment in 776 B.C. Greek time was reckoned—a central focus of Greek civilization, then. Its great Temple of Zeus was a correspondingly major monument. At the heart of that monument were illustrations of twelve labors performed, according to Greek mythical belief, by Herakles, the hero who by one account was the original founder of the Games themselves (cf.99 and pp. 206). These are by general consent among the greatest works of Greek art, masterpieces of the "severe style," milestones in the emergence of classic Greek art. Just as comparison with the Temple of Hera (49A) shows the new analytical refinement of shapes that marks the beginning of beautification proper in Greek art (q.v.), so the Herakles metopes reveal that new mind in the way they organize a mass of disparate and unrelated legends about the national folk hero into a coherent cycle to which intelligent individual spectators can relate. Relating them also to modern popular/commercial arts might seem presumptuous. But in fact it is through study of popular/commercial illustration that we can appreciate them best, I think.

In both cases we find, to begin with, illustration in the primordial sense of clarification: making clear by pictures stories told in words, and vice-versa. For that purpose it's essential that a folk hero not be an invincible superman; otherwise individuals could never relate to him. Popeye is believable as a one-eyed runt to a degree impossible were he some giant like his opponents. Superman is believable (if at all) because we can identify with Clark Kent, a timid mortal forever humiliated by the super-hero's exploits. Similarly Herakles is believable at Olympia because he is there represented not as a timeless, immortal, invincible hero of folklore, but within the time-frame of mortal lives—ours.[127] In the first metope a beardless youth, exhausted even by the relatively simple feat of killing a lion in a neraby valley, the Herakles of Olympia's metopes matures steadily and, as he matures, travels to ever more distant locales, ultimately daring even the supernatural (holding up the sky for Atlas) and the underworld (dragging the Hound of Hell from his lair); then at the last, tired and old, he needs Athen's help for the comparatively simple job of cleaning Augeas's stables—as won't we all, someday!

And like popular/commercial arts too, the "illustrator" of the Herakles scenes at Olympia probably did not invent his subject-matter, but gave form to a cycle and sub-cycles chosen by someone else—perhaps some literary man of the day, like Aeschylus, to whose plays the Olympia sculptures offer so many parallels in theme and outlook.[128] Such collaboration happened in historic arts at all times and places—including perhaps Michelangelo's with theologian Marco Vigerio on the Sistine Ceiling (III-123), and as happens still in modern popular/commercial arts—the *Wizard of Id,* for one example: Scrooge McDuck, for another (III-28).

About the Temple of Zeus at Olympia volumes could be written, and in any new survey of art history based on a methodology of social function it is a key monument. Here the point is simply this: before it was a work of art, it fulfilled social functions required at its time and place in history, specifically illustration—like so many great works of art before[129] and after. And it introduces the third major social function of historic arts—beautification proper.

Notes to Section III: Illustration

[1]The connection may also be simply one of theme. For example: Robert Short's *A Time to be Born, a Time to Die* (New York, 1973). For each verse of *Ecclesiastes,* he provides a visual image; the eye and mind make their own connections to carry the narrative. I deliberately chose George McManus' *Newlyweds* to demonstrate the "quickening" of illustrative moment: "no man," says Maurice Horn, "contributed to the basic 'look' of the comic strip as much as George McManus." *World Encyclopedia of Comics* (New York, 1976), p. 12.

[2]Defining illustration, of course, in the broadest possible way. Even within Antiquity there are important distinctions to be made; e.g., H.A. Groenewegen-Frankfort, *Arrest and Movement* (Chicago, 1951), p. 92, insists that although reliefs on Assyrian palace walls

"have often been compared with and even tentatively derived from the Egyptian battle reliefs of the nineteenth dynasty, the essential difference between 'monumental' and narrative scenic art cannot be overstressed. The nearest parallel to the Assyrian reliefs are the reliefs on Trajan's column."

[3]On the identity of writing and illustration, cf. A. Leo Oppenheim, *Ancient Mesopotamia* (Chicago, 1964), p. 235:

"Three typical uses of writing can be found in the civilization of the ancient Near East: the recording of data for future uses [i.e., substitute imagery], the communication of data on a synchronic level [i.e., illustration], and what I would like to term ceremonial use [a cross between these two, it would seem—a sacred substitute image which conveys meaning by its existence]."

See also the long discussion by Edmond Pottier, "Notes sur les vases peintes de l'acropole de Suse," *Mémoires de la Délégation en Perse,* 1912, à propos of Susa A pottery; and further, Section IV.

[4]While genuine illustrators do not distort the meaning of texts for reasons of artistic self-

expression, the meaning can be distorted for many other reasons—allegorical interpretations, contemporary political and social life, relations between Church and State, etc. Perhaps the most comprehensive study of this sort is Meyer Schapiro's *Words and Pictures: On the Literal and the Symbolic in the Illustration of a Text* (The Hague/Paris, 1974). In his generation, Schapiro was far more keenly aware of social function than, say, Panofsky, for whom "literal and symbolic" seemed to imply puzzles set for cunning scholars like himself to solve, or even Dvořak, who interpreted "literal and symbolic" as cosmic metamorphoses in history. Yet because the consequences of avant-garde principles became fully evident only after 1955, none of this generation of art historians ever fully grasped the central principle that what we call art in the 1950s and '60s was a different kind of activity from what is called historic art. So Schapiro persisted in talking about how "the artist" reads texts, how "the artist" has his interpretations affected by contemporary political, religious, and social life—a most vaguely on the model of Picasso being affected by the Spanish Civil War, or something.

⁵Evidencing this statement is the vast, the incredible increase in available archival material in every field of popular/commercial arts. On comics, to take one example, cf. M. Thomas Inge, "American Comic Art: A Bibliographic Guide," *Choice*, January, 1975, pp. 1-10, and Maurice Horn's *World Encyclopedia of Comics* (New York, 1976). Of course, mixed up with such serious work has gone an outpouring of nostalgia pieces equating popular arts with quaint memorabilia of bygone pre-TV days like raccoon coats and Stutz Bearcats. But such mixed studies have always been typical of early steps toward new understanding in any new field.

Just so, in early Italian Renaissance studies amateur and sentimental appreciation mingled with critical scholarly endeavors to attribute and sort. You can see the richness of this mixture, and at the same time realize how much serious research has already been put into this new field, via *Popular Abstracts,* index to the first ten years of the *Journal of Popular Culture, Journal of Popular Film* and *Popular Music and Society* (Bowling Green, Ohio: Popular Press, 1977).

⁶These books also have extensive bibliographies. Hård af Segerstad's study is one of several produced by Uppsala's Konstvetenskapliga Institute, all of major significance—e.g., Lena Johannesson's *Den Massproducerade Bilden* (Stockholm, 1978).

⁷Cf. Beaumont Newhall, *History of Photography* (New York, 1949), esp. ch. 13, pp. 219-240.

⁸Fred Schroeder, "Popular Culture before Printing," *Journal of Popular Culture,* XI, 3, 1977, p. 634.

⁹For illustrations of all these and date, cf. *The Unchanging Arts,* II.

¹⁰Bill Blackbeard has said, "The fundamental genius of Segar remains as implicit in his totally unaged strip work as that of Charles Dickens in his novels." Indeed there are many fundamental parallels between the two. Blackbeard has published some sequences of *Thimble Theatre* strips in Nostalgia Press (New Rochelle, 1971), and I intend to publish the "Fountain of Youth" and "Popeye's Ark" sequences in book form, as political commentaries, in a style indicated by "Remarks on Arts and Utopias in the 1930s, A Propos of some excerpts from *Popeye's Ark,* RACAR *(Revue d'art canadienne/Canadian Art Review),* I, 1, 1974, pp. 5-22. See further n. 85.

¹¹Cf. Wolfang Fuchs and Reinhold C. Reitberger, *Comics: Anatomie eines Massenmediums* (Munich, 1971), pp. 61-66.

¹²There was an empathy between Foster's illustrations and Burroughs's text recalling the relationship between Kemble and Twain ("my own dear family, just as I created them," said Twain) and between Tenniel and Dodson, who together wrestled over the form of each *Alice* illustration.

¹³Cf. Fuchs and Reitberger, *op cit.,*Ch. 9, "Sex und Satire," and Les Daniels, *Comix, A History of Comic Books in America* (New York, 1971), Ch. 8.

¹⁴For illustrations, cf. *The New Yorker Twenty-Fifth Anniversary Album* (New York, 1951).

¹⁵Cf.Thomas Craven, *Cartoon Cavalcade* (New York, 1943)., pp. 103-106.

¹⁶ Cf. Fn. II-53.

¹⁷Cf.Ralph Stevenson, *Animation in the Cinema* (London, 1967).

¹⁸A fact noted by Hellmut Lehmann-Haupt, "Animated Drawing," *Illustrators of Children's Books 1744-1943* (Boston, 1967). He deplores the change beginning c1930: "In twentieth-century America animated drawing has once more slipped back into the limbo of 'illegitimacy'... I am unable to explain why this should have happened.... Current

attempts...lack true animation.....The speech balloon in its current elaboration interferes with the basic simplicity of animated drawing...."

It is a familiar argument, based on an assumption that "the nature of process (materials, structure) should be expressive"—all animation since the earliest stick-figures by Emile Cohl is retrogressive, just as all auto design since the earliest totally exposed machines is retrogressive, etc., etc. But necessity of expressing the nature of things is a metaphysical proposition, derived from the Natural Goodness of Mankind and of Nature (hence, the more naturally expressed, the better), which forces human needs into an art mould, rather than design according to social function which moulds art to suit human needs. Animation for its own sake makes animated cartoons less effective—as any art for its own sake renders arts so treated socially useless.

[19]Cf. the appreciative article by Jay Cocks in *Time*, 17 December, 1973. Jones (b. 1911) is a relative unknown compared to Disney, though winner of three Oscars. His most fruitful years were with Warner Brothers in the 1940s and '50s. Although he never went "arty" in the Disney manner, Jones refused to go along with the limited animation necessitated by TV animation; his insistence on full animation was one reason why Warner Brothers' animation unit closed down in 1962. Cf. (94).

[20]Cf. *The Unchanging Arts*, pp. 287-89.

[21]Timothy Green, *The Universal Eye: The World of Television* (New York, 1972) surveys different types of TV "in over 40 countries on five continents" at the beginning of 1970.

[22]Similarly, in an introduction to an early 16th-century play by John Heywood in *Medieval Mystery Plays*, (Vincent F. Hopper & Gerald B. Lahey, eds., Woodbury, N.Y., 1962), p. 68, we read:

"As the drama was the major literary form of the sixteenth century, the novel is that of our time. If the reader were to cast about in the modern world for the reincarnation of the spirit of John Heywood, he might do worse than fix upon Sinclair Lewis....Sir John the priest and the Pardoner lived again in Elmer Gantry. the Pedler in George Babbitt and his pals...." And of course the successor to this kind of popular novel is the television situation comedy.

[23]Imagining Shakespeare returned to earth and attending his Quatercentenary, Muggeridge wrote:

"Perhaps Sir John Falstaff's absence, or the wine, or both together, made Shakespeare rise in his place and, to the general consternation, acknowledge the toast of the evening to himself with exaggerated courtesy; an undistinguished little man in that eminent company, wearing an ill-fitting, hired dress suit without a single decoration.

The toastmaster, with the help of two waiters, soon removed him, and then His Royal Highness could continue with his oration. I heard the roars of laughter which greeted his sallies as I made my way out to look for Shakespeare. He was telephoning when I found him. Extraordinary how quickly he picked up the use of such devices. 'I'd like to speak to Mr. Bernstein,' I heard him saying, 'William Shakespeare here. I wondered if he'd be interested in an historical series. The Kings and Queens of England Always good box office, Burbage used to say, and it doesn't seem any different now. What's that? Yes, I'll come along straight away....'" (*The Best of Malcolm Muggeridge*, p. 270).

No self-conscious genius of creative writing, he, but someone who put plays together with the demands of audiences and the resources of his company constantly in mind; who lifted plots and characters from all sorts of popular ballads, travellers' reports and town gossip; who, above all, took care to support the Establishment. No art of protest his, but a mass of warnings against the evil consequences of riot and civil commotion, exposures of demagoguery, and predictions of ruin awaiting all subverters of power by Law Established.

[24]*Journal of Popular Culture*, VII, 4, 1974, p. 985.

[25]*Ibid.*, p. 988.

[26]Agnes Nixon, quoted by Ron Townley, *TV Guide*, 3 May 1975.

[27]Tom Wolfe, *Mauve Gloves & Madmen, Clutter & Vine* (New York, 1976), p. 105.

[28]Actually this character was not invented by Walt Disney but by Carl Barks, one of Disney's artistic staff, in December 1947, and was always drawn and scripted by Barks. The Disney studio's policy of attributing all its work to Disney himself long obscured this fact. Cf. Maurice Horn, *Encyclopedia of Comics*, p.97.

[29]*Op. cit.*, III-13, p. 56. The entire episode is reproduced pp. 124-128.

[30]And provides a convenient bibliography too. Hans Jørn Christiansen and Erik Bjørn Olsen, eds. *Tegneserier, en ekspansions historie* (Aarhus University, 1974).

[31]George Orwell, *Such, Such were the Joys* (New York, 1953), p. 7.

[32]The same is true of 19th-century popular prints, as Klaus Lankheit noted so aptly in *Bilderbogen: deutsche populäre Druckgraphik des 19 Jahrhunderts* (Karlsruhe, Badische Landesmuseum, 1973), pp. 14-15:

"Modern social criticism can easily show that fixed stylized formulae [in popular prints] must have had a stabilizing—in the sense of reactionary—effect. Even the popular printmakers' open-mindedness towards the liberal-democratic movement of 1848 does not contradict this fundamentally conservative posture. Popular prints never threatened Establishments. Whoever attributes revolutionary purposes to popular prints of that epoch reads wishes from his own time into them. The essence of these popular prints is ambivalence between education through information on the one hand, and stabilizing political conditions on the other. Just for that reason, mass-produced prints have become one of the most important sources of historical revelations about that epoch.

"Getting pictures of contemporary events onto the market without delay made lengthy techniques like engraving or woodcuts unsuitable; even lithography often was too slow in times of crisis. So preparation in advance was in order...during Napoleonic wars...plates were prepared when a battle seemed imminent...after the battle captions were made up and uniforms colored according to the outcome....

"A history of Germany, indeed of Europe, in the 19th century could be made up from these prints. How valuable these prints would be for documentary history is another matter. But what does documentation mean? Specifying the actual historical sight and sound...Or rather, indicating what posterity thought of events? If it is possible to say, following Nietsche, that a human being can be assembled out of three anecdotes, then print series can show an epoch more clearly than many a learned thesis."

See further footnote V-7.

[32]Cf. Edouard Fuchs, *Sittengeschichte* (Berlin, 1904).

[34]It was Baudelaire who first cited pornography as a major function for the new art of photography, in his commentary on the Salon of 1859, "The Modern Public & Photography," J. Mayne, ed., *The Mirror of Art, Critical Studies of Charles Baudelaire* (London, 1955). There are useful observations also in Lena Johannesson, *Den Massproducerade Bilden* (Stockholm, 1978), pp. 159-165, "Scientific pornography."

[35]Pliny, *Natural History*, XXXVI, 20: "...Superior to all works, not only of Praxiteles, but indeed in the whole world, is the Aphrodite which many people have sailed to Knidos in order to see....They say a certain man was once overcome with love for the statue and, after he had hidden himself [in the shrine] during the nighttime, embraced the statue and that there is a stain on it as an indication of his lust....There is another Eros by him, this one nude, in Parium, the colony on the Propontis, which is equal to the Aphrodite at Knidos both for its fame and for the injury which it suffered; for Alketas the Rhodian fell in love with it and also left upon it the same sort of trace of his love...." From J.J. Pollitt, *The Art of Greece, Sources & Documents* (Englewood Cliffs, 1965), pp. 128-129.

[36]A typical example: the celebrated *Worship of Priapus*, by Richard Payne Knight, first published in 1783. It already has all the attributes of modern popular/commercial pornography: the underground publication that anybody interested can locate, the specious high-mindedness, the note of scientific inquiry, the unargued assumption that the ethics of derelict civilizations must be superior to his own....Curiously, this volume was reprinted by "Collectors Publications," Covina, California, in 1967, with a copyright: "All rights including Motion Picture Rights reserved under International, Pan-American, and Universal Copyright Conventions" (!) Let freedom ring!

[37]Krishna Deva, *Khajuraho* (New Delhi, 1977), p. 14.

[38]This age was the theme of the first, 1976, ISUH Institute in Cross-Cultural Studies at the University of Victoria. E.g., *Proceedings* (Watkins Glen, N.Y., 1977), p. 49:

"When Abelard talks about Celestial Jerusalem in relation to Solomon's Temple, he no longer assumes that Solomon was trying to reproduce the glories of Heaven here on earth. He assumes rather—as though it were too self-evident to expound upon—that Solomon's Temple was the model for God's 'regal palace'; it is by studying Solomon's Temple that we can understand what Heaven is like (and, by copying it in our own churches, bring Heaven down to earth—that is the logical conclusion to any such line of thought). Suger's concept of the function of this great new Abbey follows naturally from such premises—when he wishes to have his 'soul exalted to an immaterial realm' he imagines that realm in terms of St. Denis. Kings and Brahmans in India did the same—throughout all the 11th, 12th and 13th century Hindu realms, spiritual heavens were claimed to resemble the great temples which Chola and Candella rulers erected. In the case of Angkor and Java this is even more obvious. Great temples of this age there were proclaimed to be Heaven-on-earth in the most literal sense. Likewise the devout in Burma could envisage Heaven best from their great Sikhara temples, whether these were conceived as temple-mountains blazing with light, or as vases containing a lotus. Again, if neo-Confucian philosophers wanted to envisage ideal world harmonies, it was from Sung paintings that they could get their concepts—not the other way around. In Japan, Genshin and Nichiren taught that in this third and last world-age (beginning in the mid-11th century) the reality of Heaven would be realizable only through material things like sutra mounds and sentai-do (Halls of 1000 Images); hence the rationale of constructing a Byodo-in which would literally create here and now on earth the Western Paradise of Amida Buddha; hence the rationale of the Sanjusangendo in Kyoto with what John Rosenfield called its

'...awesome array of nearly life-sized statues of the 1000-armed Kannon...the sheer quantity and bristing complexity of that ensemble of images in Kyoto is one of the most sobering experiences of the irrational power of Asian imagery'."

[39]Quoted by Peter C. Dronke, *The Medieval Lyric* (London, 1968), p. 13. This verse, it seems, was long attributed to Virgil!

[40]One of those subjects where eveybody seems to have an opinion and few have many facts. One might have supposed the matter exhaustively researched; not so. Max von Boehn is as usual careful, but *Der Tanz* (Berlin, 1925), is too early to be *a propos*. Troy and Margaret West Kinney, *The Dance* (New York, 1935) has useful material on Arabic dancing, but an unscholarly approach.

[41]*New Larousse Encyclopedia of Mythology* (Paris, 1968), p. 58.

[42]Glyn Daniel, *Megalith Builders of Western Europe* (London, 1961); on Cycladic sculpture, Christian Zervos, *L'art des Cyclades* (Paris, 1957), and Sect. II, Fgr. 26 and fns. 38, 39.

[43]A.J.P. Taylor, *The First World War* (London, 1963), p. 251: "On 11 November 1918 the Allied peoples burst into rejoicing. All work stopped for the day. Crowds blocked the streets, dancing and cheering....As evening fell, the crowds grew more riotous. Total strangers copulated in public—a symbol that life had triumphed over death."

[44]"According to the Hindu view the final aim of life is salvation which lies in the merging of the *atman* with *paramatman* or the individual soul with the universal. The union of man and woman, wherein all sense of duality is lost, thus came to constitute a symbol of liberation. 'As a man in the embrace of his beloved wife knows naught, either without or within, so one in the embrace of the Knowing Self knows naught, either without or within'." (Deva, *Khajuraho*, p. 19). A.K. Coomeraswamy's chapter "Sahaja" in *The Dance of Shiva* (New York, 1957, pp. 124-134) is well known.

[45]Sura 78/34, quoted by Annemarie Schimmel, "The Celestial Garden in Islam," in *The Islamic Garden* (Washington, Dumbarton Oaks, 1976), p. 15.

[46]Herman Goetz, *Art of India* (Baden-Baden, 1969), pp. 164-165.

[47]A useful source of illustrations for this and other utopian themes is Ian Tod & Michael Wheeler, *Utopia* (London, 1978); it also has a useful bibliography for this vast theme. Typical of more scholarly studies is Dolores Hayden, *Seven American Utopias* (Cambridge, 1976), which has a massive bibliography. Curiously, I could not find a study of group sex (orgies) as a utopian activity (there are of course painfully many "studies" of the subject on the "how to do it" level). It is of course a favorite theme of Malcolm Muggeridge's; his works abound with passing allusions to sex as the sacrament of materialistic religion, etc.

[48]Orwell clearly saw the "doublethink" inherent in legalized pornography. On the one hand, Party members in *1984* were to be rigidly puritanical, so that all their efforts should be devoted to perfection of Party and society. On the other, Winston's girlfriend Julia worked in Pornosec, churning out cheap books like "Three Nights in a Girls' School" to keep the proles content. A historical precedent is evidenced by John Rosenfield, *Traditions of Japanese Art* (Cambridge, Mass., 1979), p. 361, on three leaves from an album of shunga (school of

Katsukawa Shunsho): "During the lengthening decades of peace and internal stability, the nightlife of Edo, as of Osaka and Kyoto, became ever more boisterous.... In its indulgence, color and romance the 'floating world' served as an emotional outlet for an intensely organized, rigid social order created by the military government to bring order to a nation that had known rebellion and disorder for many decades."

[49]Q.v., fn. 8. Quote, p. 634.

[50]Humorous to some; not all, apparently. There has been periodic concern about the "violence" in the Popeye animated cartoons shown on TV, and unfavorable comparisons of it vis-à-vis Disney. Ralph Stevenson's otherwise excellent *Animation in the Cinema* is surprisingly unintelligent about *Popeye* (as was Orwell in his famous essay on "The Art of Donald McGill." *Dickens, Dali & Others* (New York, 1942), possibly because they didn't know the comic. Orwell even misspelt it, "Pop Eye."

[51]*Eccl.* IX:11, using Short's 1973 translation in *A Time to be Born* (fn. 1).

[52]But in the process gaining plaudits from art critics, previously withheld; Cf. Robin Field, *The Art of Disney* (New York, 1950). A variant of the classic syndrome: "I don' min' nigras so long's they're not *too* black/ I don' min' pop'lar arts, so long's they're not *too* popular...."

[53]Q.v., fn. 19. Jones's artiness took the inverse form of anti-"elevation," blaring sound track and pointless violence for the medium's sake—if you can do it, do it, much as contemporary avant-garde architects argued that if you built with steel cage or concrete you *must* express these techniques at their rawest.

[54] Q.v., fn. 20. The Hanna-Barbera technique essentially meant a kind of Toynbean return to the original stick-figure concept of the medium. Now a single background was made to serve whole sequences with a few moving parts laid on it to simulate talking or simple action; effects of violent motion like crashing or falling were simulated simply by shaking the picture in front of the camera; correspondingly greater emphasis had to be laid on distinctive voices and clever soundtrack. However much art critics lamented sacrifices of "artistic quality," in fact the medium was so immensely improved by these gimmicks that animated cartoons of the 1930s began to look as curiously archaic, compared to TV animation, as pre-1914 newsreels.

[55]Cf. Martin Gardner, *The Annotated Alice* (New York, 1960). On p. 102 he notes, for example, the resemblance of Bertrand Russell to the Mad Hatter and his Cambridge philosophy colleagues M.E. Taggart and G.E. Moore to the Doormouse and March Hare, which led them to be known as the Mad Tea Party of Trinity—in retrospect a resemblance, perhaps, more than pen-deep.

[56]Some introduction to this huge field may be obtained from Stith Thompson, *The Folktale* (New York, 1946), especially useful in connection with the universality of folktale motifs and motives; and Mircea Eliade, *Myth and Reality* (New York, 1963) and *Sacred & Profane* (New York, 1957). I discovered Bettelheim, *The Uses of Enchantment* (New York, 1976) when this text was finished.

[57]Murray Peppard, *Paths Through the Forest, A Biography of the Brothers Grimm* (New York, 1971).

[58]Arts with the social function of promoting just this sort of class-structured State abound in 16th- and 17th-century Islam, China, Japan, Russia, etc. Cf. *On Parallels in Universal History*, pp. 49-53. These parallels were further explored in the ISUH 1978 Summer Institute

[59]Lillian M.C. Randall, *Images in the Margins of Gothic Manuscripts* (Berkeley, 1966).

[60]Friedrich Heer, *Europäische Geistesgeschichte*, I (Stuttgart, 1970), Ch.V. "Die Revolution aus Rom," pp. 49-63, also *The Medieval World: Europe 1100-1361* (New York, 1961).

[61]Elise Grilli, *Japanese Picture Scrolls* (London, 1973), "The design thus begins at the right-hand end, proceeds in sections that are imperceptibly linked to make easy transitions in the viewing, rises to a planned climax and denouement, much as happens in a well-constructed drama, and then fades away to a quiet ending."

[62]Q.v., fn. 38.

[63]In a Ballantine pocketbook reprint of *Tarzan of the Apes* (copyright 1912, first pocketbook printing July 1963, ninth, already by April 1975!) we read about Edgar Rice Burroughs: "Burroughs must have been known and loved by literally a thousand million or more people. Attesting to the unparalleled holding power Edgar Rice Burroughs maintains upon his readers are the many ERB fan clubs existing today.... Readers wishing to establish ERB fan clubs may write to ERB, Inc., Tarzana, California...."

284   Learning to See

[64]In a youthful effort, "The Master of Olympia," published after some vicissitudes in *Delaware Notes* (University of Delaware, 1957), I marshalled the arguments against the iconography being invented by any of the sculptors, and suggested that whoever paid for the temple (the Olympia priests, from the spoils of the Pisan war; or benefactors amongst Greek cities and tyrants) commissioned some intellectual to compose an iconography; that resemblances in manner of presentation, especially the East Gable's, suggest Aeschylus. To date I seem to remain the sole exponent of this theory. Nonetheless it is this "tragedian" approach which most effectively characterizes all the Olympia iconography. Herakles, in the twelve cella metaopes, for example, appears as a symbolic fulfillment of the collective wishes and aspirations of Greek society, a folk hero (rather like E.C. Segar's *Popeye*) whose hundred-odd legendary feats are quite unrelated to one another in any continuum of space or time. By contrast, the twelve Olympia metopes follow each other in a humanly intelligible sequence—three youthful exploits (in the first Heracles is a beardless boy) in the vicinity of Olympia (*Nemean Lion, Lernean Hydra, Stymphalian birds*); three feats of physical prowess in early manhood, on the geographical frontiers of the Greek world (*Cretan Bull, Brazen-footed Hind of Thessaly, Amazons)*; and finally three demanding strengths of both kinds (*Atlas, Cerberus, Augeas*) the last bringing the series to an end where it began, back near Olympia, in Heracles' old age. With a hero so existing in measurable time and space, individual spectators can identify; they can "relate" to the temple sculpture as they might to a stage presentation. Or a TV special!

On the cult of Herakles at Olympia, cf. Ludwig Drees, *Olympia* (Stuttgart, 1972), p. 35f: "Die mythische Stiftung durch Herakles."

[65]Most writers on the vast diffuse subject of shamanism dwell upon the esoteric and mystical-cosmic-unity aspects of modern practise; the mystic unity of man and animal is but one aspect of this whole. Cf. C.M. Edsman, ed. *Studies in Shamanism* (Stockholm, 1962): Mircea Eliade, *Shamanism* (London, 1967) and *Early Chinese Art on the Pacific Basin* (Columbia University Press, New York, 1968), M. Eggers, Evans, and Estrade, *Smithsonian Contributions to Anthropology* I, 1965, pp. 160ff. The question also has to do with whether there are linguistic origins common to Old World Chinese and New World Amerinds; e.g., M. Swadish, *Indian Linguistic Groups of Mexico* (Mexico, D.F., 1956).

[67]"It is interesting that we lack [in Egyptian mythology] a specific account of the creation of mankind, except in the most allusive way. . . . the reason is that there was no firm and final dividing-line between gods and men. Once a creation was started with beings, it could go on, whether the beings were gods, demi-gods, or men. . . ." John A. Wilson, "The Nature of the [Egyptian] Universe," *Before Philosophy*, p. 64. Given such a mental set, obviously there can be no firm and final dividing-line between men and animals, either.

[68]J.P. Malcolm, *An Historical Sketch of the Art of Caricaturing with Graphic Illustrations* (London, 1813); Thomas Wright, *A History of Caricature and Grotesque in Literature and Art* (London, 1864); James Parton, *Caricature and Other Comic Art at All Times and Places* (New York, 1878, reprinted, 1969). Wright's book, a classic from which Parton's was largely pirated, was reprinted by Ungar in 1968 with a long introduction by Frances K. Barasch, mainly from the literary point of view, explaining "grotesque." She is keenly aware of the significance of Wright's pioneering into fields of "art" far from accepted then (or now, for that matter):

"He believed that medieval society (lasting well into the 16th century) exerted pressure on its geniuses to reproduce the literature and art it wanted. Then, as progress took place, Wright believed, the works of art themselves began to affect society. The study of popular art, therefore, was the study of man and society, their interests and entertainments, their wishes and demands, their complaints and their criticisms." (p. xix)

She also brings out the evolution of ideas like "grotesque." But she underemphasized the fundamental principle: just as what we think funny is not necessarily what earlier times thought funny, just as what we call humorous art was not necessarily what ancients thought to be humorous, so basically: the activity we call art today is not necessarily the same kind of activity that produced "art" in the past. Medieval society acknowledged no artistic geniuses.

[69]For examples of similar misinterpretations of "grotesque" in Indian arts, cf. Partha Mitter, *Much Maligned Monsters* (Oxford, 1977).

[70]*Great Ages of Man: A History of the World's Cultures: Ancient Egypt*, by Lionel Casson and the Editors of *Time-Life Books* (New York, 1965), p. 145.

[71]*op. cit., pp. 265-267.*

[72]*Ibid., pp. 305, 306.*

[73]Perhaps the most striking example was the fantastic popularity of the big illustrated abbreviation of Winston Churchill's *Second World War* put out by *Time/Life* in 1959, lavishly illustrated by war photos from those magazines. Blood, mud, and slugging on almost every page. For many years A.J.P. Taylor's serialized magazine-type segments on the second world war have been standard magazine-rack fare. I was struck also by the success of Robert Hunt and Tom Bartman's *Swastika at War*, a photographic record of the war in Europe as seen by cameramen of the German magazine *Signal*, unabashedly identified as a propaganda vehicle for the Reichswehr which praises "the artistic skill and technical mastery of these unknown photographers who managed to convey so brilliantly the glamour of warfare as waged by the Third Reich" and informs us that the true origin of brute architecture is admiration for the artistic qualities of the Atlantic Wall's concrete bunkers. O! These are stirring times, Horatio.

[74]A tendency to this attitude is the only criticism one might make of Ken Baynes's catalogue of an exhibition of the Arts Council of Great Britain, *War* (London, 1970; Arts & Society series),otherwise by far the best treatment of popular war art.

[75]*The Complete Films of Eisenstein* (introductory essay by Eisenstein, translated by John Hetherington; London, 1973), French and German translations are also available.

[76]"...The New Comix, which originated in the late sixties and were once an expression of the same psychedelic flower child consciousness that created acid rock and love-ins (one of the earliest underground cartoon characters was a radiant daisy-faced female named Sunshine Girl), are now almost exclusively horror-porn productions, depicting in gruesome detail and with a kind of maniacal glee activities such as decapitations, castrations, and—the single most popular atrocity in comix today—cannibalism." [Harold Schechter, "Kali on Main Street: The Rise of the Terrible Mother in America," *Journal of Popular Culture*, VI, 2, 1973, p. 256]

[77]Malcolm Muggeridge, *The Green Stick: Chronicles of Wasted Time* I (London, 1972), p. 150.

[78]Duncan Williams, *To Be or Not to Be* (London, 1974), p. 70.

[79]According to André Stoll, *Asterix* (Koln, 1974).

[80]Popular Press, Bowling Green, Ohio, 1976.

[81]Cf.Robert Fishman, *Urban Utopias in the 20th Century* (Philadelphia, 1977).

[82]Cf. David Lamoreaux, "Baseball in the Late 19th Century: the Source of its Appeal," *Journal of Popular Culture*, XI, 3, pp. 597-613.

[83]Novels over two centuries and movies like *Ben Hur* (four versions) have deeply imbedded an idea that Greeks and Romans had "sports" like ours. No doubt in Hellenistic times there was some resemblance; but that was a brief interval when the Olympian, Pythian, etc., games had lost their original religious associations (cf. fn. 64) and before they had been transformed by the Romans into spectacles designed to proclaim the Emperor's cosmic power-pretensions, with stadia covered with gigantic purple dome-like coverings when the ruler was in attendance, and his command over life and death signalled by gladiators' appeal to his box.

[84]Ellery Queen, introduction to a republication of *The Celebrated Cases of Dick Tracy 1931-1951* (New York, 1972).

[85]Bill Blackbeard, in *All in Color for a Dime* (Dick Lupoff and Don Thompson, eds., New Rochelle, 1970). Q.v., fn. 10 and figure 75A.

[86]Cf. "Popeye and the American Dream," *Prospects* (New York), 1979.

[87]"Roosevelt's personality was extraordinarily complex....For all his patrician upbringing...he so much wanted people to like him that he often gave the impression of duplicity because he found it difficult to disagree with a good friend. He believed in the essential goodness of his fellow men...and few could resist his charm, which he used in the confidence that he could 'get through' to any person." Arthur C. Link, *American Epoch* (New York, 1956), pp. 390, 391.

[88]Witness the lawyer who says, "But, my good fellow, if there is no dishonesty why should I, a lawyer,go along in your ark?"—the problem being solved by Popeye's offer to bring along a "private crook" for him. Cf. "Some remarks on Arts & Utopias in the 1930s," RACAR, *op. cit.*, fn. 10, p. 12.

[89]Leopold Schwarzschild, *World in Trance* (New York, 1944). In an annotated reprinting of the "Pool of Youth" I have tried to draw out this parallelism in detail. As yet this study has not appeared.

[90]Cf. fn. 26.

[91]Cf. e.g., Eric Auerbach, *Mimesis* (Princeton, 1953), pp. 177-203, on Frate Alberto.

286   Learning to See

[92]Friedrich Heer, *Europäisches Geistesgeschichte von Augustin bis Luther* (Stuttgart, 1953), I, p. 47.

[93]In fairness it should be pointed out that Professor Heer would be far from gratified by the implications I here draw from his great work on intellectual history. In some of his *pièces d'occasion*, collected as *Das Reichere Leben* (Hamburg, 1960) he makes clear his prejudice against all forms of popular arts, which he considers kitschy opiates for democratically demoralized city masses. Elsewhere in his intellectual history (II, p. 82) he notes *en passant* the beginning of this infection:

"From the 16th century on, Italian music became a hypnotic, morbid art which produced the illusion of a mystical rapture. Soul, spirit, and responsibility went under in its streams of feeling. Everything became purely artistic. Escapism dissolved itself in a dimension beyond faith and knowledge, beyond all social responsibility and freedom. The opera houses in Venice, Rome, and Naples became the centres of cultural activity. This operatic industry with its chemically combined formula of dreamy sentimentality and the magic of the artistic star was the precursor of the film industry, the opium of the masses in the closed societies of the present."

Only consider the dates Heer was writing, and an explanation is evident: he belongs to that last generation of intellectuals before the avant-garde Establishment took over c1955, who still felt it their *métier* to uphold the "values of High Culture" against the vulgar horde and its artistic *schlamperei*, without seeming to realize that there was no High Culture left to defend. The truth is, when in Italian music "everything became purely artistic," it was not the remote beginnings of popular arts, but of avant-garde mystique.

[94]Quotes from *Journal of Popular Culture*, VII, 2, 1974, pp. 961, 958.

[95]*Geistesgeschichte* I, pp. 44-45. What Heer describes is no doubt a survival of a primordial identification of Man with Animals. Cf. fn. 67.

[96]*JPC*, VII, 2, 1974, pp. 164, 165.

[97]Cf. Timothy Green, *The Universal Eye* (New York, 1972).

[98]This "event" is reproduced by M. Horn, *World Encyclopaedia of Comics* (New York, 1976), p. 119. Under the entry "Blondie" Horn notes "It has been for a long time the most widely circulated comic strip in the world, translated into most languages and with an international audience reaching into the hundreds of millions. It has inspired 28 movies from 1938 to 1951...as well as a TV series and a novel. The strip has also given rise to countless imitations...."

[99]Peter C. Dronke provides an admirable introduction to the social function of such entertainers in *The Medieval Lyric* (London, 1968), introduction: "Medieval song has three main functions: formal commemoration, entertainment, and cult." A mid-11th century poem cited by Dronke describes how "A minstrel was brought in, his fee arranged; he took his harp out of a leather case/ and people rushed in from the streets and courtyards/ Watching intently, murmuring admiration."

[100]*Rambler*, No. 68.

[101]Like the conclusion to A.J.P. Taylor's *The First World War (op. cit.,)* which reassures us that after all, the damaged land and property in northeastern France were repaired far sooner than anyone imagined and in an overpopulated age the loss of all those young men was soon forgotten too.

[102]Cf. Sir Kenneth Clark, *An Introduction to Rembrandt* (London, 1978). This is an abbreviated and popularized version of his 1964 *Rembrandt and the Italian Renaissance* (Wrightsman lectures, New York University) which in turn he then described as "twenty-five-year-old speculations" from Oxford lectures he gave in 1947. "Not another book on Rembrandt! How can I excuse myself?" he asks rhetorically; then answers, "It is simply the overflow of an admiration for his art, and a love for his character, which is revealed in all his graphic art, that first occupied my mind when I was a child, and is still growing and expanding." A generous and noble sentiment, but one which (along with most of Sir Kenneth's books) most Dutch scholars find unacceptable in light of the facts. See, e.g. J. Bolten and H. Bolten-Kempt, *The Hidden Rembrandt* (Amsterdam, 1976). Rembrandt was *not* the loveable and noble character liberal romantic tradition (Sir Kenneth's) imagines. But he was indubitably a Founding Father of that cultural avant-garde Establishment of which Sir Kenneth has become, *via* his TV series, the leading spokesman.

[103]James H. Billington, *The Icon and the Axe* (New York, 1966), pp. 342, 343, 345, 350—I.

[104]Karl Löwith, *Meaning in History* (Chicago, 1949),introduction: "...Philosophy of history is...entirely dependent on theology of history, in particular on the theological concept of history as a history of fulfilment and salvation...Modern philosophers and even theologians like Troeltsch...arguing that the history from Augustine to Boussuet does not present a theory of 'real' history...but only a doctrine of history on the basis of revelation and faith...drew the conclusion that the theological interpretation of history—or fourteen hundred years of Western thought—is a negligible affair. Against this common opinion that proper historical thinking begins only in the eighteenth century, the following outline aims to show that the philosophy of history originates with the Hebrew and Christian faith in a fulfilment and that it ends with the secularization of its eschatological pattern. Hence the inverted sequence of our historical presentation...."

[105]*Time* 9 January 1978. As author of *Heaven & Hell in Western Art*, Hughes is more alert to such overtones than many art reviewers; time and again his will be by far the most perceptive of any on given exhibitions. In this review he can be seriously faulted, however, in one instance: when he writes "in this bright county there is no place for ghosts of doubt and running dogs of anxiety, for reclusive Cézanne and snobbish wheezing Proust, for mad Munch, crabby Degas, Baudelaire the ingrate and Picasso the egotist. And quite right too. They don't plant 'taters, they don't plant cotton, and they were born too old." That's not the right reason. The reason is that this peasant art is about something that people care about. Avant-garde art is about itself. There would be room in this bright county of Huhsien for Masaccio and Michelangelo, for the sculptors of Gothic cathedrals and the Master of Olumpia, for their art began with the same kinds of illustrative social functions as this. Going, to be sure, far beyond what these peasant painters have to offer—but at least, starting from the same place, these peasants have at least the possibilities of great traditional High Art, which mad Munch, reclusive Cézanne and company do not.

[106]*The Gospel According to Peanuts* (Richmond, Va., 1964); *Parables of Peanuts* (Richmond, 1972).

[107]Cf., Raylyn Moore, *Wonderful Wizard, Marvellous Land* (Bowling Green: Popular Press, 1974), the best of many studies.

[108]*Heil* means *whole* (complete), hale ("hale and hearty"), well, ("thy faith hath made thee whole"); *heilig* means *holy*. English thus skirts all round the meaning of *Heilsreich* (*Reich* means *realm, kingdom, State*)—unfortunately, since it is an incomparably useful concept to explain the central driving force in 20th-century geopolitics. Heer can talk about Lenin's Great Church (i.e., the Communist Party and Empire) with a chance readers will understand the allusion, but in English we cannot. Löwith's *Weltgeschichte und Heilsgeschehen* (lit. "the history of the world and the happening of salvation") has to come out lamely *Meaning of History*.

[109]The unpredictability of Science and the resultant mixture of fear, hope and derision with which Establishments generally regard it, is a theme not unique to the *Wizard*, of course. It runs all through 20th-century popular/commercial arts. Cf. Brian Ash (ed.), *The Visual Encyclopedia of Science Fiction* (New York, 1977).

[110]Some comparative quotations from Tolstoy, Erasmus, etc., are included in my article, "The Popular Arts and Universal History: New Principles for Historical Study," in *Festschrift Klaus Lankheit ., (Koln, 1973), pp. 78-95.

[111]Gillo Dorfles, *Kitsch: The World of Bad Taste* (New York, 1968). Typical denunciation of kitsch without defining it. Without defining art either, for that matter. Interesting, among other ways, for demonstrating the principle: taste is dictated by ideology—all kitsch, one gathers, is Nazi, Fascist, or capitalist. Russia, it seems, produces no kitsch; nor Labour Party Britain; nor, obviously, Maoist China.

[112]Quoted by Allan Janik and Stephen Toulmin, *Wittgenstein's Vienna* (New York, 1973), p. 97, from Egon Friedell, *A Cultural History of the Modern Age* (New York, 1948), III, pp. 299-300.

288   Learning to See

[113]Cf. Anthony Vidler, "The Modernist Vision," in *Open Plan: Architecture in American Culture* (Institute for Architecture & Urban Studies, New York, Fall 1977): "The avant-garde defined its progressive stance in opposition to the empty formulas of nineteenth-century academicism. The shining purity of machine art was rendered the more heroic by contrast to the ornamentalism, eclecticism, and pattern-making of the Academic tradition. Throughout the first quarter of this century the Modernist, confronted and threatened by the ever-present forces of reaction and archaism embodied in the Academy, proclaimed the redeeming virtues of production and abstraction. This white crusade demanded a highly visible battleground and an identifiable enemy; it found both in the brown world of 19th-century bourgeois kitsch, surviving almost intact within the dogmas and practises of the Ecole des Beaux-Arts. Underlying the programs and manifestoes of the 1920s is the continuing and implicit attack on the Ecole; every modernist principle seems to have been framed with its negative counterpoint in mind."

[114]Cf. Joan Rendell, *Matchbox Labels* (Newton Abbot, 1968). A book which unfortunately demonstrates very well how matchbooks can fall into the kitsch category. Some are commemorative, some are mere meaningless added ornament, and there is little effort to distinguish amongst them.

[115]The standard reference is André Grabar, *Les Ampoules de Terre Sainte* (Paris, 1958). For a general account, cf. John Beckwith, *Early Christian and Byzantine Art* (Hammondsworth, 1970). Like most writings on Byzantine art, there is a tendency to concentrate on stylistic "schools" at the expense of these works; thus Beckwith says the terracotta medallions from Monza have "about as much artistic value as hot-cross buns" and admires the silver phials because they more closely represent the metalwork of Constantinople; but he no more than alludes to what such works did for the pilgrims who acquired them, nor why they were made—excellent early examples of popular/commercial arts before popular/commercial times.

[116]Cf. Harold Inghold, *Gandharan Art in Pakistan* (New York, 1968) for illustrations. There is some evidence to suggest that early Christian sarcophagi and Buddhists bas-reliefs were products of the same nexus of arts in the Near East; possibly, even, some "commercial studio" served both Gandhara in the east and centers like Antioch, Alexandria and Ephesos in the west. Cf. H.H. Buchtal, Annual lecture of the British Academy, 1945, commented on by Emile Mâle, *La Fin du paganisme en Gaule* (Paris, 1953), pp. 257-258.

[117]I owe this quote—and much else—to John Maass, whose keen acumen, employed to elucidate the social function of so many diverse arts, is displayed to particular advantage in his article on Trumbull's painting, "The Declaration of Independence," *Antiques*, July 1976, pp. 103ff.

[118]*Ibid., p. 107.*

[119]Cf. Robert Dérôme, *Charles Huot et la peinture d'histoire au palais legislatif de Québec (1883-1930),* (Ottawa, 1976; Bulletin 27, National Gallery of Canada).

[120]It has been pointed out by Allan Bullock, by Albert Speer, and many other writers on the Nazi era that the people most carried away by frenzy induced during Speer's staged spectacles at Nuremburg were Party members participating in them; most affected of all, Adolf Hitler. The same is true of adolescents putting up posters in their rooms—it is they who are most affected (q.v.).

[121] Cf. Paul Hazard, *La crise de la Conscience Européenne* (Paris, 1938).

[122]By the summer of 1510 Michelangelo completed and was paid for the first half of the commission—from the figure of Zechariah over the door to the middle of the *Creation of Adam.* By August 1510 he had illustrated the rest of the ceiling to the figure of Jonah above the altar, completing the historical scenes (in reverse order to their actual chronology). In September 1510 the Pope stopped payment and Michelangelo stopped work. Finally in August 1511 they "renegotiated their contract" and between then and October 1512 the lunettes, window-heads and other details were painted to complete the job.

[123]"I do not think it presumptuous to claim for [the Franciscan theologian Marco] Vigerio the authorship of both the programs presented to Michelangelo and Raphael for execution. There is no more reason to suppose that Giotto decided which scenes were to be represented on the walls of the Arena Chapel or that Pietro da Cortona worked out personally the complex allegories of the Salone Barberini. In the Middle Ages, the Renaissance, and the Baroque period such programs were, as they still are today, decided by ecclesiastical authority. Little

interested in theology, but fascinated by the new individualism of the Renaissance, most nineteenth-century scholars saw nothing strange in the spectacle of a Pope...giving the choice of the ideological program to be presented to the world in the papal courtrooms and the official chapel of the Curia—to laymen who had no theological training and in all probability could not read Latin. This conception has placed a false emphasis on the literary originality of the artists. Its refutation by no means weakens the profoundly new and personal character of the images they created on the basis of the given iconographical material." [Frederick Hartt, "The Stanza d'Eliodoro and the Sistine Ceiling," *Art Bulletin*, XXXII, 1950, p. 214].

[124]Whether or not the features of Julius II are intentionally recognizable in some of the Prophet figures of the Sistine Ceiling is a matter of long-standing controversy. Logically, Frederick Hartt has been a leading proponent of that theory; it accords entirely with the social function of the Sistine Ceiling.

[125]Cf. Ake Nisbeth, *Hackeberga Kyrka*, Uppsala, 1977 (Uppslands Kyrkor 81).

[126]A useful summary of this important art-form is provided by David Kunzle *The Early Comic Strip* (Berkeley, 1973). By the late 14th century in France and Germany playing cards and single images of saints were being mass-produced from wooden blocks; c1450 sequences of prints were beginning to be bound together as "block books." Most popular of these was the *Biblia Pauperum*; each of its sheets had a central New Testament subject flanked by related Old Testament subjects, thus providing rich iconography for church decorators. The *Ars Moriendi (Art of Dying Well)* was another block-book frequently used for church decoration.

[127]This theme is developed at length in the lecture notes published by Karl Lehmann-Hartleben for a New York University graduate course c1946. Where he got it I have never been able to ascertain; but this outstanding scholar was quite capable of inventing it himself. I adapted it for a public lecture which I have given at many times and places, under various titles. A tentative and preliminary version saw the light of day, if that is not too euphemistic, in *Delaware Notes,* 1957 (University of Delaware, Newark) under the title, "The Master of Olympia—Creative Intellectual?" The title, alas, says it all.

[128]*Ibid.* Although the "Creative Intellectual" article is simplistic, it does raise fundamental questions. Who in fact did pay for the Olympia temple and its sculptures? It took wealthy Athens twenty-odd years to finish the Parthenon—forty, if we believe Rhys Carpenter's *Architects of the Parthenon* (q.v.). According to Pausanias (V.10.2), the temple was financed from spoils of a war between Elis and Pisa, which ended with the total destuction of Pisa in 471. Was Pisa that large and wealthy a place, especially after being destroyed in a war? Is it possible that other Greek states, like Olympia, made contributions to the national Greek shrine? If so, did they have a say in its sculptural programs? It's supposed that the iconography was worked out by the priests of the sanctuary, but no document records that, or even who these people were. There are precedents for "a plan and a design conceived by some master artist, and the carvers merely entrusted with...translating that master's designs into marble...." (Alan J.B. Wace, "Design and Execution," *Annuario* XXXIV-VI, 1950, p. 109f.) and suggestions of interrelationships between dramatists and sculptural programs (e.g. H.A. Thompson, "The Altar of Pity in the Athenian Agora," *Hesperia*, XXI, 1952). There are speculations on the financial question in G. Zinserling, "Zeus-Tempel zu Olympia und Parthenon zu Aten—Kulttempel?" *Acta Antique Hungarica* XIII, 1965, pp. 41-80 and in Tomlinson's *Greek Sanctuaries* but nobody has yet systematically addressed the fundamental question of who paid for works of ancient art and what influence their commissioning had on the artisans who carried out the required work. Ernst Kitzinger touches on it in "Ancient Art in Crisis," but makes no more than some incisive remarks; perhaps that is all anyone can do. Sture Brunsåker of Uppsala's Institutionen for Klassisk Fornkunskap to whose stimulating discussions I owe so much and whose sudden untimely death is so much to be regretted, seemed to think so. But few have approached the problem yet from the new angle opened up by learning to "see" popular/commercial arts.

[129]Since any book of this kind has to be simplistic, it's easy to think of other examples that ought to be discussed at length. The illustrations on Trajan's column, for example, so admirably analyzed by Ernest Kitzinger and compared to those on the column of Marcus Aurelius to show how a changing style reflected, or possibly helped promote, a shifting ideology. Or Dr. Groenewegen-Frankfort's discussion of Assyrian palace reliefs in *Arrest and Movement* (Chicago, 1951)

IV

Traditional Arts of Beautification in 20th-Century Form

Forms and Function: like substitute imagery and illustration, traditional beautification is a different kind of activity from avant-garde arts of Design. It is also something quite different from 20th-century Aesthetics.

LET'S BEGIN BY disentangling traditional beautification from the modern discipline of Aesthetics. Nobody has done that more summarily than Horst W. Janson, in his "Comments of Beardsley's 'The Aesthetic Point of View'," in *Metaphilosophy*, I, 1, January 1970:

Until about two hundred years ago, historians and theorists both viewed the art of the past in the light of the present-day aims, so they had no cause for quarrel. Moreover, the very concept of "art" had not yet been invented. There were *the arts* mechanical and liberal, but not "art" as a category embracing painting, sculpture, architecture, music, poetry, the dance, etc.; consequently nobody had any theories about "art" as such; they were always theories about a particular art. Vasari's *Artists' Lives* were not issued under that title, they were the *Lives of the Most Eminent Painters, Sculptors, and Architects,* since the author had no collective term for them at his disposal. Nor was there the term "aesthetics" to denote "theory of art." Unless I am badly mistaken, "art" and "aesthetics" as we use them today were born together toward the end of the eighteenth century. Indeed, aesthetics since Kant rests entirely, it seems to me, on "art" as shorthand for all those countless activities concerned with the creation of beauty, beauty being what painting, sculpture, architecture, poetry, music, the dance, etc., etc. have in common. How far "art" in this technical aesthetic sense has become common parlance is difficult to say. "Art" is also shorthand for "painting, sculpture, and architecture" (as in "art historian") and for "painting and sculpture" alone (as "the art and architecture of India," this being the pattern followed in the titles of the multi-volume "Pelican History of Art"). If aesthetics were confined to "art" in this more limited sense, art historians might find it more meaningful than they do. Unfortunately, it is not. In fact, it is not even about "art" in the broad, all-embracing sense; it's about "beauty," the creation and experiencing thereof, and more particularly the experiencing. The aesthetician's assumption, then, is that painters, sculptors, architects, musicians, poets, etc. all have a common aim; to create something beautiful. And that the beauty which is the essence of any work of art can be experienced by the beholder only if that beholder adopts an "aesthetic attitude" (or, to speak with Professor Beardsley, "the aesthetic point of view"), refusing to be distracted by all "non-aesthetic" factors such as subject appeal, symbolic meaning, etc. This ideal disinterested aesthetic beholder has been with us ever since Kant—but, I suspect, only in the minds of aestheticians....

"...ability to find the Alps beautiful is not a matter of aesthetic sensibility but of cultural conditioning. And I rather suspect that the ability to find a painting or a piece of music beautiful is similarly determined by cultural and historic factors. Maybe, then, we are mistaken if we impute to all artists the desire to create "a thing of beauty." Certainly nobody ever said so before the nineteenth century. Instead, artists were making Madonnas, setting words to music, telling stories, and the beauty of these things was a predicate, not something to be extracted by disregarding the subject, or the words, or the story. What I mean by this is that a Madonna was judged beautiful by comparison with other Madonnas, a narrative poem by comparison with other narrative poems, etc.; whereas the aestheticians demand of us that we say, "This Madonna is beautiful *quite apart* from the fact that she is a Madonna" (or, according to Sir Herbert Read, *"despite* the fact that she is a Madonna"). This, I submit, is contrary to human experience. Apparently the non-empirical character of aesthetics does not disturb the aestheticians. It does mean, however, that they can talk only to each other, thus minimizing the practical implications of their theories....

Next, traditional beautification needs to be distinguished from the avant-garde principle of good design demanding expression of the nature of materials.

Avant-garde design is in some ways the opposite of traditional beautification. Where traditional beautification begins by searching for some existing meaningful shape, then proceeds to refine it to better identify contents or use, avant-garde shapes are dictated primarily, often exclusively, by most effective expression of the nature of materials. Bottle shapes, for instance, do not necessarily result from nor necessarily serve the needs of drinking or storing liquids; like a modern musical Mass, traditional forms serve only to provide formal springboards for exhibiting qualities like texture, reflectivity, malleability, incorporation of gleaming colored threads, and the like. In traditional arts this kind of activity was an extra, coming after an analytical process of relating parts to wholes had been accomplished. It enhanced the effectiveness of beautification; indeed, such aesthetic qualities were one means of distinguishing a High Art of fine glassmaking from purely utilitarian and entirely useless Low Art glass objects alike. But it was always an adjunct to the analytical process, never a substitute for it, and never an end in itself.[1]

Or again, Picasso's ceramics are not "beautified" in any traditional sense of having ornament applied to identify use or related to the historical experience of their users. The experience they relate is the artist's own—his sensitivities to nuances of bullfighting, or Altamira cave paintings; his personal reactions to ceramic texture. Both this bottle and this ceramic (129A, B) could be adequately analyzed within the context of the discipline of aesthetics.

129A. Bottle designed by Arne Jon Jutrem for Hadeland Glassworks, Norway, 1957. From Ulf Hård of Segerstad, *Scandinavian Design* (New York, 1961).

129B. Plate signed and dated by Picasso 22 January 1957. From George Ramie, *Ceramique de Picasso* (Editions Cercle d'Art, Paris, 1974).

Aesthetics and avant-garde design both concern themselves with personal reactions elicited by objects—the one with aesthetic feelings, the other with visual sensitivities. For the avant-gardist, an object may be merely a vehicle for expression, or it may have expressive qualities of its own—texture, most commonly. In either case, what the object is made to do is of peripheral significance, if any. That is what sets both aesthetics and avant-garde design off from traditional beautification, whose primary concern is for social function.

129C. Cartoon from Saul Steinberg, *The Art of Living.*

Permission to use this drawing, which represented a woman decorating a birthday cake, was refused without explanation by Mr. Steinberg's agent.

Traditional arts of beautification did not themselves produce artifacts. They represented ways of so shaping and ornamenting artifacts—whether substitute images, or illustrations, or utilitarian objects like tools—as to identify their use and relate them to human experience, existence and values. For this purpose, arts of beautification could be employed upon any kind of object in any kind of medium, from cakes to crucifixes.

A cook who decorates a cake is not engaged in beautification merely because she is adding decoration to an object. Putting writing, or some kind of picture, upon an object does not necessarily involve beautifying it. Canvases or matchbooks are not "beautified" by having substitute images painted upon them, nor walls necessarily beautified by carrying illustrations of battle scenes carved thereon; such activities are simply variants of substitute imagery or illustration, or both (q.v., 35-39; 120-122; 125). Beautification occurs when the social function of the object itself is defined by the way it is shaped as well as by what decorations are added to it. As in birthday cake-decorating, where the intent is to make the artifact function as a commemorative object. Because the intent is so to identify function and humanize the artifact, this is beautification, whether or not the intent be successfully carried out!

Beautification in popular/commercial arts can be similarly defined and distinguished from avant-garde design.

130A. Mass-produced and mass-distributed bottles, with identifying labels: miniature liquor containers distributed by airlines, and type of Coca-Cola bottle made c1910-1960.

In designing liquor or soft-drink containers, aesthetic reaction was not a primary consideration; nor was the intent to express the nature of glass, or symmetrical harmonies. The primary consideration was social function: how to identify what the vessel contains, and how to relate the vessel in some meaningful way to its prospective users' background and experience. These goals are accomplished by finding an appropriate shape, and applying appropriate ornament (an illustration or a substitute image—including writing—or both). That is to say, both appropriate shapes and appropriate ornament were found, not "created" in the avant-garde sense. The liquor bottles are slightly adapted versions of traditional shapes going back centuries into time;[2] the soft-drink shape was consciously devised to differ from them, and evolved from there. Likewise the applied ornament was selected because it pre-existed, with appropriate associations—elegant script which suggested gracious aristocratic living (and thus, hopefully, took Coke out of the back-room sawdust-floor atmosphere of some earlier potions); crowns and coronets to suggest "Imperial Russia," thence "superior quality vodka"; Tower Guards to suggest "British tradition," thence, "superior quality gin."

These have been the principles of beautification practised at least since the first millennium B.C. To beautify a vernacular jug from 19th-century Pennsylvania or a vase from 5th-century Greece required exactly the same process of analysis as modern mass-produced whiskey or Coca-Cola bottles. In all these cases,

krater

Oinochoë   Rhyton

130B. Types of 5th-century B.C. vases from Greece, whose shape identifies specialized uses within the general category of holding wine: oinochoe for storage, rhyton for drinking, krater for mixing. See also 144B.

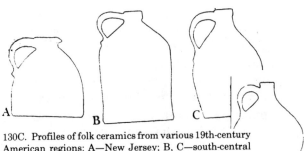

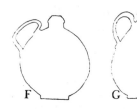

130C. Profiles of folk ceramics from various 19th-century American regions: A—New Jersey; B, C—south-central Pennsylvania; D—Massachusetts; F, G—south-eastern Pennsylvania. From Henry Glassie, "Folk Art" in Folklore and Life.

makers identified use by a shape—a shape which they found existing with appropriate significance in and for their societies, and which they then refined. For utilitarian purposes, such shapes alone, with some labelling, would be enough, but for any special use decoration was added—substitute imagery or illustration or both, relating the vessels to human life and experience. Vernacular jugs might get simple folk designs, or Masonic emblems, perhaps. Greek vases destined for export trade might be elaborately ornamented with decorative devices and illustrations from mythology, ritual games or daily life (144B). That such vessels were a major vehicle for exporting Greek culture, along with Greek wine, has never been contested. Russian, British or American culture is likewise exported along with gin, vodka, or Coca-Cola, by the bottles that contain them.

Both refinement of shapes and application of appropriate ornament require a mental capacity to analyze relationships between parts and wholes. Traditional arts of beautification are, then, as characteristic products and manifestations of analytical thought, as substitute imagery is characteristically produced by and manifests conceptual thought, and illustration a characterstic product and manifestation of analogical thinking.

The analytical thought required for beautification goes beyond merely recognizing similarities or differences, to perceive the relationship between similarities or differences. Ability to relate parts to wholes evidences, and requires, a degree of critical detachment—viewing an image or sequence of images not in isolation or related to each other only, but in relation to their setting, their outward environment.

Avant-garde principles of design not only differ (for better or worse) from traditional beautification in theory,[3] but also in practice—they involve a significantly different thought process.

Avant-garde process of Design is the consequence of repudiating the traditional social function of arts of beautification, which was to order human experience in relation to both past and present.

The principles of avant-garde design differ from traditional beautification because these two kinds of arts stand in very different sorts of relationship to society.

However diverse the forms or media upon which traditional arts of beautification were employed, they served one consistent social function—to establish order, to provide structure for meaningful human experiencing of life. That is what distinguishes beautification proper from variants of substitute imagery or illustration which from time to time may function in beautifying ways (q.v. 120-122, etc.) and likewise from arts of persuasion/conviction: while ornament was one of the means whereby architectural styles historically functioned to create visual metaphors of conviction, for example, arts of beautification are not concerned with promoting or defending or attacking any ideology, only with keeping material environments from disintegrating into existential chaos, helping humans to know themselves and find a place for themselves in the world.[4]

And they do so still. Arts of beautification still keep our world from looking like a Steinberg cartoon: "one damn thing after another damn thing." But not avant-garde arts of design. Their rationale and role in society is fundamentally different—opposite, in fact.

131A. Cartoon from Saul Steinberg, *The Art of Living* (New York, 1946). The title has significance—Steinberg's cartoons play on the theme of ornament and artifacts making the world comprehensible or meaningless.

Permission to reproduce this work was refused without explanation by Mr. Steinberg's agent, Ms. Wendy Weil. Phone calls and letters explaining the importance of having Mr. Steinberg's work represented in a study like this went unanswered.

A world where every object, human and non-human, animal-vegetable-or mineral, is given exactly equal compositional value and emphasis would be funny, because its audience takes for granted that the world should be intelligibly ordered, that the objects in it do relate to each other and to human beings in some kind of hierarchical order of importance. Many popular cartoons—Saul Steinberg's are best known, perhaps—exploit this kind of incongruity. But it would not be funny to an avant-garde audience. For precisely that kind of existential world became a favorite theme of avant-garde arts in the 1860s, and has continued so, in the name of scientific objectivity and primitive intuition, ever since. Corot claimed that milk cans and women's breasts were pictorial problems of absolutely equal interest to him. Courbet proclaimed that realism meant copying photographic form with the detachment of an emulsion-coated plate. Monet prided himself on being "only an eye" and made note of subtle color nuances on his dead wife's cheek. One of the most famous examples is Manet's *Bar*, the title itself indicating how it is to be understood—women's cheeks and gold foil on the champagne bottles, hair and lace, wine and roses, all alike problems in light and color effects.

An appeal of such art is its correspondence to a construct of the world which perceives varying forms of life not in terms of levels of evolution, some ascending line of progress from lower to higher forms, amoeba to ape to homo sapiens, but in terms of survival—and since all living forms obviously have survived, all are equal. Elephant, flea upon elephant, microbe upon flea, each in its own way is equally a culmination of the Life Force's great plan, each as perfect in its way as the rajah upon the elephant in his, or the scientist who peers at them all with supposed equal objectivity. Such art in fact has the deep purpose of inculcating ethically relativistic ways of seeing.

Carried out logically, this line of thought would reduce the world to a chaos of infantile sense impressions. But of course it cannot be carried out to a logical conclusion, for to do so necessarily implies that the carrying agent—the human brain—must be superior to the objects it is surveying. And if one thing can be superior, then a hierarchy of worth is not only possible but probable.

131B. Edouard Manet, *A Bar at the Folies-Bergère,* 1881-82, about lifesize, The Courtauld Collection, London. Precise opposite to the Steinberg cartoon, it presents a world where all objects are of equal value as a profound insight into the nature of Reality.

Hence, the kind of world Steinberg represents is absurd; hence, most people laugh at it. Not that they could consciously formulate why it's funny, or recognize what it's satirizing. They laugh because to perceive the world Monet's way takes a conditioning that the majority still have not been exposed to, or have resisted. Whereupon the existential system necessarily collapses of its internal contradictions. The notion is satirized not only by Steinberg, but long before in *Alice in Wonderland*'s "Everybody has won, and *all* shall have prizes "(95A). Only in the avant-garde world was it not satirized. There the myth of the Impressionist painter who can be absolutely impartial and objective was taken with great seriousness, with resulting internal contradictions which did indeed destroy Impressionist painting—its exponents not managing to be both totally uninvolved observers and humanity-leading seers at the same time.[5] Yet the myth itself remains, ageless and immortal, seemingly. To this day, recording the meaninglessness of the world—and so indulging futile contradictions in terms, since meaninglessness must include the recorder too—keeps its appeal for each successive avant-garde generation.

In popular arts the traditional function of beautification survives—not just to observe or document the alleged meaninglessness of existential experience, but to do something about it. The popular arts of beautification have gone on finding order in our world and keeping our experience humane and meaningful, as they did in remote centuries past.

Once understand the general principles, and the sub-functions of traditional beautification, and the continuity of modern popular arts of ornament, commercial packaging, etc., with historic arts of beautification, can easily be demonstrated.

In sum: traditional beautification had as its conscious social function the identification of use and humanization of artifacts; and as its deliberate means, combined refinement of shape and applied ornament (substitute images, illustrations, or stylized designs). The ends and means of present-day popular and commercial arts of beautification are the same.

In both historic and modern popular/commercial beautification, proportionate emphasis on shape versus ornament, and the type of ornament employed, varies according to function being performed in and for society. As reasonably well-defined categories or sub-functions can be identified within arts of beautification, as within the preceding two.

For example: among artifacts most commonly subject to beautification are revered objects, containers (e.g. vessels), objects associated with architecture, like furniture or wallpaper, moving objects (e.g. boats, vehicles), tools, machines and buildings. These do not constitute hard and fast categories. A chalice may be not only a revered object but also a container and furthermore associated with altars and architecture generally. Boats, essentially moving objects, have often been revered, frequently thought of in architectural terms, and also considered as machines (utensils for facilitating travel). And so on. What determines the kind of beautification is the basic function performed, modified by other possible functions—and this is infinitely variable.

Revered objects, for example, are effected mainly by decoration; refinement of shape can be minimal. At the opposite extreme is the utensil—tool or machine; its essential beautification depends mainly upon refinement of shape, applied decoration being sometimes superfluous insofar as its primary function is concerned (though tools and machines often decorated as quasi-revered objects, for associations with the owner's attitudes, and many other reasons).

Revered objects: an ancient category of beautification, essentially based upon additive composition and substitute imagery.

For untold ages, objects revered for any reason were beautified by ornament which glorified them, or made them splendid. This ornament might be added literally, or be painted on; it might or might not be related in some cogent way to the objects. The important point is that it drew attention to them, marked them off from others of similar type but not revered (e.g., an ordinary cup, as contrasted to a chalice). It follows that this is basically a simple art of beautification, requiring only additive composition (though in given cases it may in fact involve a great deal more!), growing out of substitute imagery.

Throughout Antiquity and well into the Christian era, distinctive decorative motifs applied to revered objects served to identify different cultures.[9] Regional character of the sort T.S. Eliot thought crucial to a healthy culture[10] continued to be provided by such ornament well into the 19th century. But since then it has been attacked by the avant-garde with special violence. It was associated with the highly visible enemy their

white crusade required, namely the brown world of bourgeois
kitsch and the Academy. And it offended, too, by the overtones of
elitism inescapably bound up with glorification. Splendor and the
like offended doctrinaire egalitarian minds, for whom the bleak
kind of life satirized in *1984* and exemplified by Lenin's bedroom
or Kandinsky Bauhaus studio was all too often the ideal. Hence
beautification of revered objects has become an activity confined
almost exclusively to the popular/commercial realm, and usually
in decidedly Low Art forms at that. But there it survives most
tenaciously.[11]

How traditional religious belief has been secularized over
past centuries and transformed into new world-saving faiths in
our own time is nowhere better evidenced than in the different
sorts of objects revered in successive ages. Almost everything so
beautified in modern times has a direct counterpart in earlier ages
and other contexts—which analysis of social function reveals.

Christmas trees, for example. Once consider not the formal
origins of this particular revered object in 19th-century Germany
or wherever but the general idea of marking some festive or
sacred occasion by decking some selected object with ornament
(especially tiny sculptures or other forms of substitute imagery),
and Christmas trees can be recognized as secularized vestiges of
Roman garlanded altars, of decorated crestings on Maya
temples, of animals decked out for sacrifice in the ancient Near
East, and so forth. And secular counterparts too of cult objects for
new 20th-century religions—like those platforms, garlanded,
strewn with roses, decked with bunting and banners, which focus
adoration of the faithful on the resident saints of Peking and
Nuremburg, Hanoi and Havana.

That utopianism and the perfectibility of mankind represent
a religion rather than a philosophy (because they are acts of faith
not provable by reason) is supposed to be too esoteric and difficult
for the masses to grasp. "You can't talk about socialism as a
religion," people will say. "Religion for your average audience
always, and only, means going to church." In that context it's
interesting to observe that almost at the same moment MAD
magazine satirized "From Old Russian Icons...to New Soviet

132A. Slabs from the Theatre of Dionysos, Athens, decorated with mythological illustrations and substitute imagery, especially sacrifice at an altar adorned with a sacred tree-form. Possibly 4th century B.C.

132B. Standard cut illustrating Christmas tree decoration from a department store advertisement, 1975. A ritual descended, via 19th-century German romantic revival of ancient Teutonic custom, from sacred tree cults of the 2nd or 3rd millennium B.C.

From OLD RUSSIAN ICONS...

..to NEW SOVIET ICONS

133. Illustration from MAD Magazine, September 1971. MAD Magazine is essentially concerned with satires on popular culture—television programs, movies, advertisements in the mass media. It therefore provides invaluable evidence as to the sorts of ideas current in mass media at any given time.

Icons," James H. Billington's authoritative *The Icon and the Axe* was being published by the Princeton University Press, including a passage which might well serve as a caption for the MAD comparison:

...The iconostasis, or icon screen [was] Russia's most distinctive contribution to the use of icons....It is only in Muscovy that one finds the systematic introduction of a continuous screen of icons extending high above the sanctuary screen, representing a kind of pictorial encyclopedia of Christian belief....Placed beneath the sanctuary and the congregation, the icon screen lay 'on the boundary between heaven and earth' and depicted the variety of human forms through which God had come from out of His holy place to redeem his people. Each icon provided 'an external expression of the transfigured state of man'....

...The spell of the icon was never completely broken. Nothing else quite took its place, and Russians remained reluctant to conceive of painting as man did in the West. Russians remained more interested in the ideal represented by a painting than in its artistic texture....

...Under the former seminarian Stalin...the icon lived on not as an inspiration for creative art but as a model for mass indoctrination. The older icons, like the newer experimental paintings, were locked up for the most part in the reserve collections of museums. Pictures of Lenin's successors deployed in a prescribed order on either side of Stalin replaced the old 'prayer row' in which saints were deployed in fixed order on either side of Christ enthroned. Just as the iconostasis of a cathedral was generally built directly over the grave of a local saint and especially reverenced with processions on a religious festival, so these new Soviet saints appeared in ritual form over the mausoleum of the mummified Lenin on the feast days of Bolshevism to review endless processions through Red Square....

Beautification thus makes the revered object persuasive. But the substitute images or illustrations which do so are not necessarily permanent parts of the artifacts decorated. When the Congress is over, down comes bunting and photos, and the building stands stark as ever. After Christmas, decorations come off and the tree reverts to what it was before. In this, such works differ from arts of persuasion/conviction like Gothic cathedral fronts or Renaissance chapels, where the applied sculpture or painting is integral to the social function being performed.

Revered objects may be anything—vehicles, books, weapons (648) vessels, people. In this kind of beautification, something like the "better the bigger" principle of child art prevails, "better" being defined as "symbolically important to the maker's or user's central value system." So when a vehicle functions primarily as a symbol rather than a transportation device, it gets decorated according to principles governing revered objects rather than those appropriate to vehicles proper. The appropriate quality for beautifying a 20th-century teenager's beloved jalopy or playboy's status-symbol yacht might be called splashiness. In the 19th century, masses of jigsawed wood and plaster made an old wagon into the glorified symbol of exotic circus life.[8] Comparable vehicles comparably decorated might be found in earlier times as funeral boats for Vikings or Pharaohs, Roman triumphal cars, Indian juggarnauts, and so on.

134A. Revered vehicle of the 20th century.

The revered object may be decorated with any type of substitute image, with descriptive illustrations, with abstract symbols, with stylized ornament, or with all of these, depending upon functional appropriateness to context. Thus the Prima Porta Augustus can be seen as a substitute image, as illustration for beautification, and as an example of arts of beautification, depending upon whether you are emphasizing its function as a "stand-in" for the Emperor and symbol of his authority throughout the empire (cf. 19A), or how the cuirass serves as a convenient surface for illustrations of his political triumphs (return of the Roman eagles captured at Carrhae by the Parthians as token of everlasting friendship, so like the North Vietnamese returning prisoners-of-war!) and promises (sun god in chariot— new day and age of peace); or the shaping of the object and its adornment with conscious intent to elucidate the meaning of individual beholders.

134B. Revered vehicle of the 19th century: English circus wagon "Dolphin Tableau," c1860, preserved in Circus World Museum, Baraboo, Wisconsin.

135A. "Prima Porta" statue of Roman emperor Octavian Augustus, in elaborate parade armour, addressing troups. Originally brightly painted, made c A.D. 1 as a model for images of the "First Citizen" to be erected throughout his dominions, functioning as a revered symbol of "Eternal Rome." (q.v. 19A)

By contrast, in this "hip" revered object (135B) associated with faith in the natural goodness of mankind being realizable once all institutions inhibiting it have been abolished, beautification is predominant. All such shapings of buttonless hookless beltless Indian-fringed dress-shape to suggest freedom in the Noble Savage sense, plus applied ornamentation of amulets, flowers, etc., is an activity comparable to dressing a Christmas tree, transforming an ordinary object into some *piece d'occasion.* Comparable too to the the various attributes by which media stars get themselves recognized: Harold Lloyd with his horn-rimmed glasses, Chaplin's moustache and baggy pants, Carson's sartorial exquisiteness, Lucille Ball's henna hair, etc.,— and to those attributes by which, in earlier ages, saints were identified: Bartholemew with his skin, Barbara with her tower, Lawrence with his rack, etc.[9] "Nowadays," a middle-aged woman was overheard to sigh, "it's Hallowe'en *every* night."

135B. "The Hippie," drawing from MAD Magazine, 1971. Another instance of a decorated human form functioning as symbol of a utopian ideal.

Closely related to this use of clothing to glorify the body as a revered symbolic object is the kind of body-painting and tattooing popular in the '60s and '70s.[10] Such arts can easily be differentiated from body-painting, tattooing, and clothing used for substitute imagery (35, 36, 37). As arts of beautification, their function is not to imitate some other form but to glorify the body to which they are applied.[11]

What constitutes appropriate decoration for the revered object is determined not by the object itself, but by the source of reverence.

136. Porcelain vase with applied painting of magnolias in underglaze blue. Ch'ing period, reign of K'ang Hsi, c1700 A.D. Salting Collection, Victoria & Albert Museum, London.

So, whether a Chinese porcelain vase holds flowers or not, has nothing to do with flowers being appropriate or inappropriate applied decoration for it; what makes flowers appropriate is association with the same ideal that makes porcelain a revered object. From time immemorial an ideal of cosmic harmony, the correspondence of Yang-Yin opposites, the *Tao* concept of the Way, has been central in Chinese religious thought, and objects evoking it have been revered. Porcelain texture and flowers alike are associated with this kind of perfection; so are birds, insects, scenes of heroism and mythological reconciliation.

Similarly with book illustration. Luxuriant Teutonic/Celtic abstract interlace has no necessary relevance for the Gospels or portraits of their Evangelist authors. But it was entirely appropriate as a way to do them reverence—and a way which recent converts from Teutonic and Celtic religions could comprehend. For countless ages past they had been accustomed to assign special sacredness to objects by covering them with profuse ornament of this sort—their funeral wagons and boats (e.g., the Oseborg find), their grave armour (Sutton Hoo), their temples.

When Christianized, Celts and Teutons glorified objects associated with their new faith just as they had objects associated with the old.[12]

137A Evangelist page of the Book of Kells, c800 A.D. Trinity College Library, Dublin.

137B. Interlace patterns on the stern of the Oseberg ship, buried as a funeral vessel (hence a sacred vehicle) c700. Oslo Museum.

137C. Prior's Door, Ely Cathedral, one of many examples of Celto-Teutonic decoration glorifying churches in the same way it once glorified sacred boats and temples. 11th-12th centuries.

On the earliest sites in Mesopotamia walls were decorated with mosaic-like cones. Down through the 18th century it was likewise taken for granted that buildings with revered associations ought to be set off from ordinary structures by some kind of decoration (amongst other devices). But by then the purpose of such decoration was gradually being forgotten, along with the traditional social function of buildings as visual metaphors. That is revealed by the well-known exchange recorded by Boswell when "Johnson expressed his disapprobation of ornamental architecture" in a coach on the way to Oxford in company with Mr. Gwyn, builder of Magdalen Bridge at Oxford "because it consumes labour disproportionate to its utility...

The spirit of the artist, however, rose against what he thought a Gothic attack, and he made a brisk defence: 'What, Sir, will you allow no value to beauty in architecture...? Why should we allow it in writing? Why do you take the trouble to give us so many fine allusions and bright images, and elegant phrases...?' Johnson...said, 'Why Sir, all these ornaments are useful, because they contain an easier reception for truth; but a building is not at all more convenient for being decorated with superfluous carved work.'[13]

"Superfluous" is obviously the key word—Johnson apparently did not realize how the function of this architectural ornament paralleled the literary ornaments he used to dignify and monumentalize his writing. In another hundred years the glorifying function of architectural ornament would be so generally forgotten that buildings were slathered indiscriminately with it—in which circumstances, avant-garde theory clamored for its total abolition.

Utensils—tools and books: another ancient category of beautification, essentially based upon refinement of shape.

Opposite in method to beautification of revered books is beautification of utensils—tools, machines, and the like. This is essentially a matter of shape identifying use. It is inherent in the activity; all utensils necessarily must be shaped to do what they are made for. But that is not the same thing as beautifying them, which involves deliberately refining shapes for aesthetic satisfaction—i.e., modifying forms without any intended improvement in physical performance, only for the purpose of pleasing eye and mind through some satisfyingly coherent relationship of parts to whole.

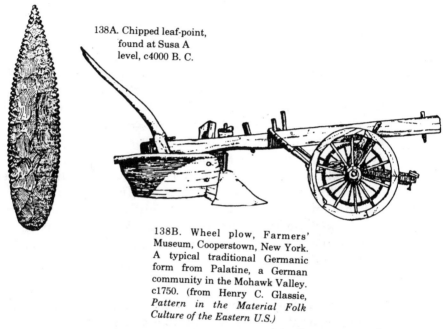

138A. Chipped leaf-point, found at Susa A level, c4000 B. C.

138B. Wheel plow, Farmers' Museum, Cooperstown, New York. A typical traditional Germanic form from Palatine, a German community in the Mohawk Valley. c1750. (from Henry C. Glassie, *Pattern in the Material Folk Culture of the Eastern U.S.)*

Twenty thousand years ago humans were chipping axes and leaf-points which look very attractive to modern eyes.That they reached their shape by a process of trial-and-error to serve their function better seems incontestable—it is logical by the nature of the activity, and a similar process can be demonstrated operating to shape every sort of tool at every era down to modern times—19th-century plowshares got their equally attractive shape in the same manner. Whether such shapes were arrived at by any search for aesthetic enjoyment in a modern sense is quite another matter.

Trained as we have been for three generations to appreciate products of the form-follows-[physical] function doctrine, we naturally take aesthetic pleasure in any form well suited to its purpose, from prehistoric leaf-points to 19th-century plowshares. But was there any aesthetic motivation in shaping those forms originally? Not in the leaf-points, apparently; their discoverer specifically denied aesthetic motivation even to the Susa A pottery discovered alongside them.[14] Nor in the plowshares either, it seems.[15] Why then can Germanic-type shares be distinguished from traditional English ones, and both from Japanese types? Isn't that evidence for national aesthetic preferences? Not really. It is evidence for absence of any deliberate or conscious designing in the modern sense. A plowshare's shape may be varied within certain limits without measurably affecting its efficiency; instead of taking advantage of this flexibility to experiment with pleasing aesthetic variations, the makers of traditional plowshare types went on reproducing whatever forms they inherited, mindlessly. This same immutability argues that the shapes of ancient utensils like leaf-points, which so delight the modern eye, may not have been aesthetically motivated either. For once having arrived at a form seemingly adequate for their physical function, they undergo only minor variations for ages—leafpoints found on 4th-millennium levels at Susa differ hardly at all from Soutrean points twenty-odd millennia before, nor from specimens found at 19th-century North American Indian sites or Polynesian villages in the South Seas.[16]

Different from deliberate aesthetic appreciation also is the treasuring of utensils as revered objects. Axes, for example, were so revered early, long, and in many different civilizations. And as revered objects, axes lavishly decorated with applied ornament appropriate to revered objects have been found from all times and places.[17] In this category come jade axes from China and axes from Indo-European peoples chased in precious metals as well as axes with handles decorated by frontiersmen on long winter nights. In all these cases the shape is revered for its associations, not consciously designed to identify function in some aesthetically satisfying way.

Utensils of beautiful shape—i.e., shaped with a deliberate intention of gratifying eye and/or mind, are rarely if ever demonstrable before the first millennium B.C. Then, from c600 onwards, examples are abundant and universal. Swords, for instance.

139A. Sacred Minoan double axe. Crete,
c1600 B.C.

139B. Ceremonial axe-head from
Luristan. Early first millennium
B.C.

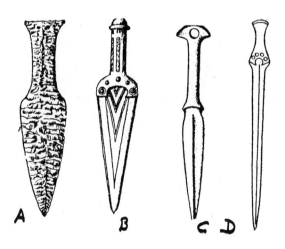

140A. EVOLUTION OF SWORD FROM HAND AXE: (A)
Prehistoric type of handaxe with leaf-shape point. (B) Bronze
ceremonial dagger ornamented as revered object, in shape a
mimetic version of "A," additively composed of several parts.
This type could also serve as a lance-point. c 3rd millennium B.C.
(C) Dagger cast in one piece, c. 2nd millenium B.C. (D) Heavy
sword, cast in one piece, c. 1st millennium B.C.

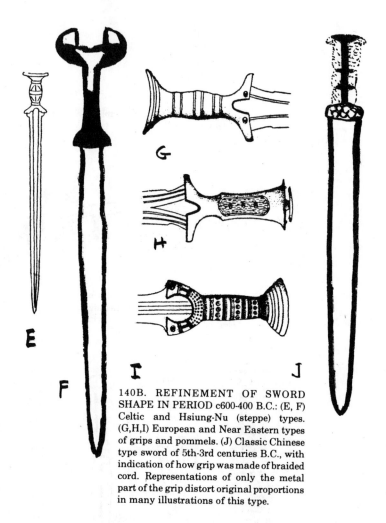

140B. REFINEMENT OF SWORD
SHAPE IN PERIOD c600-400 B.C.: (E, F)
Celtic and Hsiung-Nu (steppe) types.
(G,H,I) European and Near Eastern types
of grips and pommels. (J) Classic Chinese
type sword of 5th-3rd centuries B.C., with
indication of how grip was made of braided
cord. Representations of only the metal
part of the grip distort original proportions
in many illustrations of this type.

In a strictly utilitarian sense, the sword is a specialized
adaptation of the hand-axe, which as a stone utensil functioned
for untold prehistoric millennia variously as a pick, axe, hammer,
dagger, spear or arrowhead, depending on whether thrown or
held, and from what end. Specialization began around the 4th
millennium, and resulted by the 2nd in a variety of implements
and weapons, each of a distinctive shape dictated by trial-and-
error testing of what it was made to do—a process extending over
a long period and not much affected by introduction of metal,
apparently. The really significant change in utensil-making
occurs in the first millennium when the shape of all these utensils

begins to be modified and refined in a way hardly to be explained either by improvements in physical functioning nor function as a revered object. This change, well demonstrated by swords of the period c600-c400 universally, has to do with the way shapes of handle, blade, pommel, and lugs are refined in proportion, and its purpose is unmistakeable. Obviously swords are now no longer thought of as assemblages of individual parts each serving its own function and/or perpetuating some mimetic shape, but as unified shapes with each part made to contribute visually and intellectually. And no longer are their forms determined by a millennia-long process of trial-and-error, but by a process of deliberately analyzing how best to relate parts to whole so as to identify the artifact's total use and relate it to users' perceptions— i.e., relate the parts in a living and inseparable way like the parts of its users' own bodies.

Similar analytical processes, comparable arts of beautification, can be read in artifacts universally in this same period, and for millennia thereafter, down into modern times. Then the meaning of beautification changes; the word goes out of fashion, replaced by Design, which is concerned with expressing the nature of materials, honestly revealing construction, and thereby evoking various types of emotional and sensuous responses in spectators.

But though the word goes out of fashion, the activity of beautification continues, in other contexts. In ours as in every past age, it is most evident in objects most central to prevailing life-styles. In the first millennium weapons got the most attention, because they were central to the life-styles, indeed the survival, of peoples during the great population upheavals and migrations of that age. Now the comparable utensils to swords is machines—and that is where our action is. *Not* industrial design, but commercial design—the kind intended to make machines attractive to users, to fit them into a humanely ordered environment—that is where the traditional arts of beautification still flourish and do their civilizing work.

"a locomotive...has its peculiar physiognomy, not the result of caprice, but of necessity. It expresses controlled power; its movements are terrible or gentle. It advances with awful impetuosity, or when at rest, seems to tremble with impatience...its exterior form is but the expression of its power. A locomotive, then, has style. Some say it is but an ugly machine. And why ugly? Does it not have the true expression of brutal energy? Is it not a complete organized mass, possessing a particular character? A thing has style when it has the expression appropriate to its use.... We who in the fabrication of our machinery, give to every part the strength and form it requires, with nothing superfluous, nothing which does not have a necessary function, in our architecture foolishly accumulate forms and features taken from all sides, the result of contradictory principles, and call this art....[18]

The great instrument of European expansion into Asia and Africa and the Americas, comparable in effect and worth to the Indo-European sword four thousand years before, was the steam engine. This was the machine which inspired Ruskin along with Viollet-le-Duc, Marx and Monet, to rhapsodies on the powers of science to transform human arts, society and life itself. Most visible and dramatic form of the steam engine was the railway locomotive—invariably thought of not as a vehicle but as a hauling machine.

Yet the actual design of locomotives was not done by avant-gardists. Few of these enthusiasts for Science in general mastered specific principles enough to tackle the design problems of such machines; that had to be done by people employed by the companies responsible for manufacturing them, and so accountable to customers' (and through customers, of public) taste. Locomotive shapes thus evolved in a way directly contrary to avant-garde principles, by a process typical of traditional arts of beautification. What by avant-garde standards was the satisfying direct and dramatically open design of 19th century locomotives had become by the 1930s a theme for public derision, known (from the great satirist of such machines) as "Rube Goldbergs." Working parts and materials once exposed defiantly black and stark were sheathed in smooth casings. No longer the sum of its parts, the locomotive was made to have a distinctively unified shape of its own—a shape, furthermore, which in terms of those parts, was artificial and deceptive.[19]

What happened is easy to see: locomotive shapes evolved along lines and principles similar to those which shaped swords in the centuries c600-400 B.C. Visual unification was achieved by deliberate proportioning of parts to the whole (some exaggerated relative to others, like the wheels; others subordinated, like the steam boilers) so as to produce a nicely ordered package, controllable and experienceable as the extension of a beholder's personality and powers. Obviously there is no formal connection between locomotives and swords. They relate on the level of social

141A. "Countess of Dufferin" locomotive built in the United States c1870, barged up the Red River to frontier Canadian prairie city of Winnipeg, now preserved as a monument by the Manitoba Museum of Man and Nature.

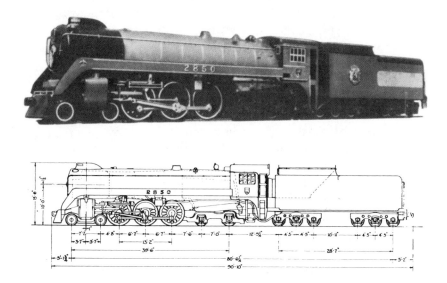

141B. "Royal Hudson" locomotive, built in the United States in 1938, used as Canadian Pacific Railroad No. 2850 to pull train for visit to Canada of King George VI and Queen Mary in 1939. Restored by British Columbia government as historical project, 1974.

function. Both did things which were necessary in and for their respective societies terrifying in implication. Only shapes that emphasized humane uses and mitigated terrifying associations could have broad appeal.

Few thoughtful people rejoice in the contemplation of a machine-like world, any more than in the thought of a world dominated by the sword—except of course such as envision themselves masters of such an instrument and using it for domination. Most, who begin or end by realizing that in such worlds nobody rules, all are victims, find the idea terrifying: "We did not imagine," Lewis Mumford wrote in sober afterthought of his early enthusiasms, "what the whole world would look like when made over into the image of the machine." Hence avant-garde failure, despite near-total control of grant- and recognition-giving agencies, to impose its Establishment concepts on Design on mass markets; hence relegation of "Rube Goldberg" machines to the category of "works of art" in Galleries; hence prevalence of traditional beautification everywhere outside direct or indirect avant-garde control.

Another powerful agent of civilization has always been utensils for writing. The pen is mightier than the sword; the mechanical pen, the typewriter, mightier yet—and more dangerous. Its shape too has been subjected to the humanizing and ordering process of traditional beautification.

Frank exposure of working parts was characteristic of the Model I Remington typewriter, as of most 19th-century machines. As long as utilitarian improvements were still being made, such exposure continued, keys being frequently displayed in front like fans or pipe-organ pipes. But as soon as the machine was perfected, its appearance began to change. Proportions of the parts were related one to another; many were hidden; all were subordinated to a single simplied non-mechanical shape, seen and made as an extension of the user, easily graspable by hand and mind alike.

So with every common 19th-century machine. Sewing machines, lantern-slide projectors, telephones, the 20th century shaped them all into similarly simplified shapes comprehensible within an ordered environment. Even devices like refrigerators and lamps which originally had been modelled on 18th-century furniture and given claw-and-ball feet or cabriole legs, were "modernized" on principles of traditional beautification, not

142A. First typewriter, manufactured by E. Remington and Son, gunmakers of Ilion, New York, in March 1873, on a model designed by John Sholes.

Mass-produced electric typewriter, sold through catalogues in the 1970s.

143A. Bronze inkwell in the form of a globe held by statuette of Herakles, with twin candlestick holders. The work consisted of five separately cast pieces—one, the penholder, now missing. Robert Hull Fleming Museum, University of Vermont, Burlington. Attributed to Andrea Riccioi of Padua, c1450.

expressing materials and construction (it became common to paint metal so as to suggest cloth, for instance) but rather as manageable shapes related to owners' personalities. All had their mechanical aspects disguised. All were so treated as to emphasize the essential nature of their operation. All were premised on an implicit assumption that good design means order and relatedness—in artifacts and in the universe. All, in other words, were products of traditional arts of beautification functioning to humanize the world.

And it is by this principle that continuity of ancient and modern arts of beautification can be recognized in utensils (and other objects) vastly different in outward forms.

143B. Promotion Photograph supplied by General Electric Corporation, dated February 1961 and captioned: Squirrel cage induction motor, rated: K-OL-6-4000HP-1200RPM-4160V, completely assembled prior to shipment. Hinged accessory cover for filter compartment is shown just above motor nameplate. Conduit entrance place on end of terminal compartment may be rotated 90 degrees when motor is installed. Model 109x862, EN 696118 E312.4

Other than both being in the technical category of utensils, what has a tiny Renaissance pen-and-ink-stand in common with a huge induction motor of the 1960s? In outward form, nothing. One is elaborately sculptural, with literary connotations; the other, plainly matter-of-fact. Nor could it be argued that both "express power." True, Herakles holding the globe does recall Renaissance fascination with power symbols and could be considered symbolically akin to equestrian figures like Gattamellata and Colleoni with their overtones of Man dominating brute Nature, or Reason triumphant in the forms of

324 Learning to See

Judith with Holophernes's head, David subduing Goliath. And the blocklike appearance of the motor housing might be interpreted as an abstract image of brute strength *a la* Henry Moore. But that would impute to their makers intentions of expressing themselves and their age in a modern manner to a degree unlikely in one case and preposterous in the other. Both are in fact shaped according to the quite different principles of traditional arts of beautification. They were not designed to express power, but to modify it—or more exactly, to make power comprehensible in the original sense of graspable, controllable. So the Renaissance pen-and-ink ensemble allegorizes the power of words in an anthropomorphic way, stating in effect that it is a good servant but a bad master; that they who possess it have Herakles' strength but also his responsibilities and vulnerabilities.

Likewise the great motor's brute strength, nakedly displayed, would be terrifying rather than inspiring to most people—not least because it would be incomprehensible. So again the utensil is given a simplified, coherent shape at the expense of expressing its nature and materials literally, but enabling the essential function to be grasped by the eye and related to by the mind. In both cases, then, beautification operates to humanize—literally, make humanly comprehensible and hence comfortable—an environment.

Once recognized in continuity, similar operations of traditional beautification can be recognized everywhere through all variations of place and circumstance. A medieval astrolobe for charting the stars may combine the names of dozens of remote stellar bodies, with stereographic projections of the horizon and circles of altitude on the celestial sphere with zodiac tables and calendars giving Church festivals—relating vast stellar spaces to humanly comprehensible order. A Renaissance equatorium may bear markings related to medical astrology. And so on.[21]

For containers, architecturally related objects, or vehicles, shape and applied ornament combine in varying degrees in the identifying and humanizing processes of traditional beautification.

Between utensils, whose beautification is primarily if not exclusively a matter of refining shapes to identify and humanize function, and revered objects set apart primarily if not exclusively by applied ornament, come other categories whose beautification involves both those activities in varying proportion: containers, architecturally related objects and vehicles.

Oldest and most famous of these types is the container. Revered containers go back to vast antiquity, possibly prehistoric times, though at what point disengaged from simple substitute imagery at all, and when consciously so, would be crucial and unaswerable questions. Quite beyond argument is the fame of the first objects demonstrably beautifed in a mature sense: Greek vases (144B).

144B. Attick black-figured amphora, 3rd quarter of the 6th century B.C.: National Gallery, London: Felton bequest. Cf. 130B.

144A. Chalice of the Last Supper (the Holy Grail).
Valencia Cathedral (Spain).

Oftentimes such containers, like any other objects, become revered for reasons alien and incomprehensible to their original makers—a process by no means contemptible, simply part of the shifting nature of things. A utilitarian vessel of hollowed stone, of a type common throughout the Near East for millennia, gets associated with a sacred event and so in due course set off with handles and base, chased gold and jewels (144A). A Greek pot painted for Athenian export trade gets put on exhibition in a pedestalled glass case as a revered symbol of Human Creativity (144B), or a piece of Chinese porcelain (136) inheriting status as revered object from remote prototypes in bronze ritual vessels, becomes a revered object of aesthetic contemplation.

Not as comprehensible, or excusable, is the truculent claim sometimes put forward, that avant-garde expression of the nature of materials is the *only* way to design. This would mean, presumably, a world in which every bottle (for instance) opened would afford an experience of the nature of glass to the opener. Quite apart from the practicalities of experiencing the nature of things to the full all the time (like a bloodhound with his nose to the earth) there would be the practical difficulty of always opening the wrong bottle. So we continue to have arts of beautification which identify use and relate to human experience in the traditional manner—arts of popular/commercial packaging, we call them.

144 Bottles containing
(a) wine
(b) whisky
(c) liqueur

a   *b*   *c*

Closest relatives in modern times to ancient Greek vases are wine bottles. They too are shaped to identify function, usually by inherited types of shape (q.v., 130A, 130C)—who cannot tell a wine from a whiskey, and both from a liqueur bottle by shape alone?—and always by applied ornament (including lettering) background (vaguely Spanish leatherwork, monastic bulla, royal insignia, etc." And like Greek vases too, this type of container varies from near-completely utilitarian to near-revered object, and its style of beautification varies correspondingly. Comparable to the ordinary mass-produced plain mass-produced terracotta vase ordinary Greek wines were put into (130B) is the ordinary mass-produced green-glass wine bottle of the present day; comparable to presentation pieces made by ancient Greek potters (144B) are elegantly packaged expensive liqueur containers seen on store shelves most frequently around Christmas—sometimes sculpturally shaped, sometimes wrapped to simulate felt, sometimes tasselled, boxed in gilt, etc.

Vehicles furnish particularly good demonstrations of the principle that appropriate beautification of any object varies with its social function. Insofar as vehicles involve some kind of power plant (sails, engines, etc.) they could be thought of as a kind of utensil, and be beautified accordingly. But were they considered a kind of architecture (because people not only ride but on occasion live in ships, campers, etc.), another sort of beautification would be called for. And yet another would be appropriate to the degree that a vehicle constitutes a revered object (134B).

Automobiles are the classic case of beautification being determined by how a vehicle is perceived as functioning in and for society.[22]

Historically, automobile design evolved as a compromise between two quite different, even contradictory, assumptions of function—one, that it was essentially a carriage, i.e., an object revered as a prestige symbol; the other, that it was a machine, a powerful new kind of tool placed at mankind's disposal.

Throughout the 19th century "carriage" meant "prestige." "Carriage trade" referred to the rich, the well-mannered.

Upper classes in all Westernizing nations eagerly acquired carriages as European status symbols; you can see them lined up in the Imperial museums of Russia, Iran, Hawaii, Japan. Middle and lower classes in those Western nations themselves were just as eager to acquire carriages, for similar reasons. Only theirs were horseless.

models alike—should take a carriage form first was practically inevitable. Not only was there an immediate prestige association; also operative was the ancient principle of mimesis, whereby in all times and places, from the beginning of civilization, forms originating in older techniques and familiar in older materials have been perpetuated in new materials when technologies changed (Cf. 43). Consciously used in beautification, mimesis can be an effective means of counteracting "future shock" (q.v. Sect. V). Mimesis explains why the very first mechanized carriages still carried reproductions of whip-sockets for the now non-existent horses; and why, though the whip-sockets soon vanished, the first Model "A" Ford still in 1903 had carriage

A. Official carriage made in 1909 for use by the Royal Family and important National Guests of Japan.
served and exhibited in Meiji Village, Inuyama, a museum dedicated to tracing penetration of Western
uences into Japan through architecture and artifacts of all sorts.

145B. Model "N" Ford, 1909. Essentially a buggy type
of carriage, open on all sides.

C Model "T" Ford, 1922. The same, closed in by
rs and windows.

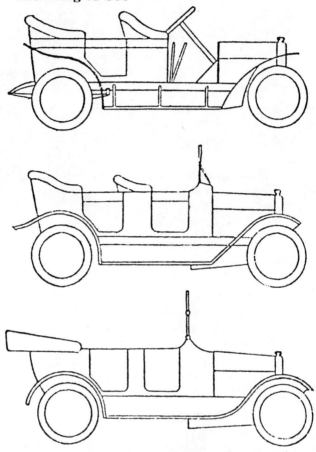

146. Development of Benz automobile forms over the first decade of the 20th century, schematic drawings from Clement Edson Armi, "Formation of the Torpedo Tourer." To illustrate how "a new and complete aesthetic of the torpedo tourer" came about as the result of a "sequence of changes that resulted in the straight hood-to-rear line."

lamps set at the side rather than directly in front; and why to this day the principle of power plants properly belonging up front stubbornly persists, no matter how obvious the practical advantages (no long driveshaft, less noise and smell) of putting them at the rear.

With this kind of shape went appropriate ornament—i.e. applied decoration appropriate to a revered object, both literal and abstract symbols, as always. Small sculpture, three-dimensional or inset, decorated radiator-and hub-caps on even the cheapest vehicles. For the more luxurious, symbolic if not actual tassels, coronets, stripings, crests and plumes provided requisite glorification.[23]

Only in the 1930s did the square carriage shape and the applied decoration of a revered object begin a slow disappearance. And then the reason was less "public education to Good Design," as often claimed, than simply fading prestige associations, as new generations grew up for whom "carriage trade" was an empty old-fashioned expression, and "coach" somebody who taught football.

That a major innovation in automobile form began around 1910 is a commonplace. Not so common is an understanding of how it came about.

"Art historical methods can be used to analyze the formation of the torpedo tourer," writes Clement Edson Armi in his 1970 article on that subject in the *Journal of the Society of Architectural Historians* (XXIX, p. 339f):

> For example, the same methods traditionally proposed for describing the development of the Gothic cathedral can be applied to the formation of the torpedo tourer. That the changing aesthetics of mediaeval architecture had been due largely to structural alterations was a position held by prominent German architectural historians, led by Franz Kugler. However, to present the new aesthetic and body improvements of the torpedo tourer as determined by internal structural or chassis changes is a method that does not apply (although a car is a particularly functional object and, therefore, is perhaps especially subject to mechanical changes). For although detachable rims, front wheel brakes, and shaft drive were developed between 1905 and 1915, during this period there was no functional or structural innovation important enough to have changed the entire outline of the standard gasoline car. The French approach to the development of the Gothic cathedral traditionally has been archaeological and descriptive. For example, de Caumont explained the formation of the Gothic cathedral as a development of architectural parts from the Early Christian basilica, a triforium added here, an expanded clerestory there; while Focillon described it as an aesthetic turnabout involving a new concept of light, space, and form, that depends on collective changes to produce new effects. Similarly, the torpedo tourer formation can be seen as a continuous development of changes, of added and subtracted parts, that at one point meant a substantially different car. Or, the torpedo shape can be seen as a new aesthethic thing, a design different in essence from the car designs of the past.
>
> In analyzing the development of the torpedo tourer, a method similar to the one used by Focillon is the most meaningful. The classifying approach of de Caumont, listing body changes from about 1905 to 1912, is necessary but misses the main point: the abrupt aesthetic departure of the torpedo tourer is well documented.

The problem is that neither of these French art-historical methods explains why anyone should build any kind of cathedral in the first place. You can, after all, hold Mass in a barn and seat your bishop on a barrel; the service will be no less valid. You will not in fact fully understand the change from Romanesque to Gothic until you understand it in terms of what the buildings' forms were meant to do—i.e., in terms of the methodology of social function (q.v. Sects. I, VI), as expounded by art-historians like Otto Von Simson or Norris Smith: how the Romanesque perpetuated an Early Christian style of simple Roman republican basilica in contrast to pompous and sophisticated Late Imperial building styles, as a visual metaphor of virtuous Roman republican society restored and rejuvenated by an established Christian church; how this Establishment was challenged by enthusiasts for ecclesiastical supremacy, who promoted their visions through a new image of the Church as agent for transforming the world into heaven-on-earth and sought a higher, lighter style of visual metaphor to present it in—the change from Romanesque to Gothic is fully comprehensible only in terms of social function.[26]

So here. You cannot fully or properly understand the new style of automobile in terms of aesthetic formalism—as Armi very perceptively realizes; its real motivation was a different concept of what an automobile is. Rather than a revered object, the "torpedo tourer" makes it out to be a machine. And once so conceived, arts of beautification appropriate to utensils immediately apply.

A new style, new form, is called for: a form which will minimize the terrifying implications of machines, humanize their alien mechanical nature—a form that will suggest speed under control, by in effect integrating driver and vehicle into a symbol of human comprehension extended. The car thus is not a machine existing on its own which a driver enters and propels; rather, the machine becomes an extension of the driver. Admittedly, the resultant sense of power was abusable—by the insecure, the immature, the drunk. But for most people, driving a machine so shaped would provide a satisfying sense of being in control of some aspect of their lives, some compensation for rapid erosion of personal control in so many other areas of increasingly regimented modern life. A machine so shaped was humanized, related to the individual beholder and user—a typical product of traditional arts of beautification.

Such a machine was in no necessary conflict with a

onception of the automobile as revered object. But it was undamentally incompatible with the avant-garde Design oncept of automobiles as "hollow rolling sculpture."

Shapes resulting from automobiles conceived as machines ad many outward points of similarity with avant-garde Design, o that in any discussion of automobile evolution "rolling culpture" by Norman Bel Geddes and Walter Gropius, lorifications of stark efficiency by Buckminster Fuller or Walter 'orwin Teague are almost ritualistically displayed. Yet their ifluence was demonstrably minimal. No such influence is ecessary to explain the evolution of commercial automobile rms. Furthermore, in every specific case those forms appear efore the avant-garde designs acclaimed for having inspired

147A. "Airflow" Chrysler sedan, designed by Carl Breer and Chrysler engineering department, 1934. Advertised as "organic": "Old mother Nature has always designed her creatures for the function they are to perform. She has streamlined her fastest fish...her swiftest birds...her fleetest animals....You have only to look at a dolphin, a gull, or a greyhound to appreciate the rightness of her tapering, flowing contour of the new Airflow Chrysler. By scientific experiment, Chrysler engineers have simply verified and adapted a natural fundamental law." This was the first production car to have body and chassis fused into a single unit. It sold only 11,292 units the year it appeared and had maximum publicity (1934); by 1937 only 4,600 were sold, the model was becoming a national joke, and was discontinued.

147B. "Dymaxion (dynamic plus maximum) Car," three-wheeled, rear-engined, teardrop-bodied image of pure rational action, symbol of the future world where every social and industrial operation will be done with maximum efficiency per unit of input by man, beast or machine. Designed by Richard Buckminster Fuller in 1933, exhibited at the Century of Progress Exhibition in Chicago where driver was killed in an accident at the Fair gates entrance.

them.[24] Clement Edson Armi points out, for example, that Buckminster Fuller's Dymaxion Car of 1933 which the Museum of Modern Art's 1968 *Machine Art* exhibition catalogue called "the most original reconsideration of automobile construction" and "revolutionary" was in fact anticipated in every important respect by the 1909 torpedo tourer, and in all specific details by the "Future-Car" published in the 1913 *Scientific American.* Likewise with the rest.

As for educating public taste, the Chrysler "Airflow" design of 1934, customarily cited as the great and dramatic evidence of avant-garde influence on commercial design, in fact proves exactly the opposite. Only Raymond Loewy's bullet-nosed 1950 Studebaker which to critical acclaim (dynamic expression of power, etc.) displaced the classic "Champion" line and in retrospect can be held responsible for putting Studebaker Corporation out of business, rivalled the "Airflow" as a legendary flop as far as public acceptance was concerned. And the reason was not really that these designs were "ahead of their time" as so often alleged. The truth is, they were out of touch with their time— i.e. its human needs. They were practising art in the avant-garde sense of expression—expressing their own sensitivity to speed and power, expressing the nature of metal, creating shapes evocative of Science,[25] or of the "spirit of the age."[26] The needs of those who bought and drove cars, whose lives were beginning to be shaped by cars in countless ways, were different. They did not want to be reminded of ominous, intangible forces, outside their control, irresistibly moving them to uncomprehended destinies— these were, after all, the 1930s, the years of the Great Depression. If adoption of a design like the "Airflow" by a great business corporation in 1934 proves anything, it is that in what Arthur Schlesinger called "The Crisis of the Old Order" which opened *The Age of Roosevelt,*[27] great American capitalists were as shaken in their self-confidence and common sense as intellectuals in England, middle classes in Germany, poets in Italy and Russia; all alike were apparently prepared to jettison traditional values at the call of any persuasive form-giver, artistic or political.

Whereas there could be no significant interchange between avant-garde principle of Design imposed upon people by form-givers, and traditional beautification by form-finders refining existing meaningful shapes and decoration to make objects more humanely coherent, the common assumptions of traditional arts

' beautification were shared by those perceiving automobiles as
vered shapes to be adorned, and those perceiving them as
achines to be humanized. Fusion of these two kinds of design
as, therefore, easy, natural and inevitable. It occurred in the
'30s.

148A. The 1929 Dodge still perpetuates the carriage form, almost mimetically, and thus
remains a revered object, beautified with decoration accordingly.

148B. The 1942 Plymouth still conserves features of the decorated revered object; but fuses it
with beautification appropriate to a humanized machine, to produce the classic automobile
form.

The process can be demonstrated by comparing almost any pair of commercially-manufactured cars from 1929 to 1940. The Dodge illustrated here, for example (148A), not only preserves the old carriage's square shape, but its running-board, its coach lamps (useless both for parking lights and for assisting passengers, since its location doesn't suit either purpose), even the old carriage's back window-shade with tassels. It has the same additive sort of design—spare tire put awkwardly into the front fender, spoked wheels, headlights set onto a separate bar, taillight on its own support attached to bumpers, which in turn are separate from the body. The 1941 Plymouth (148B) retains elements of the decorated revered object. Its chrome stripping adorns as much or more than suggests speed. The hood ornament too suggests a revered object, like the figurehead on oceangoing sailing-ships. But the additive composition is gone, replaced by a unification of all parts into a single whole suggestive of a tool which can be controlled by the hand (like a hammer, or an axe)— or alternately, an extension of the driver's body and mind. In a word, the machine has been humanized, made Man's servant, not his idol or master. So appeared the classic automobile form (classic=perfect of its kind), a fusion of revered prestige object and humanized machine.

149A. 1975 Mercedes-Benz 280S. This car retains fusion of carriage and humanized machine images approached by Benz before 1914 and standard for all successful cars since the 1930s.

Ever since the 1930s, the classic automobile form has remained basically unchanged. There have been occasional efforts to swing fashion in one direction or another. Ferdinand Porsche's design for a "Volkswagen"="people's car"—was well received, but in spite, not because of its unorthodox design, as the failure of all attempts to popularize higher-priced versions of it like the Porsche proper (so obviously "hollow rolling sculpture") conclusively proved. The Porsche couldn't catch on even though its suspended ride was, and is, uniquely comfortable. Conversely, an opposite wave in the later 1950s toward glorification of cars by applied ornament on aerodynamic themes—sweeping fins and the like—soon petered out. Throughout, the mainstream remained constant,[28] and this classic balance of revered object and humanized machine seems likely to remain stable indefinitely.

149B. Symbolic applied ornament used in Mercedes advertising.

This is simply another demonstration of the principle of the "unchanging arts": forms in living arts do not evolve according to some Focillonian or Wölfflinesque life-cycles of their own, but in accordance with the life of society. If social function does not require change—i.e., if an art has fulfilled its social function satisfactorily and society continues to require the same functions of it—art form won't change either. (The long life of "Catholic art" forms established in the High Renaissance is another example.[29])

The design of any type of vehicle can be similarly analyzed in terms of social function. What determines the form of ships and boats, for instance—apart from necessary physical function—is the relative degrees to which they are conceived as utensils (devices for accomplishing some task), revered objects, or a kind of architecture for people to live in.[30]

So in a 15th-century Chinese junk or English ship-of-the-line, basic shape is determined by essential function. A dramatic change in shape occurred when rudders were fixed to sternposts rather than on the starboard or steering-side, as for millennia preceding. Aft was now decisively distinguished from bow by its squarish shape; the available "dead" space (as far as navigational purposes were concerned) naturally became living quarters, which now moved from their previous location in the center of the boat. The resulting shape was then further refined according to traditional principles of beautification by relating the artifact to human experience, visually and intellectually, so humanizing the material environment. Specifically, aft hull and platform or cabin walls were built as one integral unit by the end of the 15th century—just as separate working parts of automobiles and trains and typewriters coalesced to make a humanly coherent type of utensil hundreds of years later.

What most obviously distinguishes Chinese from comparable European ships is the applied decoration on hull and sails—heraldic devices, colors, patterns, referring to the social and historical setting for and from which they respectively were made. To an educated eye other differences in relative proportion would be at once apparent also, which result from subtle refinements in shape dictated not by necessity but by appeal to beholders' perceptions of what is right, hence consistently reflect and mould national and racial qualities. And the same principle has applied in every century since, to every kind of ship. Over the past millinium all sorts of technical improvement have been made in the art of sailing, and specialized types of ships with distinctive forms have proliferated. But the principles of traditional beautification applied to them have not changed. Whether conceived as utensil, revered object, or architecturally, and in what proportion, has determined the ultimate form of any and all.

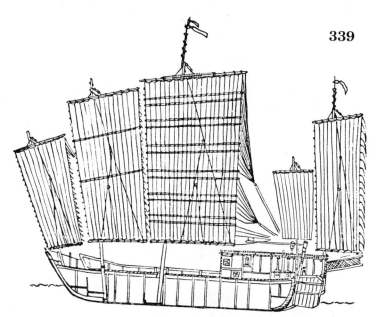

150A. Chinese junk, c1300. The basic shape is determined by rudder being attached to vertical sternpost on the ship's axis. Claims that this arrangement developed earlier in Chinese ships than European ones seem motivated more by ideological enthusiasms than factual observation.

Reconstuction of an English ship of the early 15th century from representation on a seal of John Duke of Bedford (1389-1435), Lord High Admiral of England 1428-1435. Rudder attached to sternpost produces squarish end like Chinese junk's, and sets off bow from stern. Square after-castle accommodates cabins, fore-castle (fo'csle) used as fighting platform.

151A. H.M.S. "Rose," British Navy frigate in service 1756-1779, used to blockade New England coast in Revolutionary war, a replica built in Canada in 1970 and kept as museum piece at Long Wharf, Boston Harbor, Mass.

151B. "Fireball" sailboat, type invented by amateur boatbuilder in 1971, later marketed commercially in British Columbia for racing.

Frigate from the 1770s and pleasure sailboat from the 1970s are basically similar in form because they are basically similar kinds of utensils—devices utilizing wind for propulsion. Within that framework, there are differences resulting from social function—size and weight are different because these craft were made to do different things in and for society: shapes of sails, type of hull, etc. But proportion of mast height to body remains roughly similar; and there is in each case an adjustment within limits to subtle variations of makers' and users' preferences.

The real differences between the two are in kind and degree of ornament. Small sailboats like this get slight and relatively minor decoration—a "fireball" dot; variously colored sails; small personal transfer patterns on hulls. The frigate gets flags and banners, bold painted stripes; an elaborate figurehead; and on its stern, where the captain's cabin is located, carved cornices, ornamental sculpture of various kinds. Again the reason for the difference is social function. The frigate functioned as a revered object both when built (as all major battleships in a country using seapower for world domination would necessarily be) and as restored (symbol of past glories). Further, it functioned architecturally—not only was the cabin a kind of building and hence taking ornament appropriate to buildings rather than utensils, but it had class status to proclaim (q.v. 154). Neither of these considerations affected the sailboat's beautification to any significant degree.

152B. Souvenir photograph postcard of small aircraft carrier U.S.S. *Kula Gulf*, CVE-108, 1951.

152A. The "Fighting Temeraire" towed away for scrapping by a steam tug, centre section of J.M.W. Turner's illustration of an event of 1839 in the National Gallery, London.

In some recent art history Turner's *Fighting Temeraire* figures as a classic early case of the prophetic Artist perceiving Realities hidden from duller contemporaries— an image of the coming Age of Technology, the end of four thousand years of sail, the beginning of Science's Brave New World. So read, it has much appeal. It becomes a painted document of inevitable change and/or progress. Whether Turner himself intended anything like that is another matter— he seems in sober fact to have been combining the traditional painter's eye for dramatic visual effects with the traditional painter's nose for a salesworthy subject—as he did when painting several versions of the Houses of Parliament on fire, a slave ship foundering, and many else such. Nor does that interpretation get much support from the historical evolution of ship forms. For the changeover from sail to steam in the 1830s has dramatic ideological implications only if you think of ships exclusively as utensils for moving objects about on water—i.e., in terms of their propellant devices. Then indeed the contrast is stark between majestic frigate and dirty snorting paddle-wheeled tug; then indeed the line is straight from tug to graceless floating heaps of machinery like a small aircraft carrier, from Romantic to Existential worlds.

But these are not valid comparisons. This is not what happened in history. You cannot compare a utilitarian tug built strictly for hauling ships about the harbor with a man-o-war built for fighting on the high seas; they do totally different things. You cannot compare such a man-o-war with an aircraft carrier, either, because it is not a fighting ship, but a platform and garage that happens to float. Once make remotely appropriate comparisons and the shift from sail to steam will be seen in proper perspective as no more era-shaking than the shift from starboard to sternpost rudder—a technological change comfortably cushioned by traditional arts of beautification perpetuating familiar forms.

153B. Scale model of ocean liner design published in Norman Bel Geddes's *Horizons* in 1932, completely enveloped in steel and glass envelope of teardrop form. Model exhibited in Norman Bel Geddes Collection, Hoblitzelle Theatre Arts Library, Humanities Research Center, University of Texas at Austin.

You frequently hear claims that ships of the 1960s and 1970s are one place where "visionary" designs of the 1920s and '30s made a decisive impact on modern life. And it is not entirely untrue; avant-garde Design did have some mass influence here. But neither direct, decisive, nor indispensable.

For avant-garde Design of the '30s thought of ships almost exclusively as machines—i.e., as power symbols of the New Age. So Bel Geddes wrapped his model liner entirely in a tear-drop-shaped shell of glass and steel; LeCorbusier preached the liner as machine for living, model *unité d'habit ation*. But real ships built by real shipwrights were never considered exclusively as machines, rarely thought of primarily as machines either. Still less as self-renewing ecosystems, model terrarria.

153C. "Motor Ship 'Braemar', 5000 tons, 294 passengers, Fred Olsen Norway Lines, Newcastle-Oslo." Postcard   distributed on board this motor ferry, 1964.

Among modern types of ship, ferries come closest to avant-garde ideals, because they are closest to machines in social function—least lived in and hence least concerned with architectural types of symbolism for human life and values, most concerned with serving a single specific purpose. But even they were never wrapped in envelopes; even they never were conceived as hollow floating sculpture. Still less the big ocean liners. Historically, they evolved along another track; like autos, they would have arrived at their mature shape had avant-garde Design never existed.[31]

A sign of changing times in art history was Holle's *Kunst der Welt* series generally, and E.G. Evers' contribution to it on *The Art of the Modern World* (1967). For he wrote not only about the line of progress from David through Courbet and Impressionism to Picasso and eschatological consummation; he also wrote about

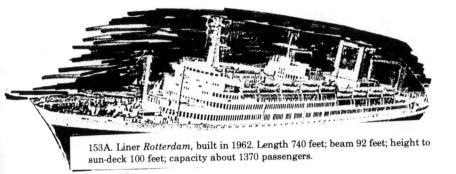

153A. Liner *Rotterdam*, built in 1962. Length 740 feet; beam 92 feet; height to sun-deck 100 feet; capacity about 1370 passengers.

railroad marshalling yards, public statuary, even ships. Turner's *Fighting Temeraire* interested him not alone for its color handling, but for its subject. "The *Temeraire*," he wrote,

> ...succumbed to the fate of all ships. The materials of which she was built were still so valuable that she was broken up. (That is why there is almost no memorial to the great ages of shipbuilding; that is why it was so splendid that the *Gustavus Vasa* could be raised, and so praiseworthy that ten years ago the British Navy did not allow the battleship *Repulse* to be broken up, but decided to preserve it as a memorial for posterity). (p. 35)

About the same time Lawrence Brown wrote to similar effect in *The Might of the West:*

> We have another great though esoteric art in the West which has escaped classification as such...naval architecture. Other societies have built ships for practical purposes, as we use porcelain without making a great art of it, but only to the West did shipbuilding approach—even though it never reached—the status of architecture. Unfortunately, since this art, like acting and dancing, deals with a perishable medium, knowledge of it outside its own time can be derived only from records, never the creation itself.
>
> The art of naval architecture necessarily dealt with the mechanics of buoyancy and sailing, as the art of architecture dealt with the mechanics of load and stress. Art entered in the means of solution. The problems of the ship were solved by making her lines and riggings more powerful and graceful, her motions in the sea more sure and delicate. And the ship, the mistress of the endless oceans, became a true artistic symbol to all the maritime people of the West—and most of them are maritime—a symbol of all that is far and lonely.... (p. 27)

In such passages is the key to how shipbuilding has actually been conceived down through the centuries. Not just machines, but also revered objects, a variety of architecture. And though

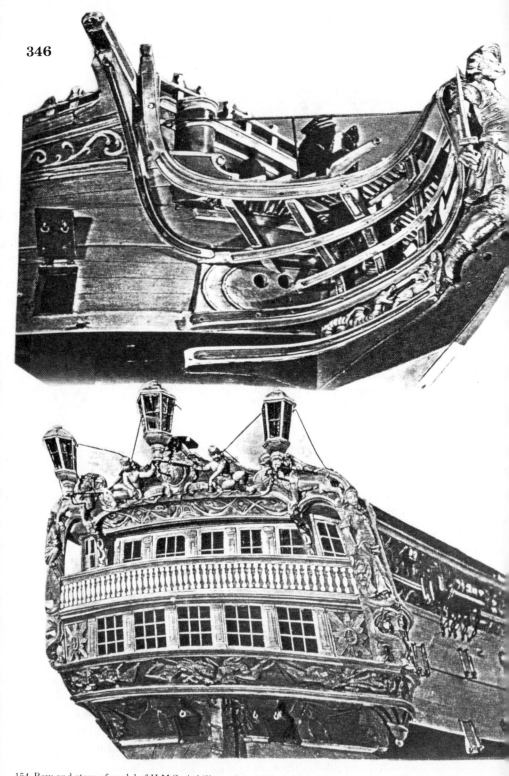

154. Bow and stern of model of H.M.S. *Achilles*, a Second Rate ship of the line built c1750, in the Sailing Ships & Small Craft Collection of the Science Museum, London. Cf. 137B.

originals have vanished, you can see this perfectly well in models—especially if enlarged on a screen. In museums this essential character of ships is often harder to visualize because ship figureheads and ornamental sculpture get classified as a kind of folk art, and self-consciously separated from their "utilitarian" context, as bits of altars, statues, glass, etc., get torn out of churches and similarly set up for connoisseurs' delectation. But that very circumstance dramatizes how close ship design is to church architecture.

Once understand how ships were conceived as revered objects associated with architecture, and the principles of traditional beautification in ship design through the centuries will become obvious. Figureheads and architectural decoration had special roles. Figureheads (by no means unique to Western ships—you see them on Greek galleys, Chinese junks, Viking longships—they may be as old as shipbuilding itself) served to identify, to personify (ships are one of the few inanimate things to have gender in English, always "she"), hence to humanize, to relate to history and experience. Architectural decoration, in addition to this function, had the special function of emphasizing hierarchical social rank on shipboard.

For ages—perhaps since the beginning of sea travel—discipline has been stricter, hierarchical authority more rigid on ships than in corresponding social settings on land. The reason is plain: life in too close quarters over too long periods, and the constant alternation of boredom with tension, fosters outbreaks of rebelliousness which could bring disaster on all concerned much more quickly and totally than in civilian settings; hence the heinousness of mutiny and the legendary severity of shipboard discipline. Architectural decoration served to reinforce this discipline, by lending visual support to shipboard hierarchy.[32] Degrees of lavishness and arrangement of access patterns to captains', officers', mates' and crews' quarters, all were dictated by what was universally perceived as an overriding imperative for clear distinctions between rulers and ruled in the microcosmos that was a great ship.[33]

And despite all allegations to the contrary, ship design is based on these principles still.[34]

Beautification can be an art of persuasion/conviction. Example: furniture.

Quintessential example of architecturally related arts of beautification is the chair.

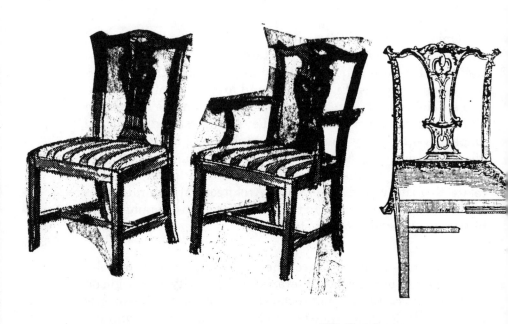

155A. side- and arm-chair, from a set of six "Chippendale solid cherry chairs" advertised for $499 in the *New York Times* for 29 April 1973.

155B. Chair from Thomas Chippendale's *A Gentleman and Cabinet Maker's Director,* 1954.

For almost two hundred years now the mass market has been dominated by varieties of "traditional" furniture, that is, by furniture more or less directly descended from 18th-century styles (155, 159). In recent times this preference has been maintained in the teeth of promotion by every conceivable means (including near-total control of design schools) of furniture designed on avant-garde principles to directly express materials and structure. It's a curious situation.

In theory, modern furniture should be an overwhelming favorite: it can offer originality versus imitation, honesty versus artificiality, the new and fertile versus the old and exhausted, the straight-forwardly scientific as against fake folksiness. In practise, popular/commercial "traditional" styles are overwhelmingly favored. Because, I think, people sense that the real contrast between avant-garde and traditional is between mechanistic imagery and beautification on traditional principles according to social function.

The great talking point for all avant-garde arts has been their claim to be "scientific"—the 20th-century's great shibboleth to silence doubt. In fact, neither the purposes nor the principles governing a design like the armchair exhibited by the Italian Ministry at MOMA in 1972 (156) could be called scientific. They were closer to cult objects—a cult not shared by the prospective users, furthermore.

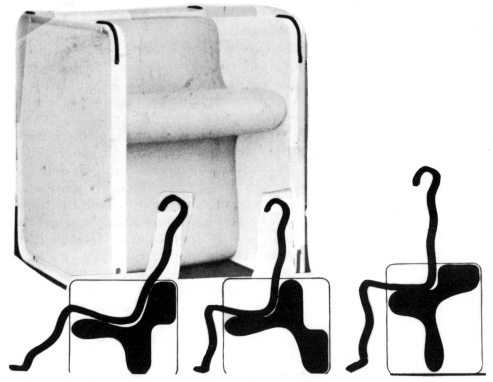

56). Rocchetto ("Bobbin") three-position arm-chair designed in the mid-1960s by Cesare Casati and C. Emanuele onzio, to be made of fibreglass. Model and diagram from E. Ambasz, *Italy: The New Domestic Landscape,* istributed by Italian Ministry for Foreign Trade as a catalogue for the 1972 exhibition at the Museum of Modern rt, New York.

Emilo Ambasz's exhibition catalogue on *Italy: The New Domestic Landscape* begins with approving citations from David Cooper's *Death of the Family, in which this intrepid Doublethinker from 1984* manages to maintain simultaneously that the present "nuclear family" is doomed, and that it must be destroyed, because if it is not destroyed it may last forever, to the great detriment of future utopian plans. Wherefore, in furniture, avant-garde designers must work for

abolition of the rigid structure and the hierarchy of the family, and the consequent abandonment of authority as the principal coordinator of human and family action. To complement these objectives, any proposed design would have to contemplate individual needs for adaptable and fixed spaces in which to enact private roles, as well as communal spaces in which to express previously unrealized and unthought-of relations....

But this is not designing furniture. This is restructuring society—a favorite avant-garde dream since Jacques-Louis David's dictatorship of taste of Napoleonic France, but persistently unrealized—as it is still. The living art of traditional beautification functions to make the world more liveable here and now, for people as they are, not as they ought to be. And in fact traditional chair design has always been related to gradations of authority, because in the family gradations of authority are natural—i.e., proceed not from cultural conditioning, but from the nature of things.

A baby is not subordinate in family rank to a mother because of some arbitrary social custom or mores of law; but because a creature who is a few months old must in the nature of things know less than and be dependent upon a creature who is twenty or thirty years of age. (Many people now and in all civilizations past have maintained that there are physiological differences between men and women that establish relationships between them comparably determined by the nature of things—but that contentious point is not so germane to the argument here.) Artifacts so designed as to express this nature of things would therefore be more humane. That is a logic followed, consciously or not, by the great majority of people living in families today—and they constitute the great majority of people, period.

Traditional furniture design (i.e., what we might call variants of 18th-century styles) expressed gradations of authority. Most authoritative was the arm-chair; its descent from the throne is plain. Ultimately arm-chairs and thrones are

157. Tutankhamen's throne, c1340 B.C., Cairo Museum. Wood, gold-plated and encrusted with scene of Tutankhamen and Ankhesenpaaten adoring Aton, the sun's disk. Dais functions as chest, with appropriate symbolic decoration.

158 Coronation chair in Westminster Abbey, London. Possibly 13th century in this form, with the Stone of Scone, coronation spot for the kings of Scotland, in the chest space below. Lions support this throne, like Tutankhamen's.

variants of the same symbol. All chairs originated as chests, or more exactly, what we might call foot-lockers, which held clothes and worldly possessions and could be sat upon. Out of ordinary chests of this type benches evolved by natural stages; then, by adding backs, ancestors of the side-chair; by adding both backs and arms, the arm-chair, of which the most elaborate type was the throne, seat of ultimate authority. Thrones go back to vast antiquity, Achaemind kings of Persia and Pharaohs of New Kingdom Egypt sitting upon thrones not essentially different in concept from the coronation chair of medieval English kings in Westminster Abbey.

When democratic notions of "every man a king" began to spread, chair symbolism began to shift accordingly. If chairs were not exactly mass-produced in 18th-century England, they certainly were produced in far larger quantity than they had been before, and used by a far greater range of people. Responding to the new demand, 18th-century furniture designers created chairs which kept something of the old gradations of authority—arm-chairs for heads of households and distinguished guests, side-chairs for ordinary members—and something too of the ornament appropriate for such a purpose. At the same time, they refined shapes and proportions to create images of reason and balance—i.e., civilized living.

About 18th-century furniture as cultural expression volumes could be written, and have been. In *Images of American Living,* for instance, I observed that the development of classical forms in 18th-century American architecture and furniture is "remarkably consistent. It is possible, in fact, to compose a table roughly correlating points of stylistic development with dates and regions."[35] But I did not then understand what this consistency implied. I thought it had to do with the "depth, pervasiveness, and power" of the classical mind—implicitly meaning the mind of the artist, first, and secondarily "reflections of the spirit of the time." What that table in fact demonstrates is how traditional arts help *create* the "spirit of the time." Eighteenth-century classical arts functioned to fortify aristocratic convictions. That is why 18th-century classicism developed earliest and was consistently most advanced in the aristocratic South, latest and least in bourgeois New England. The table is an instance of beautification being dictated, like all other traditional arts, by social function, hence varying in accordance with shifting social patterns.

And the applicable point here is that still in later 20th-century society social patterns are not so different from what they were as to make 18th-century furniture obsolete. Its forms still seem satisfactory enough for clarifying natural patterns of family life as to be mass-produceable for middle-income and low-income groups; even among intellectuals and higher-income people as taste for it is acceptable, if suitably disguised as passion for Antiques.

Once grasp the principle that the workings of traditional beautification are now and always have been determined by social function—by what an object *does* in and for society, rather than what it *is*—and many more aspects of popular and historic furniture, otherwise mystifying, stand clarified: why some household furniture retained traditional architectural character and other types did not; why applied ornament remains so persistently popular; and problems in historic furniture interpretation as well.

In early 20th-century homes, furniture proper was by no means the only perpetuation of 18th-century forms. Bathtubs and stoves commonly had claw-and-ball feet. Refrigerators had vaguely cabriole legs. Radios had classical colonnettes, or what the 18th century would have called "Gothick" tracery over their speakers. And so forth. By mid-century all furniture but chairs and tables had been generally "modernized"—i.e., simplified, unified, most working parts sheathed. Social function explains what happened.

Mass-produced bathtubs, stoves, refrigerators and radio sets came to be seen as related to the microcosmic society of the household in a different way to furniture. They were thought of as tools, hence subject to operations of traditional beautification similar to those shaping typewriters or telephones—not "designed" to express materials, construction or powers of Science, but refined in shape to relate better to owners and users, to function as extensions of human personalities and under human control. And they were thought of as tools because they were seen to be equally usable by all; hence associations with rank within the family society, which still affected and dictated furniture forms, did not apply to them.

When father, mother and children sat down at the dinner-table or met friends in the living-room, a natural gradation of position in the family and specialization of function began operating, for which traditional chair-types provided appropriate settings and symbolism. A three-year-old may be the equal of a fifteen-year-old or of mother and father in the sight of God, and to devout egalitarians. But not at the family dinner table. There, inequality inherent in the nature of things, prevails. One family member—or some family members—have the ability to provide the food; some have the ability to cook it; others are able—again, simply by the nature of things, only to eat what is set before them. Contrariwise, listening to the radio or getting food out of the refrigerator or having a bath is an activity of another sort. In them all family members are on approximately an equal level, and traditional beautification shows it.

Popular/commercial arts of beautification, then, do in and for our society what traditional arts of beautification have always done—they make the environment more structured and hence more humane, less machine-like and hence less alien. This they do by creating new forms where altered social functions require them, and by perpetuating traditional forms where older social functions remain unchanged. Of the latter, another good example is the "Hitchcock" chair which has been manufactured in more or less the same form, and in the same place, for almost a century and a half.

L. HITCHCOCK.

HITCHCOCKS-VILLE.CONN.

WARRANTED.©

233, Turtle, side chair

159. Advertisement for a modern reproduction No. 233, "Turtle" side chair, of "Hitchcock chair" made for mass distribution in Connecticut c1820-1840.

If ever there were a chair-type assembled by a committee, the "Hitchcock" would be it. Spindles from the 17th-century High Style furniture are combined with imitations of rustic folk-woven seats and vestiges of 18th-century crestings and splatted chair-backs, the whole painted shiny black set off with bands and tips of gold, completed by stencilled patterns inspired by lithographed prints of Renaissance still-lifes. Here is a melange which violates every single canon of avant-garde Design, violently and dramatically, yet has survived last century and may well live on through ours. Can this be merely an instance of Bad Taste, curable through proper Education in Design? Hardly. The explanation goes deeper.

Recall first how chairs functioned as status symbols in the preceding century, and indeed throughout history. Recall then De Tocqueville's famous words about the 19th century being the time of democracy's irresistible march in America. Recall, third, how democracy promised to make Every Man a King, provide princely perquisites and privileges for all. And, finally, recall the egalitarian nature of life on the American frontier—and that to cultivated Europeans all American life was frontier. If you wanted to make furniture appealing to such a market, how would you go about it? Give rough and rude expressions of the raw nature of materials and structure? Hardly—that would be like selling books extolling the Noble Savage to the Ingalls family. Elegant reproductions of 18th-century Chippendale or Queen Anne? Not for people trained by Revolutionary rhetoric to think all aristocrats effete oppressors of the People. What you need is something as simple to make as folk furniture, yet keeping the kind of associations with genteel dignity attached to 18th-century furniture shapes and ornament, and cheap enough to be bought for the front parlor of a "Common Man's" home. What you would get from that recipe is a "Hitchcock chair."

Similar processes would produce the 19th century's most typical wallpapers smothered in gross gilt garlands, descendants of flock papers imitating velvet and back of them, tapestries adorning the feudal lord's Great Hall. Or teacups wreathed in roses, recalling in both shape and decoration the tea service as "revered object" in original Chinese and Japanese tea ceremonies.

Evolution of such popular forms can be explained at another, deeper level also—as evidences for free choice and individuality. That is not as paradoxical as might seem from the surface contrast of poorly imitated outmoded models with avant-garde freedom to express material, structure, spirit and essence. For in what does avant-garde freedom consist? Freedom to choose one alternative only—one way only to approach every problem; and if the world rejects your solution, then you change the world—force people to choose your free solution, as Rousseau and Marcuse put it. And what does tyranny of imitation involve? Insistence on choosing what form among countless possibilities from the vast range of past solutions can most meaningfully be transformed to suit present needs, can most effectively sustain and further an orderly framework embracing both past and present.

For something like a Hitchcock chair is not blind or dumb imitation. It is adaptation—adaptation of symbolically significant forms to changing needs. Once chairs got ornamented with details symbolizing a divinely ordained monarch's special kinds of earthly and spiritual power: Gothic crockets relating the chair to ecclesiastical architecture of its age and thence to imagery of Heaven, lions as timeless images of kingly qualities. Now chairs symbolize the Common Man's elevation to the old peerage—anyone can command the means to "rule, and set in a chair" (to be Shakespearean); every home can be a palace. Forms so nicely suited to social functions can hardly be dismissed as decadent or tyrannical. Quite the reverse. By forms like these human beings have protected themselves against "Future shock" for thousands of years.

Ultimate social function of traditional beautification: to protect against "future shock."

Everybody living in modern times is aware of technological change. Usually it's hailed as a grand thing, harbinger of new tomorrows, and all that. But increasingly nowadays the dangers and difficulties of technological change are becoming evident too. Alvin Toffler's *Future Shock* summarized the problem in its title: too much and too sudden technological change is bad for people. All sorts of ailments, psychic and physical, result from people's familiar environments changing too abruptly. Uprooted too suddenly, people wither from shock, just like plants.

Sometimes modern people imagine that technological change is a peculiarly modern problem. In its acute and endemic form, it obviously is. But throughout history, technological changes have been going on, and suddenness is their prime characteristic. Suddenly fired pottery appears, six or seven thousand years ago. Metals, replacing wood or stone in dozens of familiar usages. Horseback riding. New weaving techniques. New techniques of navigation. And so on and on. And all these changes have also carried with them risks of future shock. Since time immemorial technological change and future shock have affected humans, then. And since time immemorial, cushioning it has been one of the great functions of arts. Always human beings have felt a need for change; always they have a felt a need for stability. Traditional arts balanced these needs to make change orderly and constructive rather than a psychically disruptive upheaval. Mimetic forms were a principal means. Old familiar shapes perpetuated in newer materials and contexts gave populations time to adjust when pottery replaced clay-smeared baskets, when chariots replaced wagons, when buildings were made out of stone instead of wood or reeds (46-52). But in those remote times, simple mimesis, based upon predominantly analogical thought, was the principal and probably the only motive. By Greek times this kind of designing became consciously directed at the perception of individual beholders— that is one of the characteristics of historic beautification as the Greeks developed it (q.v. 49-52). It remains so still, in popular/commercial arts. And it is to popular/commercial arts that we must look nowadays to cushion the shock of one-sided exaltation of technology that bids fair to turn our environment into a mechanical wasteland. Truly, salvation through design!

Notes to Section IV: Beautification

[1]A principle apparently overlooked by Erwin Panofsky when he took up the question of beauty in *Meaning in the Visual Arts: Papers In and On Art History* (New York, 1955), pp. 2, 322, and there expounded how there are "certain man-made objects to which we assign a more than utilitarian value" which "demand to be experienced aesthetically." For he did not explain who are the "we" that "assign more than utilitarian value." Nor on what grounds "we" assign it. Nor by whom and on what principle is the difference to be determined between objects that "demand to be experienced aesthetically" and those that do not. This is in fact a form of the old closed circuit: "Art is what the artist says it is. Who are artists? Artists are people who make art." Hence, "What is Beauty? Beauty is defined by aestheticians. Who are aestheticians? Aestheticians are people who define Beauty."

[2]One of the most ambitious attempts to define an aesthetic for folk art is Henry Glassie's "Folk Art," in *Folklore & Life* (R.M. Dorson, ed., Chicago University Press, 1972). Glassie has the perception—still rather rare—to realize that there is a difference between folk and popular art, and that both are properly judged on premises different from those of Fine Art. His heroic effort to disentangle them is not consistently successful, I think, because he does not keep consistently aware of their divergent social functions.

[3]In Japanese the word for Fine Arts is *bi-jutsu*, of which the root character is *bi*—"beauty." In French it is the same; *beaux-arts*—"arts of beauty." Language thus demonstrates how beautification has been the irreducible core of the traditional concept of what art does in society. Abandonment of any concern for beauty, which is explicit in Courbet's manifesto and implicit in the avant-garde thereafter, marks a decisive and final break from traditional concepts of what art is and does.

[4]Gregory Keypes, *Sign, Image, Symbol (p.208).*

[5]"That this concept of the artist as a mechanical, impartial observer is quite incompatible with the artist as an inspired seer, prophet, interpreter and determinant of Reality to men seems very obvious to us. Either the painter is a master who imposes himself and his ideas on nature, or he is subservient to Nature, and lets Nature impose itself on him; you can't have it both ways. . . . Impressionism as a movement foundered on this very rock." *The Restless Art,* p. 175).

The notion of total objectivity applies not only to impressionist painting, of course, but to every other art, including the art of historical writing. A classical example was Hippolyte Taine's introduction to *History of English Literature* of 1863 (the same year as Viollet-le-Duc's *Discourses* and Edouard Manet's *Luncheon on the Grass,* which ". . . stated his full philosophy and program: In dealing with the works of literature, 'as in any other department, the only problem is a mechanical one: the total effect is a compound determined in its entirety by the magnitude and direction of the forces which produce it.' The only difference between moral problems and physical problems is that, in the case of the former, you haven't the same instruments of precision to measure the quantities involved. But 'virtue and vice are products like vitriol and sugar': and all works of literature may be analysed in terms of the race, the milieu, and the moment." (Edmund Wilson, *To the Finland Station,* New York, 1940/1953, p. 48).

[7]Extraordinary art-historical erudition, virtually no consideration of social function—that is Joan Evans' classic study of ornament in Western Europe from 1180 to 1900, *Pattern* (London, 1931). The blurb for a reprint in the 1970s explained that according to this author, "Far from being an afterthought, decoration is an integral part of an object, be it a religious building, a drinking vessel, a tile, or a piece of furniture, always enhancing its effect without hampering use." That it might have something to do with the use of an ojbect as a revered thing, seems rarely to have entered either copy-editor's or original author's head. Therefore it seems curious to neither that after 800 years of ornament "concluding discussions of the theories of Ruskin and Morris and the character of Art Nouveau bring the reader nearly up to the point when, historically, ornament began to 'fall of its own weight' from objects, and industrial designers, led by such genuinely creative centers as the Bauhaus, began to adapt to industrial processes and requirements—and, in so doing, generated our nearly ornamentless modern environment." That this might have something to do with a basic change in underlying values held by people like Ruskin and Morris seems again never to have been considered—still less, that only in the narrow confines of the avant-garde world is ours a "nearly ornamentless environment."

[8]The traditional concept of ornament functioning to make an object revered is still perfectly well understood throughout our society, whenever the question is taken out of context including the word "art." Thus this use of ornament is excellently described and sympathetically applauded in an article by Armand B. Ferrara, "Old Circus Wagons Restored to Glory in Baraboo," in the *Smithsonian Magazine,* III, 12, 1972.

[9]Cf. Josef Braun, *Tracht und Attribute der Heilingen in der christlichen Kunst* (repr. 1943).

[10]Typical was the work of Kenneth "von Dutch" Howard, who attained local fame in the Los Angeles area as painter of automobile fenders, human skin and everything in-between. His work was illustrated and discussed in the popular, not the academic press, needless to say. Cf. *True Magazine,* Sept., 1967.

[11]Dress as glorification of revered objects with an inherently persuasive function is often overlooked in books on clothing. One of the few to bring out this character effectively is Geoffrey Squire's *Dress & Society 1560-1970* (New York, 1973). It is a good example of how a serious study of popular/commercial arts ought to be carried out—much more so than the light and "slumming" approach to the same subject in books by Bernard Rudofsky or James Laver.

[12]Cf. Gerda Boethius, *Hallar, Tempel och Stravkyrkor* (Stockholm, 1931): Roar Hauglind, *Norske Stavkirker, Dekor og Utstyr* (Oslo , 1973 , Birger Ree, *Stavbygg-basilika-stenkirke* (Oslo, 1935).

[13]*Life,* 19 March 1976. Admittedly, Johnson was never very perceptive in matters visual.

[14]Cf. Fn. III-3.

[15]The process whereby 19th century manufactured tools reached a shape best corresponding to their function can be traced through advertisements from successive decades. This technique has been employed to some extent in Henry Glassie in his *Patterns of Material Folk Culture in the Eastern United States* (Philadelphia, 1968).

[16]Another useful source for tracing evolution of forms for tools is museums, of which a surprising number and variety exist—all the way from the Mercer Museum in Doylestown, with its miscellaneous arts-and-crafts emphasis; to regional, like the Farmer's Museum, Cooperstown, New York, associated with American Studies; to the more scientific museum of history and technology at the Smithsonian Institution in Washington. Most universal, perhaps is the Musée de la Technique in Paris, where the continuity of tools from Palaeolithic times down to the 17th is plain.

[17]Evolution of forms in tools is also dealt with by archaeologists. A good example is the sequence of evolution in "dagger-axes" worked out by Berhard Karlgren in which shape is derived not only from physical use but also ceremonial—jade versions of bronze tools losing their practical features such as lugs. Here the basic principle that social function determines form is implicitly, and occasionally explicitly, accepted; but the principle is never transferred, apparently, to discussions of later Chinese arts, let alone modern European ones.

Eugène Viollet-le-Duc, *Discourses on Architecture* (Boston, 1881), II, pp. 182, 186, a translation of the original (Paris, 1863) by Henry Van Brunt. In the early 1860s when Viollet-le-Duc was giving these *Discourses,* Hippolyte Taine was writing his famous introduction (IV-5) and Manet painting his didactic pictures demonstrating how to paint "modern," a revolution in values began, consolidated in the later 1880s. Sometimes this shift in values can be observed in a single work, like Eastlake's *History of the Gothic Revival* (as was pointed out in my introduction to the 1974 American Life Foundation reprint). This same shift replaces traditional Beautification with modern Design. A fruitful field of investigation for social psychologists, perhaps.

[19]A very convenient and competent survey of the streamlining fad of the '20s and '30s is Donald J. Bush's article, "Streamlining and American Industrial Design," *Leonardo,* VII, 1974, pp. 309-317. He points out that the major influence on American locomotive design was Otto Kuhler, "a German mechanical engineer who had supervised railroad construction and had acted as a styling consultant to German and Belgian automobile companies...his sketches of a proposed streamlining of the New York Central *J-1 Hudsons,* published in 1928, were intended as a dramatic symbol to excite the public rather than an exercise in aerodynamics" (interview of Mr. Bush with Mr. Kuhler, 13 Feb., 1973). The next most important figure, according to Bush, was Henry Dreyfuss, who designed the engine that hauled the New York Central's *20th Century Limited* in 1938. Bush says that "Dreyfuss combined the beauty of motion of the running gear with a sculptured symbol (in the streamline superstructure) of a 20th-century machine designed for efficient motion through a resisting medium. Thus the purpose of the machine was clarified and its mechanism revealed. The complex of thermal and hydraulic systems and their attendant control systems and hardware, all of which would have been visually incoherent, was contained within a handsome shell." This is a matter of degree. If we comp ire an illustration of Dreyfuss' engine with the avant-garde concept of Normal Bel Geddes in 1931, which "stretched an air-foil of steel and glass over a conventional steam engine, placing the cab in front for greater visibility," it will be seen that in fact Dreyfuss played down the symbol of power, and retained a great many elements of decoration appropriate to a revered object and a humanized artifact.

[20]It may be more than a passing curiosity that the typewriter and the slide projector (or magic lantern, as it was originally known) both originated in the same decade of the 1870s. The first slide lecture in history was given at the Technische Hochschule in Karlsruhe (now the University) in 1873, and its centenary celebrated with appropriate ceremony in 1973.

[21]There are some particularly good examples of early scientific instruments in the Museum of Science at Oxford. For example, an astrolabe of about 1370, closely resembling drawings in the extant manuscripts of Geoffrey Chaucer's *Tractatus de conclusionibus astrolabii* of 1391, referred to here.

[22]For a good general survey of the automobile as a sociological and economic phenomenon, see John B. Rae, *The American Automobile* (Chicago, 1965). Also noteworthy

are Frederick A. Talbot, *Motor-cars and Their Story* (London, 1912) and Kent Karslake and Lawrence Pomeroy, *From Veteran to Vintage* (London, 1956). The latter is remarkable for its grasp of the automobile as a revered object; the former, because Talbot as a manufacturer of English luxury cars, was seriously concerned to define what kind of shape appealed to the public. His basic objection was that the American mass-produced car was too much of a machine, offered too little human satisfactions to its owner.

[23]An outstanding example of how *not* to write about popular arts—so outstanding, indeed, that it almost seems a spoof—is Erwin Panofsky's, "The Ideological Antecedents of the Rolls-Royce Radiator," in *Proceedings of the American Philosophical Society*, 107, 4, 1963, p. 273f. In this article Panofsky gives his usual dazzling display of erudition, ranging over matters art historical from the early Middle Ages through the 18th century, in what seems almost (and may indeed have been intended as) a parody of Nikolaus Pevsner's *The Englishness of English Art*. Nowhere is an automobile even mentioned until the very last paragraph where we learn that the radiator ornament, designed by Charles Sykes, R.A. "was added as early as 1911 to the Rolls-Royce." Panofsky's point seems to be that in some manner Rolls-Royces are typically, English, product of the same people who gave us Lincoln Cathedral and Chiswick House. Nowhere is there the slightest hint of any awareness that the design of a vehicle involves the traditional art of beautification, or that one might consider the radiator ornament of a Rolls-Royce with the same seriousness as the pinnacle on a cathedral. But then Panofsky was always curiously blind in this area, assuming acceptable avant-garde positions without ever investigating them.

[24]Anticipation of avant-garde forms in popular/commercial arts, rather than the other way round, is the rule (cf. *The Unchanging Arts;* fn. I-48). In automobile design, it seems that avant-garde designers picked up, and made metaphysical symbols out of, forms originating in commercial airplanes which were *not* designed by the avant-garde. Thus Walter Dorwin Teague pushed aerodynamic symbolism in *Design This Day* (New York, 1940) talking about the contour lines of Boeing 247s and Douglas DC-1s

Several other examples occur in Sterling McIlhany's *Art As Design: Design as Art* (New York, 1970), outstanding among the few attempts to deal with the interrelations of commercial design, Fine Art, industrial design, pop art, and other kinds of avant-garde painting. McIlhany has the great merit of taking commercial art seriously, and in so studying it, has discovered that it precedes avant-garde artists in the invention of almost every form (for example, on p. 30 he cites a trade sign in the form of spectacles, "designed long before the advent of surrealism or pop art, this hypnotic sign is a marvelous example of both styles.") But he never develops the principle thus revealed—hence never speculates on why commercial arts, serving a social function, might necessarily precede avant-garde in invention of new forms. That is because he never emphasizes how the function of avant-garde Establishment arts in and for society is totally different from the social function of commercial design, even though this can be abundantly demonstrated from the material he has assembled.

[25]Donald Bush in "Streamlining and American Industrial Design" quotes the Chrysler Corporation advertisement for the "new air-flow Chrysler" in *Fortune,* IX, 4 (1934) and points out that fashionable torpedo-type stream-lining of the 1930s was not in fact scientific. Avant-garde promoters simply ignored the evidence against it. Bush points out that "a dispute over the need for stream-lining automobiles raged amongst knowledgeable contributors to *Scientific American,* the *American Mercury,* and other American magazines. Wind-tunnell tests run by the Bureau of Standards in 1934 indicated a considerable reduction in drag was possible with an *Airflow*-type body but that a true tear-drop shape body offered only a very slight improvement over it...little attention was given to the discovery in 1935 by Georg Madelung that at higher automotive speeds a tapered rear was unnecessary, or to the results of tests by Wunibald Kamm that led to the Kamm-back or K-form, smoothly contoured in front but ending abruptly in a vertical flat surface (the reference here is to K. Ludvigsen, "Automobile Aerodynamics: Form and Fashion," *Automobile Q,* VI, 2 [1967]). The shape was so ugly nobody then adopted it. But there have been a number of quasi-avant-garde designs marketed in the '60s and '70s, both of the "hollow rolling sculpture type" and the Kamm-back (most notably American Motors' *Gremlin.*). Predictably, their sales have been limited.

[26]Bush makes an interesting analogy of streamlining with certain fashionable avant-garde trends in the 1930s.

"A number of authors, notably James Joyce, have used the stream-of-consciousness technique to reveal the thoughts of their characters, their assumption being that the mind is a mixture of various levels of awareness, an unending flow of sensations, thoughts, memories, associations, and reflections. The technique emphasizes the active character of the mind and the merging and blending of thoughts. The philosopher John Dewey regarded experience as a smooth continuum. In his *Art and Experience* (1934) published the year the *Airflow* and the *Zephyr* appeared, he wrote of memorable experiences that: '...every successive part flows freely, without seam and without unfilled blanks into what ensues...there are no pauses, places of rest, but they punctuate and define the quality of movement, they sum up what has been undergone and prevent its dissipation and idle evaporation. Continued acceleration is breathless and prevents parts from gaining distinction. In a work of art, different act, episodes, and occurrences melt and fuse into a unity and yet do not disappear and lose their character as they do so'."

[27]It is worth keeping firmly in mind that at the same time streamlining was being introduced and symbols of power and efficiency promoted by the avant-garde, the Old Order of American society (accepted since the Civil War, perhaps since the founding of the Republic) was undergoing a nervous breakdown. Arthur Schlesinger described it in the first volume of his *Age of Roosevelt—the Crisis of the Old Order* (Boston, 1957):
"In February 1933, the Senate Finance Committee summoned a procession of business leaders to solicit their ideas on the crisis.... As they spoke their lusterless pieces, the banks be, an to close their doors. 'Our entire banking system,' said William Gibbs McAdoo in exasperation, 'does credit to a collection of imbeciles.'

"But bankruptcy of ideas seemed almost as complete among the intellectuals. 'My heart-break at liberalism,' wrote William Allen White, 'is that it has sounded no note of hope, made no plans for the future, offered no program'....Others, in their despair, could only yearn for a saviour. Hamilton Fish, the New York Congressman spoke for millions when he wrote to Roosevelt late in February that in the crisis we must 'give you any power that you may need.'

"The images of a nation as it approached zero hour: the well-groomed men, baffled and impotent in their double-breasted suits, before the Senate Committee; the confusion and dismay in the business office and in the university; the fear in the Country Club; the angry men marching in the silent street; the scramble for the rotting garbage ·n the dump; the sweet milk trickling down the dusty road; the noose dangling over the barn door; the raw northwest wind blasting its way across the Capital Plaza." (Prologue: 1933, pp. 4-5)
These were the people who within a few years would be sponsoring avant-garde painters and architects; as Wolf von Eckardt noted cynically in *Back to the Drawing Board,* mechanistic formulas for urban renewal which had been rejected in Russia and ignored in Western Europe were rescued from oblivion by American corporations, to whose ideology (if not, indeed, existence!) Gropius, Corbusier, Giedion and the rest were so scornfully opposed.

[28]Useful illustrations and brief summaries of trends can be found in the section on automobiles (especially pp. 89-95) of Sterling McIlhaney's *Art as Design: Design as Art* (New York, 1970).
[29]Cf. Fred Schroeder, *Outlaw Aesthetics, op. cit.*
[30]The following paragraph from Lawrence Brown's *Might of the West* (p. 28) is worth reproducing, without necessarily agreeing with his premises or conclusions as to any implications for cultural history:
"We know very little about the early ships or their builders as we know little about the early architects of the West, but by 1400, the fundamental form of the ocean-going ship had been designed and that form remained the type of the ship for as long as the art lasted, that is, until it became purely practical engineering in the days of iron and steam. This type was the three-masted, square-rigged ship, still showing the marks of the galley and the Mediterranean in her latteen-rigged mizzen and the ancient Roman rostrum, the galley's beak, at her bows. From then on aesthetic refinements took place, many with only incidental practical significance. There was a maze of inter-related problems in proportion: the spacing and rake of the masts, the proportion of the lower masts to the beam and length of the vessel, the

proportion of the upper masts to the lower, the proportion of the three masts, one to another, the angle and length of bowsprit, the length and vertical spacing of the spars. In these problems, within wide ranges, aesthetic not practical considerations determined the final design as Sir Henry Manwayring point out in 1644. 'There is no absolute proportions in these, and the like things, for if a man will have his mast short, he may the bolder make his topmast long.' The ultimate proportions arrived at were those that created a moving object of great beauty and symbolic content. Viewed abstractly a ship is simply a building designed to move over the water rather than to stand firm on the land. To a society that feels at home on the sea, it is as natural a means of artistic expression as land buildings have always been to all societies."

[31]It might be more accurate to classify avant-garde Designers of the 1930s in with Science Fiction rather than practical arts of any kind. They were persistently futuristic. That is not necessarily the same thing as having a profound influence on the future. To be sure, it could be pointed out that Bel Geddes envisaged a transatlantic airliner carrying hundreds of passengers and crew, which got lots of play in the press, and might be called premonitions of "Fat Alberts"(747s) introduced in the '70s. But there is no reason to suppose that the 747 would not have been invented had Geddes never lived. It was the logical culmination of a line of evolution instituted by practical engineers and scientists. Avant-garde Design of the '30s could be better described as pseudo-scientific, simply extrapolating from existing data, like the prognostications satirized by G.K. Chesterton—dandelions being a quarter-inch taller this year than last, within 30 years dandelions must grow higher than the housetops, etc. In fact, the most futuristic of all designs of this period probably can be found in *Buck Rogers*, the first American science-fiction comic strip (1929-1965— i.e. from the Depression to the time rocket ships became commonplace!) In it were anticipated fashionable torpedo shapes, "Streamlined Modern" and all the other day-dreamings of a totally different kind of existence brought about by miracle-working Science.

[32]Historically, there seems to be an inverse compensating relationship between regimentation of military force and humanizing of equipment. For example, up to the late 17th century, all navy vessels except First-Rate used only the Crowned Lion as a figure head. Individualized and personalized figureheads began to appear on second rates around 1700; in 1727 smaller ships were authorized to use appropriate figureheads, and by 1760 all ships were personalized. It was precisely during these years that drill in the army became more and more mechanical, under the influence first of Calvinist Holland and then Frederick the Great's free-thinking Prussia. In World War II, flights were dispatched by radar and controlled by ground radio, but airplanes were decorated with individual insignia; the same with tanks. It is the nature of human beings to compensate, if allowed any freedom at all.

[33]That ships and shipboard life are microcosmic is a commonplace in literature: *Moby Dick; Mutiny on the Bounty; The Caine Mutiny*, etc.

[34]"The shipbuilding art reached its final development in the first half of the 19th century," Lawrence Brown wrote (*Might of the West*, 29-33), "and was one of the few arts flowing late enough in Western life
"...to include Americans among its great practitioners. The two greatest of the American naval architects were Joshua Humphreys of Philadelphia who designed John Adams' frigates and Donald McKay of Boston who established the type of American clipper. Then the art died, as architecture as a great creative art died a generation before. The two techniques are today almost completely parallel: deliberate archaism as in sailing yachts and ecclesiastical and academic building, eclecticism or modernism spread thin over minimum mechanical workability as in passenger vessels, power yachts, hotels and domestic construction, and unadulterated, undisguised engineering in war ships and freighters, bridges, highways, and industrial plants."

A common enough view. Brown, like too many others, here and elsewhere assumes that avant-garde Design is the only art of beautification we have left; compares it to traditional beautification; comes to the inevitable conclusion that all is over. *Homo, circumspice!*

[35]II, 7. "Diversity Within Unity, The Classical Mind as Regional and Class Expression," pp. 173 ff.

V

Traditional Arts of Persuasion/Conviction In Twentieth-Century Forms

Definitions and Distinctions

Historically, arts of substitute imagery, illustration and beautification all may and on occasion have had persuasive/convictive functions. But arts of persuasion/conviction proper are very specialised, distinguished by two characteristics: forms having full meaning only with reference to some body of ideas or ideology outside themselves; and conscious styles associated with and shifting in response to such ideologies.

PERSUASION AND CONVICTION are complementary functions. The language proves as much. Despite the dictionary definition that "conviction" means "assent founded on satisfactory proofs which appeal to reason" while "persuasion" means "assent founded on what appeals to the feelings and imagination," for practical purposes, "I am persuaded," means "I am convinced," in English (and most other languages). "You'll have to convince me of that," means "You'll have to persuade me by logic and facts." Arts of persuasion/conviction are correspondingly complicated and interrelated, and complicated by being on occasion either implicit or explicit, or both.

All arts anywhere can have an implicit function of persuasion/conviction in given circumstances. Persuasion, by the very fact of their existence; conviction, by the fact of somebody's expending the time, energy and resources to make and/or pay for them. In that sense, persuasion/conviction was the first reason for artistic activity in history, and the earliest motive for child art. In that sense we have on occasion already considered substitute imagery, illustration and beautification as variant arts of persuasion/conviction (q.v.).

Arts with explicit functions of persuasion/conviction have two distinguishing characteristics. First, forms which have no meaning or only partial meaning except with reference to an outside body of abstract ideas, or an ideology; and second, deliberate styling of forms to create effects or establish associations pertaining to such ideas or ideologies. On reflection, it will be self-evident that these characteristics are interrelated.

Proof of deliberate styling is only possible when there is some extrinsic framework of reference by means of which the forms derive their meaning and communicate. Self-evidently, arts which so subsume, use and depend upon all the others, and which demand a complicated mental process of transference from tangible symbol to abstract idea or value-system and back, will appear last in child development; and there is some reason to believe that they appear last in history too (q.v. Sect. VI).

Obviously a given persuasive style will, if its persuasion be successful and the ideology it promotes be generally accepted, in its turn become a/the style of established conviction. Whence it follows that persuasive arts will more commonly be ephemeral (song, sermon, ballad, drawing, painting), arts of conviction more commonly solid, like sculpture and architecture.

In this social function, too, popular/commercial arts of our time are the successors of traditional and historic arts; here again, avant-garde arts are of a different order from either.
Comparisons will make the point.

The ancient Assyrian battle reliefs, though we assume they must have been put up to strike terror into enemies of Assyria, in fact don't actually persuade viewers to any conclusions (160A). They present facts, relate stories, whence viewers draw their own conclusions. There is plenty of symbolism, but it is all related by logical sequences to the main theme; it is all intelligible without any reference being required to anything outside the picture itself.
Specifically: lines of battlements commonly appear in Assyrian battle illustrations as symbols of a city. An abstract symbol thrice removed from actuality—shorthand representation of a brick form mimetically reproducing

160A. Scenes of the capture of the city of Lachish, from an 8th-century B.C. Assyrian palace relief. Siege engine with battering ram; ruins raining down from the walls; refugees fleeing; resisters impaled on stakes.

primaeval mud and wood and wicker shapes. But all logically related one to the next, all quite intelligible without reference to any ideas outside themselves.

Like all ancient illustrations of this type, their clarification and elucidation of triumphs in battle necessarily affirmed the powers and glory of kings and pharaohs. But whatever persuasion/conviction they effected was by deduction on the viewers' part—in this respect anticipating 19th-century academic narrative paintings, 20th-century war movies, and advertising, none of which require an outside frame of reference for intelligibility either, nor afford demonstrable proof of persuasive/convictive function from external evidence (q.v. 214f.)

I'M BRINGING PEACE TO THE
POOR SUFFERING BASQUES

160B. Cartoon by David Low protesting the bombing of
the Basque town of Guernica during the Spanish Civil
War, by planes under the command of General Franco,
who is represented standing in the midst of the ruined
city, which appeared in the *London Daily Express* on 22
June, 1937.

By contrast, David Low's cartoon makes almost no sense in
itself. A dumpy military officer stands amidst desolate ruins
saying, "I'm bringing peace to the suffering Basques." So what?
So nothing—as it stands. For intelligibility, the picture must be
seen in reference to a set of ideas outside itself. That is what
distinguishes it as persuasive art proper. Its purpose is not to
make a substitute-image picture of the town of Guernica nor of
Franco, nor to illustrate an event; its purpose is to use these
images to persuade you that Fascism (the cluster of ideas
subsumed under that word) is wicked. It uses substitute images
and illustration for that purpose.

To effect its purpose, Low's cartoon relies upon more complex
thought processes than those involved in the Assyrian relief (or
any ordinary illustration). The Assyrian relief is related to the
city of Lachish, and to neighboring reliefs of other conquests and
doings of kings, as spokes are related along the rim of a wheel: one
symbol leads logically to the next, "this thing is like that thing."
But Low's cartoon is related to the town of Guernica and to other
arts dealing with Fascism only indirectly—as spokes are related
to each other *via* the hub of the wheel. The hub in this metaphor is
the abstract cluster of ideas, principles and attitudes called anti-
Fascism.

So thinking in terms of abstract causality—relating facts to abstract systems of ideas, reducing them to principles, then re-introducing them to material contexts—employs and subsumes all earlier levels of thought. The kind of analogical thought involved in ordinary illustration, the conceptual thought involved in substitute imagery and the analytical thought on which beautification depends, all are involved. Historically, abstract causal thinking could not, then, have appeared before the others; and indeed the first unequivocal demonstrations of it occur in dramatic shifts of style from literal and naturalistic to abstract and symbolic which occur in arts of the early centuries A.D., both in the Christian West and the Buddhist East.[1]

Avant-garde art employs abstract causal thought also.[2]

160C. Postcard distributed by Museum of Modern Art, New York, of Picasso's 1937 painting "Guernica"—which he called a "weapon in the struggle against Fascism" generally, and specifically a protest against German and Italian planes bombing the Basque town of Guernica during the Spanish Civil War.

Here, surely, is one area where avant-garde arts have an objective social function comparable to historic arts. One can even point to a change of style for purposes of ideological impact:

Guernica's surrealism is supposed to make a deliberately total contrast to earlier styles of bourgeois war pictures (cf. 103B). Juan Larrea in his book on *Guernica* meant it as the highest compliment that

> Everything has been considered inherent in the art of painting, even by the most advanced schools: light, color, precision of plasticity, of drawing...are here conspicuously lacking. The most that can be said to remain is a clean surface upon which we follow the alternative syncopations of blacks with greys and whites, in a mysterious drama of vital disorder, with a marked tendency towards triangulation....[5]

The trouble is, that in traditional arts of persuasion/conviction style is inseparable from content and vice-versa. To lack either component is to lack persuasion/conviction. Each made the other intelligible and relevant. But in an art like Picasso's, content is by the artist's own admission and intent insignificant and solipsistic. It follows, as Larrea says,

> Clearly, then, the reality conveyed by the *Guernica* is not a physical but a mental reality...a dream world, with images flowing together, not related particularly to Guernica, Basque country, or anything else.

Necessarily; for by definition avant-garde art is a private language. "Avant-garde" in theory meant "vanguard," "ahead of the pack," thence in practise to be avant-garde is to employ art forms unfamiliar to the common horde, validated within the closed system of Art-Is-What-Artists-Say-It-Is-And-Artists-Are-People-Who-Create-Art, not by trial and error use for persuasion in the marketplace. Expressing, not communicating, has always been the avant-garde's fundamental business, and becoming a powerful Establishment has not changed that. The forms remain private and the system remains closed. Painters may call their works "love letters to the world," but if they won't speak the world's language, their love must go unrequited, and they resemble those 19th-century missionaries who professed overflowing love for the heathen but refused to preach in barbarous tongues. However many government subsidies they get to teach the natives more elegant speech, it will do no good.

Only the "vulgar tongue, comprehended of the people" can carry conviction, as all good missionaries have always known. And that means communication employing traditional arts of substitute imagery, illustration and beautification.

Picasso's art in the 1930s was of course only an anticipation of automatism, abstract expressionisms, formalisms, conceptualisms to come, all protesting by style—"artists in permanent revolt against their own style," as James Johnson Sweeney once put it so felicitously[6]—with ever less content. And as this went on, the fundamental principle of living arts operated ever more demonstrably: if society's unchanging needs for arts fulfilling traditional social functions is not met by activities going on under the name of Art, then other activities performing those traditional social functions must and will be found.

Picasso's *Guernica* is assuredly a much greater work of art by 20th-century standards than is David Low's cartoon of the same subject. Liberal opinion of all shades having seized upon the Guernica atrocity as a rally-point, and Picasso having promised a great emotive painting on that theme for the Barcelona exhibition of 1937, it was proclaimed a masterpiece long before it was completed—indeed, long before it was begun. That it has been a stylistically compelling "weapon in the struggle against Fascism" is incontrovertible. But only for those already converted. Nobody not already convinced of Franco's turpitude would be persuaded by Picasso's *Guernica* that Franco was a monster—least of all any proletarian. For it totally lacks objective content. As Picasso himself said, when asked whether the dying horse signified Spain and the rampant bull Franco, or vice-versa, or something else entirely, "It means what you want it to mean." And quite rightly, since the subject of the painting is, as usual, the painting itself: "What is Art?—" or more precisely here, "How should a Great Artist Protest?" The particular occasion for the painting or for the protest is immaterial. It is the same with protest in avant-garde music or poetry—protest is smothered in self-expression, conceptualized to death.

In effect, Picasso's *Guernica* has returned to the simpler kind of persuasion represented by 19th-century battle paintings or Assyrian reliefs (q.v. 160A). It is inherent, that is to say, something deduced by the viewer. Only, instead of making the deductions from the content, viewers are supposed to make it from the style. Since the style is by definition a private language, "a secret," as Conceptualists were fond of emphasizing, between Artist and Art, it follows that this kind of art is not merely potentially ambiguous (as deductions from illustrative content alone necessarily must be),[7] but necessarily solipsistic. It means what you choose it to mean.

Needless to say, arts with such an ethically relative outlook as this have been welcomed by authority at all levels. Funds and friends have poured in upon the art world ever since 1955, when this kind of art became dominant. All threat of subversion is gone from it; governments all over the world can subsidize art with carefree minds, knowing that nothing artists do will disturb any important State enterprise.[8] But that is also the reason why popular/commercial arts of persuasion, like David Low's political cartoons, are so much more effective as persuasion. Whether or not qualities of traditional High Art may be claimed for them, their effectiveness as Low Arts of persuasion/ conviction is beyond question.

No elaborate commentary is needed to explain what a good political cartoon is or does in and for society. Nor does it require subsidies. Low's cartoons in the *Daily Express* (to pursue this example) were read by all classes of the population; and if to this day public opinion in Britain amongst all classes remains convinced that somehow Franco's regime was a disaster to progress and light in Spain, that is surely due to Low's, not like Picasso's, kind of arts.

Variant Types of Modern Arts
Of Persuasion/Conviction

DIVERSE WAYS in which substitute imagery, illustration, and beautification function for persuasion/conviction have been treated in sections dealing with those popular/commercial arts. Within arts of persuasion/conviction proper, at least three main types are identifiable.

First, advertising. Of course not all advertisements are arts of persuasion/conviction, strictly speaking. Far from it. Much advertising consists of simple substitute imagery (the repetitive symbol, e.g.), and much more of various kinds of illustration in which persuasion is effected by the viewers' own deductive powers. Very little advertising consciously employs style for ideological persuasion. In short, in only the smallest percentage of advertisements is persuasive intent demonstrable from forms themselves. But since the intent of this art is known, and demonstrable from context, advertising can be classified as a type and all its kinds discussed together here.

The other two main types of modern arts of persuasion/conviction are political cartooning and popular/commercial architecture. The deaths of both as viable arts have been announced periodically for many decades now, but they continue to flourish. Both exhibit characteristics of persuasive/convictive arts proper: full meaning deriving only from an abstract body of ideas not necessarily represented by either the substitute images or the illustrations employed; and forms shifting in style according to ideology.

Advertising

Evolution of advertising forms: inherent persuasion in substitute imagery and illustration; compulsive symbols; irrational association; psychological hard-sell.

Nowadays, advertising is the most prominent of all persuasive arts in both Western and Communist worlds. It has been so for as long as anyone living can remember. In fact advertising has surrounded everyone inescapably for a century and more, and may continue for longer than we like—Orwell's *1984* began with a torn poster flapping in the harsh wind. But in the long sweep of history, advertising is a quite recent art. Essentially it is a tool and product of the Industrial Revolution and capitalism—originating for all intents and purposes in the 16th century, maturing with late 19th-century commercial advertising (the matrix of posters), used in the 20th century proportionately more and more for political and social persuasion of various sorts—of which persuasion for avant-garde tastes in art is one. Broadly then, advertising is the link between medieval allegory, and modern social and political cartooning; by perfecting deliberately persuasive forms, it effected the transition from medieval to modern arts of persuasion.[9]

Advertising originated in simple substitute imagery—informative announcements like tavern signs ("Pig & Whistle"), guild emblems (striped barber poles are survivors) and the like. So taverns and butcher-shops were identified and advertised in first-century B.C. Pompeii; so chairmakers and wigsellers "advertised" by signboards and trade-cards in the 18th century A.D.

Strictly speaking this kind of simple substitute imagery was not an art of persuasion proper. Its meaning was self-contained, requiring no reference to anything outside itself. Nor was there anything persuasive about either words or pictures; they simply presented what was available where persuasion (if any) happened independently. Deliberate persuasion only began in the 19th century when these substitute images were made into compulsive symbols.

The repetitive compulsive symbol was a response to social needs in the period c1830-1880. Mass luxury goods had begun to come off assembly lines in quantity, democratic franchise was broadening, and money filtering down to more and more potential purchasers; but mass public education had not yet been legislated, so that trying to sell goods by written advertisement of their merits was useless. The answer was to keep a few simple words, brand names especially, so continuously before the public eye as to provoke automatic buying responses at the counter in due course. P.T. Barnum (1810-1891) and Thomas Holloway (1800-1883) were two great masters of the compulsive symbol, Barnum emphasizing repetition in his seven-step philosophy of advertising, Holloway public exposure. In every mid-19th-century American newspaper Barnum's ads proliferated; on every 19th-century European surface the words "Holloway's Pills" were apt to appear, from stones in Switzerland's Reuss River to clouds above London's Strand—and along the streets of Lima and Delhi too, in Peking and Sidney, and on the Great Pyramids.

MUNDY'S

PHOTO STUDIO

PORT HOPE.

J. H. Mundy, late of Montreal and Toronto.

ALWAYS AT HOME AND IN GOOD HUMOR.

161. Two examples of the informative announcement type of advertising, from a Toronto newspaper c1907. Descent from traditional tavern signs is obvious.

All over the civilized world
THE IMPROVED

BOSTON GARTER

IS KNOWN AND WORN

Every Pair Warranted

The Name is stamped on every loop —

The *Velvet Grip*

CUSHION BUTTON CLASP

Lies flat to the leg—never Slips, Tears nor Unfastens

ALWAYS EASY

Send 50c. for Silk, 25c. for Cotton, Sample Pair.

GEO. FROST CO., Makers, Boston, Mass., U. S. A.

REFUSE ALL SUBSTITUTES

Examples of repetitive compulsive symbols, two from c1850 (above and two more modern w). The objective in all cases was to create something (image, symbol, trade-mark, brand, which would automatically bring a product or service to mind and provoke some positive nse uncomplicated by thoughtful reflection.

The repetitive compulsive symbol technique is infinitely adaptable, to all sorts of purposes. Its political possibilities are conspicuous: the same invokings of automatic response that leads purchasers to pick brand-names can be generated in favor of candidates with Presidential profiles, and two-legs-bad-four-legs-good types of mindless slogans: "Power to the People," "Kill Pigs," and such.

It also can be adapted to architecture. Best-known present example, perhaps, is McDonald's golden arches. But their inspiration goes back to an earlier hamburger chain, the White Towers.

Architecture like the standardized types of White Tower Hamburger stands cannot really be described as mimetic. It is not a replica in larger or more durable form of some shape acquiring revered associations in an earlier and more perishable form (q.v. Sect. I); if anything, its texture and form are shaped more on avant-garde principles of expression, since they derive basically from its prefabricated skeleton and the practice of attaching exterior panels to it for efficiency, an anticipation of the famous Alcoa Building in Pittsburgh by some thirty years.[10]

Nor can it be described as eclectic, since its forms are about as devoid of symbolism as the avant-garde's. Whatever the varied associations of the Gothic style and its diverse Revival manifestations—including the vaguest sort of allusions to civic enterprise like the Chicago Water Tower whence the White Tower's inspiration allegedly derived—they cannot possibly be stretched to include anything relevant to the eating or cooking or selling of hamburgers. This architecture cannot be considered in the same category as the "Chuck Wagon" (59), a popular/commercial descendant of some traditional form. It is in fact a kind of advertising—a repetitive compulsive symbol, just like a logo. To judge from the founder's own account, it also involved the next kind of advertising, by irrational association:

To make [the business] distinctive, I suggested that we use the name White Castle, because "White" signifies purity and cleanliness and "Castle" represents strength, permanence, and stability. The building itself was of cement block construction, designed with battlements and a turret in keeping with the Castle idea, a style of architecture still in use.[11]

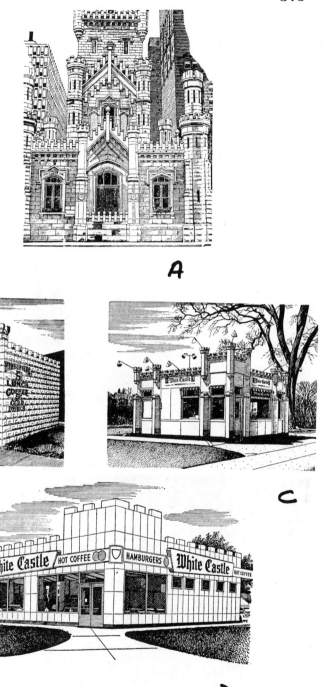

163A. Chicago Water Tower, one of several municipal amenities erected in the 1880s in a whitish stone with Gothic etails. 163B. First White Tower Hamburger stand, erected 1921 in Wichita, Kansas, of cement block, 15 x 10 feet, ·ith five counter stools and wooden fixtures. 165C. Standard White Tower stand of the 1930s, prefabricated of steel ate with hung enamel porcelain panels, patented 1928. Fifty-five in all were erected.   163D. "Modern" ost-1945) White Tower Hamburger stand type.

Already by the 1870s compulsive symbols were being so widely used as to cancel each other out. To make one more compelling than another was the immediate stimulus for developing advertisement by irrational association.

164. (A) Example of advertising by irrational association, c1885. (B) Ditto, c1970. In either case it would be difficult, without the caption, to guess precisely what might be advertised.

When you can endure all the burdens and pressures of life, that is called strength.

Juxtaposition was the operative principle here, words and/or pictures referring to a product set next to words and/or pictures totally unrelated to it, beholders connecting the two in their minds by referring both to a third, abstract, concept. So (164A) a compulsive slogan symbol: "White: King of Sewing Machines," gets set into a waterscape with willows and boats; the common connection is with leisure and quietness. On a trademark, "Talon the Quality Zipper" (164B) is juxtaposed with a gnarled oak silhouetted against the sky. The connection? "Strength, Endurance." Without this abstract idea, the juxtaposition would be incomprehensible, since words and pictures have nothing literally to do with each other.

165. Bovril advertisement, 1919. From *History of Bovril Advertising,* London, 1968.

Inasmuch, then, as the full significance of advertising by irrational association is derived from some frame of reference outside itself, it has a definitive characteristic of arts of persuasion which compulsive symbols by themselves lack.

Like compulsive symbolism, advertising by irrational association too contains inherent elements of political and social persuasion, like it or not. Sometimes those elements work at cross-purposes with the whole principle of commercial persuasion.

This advertisement sells Bovril by compulsive symbol (the distinctive bottle shape and capitalized trade-name) and by irrationally associating Napoleon, Cromwell, Dempsey and Disraeli with Bovril through the abstract idea of tirelessness. But it also sells a certain view of life. Greatness, it intimates, consists in mastery over other human beings, by whatever means (war, boxing, revolution, demogoguery, flattery). Money is another means, not mentioned, but obviously sanctioned. The advertisement in fact depends upon, and supports, a whole set of political and social presuppositions without citing any.

Similarly with a typical 1975 advertisement based upon irrational association with a compulsive symbol for cigarettes (distinctively colored and lettered package) and fashionably holidaying youth, through the abstract idea of "cool" behavior (in two senses). But social and political implications here are quite different. This kind of "cool" behavior repudiates the Puritan work ethic. Freedom is its ideal, from work as well as from bourgeois clothes and sexual habits. It is the 1960s version of the "American Adam"—that Garden-of-Eden vision where, thanks in this case to beneficent Science and the Machine, mankind enjoys eternal holiday, leaping from brand-new Volkswagen van in brand-old 1984 Outer Party blue jeans, uniform of the well-connected play-worker.

166. Salem Cigarette advertisement, back of an April, 1975 issue of *TV Guide.*

midnight

VOL. 21 — NO. 46 ® MAY 19, 1975 ⟨F⟩ 30¢

MIRACL
Wom
Blee

Onassis Family Has Last Laugh:
Jackie To Lose Ari's Millions
Deathbed Will Forces Her To Remain

Hundreds Brought Back To Life Confirm:
Friends & Relatives Wait
Beyond The Grave For Us

George C. Scott
Wrecks Home In
Drunken Binge

PSYCHIATRIST WAR
Women Kill
Kill Your Marri

CONGRESSMAN REVEALS:
Doctors Cheat Poor &
Out Of $1.5 Billion Ever

167. Typical front page of a 1970s tabloid, reproduced so as to bring out key words that catch the eye—i.e., the hopes and fears and fancies—of Mankind.

Commonest form of irrational association is the motion picture. David Wark Griffith is frequently credited with first seizing the full possibilities of juxtaposing images of someone firing a gun (say) and a bird falling (say), and leaving it to audiences mentally to connect the two, sometime around 1908-1912. Precisely in those same years the sometime director of the Psychological Laboratory at Northwestern University outside Chicago, Walter Dill Scott (1869-1955) put advertising on a systematic, scientific basis with his books *The Psychology of Advertising* (1908) and *Influencing Men in Business* (1911). The coincidence is not fortuitous. Illustration and scientific calculation are the two principle ingredients added to compulsive symbols and irrational association to concoct one of the 20th century's most potent moulding forces—psychological hard-sell advertising.

It may well be that the earliest deliberate scientifically researched psychological hard-sell occurred amongst 19th-century novelists competing for the vast new market which mass literacy had opened up. Certain it is that one of its fine 20th-century flowers is the modern tabloid, which is well worth perusing on that account if for no other. It can provide lots of insight into the popular mind if you approach it with speculations like the cause that moves the populace at large most readily. What are the real concerns of the mass of the population? These are the kinds of insights which academic intellectuals, especially, all too often assume to be beneath serious notice. But advertisers *must* be aware of them. And they are.

Walter Dill Scott, synthesizing empirical discoveries of the preceding two or three decades, declared callously that advertisers should

appeal to ruling interests and motives...the desire to be healthy, to hoard, to possess, to wear smart clothes, to get something for nothing, to be like the more privileged and successful classes.

Or in plainest language, base advertising on vices—envy, shame, greed, jealousy. Suggest not so much how happy people will be with your product, as how miserable they will be without it.

Experiment with psychological science to ascertain precise degrees of unhappiness and misery, and their palliatives.

Next the formula calls for a vehicle, a means of channelling and focussing those hopes and fears and foibles on some particular product, some predetermined end. The implicit persuasion of substitute imagery is not enough. Nor even compulsive symbols, irrationally associated. The solution: participatory illustration, advertising anecdotes in which modern Everyman can play this secular century's Divine Comedy.

Tinkly triumph, homely heartbreak—such is the stuff of psychological hard-sell advertising anecdote. *"That might be me!"* In it, the history of 19th- and 20th century evolution of illustrative arts is recapitulated.

First, book illustration: the picture with text (but neither fully intelligible without reference to an outside system of values and ideas, as persuasive arts demand). It appears first in the journals and newspapers put out to meet the new mass-educated market of the 1870s, and in the posters advertising by irrational association appearing in Paris by Jules Cheret in that same decade. Thence it becomes a standby of monthly magazines like the *Saturday Evening Post* and Edward Bok's *Ladies Home Journal.*

Next, the comic strip format: before-and-after sequences, hopes and fears put into motion by sequential boxes.

Finally, the television commercial: "the hopes and fears of all the years are met in thee tonight!" Compulsive symbol, irrational association, participatory illustration all set in motion and put to music, television realized what to earlier generations of advertisers would have seemed the utopian dream of direct, face-to-face psychological hard-sell in the victim's own living-room; all the advantages of hardened bazaar-haggling and supersonic technology.[12] But for the saving switch to another channel or to silence, the public would have been totally at the advertisers' mercy. In *1984,* sets had no switches.

Psychological hard-sell, like preceding advertising arts, has inherent political implications. But whereas compulsive symbols inherently promoted Adam Smith's kind of vision of capitalism manufacturing abundance, and irrational association lent itself

"Don't make a monkey of yourself"

cried Bob as I sat down at the piano

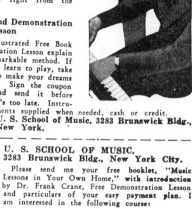

IT was love at first sight when I met Helen. Unfortunately, she didn't feel the same about me. "You need a little publicity," Bob said, when I confided my troubles. The very next day he had a long talk with Helen.

"She's crazy about music," he told me later, "so I conveniently forgot you can't play a note and told her you are an *accomplished pianist!*"

"But Bob . . ."

"Not a word! If you're asked to play, just say you've sprained your wrist!"

That evening we were all gathered around the piano.

"Won't you play something?" said Helen.

I smiled and replied that *it would be a pleasure.* Bob's grin changed to amazement. "Don't make a monkey of yourself!" he whispered excitedly. Instead of replying I began the first notes of Berlin's "Russian Lullaby." On and on I played until thunderous applause shook the room.

Bob cried amazed "When did you learn to play?"

I laughed. "That Free Demonstration Lesson in Music I sent for last summer showed me how easy it was to learn without a teacher, so I took the complete course. That's all."

This story is typical. You, too, can learn to play your favorite instrument at home, in your spare time, this easy new way. First you are *told* what to do—then a picture *shows* you how to do it—then you do it yourself and *hear* it. There are no tiresome scales—no laborious exercises. You play simple, familiar melodies *by note* right from the start.

FREE BOOK and Demonstration Lesson

Our wonderful illustrated Free Book and Free Demonstration Lesson explain all about this remarkable method. If you really want to learn to play, take this opportunity to make your dreams come true. Now! Sign the coupon and send it before it's too late. Instruments supplied when needed, cash or credit. U. S. School of Music, 3283 Brunswick Bldg., New York.

Pick Your Instruments

Piano	Violin
Organ	Clarinet
Ukulele	Flute
Cornet	Saxophone
Trombone	Harp
Piccolo	Mandolin
Guitar	'Cello
Hawaiian Steel Guitar	
Sight Singing	
Piano Accordion	
Italian and German Accordion	
Voice and Speech Culture	
Harmony & Composition	
Drums and Traps	
Automatic Finger Control	
Banjo (Plectrum, 5-String or Tenor)	

Gray Hair

Cheated Her Out of the Job

Now *Comb* Away Gray This Easy Way

WHY endure the handicap of Gray Hair? Just comb Kolor-Bak through your hair and watch the gray disappear. Kolor-Bak is a clean, colorless, scientific liquid that leaves the hair lustrous and full of life. The one bottle does for blonde, auburn, brown, black. Already hundreds of thousands of women and men have used it.

Make This Test

Test Kolor-Bak on our guarantee that if it doesn't make you look ten years younger your money will be refunded any time you ask. Get it from any drug or department store today.

Kolor-Bak

Imparts Color to Gray Hair

168. Two examples of psychological hard-sell from magazines of the 1930s. A dramatic scenario is concocted by text and illustrative picture to sell by inciting fear and shame.

to Wellsian fantasies of luxury without limits and without labor, the implications of psychological hard-sell are all totalitarian. In *The Unchanging Arts* (1970), I wrote about this at some length:

> ...it is not so much the ends advertising has been devoted to as its means of attaining them that have been so poisonous—and particularly the twin techniques employed on television. The kind of mentality they foster could support no civilized society at all.

But fortunately mankind has been provided with two great defenses against the TV commercial—at least in the free world. Freedom means freedom to sleep in front of the thing, or to turn it off, at will (169).

Compulsive symbol, irrational association, psychological hard-sell—all these forms can be found in avant-garde arts, developed as expressive ends in themselves, cut off from social function; another instance of the disastrous split in 20th-century arts.

Advertising arts exemplify everything that disgusts so many thoughtful people about popular arts in general. Need they be so banal? Was the perception of Jules Cheret's lithographed posters turning Parisian boulevards of the 1870s into picture galleries, and so many comparable aspirations, necessarily hopeless and hypocritical from the start?

Insofar as greed and envy can never be beautified, arts promoting them can never be instruments of beautification. But insofar as a decent living standard is no contemptible ambition, arts furthering it don't necessarily de-humanize or uglify. If such has been their effect, surely one reason is that the best artistic sensitivities of our age have been employed elsewhere. Advertising in fact provides probably the most instructive example of what spiritual havoc and environmental improverishment has been wrought by the split in our 20th-century arts between expression and social functions. For every one of the distinctive persuasive devices evolved in arts of commercial persuasion has been picked up by the avant-garde and developed with extraordinary skill—but as ends in themselves, with little social point or purpose, hence with little environmental impact.

169. "Momma" exercises her democratic freedoms. Sunday page by Mell Lasarus, 3 July 1976.

Paul Klee's set of compulsive symbols all came, consciously or not, from the repertoire devised long before his time for advertising. Arrows, pointing hands, gradations of color, type tone and sequential shape used to attract eyes to one area or another—all of these were invented in the service of commercial persuasion, and developed by Klee most intricately, delicately, feelingly. But to no effective end—as Saul Steinberg's satires of them so amusingly pointed up. Applied to some definite social end, they might have improved the environment enormously; but that never happened. Nor did anything come of Al Held's imitations of the effects of billboards. "Pop" artists made Precious Objects out of rows of brand-labels on soup cans and the like; and so what? It never softened the stridency of advertising by compulsive brand-label symbols.

Before 1914 James Ensor was already appropriating techniques of advertising by irrational association for subtle visual experiences; Dada and Surrealism in the 1920s and '30s explored all sorts of intricate variations. How these efforts may have hastened the anarchist millennium of non-verbal non-logical communication remains yet to be seen; immediate practical effects on society at large were nil, although Dali and Arp and Ernst made a lot of money.

"Happenings" likewise got lucrative reputations for their inventors; but this immersion in hard-sell psychological persuasion for its own sake affected nobody not already committed to its propositions. Some of the techniques might well have helped humanize commercial selling. But no attempt was made by the artists to put themselves in a position where their ˒ talents might have been so employed. "Pop" is not popular— though it definitely is commercial.

So their talents were wasted. And so long as these persuasive forms remain ends in themselves, avant-garde talents will remain wasted and void, as far as society at large is concerned. Nor is there much point in that case complaining about the banality of advertising arts.

Political Cartooning

Political cartooning employs didactic substitute images and/or illustrations, compulsive symbols, and irrational associations.

REVIEWING A BATCH of new books on political cartooning for *Time* in a major essay ("Editorial Cartoons: Capturing the Essence," 3 February 1975)—itself somewhat of an event—Stefan Kanfer concluded,

Whatever the reasons, the editorial cartoon is one of America's liveliest and most permanent art forms. As Watergate proved, politics cannot eradicate or even tame journalism. As subsequent events have demonstrated, the reverse is also true. Them damn pictures are likely to enliven the next hundred years—and more.

Let's begin an analysis of arts of social and political persuasion, then, with a "Watergate" cartoon—Paul Conrad's of 24 March 1974. How does it work, in and for society?

RETREAT TO MOSCOW

171A. "Retreat to Moscow." Cartoon by Paul Conrad, published in the *Los Angeles Times* for 24 June 1974, republished in Richard B. Freeman, *Graphics '75: The Unmaking of a President,* University of Kentucky, Lexington, 1975.

There is nothing very persuasive about the cartoon in itself. In fact, the cartoon in itself is nearly meaningless: an unknown person in old-fashioned costume riding a horse into a nondescript landscape. Its meaning derives entirely from things and ideas outside itself: first, from its resemblance—vague but still perceptible—to a well-known 19th-century painting of the Emperor Napoleon retreating across the interminable steppes of Russia after his disastrous invasion of Russia in 1812; second, with a State visit to Moscow by U.S. President Richard M. Nixon in June, 1974. Only when these two associations are grasped can we know what the picture is *about:* namely, a complex of abstract ideas—overweening ambition and retribution, escape from domestic problems by grandiose foreign adventures, and the like.

This is how cartoons, both social and political, typically get their meaning. It's also how great traditional arts for the past two thousand years typically got their meaning. A certain level of intelligence, powers of reflection, ability to think in terms of abstract causality, to make connections, is presumed and prerequisite on the spectator's part. Here's a second example, in a different style (171C, D).

171B. "1814" (Napoleon's Retreat from Moscow) painted in 1864 by Jean-Louis-Ernest Meissonier (1815-1891). Best-known of a series of Napoleonic pictures begun in 1859, and still the best-known of all Napoleonic subjects.

171C. "Let Us Prey (after Thomas Nast)," cartoon by David Levine in the *New York Review of Books*, 20 September 1973.

A GROUP OF VULTURES WAITING FOR THE STORM TO " BLOW OVER."—" LET US *PREY*"

171D. A famous cartoon from the prolific 1871 series on "Boss" Tweed and the "Tammany Ring" in New York City: "Let us Prey: Waiting for the Storm to Blow Over." From Albert Bigelow Paine, *Thomas Nast: His Period and His Pictures* (New York, 1904).

Again, the meaning comes from outside, the cartoon in itself being no more than a representation of some hybrid creature, like those on old Mesopotamian seals (38A). Levine's cartoon depends upon an association with Thomas Nast's, and both derive their significance in relation to a high ideal of political life: politicians should be servants and not robbers of the people. Again, a high degree of intelligence on the spectator's part is presumed: enough to connect a famous earlier cartoon campaign against corruption in high places with the present "Watergate" scandal, and draw parallels. It's often said that modern political cartoons are highly simplified, compared to its predecessors[13] but in fact that is not true of their content. Only their improved style makes them more effective than earlier complicated allegories.

PUNCH'S ILLUSTRATIONS TO SHAKSPEARE.

" Is all our travail turn'd to this effect ?
After the slaughter of so many peers,
So many captains, gentlemen, and soldiers,
That in this quarrel have been overthrown,
And sold their bodies for their country's benefit,
Shall we at last conclude effeminate peace ?"

Henry VI., Part 1, *Act* v., *Scene* 4.

172A. Political cartoon by John Tenniel, *Punch*, 12 April 1856.

In popular/commercial cartooning style is associated with ideology, just as in all historical arts of deliberate persuasion/conviction.

Superficially, there would seem to be two styles of cartooning during the 19th and 20th centuries—a linear pen style represented here by David Levine (171C) and in the 19th century by Nast (171D) and Tenniel (172A), and a pencil or lithographic style, represented here by Conrad (171A) (perhaps better by David Low, 160B), which goes back to Daumier (172B), and is more closely related to painterly effects.

172B. "L'Empire c'est la Paix." political cartoon by Honoré Daumier, first published in *Le Charivari,* 19 October, 1870, and republished in the state above in *Album du Siège.* The reference is to a famous promise of Emperor Napoleon III when he seized power two decades before.

This is deceptive. In fact both styles derive from 19th-century naturalistic styles of painting and drawing; both are expressions of and instruments used by democratic politics. Both are above all concerned with communicating with, persuading, convincing individuals; for that reason, they must above all use the mutually agreed-upon formal language of art amongst Western peoples.

What this common style contrasted with—deliberately—was the Rococo vagueness of 18th-century aristocratic arts. It's sober, plain and direct. Style is dictated by content and social function—as style in High Art always was. The social function changed from serving hereditary dynasts to serving democracy; therefore the style changed.

In theory arts serving socialism should contrast with arts serving democracy; in practice they don't, first because much socialism is democratic; second, because authoritarian socialism, as represented by Leninism in Russia or Maoism in China, needs to communicate with people and can only do so in a commonly accepted stylistic language.

After the Bolshevik Revolution of 1917, committed socialist artists naturally wanted to express the change of regime by a change of style. The "March of the Moderns" having been so closely associated with social and political radicalism—as Donald D. Egbert so conclusively demonstrated[14]—abstraction of some sort seemed logical and inevitable: "a new art for a new world."[15] So all the theories of non-verbal communication and pure spiritual art propounded by radical enthusiasts in pre-1914 Europe flowed into Moscow in 1919 and the early twenties, like tea leaves swirling down a toilet. They produced posters still admired by progressive theorists; projects later copied in France and Germany, and still later executed by great American capitalist corporations.[16] But they didn't produce much admirable from Lenin's point of view. Lenin and Trotsky were faced with winning a civil war, with destroying their enemies however they could; and these posters and radical buildings—a Pravda headquarters in Petrograd, where winter temperatures regularly fell to -40, whose machinery was exposed for purposes of ideological expression, for instance—were not helpful. Denouncing the "infantile disorder of Leftism," Lenin sent most enthusiasts packing, back to their radical chic capitalist patrons. From those remaining he commanded "socialist realism." That is, naturalistic art and cartoons like those 19th-century bourgeois democratic artists made, which would exhort workers and peasants to resist the Bolsheviks' enemies; buildings which workers and peasants understood as "palaces for the laboring masses," however avant-gardists might deplore it. In the long run, of course, a serious error in judgment. The right art for the kind of regime Lenin was setting up was not democratic-style posters and painters, which encouraged reflective association of ideas for full significance. Rather, it was the avant-gardists' abstractions—arts which required only visceral reactions, knee-jerk responses to stimuli; arts which could be judged by no objective standards and which therefore provided no firm ground for any kind of resistance to authority. Only in the later '70s when the need for persuasive arts was long past and the Communist regime was firmly established, would that realization begin coming to Russia's rulers. That, however, is another story. For now the point is simple: political cartooning is, like other popular/commercial arts, the legitimate descendant and perpetuator of traditional historic arts of persuasion—persuading by style dictated by ideology, and content imparted by association with abstract ideas via abstract causal thought.

Popular/Commercial Architecture:
The Continuing Art of Architecture
as Visual Metaphors of Persuasion/Conviction

In popular/commercial building, traditional concepts of architecture as the art of creating visual metaphors of convictions survive, in contrast to the avant-garde Establishment view of architecture as an expression of Master Builders creating visual and emotional experiences for spectators.

IN THE EARLY '60s the United States government began a multi-million-dollar transformation of the Pennsylvania colonial assembly's simple 18th-century meeting place into a monument to American national ideals. The project was justified on grounds that here was a building which for Americans everywhere had come to symbolize Independence and Liberty. And there was historical precedent—Independence Hall was possibly the first American building to be restored as a monument. Its tower and cupola, which in typical 18th-century usage had set off the otherwise utilitarian structure as having civic and ceremonial functions, had been repaired in consciously Colonial style by William Strickland in 1827, and self-consciously on several occasions thereafter as well. The 1960s project in effect consisted of putting this unpretentious and (in its own time) not particularly remarkable structure into a grandiose frame—an axial avenue down which proud citizens were to promenade with a gravity appropriate to monumental occasions.

On this reconstruction no end of distinguished scholars and architects labored. And it would be fair to say that, while there was considerable disagreement as to the appropriateness of such a monumental axial approach, nobody disputed the general principle of restoring the building to its 18th-century shape as something meaningful to all Americans.

In these same 1960s, one Emilio Capaldi began a series of shopping malls. Capaldi was a contractor who, as explained in newspaper interviews at the time, had risen from humble origins to become well-to-do and civic-minded, and accordingly chose for his chain of shopping centers eclectic forms which for him

173. Independence Mall Shopping Center, on the Concord Pike, Wilmington, Delaware. Designed by owner and operator Emilio Capaldi in 1963.

constituted meaningful symbols of the government and economic system to which he owed his success. Result: a series of "Independence Malls," each consisting of a U-shaped block centered on a replica of Independence Hall. Or more exactly, on an Independence Hall facade, for both the central feature and flanking Philadelphia-vicinity landmarks are facades only, attached to a red brick shell. The whole provides, according to a caption on the postcards distributed at the Malls (173), "a stroll through 'historic Philadelphia' with its quaint shoppe fronts and colonial atmosphere....Independence Hall, Betsy Ross House, Liberty Hall, Letitia Penn House...all recreated from golden moments of the past to implement and serve the present."

Technically, this is eclectic architecture, meaning (as its derivation from the Greek "ek-lektos," "out of the best" implies) picking and choosing from the best, or what someone considered to be the best, styles and forms from past architecture to create combinations or imitations for some present purpose. What it really means nowadays, to anyone of architectural sophistication, is scrapbook architecture. Designs for many such buildings were in fact quite literally put together with scotchtape, by builders who never went near any school of architecture.

What scholars and experts engaged upon the Independence Hall project thought about Mr. Capaldi's "Independence Malls," when they thought about them at all—which was hardly often— has not been formally recorded. But unofficially we may hazard a guess. The idea that Mr. Capaldi was engaged in anything resembling the art of architecture was too ridiculous to consider even for a moment.

Great Architecture is what Great Architects say it is. How can we know a Great Architect? By the Great Architecture he designs. At least, that's the implications of an article by Philip Johnson in *The Inland Architect* a few years ago[17] where he listed the best buildings of the last decade as those "which gave me the greatest thrill when I entered them." Amongst this Great Architecture, Gund Hall figures prominently.

Nobody would dispute Philip Johnson's vast experience, his demonstrated sensibility, his seminal role in shaping our modern architectural environment. Nor would anybody deny Johnson's contention that Gund Hall constitutes impressive visual space. What more and more critics nowadays are coming to disagree

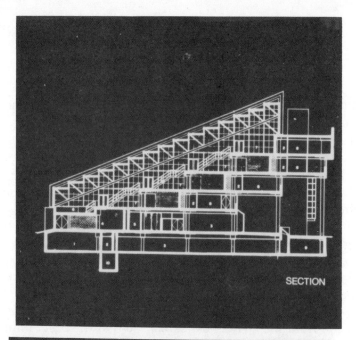

SECTION

174. Section and detail of interior of Gund Hall, built for the
Graduate School of Design, Harvard University, 1969-72. John
Andrews/Anderson/Baldwin, architects.

with is his assumption—or more exactly, the fundamental assumption behind the Modern Movement—that impressive visual experience is the whole of Architecture; that its only and primordial function is to provide opportunity for personal creative expression by Master Builders, and private aesthetic experience by beholders.

Such a definition of architecture diverges as widely from traditional ideas of what this art involved, as avant-garde painting differs from traditional arts of substitute imagery, illustration or beautification. Not that modern architecture has been devoid of social purpose—far from it. A social purpose is unmistakeable in the description of Gund Hall from its official handout brochure, for instance, however circumlocutiously stated, and however vigorously disputed by its creators. They claim that Gund Hall and buildings like it are simply spatial experiences; that any resemblance to those wide factory interiors spanned by struts and plates and beams illustrated in Siegfried Giedon's *Space, Time, and Architecture*—mandatory and ofttimes sole reading in architectural schools from the 1940s through the 1960s—is merely fortuitous. They maintain that all those struts and beams and pipes and sprinklers, which so resemble those early industrial features o'er which the worthy Siegfried was wont to wax so lyrical, are just honest expressions of structure carried to fashionable ultimate nakedness; that they have no metaphorical associations with French student-and-worker movements going on while Gund Hall was on the drawing-boards, in the late 1960s. The handout implies otherwise. "Gund Hall," it proclaims, by centralizing facilties,

allows for improved collaboration....The interdisciplinary collaboration essential to the school's goal in providing a comprehensive approach to the study of environmental design is given expression in the building's central studio space which extends through four levels under a vast sloping clear span roof.

That is to say, the building is *about* work, or more exactly, the work-process—which according to Adolf Max Vogt,[18] is *the* subject of revolutionary architecture. In other words, it inculcates, by actualizing, a whole ideology of collective salvation through scientific design which has been avant-garde orthodoxy lo these many decades past: Tony Garnier's *Cité Industrielle* sans law-courts, sans police stations, sans jails and insane asylums because, Garnier explained, "in the new society under socialist law there would be no need for churches, and that as capitalism would be suppressed, there would be no swindlers, thieves, or murderers[19]; Louis Sullivan's lofty skyscrapers fit for a society where "every infant born in what is generally called normal health, is gifted by Nature with a normal receptivity which if cherished and allowed to be developed will unfailingly develop those normal, natural and sane qualities of mind to which we today give the name Genius...."[20]; Corbusier's *Ville Radieuse,* with its "totally engineered environment" bringing in "the final age, when ignorance and darkness will be forever dispelled and when history would cease;"[21] Taut's *Stadtkrone* and Gropius's Bauhaus microcosm and all the rest.[22]

None of this has much to do with Mr. Emilio Capaldi and his Independence Malls. But then, it really doesn't tell us, either, why restoring Independence Hall is fit work for Great Architects but reproducing Independence Hall in the life-and-work setting of a shopping center, for exactly similar symbolic reasons, is a trivial travesty. All that has been established is in fact that most people educated in architectural schools do not consider Mr. Capaldi a Great Architect, hence that his Independence Malls do not qualify as Great Architecture whether or not he gets a thrill when he enters them. Could we but find someone to give either Mr. Capaldi or his shopping malls the necessary certification the whole situation would presumably be transformed. But alas! distressing thought! should Mr. Johnson somehow lose the certifying powers he presently possesses—i.e., should his authority as a Great Architect be questioned (because some other Great Architect failed to be thrilled on entering Johnson's buildings, for instance!), then presumably Gund Hall would flunk the test of Great Architecture too, be demoted to obscurity, oblivion even.

Clearly, an unsatisfactory situation. We need to go back to fundamentals—specifically, to the fundamental difference between our idea of defining architecture primarily or exclusively as the art of evoking emotional responses, and earlier, historic definitions of what architectural art was about. Our present definition is subjective. Its validity depends upon a contemporary climate of opinion, upon certain unspoken hopes of a better society, and associations therewith of certain forms and ways of handling materials—brute forms somehow imputing ideals of simple unspoiled life free of artificial restrictions, factory aesthetic imputing one-class egalitarian outlook, and so forth.

In the traditional High Art of architecture, style was not a self-justifying end in itself, and aesthetic response was only a means to an end. As Norris Kelly Smith put it so well in *Frank Lloyd Wright: A Study in Architectural Content,* "the buildings that have traditionally been regarded as works of architectural art have invariably been bound up with an organized social group, an established institution":

According to Nikolaus Pevsner, 'A bicycle shed is a building, Lincoln Cathedral is a piece of architecture.... The term architecture applies only to buildings designed with a view to aesthetic appeal.' [Bruno] Zevi disputes this, contending, rightly enough, that a bicycle shed may be designed so as to be aesthetically appealing. But would this make it a work of architectural art? I think not, because it would still be unrelated to any area of institutional meaning. Palace, house, tomb, capitol, court, temple, church—these, mainly are the buildings which stand for the institutionalized patterns of human relatedness that make possible the endurance of the city, or of society, or of the state; and these have provided almost all the occasions for meaningful architectural art for the past five thousand years. They bear upon realms of experience which have given rise to great quantitites of painting and poetry; but one would be hard put to find either a painter or a poet who could make much out of the occasion or the experience of bicycle-parking. Nor can the architect endow it with significance....

To put it bluntly, architecture has always been the art of the Establishment. It has been bought and paid for exclusively by successful, prosperous, property-owning institutions with a stake in the preservation of the status quo, and it has generally exhibited its greatest power and originality at times when those institutions have been threatened and in need of support. Needless to say,the other arts have also been patronized by members of those institutions. The uniqueness of architecture lies in the fact that it is *about* the institutional establishment, as the other arts generally are not, though on occasion they may be....

A building may be said to be a work of architectural art, then, insofar as it serves as a visual metaphor, declaring in its own form something (though never everything) about the size, permanence, strength, protectiveness, and organizational structure of the institution it stands for (but does not necessarily house).[23]

This is a definition of architecture in terms of social function—what buildings *do,* in and for society. And that is the way works of architectural art historically were conceived and evaluated for two thousand years past.

Of course Great Architecture always provided a thrill for those who entered it—and not to their Master Builders alone. "Rude ambassadors from the Germanic north fell unconscious from awe," according to Procopius, when ushered under Justinian's great dome of Holy Wisdom in Constantinople. A visitor to Cluny, mightiest of medieval monasteries, records: "At mox surgit basilica ingens"—now surges up the mighty basilica. Anyone who can walk into the Royal Chapel at Granada or the court of the Bandshahi mosque at Lahore and feel nothing, must be totally without sensibility. But in all such cases, aesthetic effects of vast space and sequential masses and decorative materials were subordinated to a visual metaphor of the institution which had these structures erected—to ideas of the sustaining nature of things that justifies all authority, to monastic or princely or ecclesiastical institutions. Great Architecture historically was not erected to provide aesthetic experiences for the visitors; rather, visitors' aesthetic experiences were contrived so that convictions embodied in the architecture might be more compelling.

According to orthodox architectural-historical theory, that concept of architecture as meaningful visual metaphor began disappearing in the 18th century and by now is totally gone. Its last exponent is supposed to have been Frank Lloyd Wright. He, according to Norris Smith, conceived of factories (for example) like the Larkin or Buffalo or the Johnson Wax in Racine, as sacred centers of communal life analogous to Greek temples or Gothic cathedrals in their time and place[24]; he understood how to make houses metaphors of the family. *Mais après lui, le déluge.* That kind of architectural thinking is no more, Kaput. Fini. And that is certainly true as far as architectural schools are concerned. Where now can you find a professional school of architecture or design that teaches any such approach to their art? Wright knew (as his bootlegged houses show) how to design in Tudor or Colonial or chalet. What architectural school offers courses in eclectic architecture nowadays?

But—striking contrast!—what architectural landscape *doesn't* still have dozens of examples to show, of buildings conceived as metaphors of value, and decked out in eclectic style correspondingly. For, like those bumblebees which go happily

175. "Certainly you want the greatest freedom of choice, and that you will get..." illustration from a catalogue of quasi-prefabricated "villas"—i.e., development houses in different provincial styles of Sweden, issued by LB-Hus AB, Bromolla, 1978. Recognizably not American in style—but recognizably belonging to the same category of popular/commercial building.

zipping about all unaware of aerodynamic principles which pronounce them unable to fly, popular/commercial builders all over the world have gone on perpetuating a kind of architecture which is supposed to have died long ago.[25]

Which corresponds better to the traditional definition of architecture in terms of social function: development houses like these (175), shopping centers like Independence Mall (173), or an existential experience like Gund Hall (174)? The question answers itself. However impoverished or banal popular/commercial architecture may aesthetically be, it remains conceived on traditional principles of High Architecture as an art of persuasion/conviction: full significance deriving from a body of ideas outside itself, style deliberately used to assert ideology.

The ideology being asserted in this case is, of course, a traditional one—the concept of a nuclear family in free possession of its own domain, the principle of free enterprise, the prizing of liberty above equality. These values are asserted by means of eclectic styles whose very persistent use defies established avant-garde canons of taste-and thereby, the ethical relativism which they inculcate. By however dumb instinct, impoverished proportions, confused spatial organization and bastardized eclecticism, the development house still manages to perpetuate a deliberate visual metaphor of institutional values. In its own form, as a one-family dwelling, it represents a metaphor of the traditional basis of Western society. By applied and secondary forms borrowed from various folk and vernacular building sources in past ages, it proclaims values and ideals held by the nuclear family that lives within: roots, if you please. Swedish heritage; American ideals of spacious and independent life; the common Indo-European conviction traceable for ages past, that the landholding family is the stable and successful family. Whether or not these assumptions are true is not at issue here (though one might venture, parenthetically, they are no falser than the *Ville Radieuse's*). The important thing is that popular/commercial builders and their clients hold them. Hold them, indeed, so firmly that, despite the obvious interest of both private builders and buyers to keep costs low as possible (in distinction to big-government and corporation clients who subsidize—in effect—avant-garde architecture), extra money is spent on eclectic ornament, on folk textures, on other "frills," thus manifesting in the most practical possible way their deep aversion to the ethically neutral flat roofs and bare walls of fashionable avant-garde taste.

That the ethical stance of avant-garde architecture—not to mention its aesthetic—is far from an unmixed blessing for Western civilization has long been realized, and ever more fiercely put forward over the past ten or twenty years. That the stubborn perpetuation of eclectic styles in popular/commercial building might be a solution to the problem is only beginning to be suggested.

Judged by proportionate numbers alone, traditional architecture as presented by popular/commercial building is thriving amongst us. According to some surveys, at least 90% of all buildings belong in this popular/commercial category, erected without benefit of professional architectural advice. Some say it may be as high as 95%.

Quality is another matter. Ours is an urban landscape by and large devoid of architectural graces—by turns barren, banal, brutal. But what can be expected? Sensitive and skilled designers are being taught to ignore social function, to put up buildings which give no indiction from shape or proportion or ornament whether they are apartments or office buildings or warehouses or beehives or bandstands, which express only their components in (theoretically anyway) purely architectural language. Society's need for unifying visual metaphors will, therefore, and must be served by others—by people who for lack of education or lack of native abilities or whatever seem far too often insensitive to proportion, massing, voids, texturing and the like, who put buildings together scrapbook-style. If ever we are to create a living counterpart to the urban graciousness of ordinary 18th-century building like Independence Hall in its original Philadelphia setting, let alone other Great Architecture, then somehow we need to put aesthetic expression and social function back together again, as they were in earlier ages.

In historic architecture, aesthetic impact and visual metaphor of social values linked together; architects' expression and sensibilities were subordinate to and supportive of social function. Our separating these two elements has impoverished both. Even more disastrous has been the campaign against eclecticism.

All architecture from the beginning of history until quite modern times employed eclectic forms to indicate the uses and social significance of different kinds of buildings. The idea that each period had a style of its own which could be found in all its buildings—the *Zeitgeist* principle of cultural expression—is true only in the broadest sense. Buildings of many different styles co-existed throughout history—and more than co-existed, worked together to structure built environments meaningfully. Almost within memory, the classic European village had its manor house and its peasant cots in very different styles, its town house somewhere in-between, its church composed of several different building periods, and its utilitarian buildings like foundries or smithies or sheds.

Objections to the class-structured state, pressed in the 19th century with all the passion of inverted religious fanaticism extended to the architectural symbolism which proclaimed class

distinctions. But instead of developing a symbolism of their own
or building styles to express the successive reforms of society
which liberalism achieved, the pioneers of modern design,
generally speaking, promised to abolish all eclectic styles and all
ornament. Filled with missionary zeal they launched a white
crusade against the bourgeois world of brown kitsch (as they saw
it) and all its works. Hence the negative character of so much
avant-garde design—they simply advocated the opposite of
whatever wicked beaux-arts academics taught. That left us our
present barren environment, wherein whatever isn't dominated
by factory aesthetic is a monument to some Form Giver's
sensititivity. Or so one would gather from the plethora of recent
denunciations of avant-garde architecture, which has become a
sort of parlor game: Peter Blake and Wolf von Eckardt have
proclaimed "abstract architecture" a failure because it doesn't
correspond to human needs; Robert Fishman's *Urban Utopias in
the Twentieth Century* concludes " 'Tomorrow,' observed Samuel
Johnson, 'is an old deceiver, and his cheat never grows stale.'
Howard, Wright, and LeCorbusier believed that the 20th century
would be a period of social reconstruction crowned by the creation
of magnificent new cities. They were wrong...."[26] Robert Hughes
described the interiors of Stanley Kubrick's *Clockwork Orange* as
a "cultural satire...making exquisitely chilling predictions
about the future role of cultural artifacts—painting, buildings,
sculpture, music—in society:

At issue is the popular 19th century idea, still held today, that Art is Good for You,
that the purpose of the fine arts is to provide moral uplift. Kubrick's message,
amplified from Burgess's novel, is the opposite: art has no ethical purpose. There
is no religion of beauty. Art serves, instead, to promote ecstatic consciousness. The
kind of ecstasy depends on the person who is having it. Without the slightest
contradiction, Nazis could weep over Wagner before stoking the crematoriums.
Alex grooves on the music of 'Ludwig van,' especially the *Ninth Symphony,* which
fills him with fantasies of sex and slaughter.[27]

They join earlier critics like George Nelson and Norris Smith who
have recognized the moral vacuum of modernism, who complain
that its not being *about* anything makes it monotonous to a
degree no architecture in the world has ever been; and who
observe, rightly, that you cannot design a humane environment
on the same principles you apply to zoos, because humans live by
ideas and associations, not merely air, light and water.

Dean of this movement is Lewis Mumford, who for years has been denouncing mechanistic excesses in avant-garde architecture. In the *Architectural Record* for February 1968 he made an especially noteworthy statement of his case, regretting that "our youthful dreams of a truly modern architecture. . .came true" because

In our admiration for the entrancing constructive feats made possible by modern technics, we did not imagine what the world would look like if every part of it were made over into the exact image of the machine. . .modern architecture. . . .has revealed the real nature of our civilization: its compulsive irrationality, its mechanized barbarism, its psychedelic fantasies. . . .Our generation. . .should at last understand that unless we preserve human continuity. . .our scientific and technical advances will be not merely menacing but meaningless. . . .

None of these critics, however, seems to have seriously reflected on the fact that avant-garde architecture is not the only building we have. They all take it for granted that we must look to the great architects who have got us into what they feel is so great a mess, to get us out. And they are far from certain, let alone agreed, as to how that might be accomplished. Perhaps these two circumstances are related. For, while Mumford gives no clear idea of precisely how that "human continuity" can be preserved, without which "our scientific and technical advances will be not merely menacing but meaningless," in fact such a continuity has been preserved—in our popular/commercial arts. Von Eckhardt likewise demands a new humane kind of building but cannot seem to see that "cheap colonial town houses" that "disfigure" those building lots not occupied by high-rises, might be the beginning of a means toward his desired end.[28] It's time to examine this possibility more closely.

To re-create a meaningful environment we need to study principles by which older architecture was invested with meaning, to see whether it is possible to re-create something similar for our convictions. Popular/commercial building provides a means to this end.

Traditional architecture was invested with meaning in three ways: (1) Mimetic shapes and textures; (2) Proportion: folk traditions and behavioral space; (3) Eclectic styles: forms and proportions borrowed from earlier architecture because of associations they carry with appropriate ideas and values. None of these ways of making meaningful visual metaphors has survived in avant-garde architecture. Popular/commercial building preserves all of them.

Mimetic shapes as found in popular/commercial architecture perpetuate possibly the earliest means of making architecture in history. If contemptible nowadays, it is because the occasions for building mimetic shapes are usually trivial, not because the principle is contemptible in itself.

Popular/commercial architecture preserves mimetic shapes especially commonly in roadside architecture: diners shaped like chuck wagons, banks shaped like piggies, and so forth. We have already considered these in the section on substitute imagery (59, 61A, 62). And we have observed that such a concept of architecture is not in itself contemptible, many great architectural monuments of the past having been so conceived (e.g. Pyramids, Sainte-Chapelle, Surya Temple Konarak, etc., q.v. 60, 61). They are usually trivial because they do not involve metaphors of those "patterns of human interrelatedness on which depend the endurance of the family, the State, and civilization" which Architecture has to be *about,* if it is to rise above triviality. Unfortunately, modern buildings in which such visual metaphors might be possible are nowadays almost always commissioned from avant-garde architects, and what results is usually trivial for quite a different reason—like Saarinen's arch in St. Louis inspired by a bent pipe-cleaner or his TWA Terminal arches modelled on grapefruit peels,[29] they are visual experiences lacking any effective intellectual component.

Yet no great acquaintance with architectural history is required to perceive that mimetic forms are not necessarily trivial in themselves; that they have been used effectively in public buildings, not solely in Antiquity or the High Middle Ages, but right up to modern times. Schools don't have to look like factories or jails, for instance; in the very recent past they looked like civic monuments, by use of mimetic shapes.

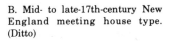

176A. Early 17th-century type of New England meeting house. From J. Frederick Kelly, *Connecticut's Old Houses*, 1933, p. 64.

B. Mid- to late-17th-century New England meeting house type. (Ditto)

C. First Meeting House, West Springfield, Massachusetts, built 1702, as it looked before demolition, c1870.

In Old England, a meeting house for dissenters from the Established Church of England was quite literally a "house for meeting." It was supposed to distinguish Puritans, who preserved the pure early church practise of gathering together in one or another of the homes of the Elect, from those corrupt Anglicans who met in a steepled public building. But no sooner had Puritans arrived in the New World than they themselves began to develop a form of meeting house which, by its distinctive shape, soon set their gathering place apart from ordinary dwellings quite as decisively as any steeple. Squarish ground plan, pyramidal roof, gables on four sides and medieval verticality made the town meeting house instantly recognizable, from the early 18th century on (Old Ship Meeting House at Hingham, Mass., is the only survivor of the type today, and it is much altered; but there are numerous illustrations, for these buildings were too distinctive ever to be overlooked).The precise origins of this shape are irrelevant to our point here. Perhaps it owed something to traditional town-house-cum-market types, and ultimately, however unsuspected by its builders, to the atavistic appeal of ancient sacred and royal dome symbolism; no matter. Four or five generations of use attached ineradicable associations with the idea of "public life" to this shape. For here were held meetings not only for worship but for regular debates over community policy. Here the young were educated in congregational doctrines. Here law-enforcement and trials took place. So it was that, when in the early 18th century Puritan congregations began to build churches proper—i.e. buildings indistinguishable for all intents and purposes from Anglican churches (!) the old meeting-house shape did not disappear. Instead, it got transferred, in the manner of mimetic shapes from time immemorial, to other public forms—courthouses, capitols and schools.

Time and again the first specific symbol of organized civic life on the expanding American frontier was a meeting-house shape. It served in several instances as a capitol—in Chillicothe and Zanesville in Ohio as well as in Columbus (177B); also the second Indiana state capitol at Corydon (1813—, restored 1968)—an almost perfect example, the only stone building in the town, and oriented Westward (perhaps a vestigial connection with church tradition?). Courthouses copied capitols: there is an almost exact copy of the Corydon capitol at Rome, Indiana, in the Perry County courthouse on the Ohio River, for instance. Another example is the Ohio Village in Ohio Historical center in Columbus, "a typical Ohio county seat as it would have looked during the years 1800 to 1850." The visual effect of such courthouses, set in squares of late Georgian town-houses, was to image order and structured life in what had only recently been howling wilderness and formless prairie. There were dozens of examples.

177B. Third Ohio state capitol, Columbus, in use 1816-1851.
Later used as a schoolhouse.

In due course many of these courthouses and capitols became too small and new ones were built. Most big capitols imitated the United States capitol, for ideological reasons (q.v. 56, 57). The surplus buildings were commonly used as schoolhouses—that happened in all three Ohio capitols. But many schoolhouses were built in this shape from the first. Examples are, again, abundant.

Emily township district was one of many in eastern Ontario with considerable early immigration from New England and New York. Its schools showed that heritage. They were like many such schools all over North America. You can find examples like the first three of these in Minnesota, Nebraska, Kansas, California. Wherever they were built they proclaimed a philosophy of education which saw schools as training grounds for civic responsibility. Could such shapes have been perpetuated in other, larger forms? Certainly; there were many ways to do it.

178A. S.S. #1 Omemee-Emily (Williamson's *Omemee*)
c. 1840 – 1884

178B. S.S. #1 Omemee-Emily (Williamson's *Omemee*)
1884 – 1904

178C. S.S. #1 Omemee-Emily
1904 – 1964

Lady Eaton Elementary School
1964

178D. Four county schools for the township of Emily and the town of Omemee, midway between Lindsay and Peterborough in east central Ontario. From Howard T. Pammett, *Lilies & Shamrocks: A History of Emily Township, County of Victoria*, Ontario, 1818-1973.

What caused the abrupt change from precedent in the new school of 1964 was not technical considerations. The new school holds hardly more pupils than the old one. Responsible was a different aesthetic: the levelling aesthetic, reducing everything to utilitarian factory mode, in the name of honestly expressing materials, sculpture and the like. And behind that, a deep shift in educational philosophy: this style, here and elsewhere, inculcates an ethical relativism that is not interested in training for civic responsibility, the "when we are grown and take our place as men and women with our race" outlook. It trains for egalitarian participation in a consumer, collectivized economy. Its philosophy is closer to the old theory of teaching slaves to read and write just a little, enough to make them more useful on the plantation—but not enough that they are capable of probing thought. Much—too much, indeed—like the informing ethos of abstract logos and compulsive symbols as compared to the democratic political cartoon (q.v.).

Another, somewhat earlier example, is provided by tollhouses.

179A. Tollhouse of 1801 in Bewdley, Worcestershire.

179B. Mount Clare railroad station, Baltimore, Maryland, 1830. A comparison made by Carroll L.V. Meeks in *The Railroad Station* (New Haven, 1956) showing translation of octagon form from toll-house to early railroad station.

As late as the beginnings of the railway age, the principle of employing mimetic forms to make an environment more intelligible was understood. You need to design a new kind of building, a place where people start their journey by rail? Very well; the procedure is not to hire some Form Giver to build a monument to his own sensitivities, but get a Form Finder who can find some form that will make the purpose of this new building immediately intelligible to prospective users (and in the process, hopefully, also provide them with an aesthetic experience). What better form than a toll-house? There, fares were paid and journeys begun on the old road-way. For the new railway, that shape instantly proclaims a similar function. And an octagonal form retains, furthermore, a whole set of early associative meanings appropriate to the idea of journeys and beginnings. By a string of intermediaries, it was connected—to go back no further!—to those traditional baptistries where, in early Christian culture, new beginnings—i.e., new starts on life's journey—were made.

Because in medieval number theory "8" symbolized the beginnings of a new cycle or of life, baptistries were usually octagonal; or if they were not, the font was sure to be. Would designers of 18th-century toll-houses have remembered this

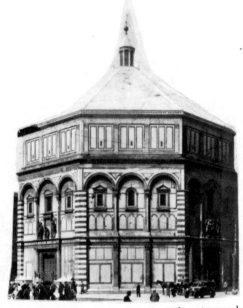

180A. Baptistry of Florence, built in the 11th century and completed in the 15th by Ghiberti's "Gates of Paradise"

symbolism? Hardly. But it could well be that the association of "8" and hence of eight-sided buildings, with the idea of new beginnings could have survived, for it was pervasive throughout Christian culture.

The mystical significance of "8" derived from its following "7," a preeminently important number. Not only is "7" in number theory proper a combination of "4" ("body," i.e., the 4 elements of which the body is composed) and "3" ("soul," image of the Trinity), whence 4 plus 3 equals "Humanity," but so many things in human life come in sevens: seven days of the week, seven notes of the scale, etc., whence "8" is the number signifying new beginnings.

"Symbolism in an art as abstract as architecture was most effective at a popular, instinctive, and illiterate level," Baldwin Smith was fond of repeating.[30] The ways such a form as the octagon would survive in association with beginning and with journeys would be by builder and commissioner alike feeling, "something about that form seems right," without putting it into words. "Looks fine to me—go ahead." And that, I think, may well explain how very often you find vestiges of old symbolism in highway markers erected by government road departments,

180B. Rogers Pass marker on the Trans-Canada Highway marking the Great Divide.

operating without benefit of Form Givers—Form Finders reappear. An example, perhaps, is the continental divide marker on the Trans-Canada highway at Rogers Pass (180B). Superficially it looks like Saarinen's arch in St. Louis; some inspiration may possibly may have come from there.[31] But, whether by accident or design—perhaps a bit of both—the symbolism is better. This actually is a place of beginnings— rivers and watersheds, specifically, and thence a decisive point on the highway, as well as on the trails that preceded. And if you draw out the ground-plan, you find that it actually is an eight-sided inverted star. Further, it is associated with a fountain. That too has rich precedent (180C).

The designers of the Rogers Pass marker had certainly never heard of the town fountain at Chiapas. Few people had, until Professor Markman found it. Is it then entirely fortuitous that this astonishingly (for the time and place) elegant monument, marking the beginning and/or end of journeys to this town, should be so curiously similar in plan (eight-sided inverted star), effect (domical) and social function? In one sense, yes; quite possibly the Rogers Pass monument made no intentional

180C. Fountain in Chipa de Corzo, Chiapas, Central America, west side. (photo and data, courtesy Sidney Markman). A *mudejar* building tradition translated transplanted from Seville to Central America; and a secularization of domical symbolism, from baptistry (eternal life) to civic fountain (life-giving water, community center, etc.). Begun 1557, completed 1562, restored 1944.

allusions to "8" as a symbol of beginnings or to domes as a symbol of authority (sacred or royal, as the case may be). Quite possibly the taste for these forms, which obviously led to this design being commissioned in preference to some other, was entirely instinctive. Nonetheless that taste did obviously exist; this design was in fact chosen over others. It "looked right," somehow. That's how living architecture works.

Mimetic materials, widespread in modern popular/commercial arts, likewise were historic devices for perpetuating familiar associations and continuity of ideas.

In modern popular/commercial building, perpetuation of earlier shapes rarely involves perpetuating the original materials of those shapes as well. Far from it. It often happens that almost every material in a popular/commercial building will be so designed as to look like something else. Mobile homes are particularly striking examples of this pervasive practise.

Lightness is an overriding consideration in mobile homes. It follows that, wherever practicable, aluminum and plastic will be employed. One might further expect that, since there are preeminently modern materials and any or all superfluous ornament would add undesired weight to the load, the characteristic stripped-down shapes favored by avant-garde design since Loos and the Bauhaus, would be used throughout. Not at all. Plastic and aluminum are treated to resemble traditional shapes and textural effects of wooden bargeboarding and timber struts, cornices and shutters; even flagstone terraces. Precisely the sort of "dishonesty" most ranted against by three generations of avant-garde theorists—and most confidently predicted to disappear once the mighty had been turned out of their Beaux-Arts academy seats and the pure in aesthetic heart had been exalted in their place. All of which happened a very long time ago now.

Worse, from the avant-garde point of view—if possible—are the interiors of typical mobile homes (181B), which usually come as a package with the home itself. Typically, plastic is made to look like wool carpeting, inlaid stone flooring, fancy stonework, white leather, polished blonde oak, lace curtains, and decorative

181A. Designers' presentation rendering of a Tamarron Doublewide Home, from a 1975 promotional brochure.

tile—versatility indeed! Aluminum is made to look like cherry cabinets, like brass, like steel. About the only thing "in the nature of materials" is the glass ashtray.

Why so much "fakery"? For the same reason that Parthenon builders "faked" carpentry in marble.[32] Throughout all historic architecture, textures originating in earlier materials have been perpetuated in later ones, for their symbolic associations. So mimetically recalling revered human values and historic experience (cf. Sect. II), has been an effective—perhaps *the* most effective—means of maintaining human continuity from generation to generation. For precisely this reason, popular/commercial architecture continues the practise. Mimetic materials help owners of mobile homes to think more of their being in a home than of their being mobile—which is to say, they remind owners of what, throughout history, homes have always been *about*. "Mobile home" is a contradiction in terms. "Home" means *non*-mobile, it means permanence. Whence—you want a home, but for whatever reason all you can manage is something which can be erected on a lot at minimum labor charge? There's a solution: materials textured to remind you of that more permanent base you really want and which you hope to have someday. Because their products are so treated Tamarron can advertise: "Share in the GREAT AMERICAN DREAM...A spacious home of your own"; or Marlette: "Walk in and Start LIVING."

181B. Kitchen area in a Marlette mobile home (manufactured in Michigan, Georgia, Kansas, Pennsylvania, Oregon, and Ontario. From an ófficial brochure c1975.

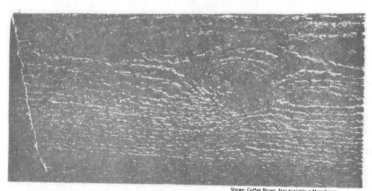

Shown: Coffee Brown. Also available in Moss Green.

It used to take 70 years to get a look this warm and weathered. Masonite has it now.

If you have the time, you can wait for the sun, wind, and rain to work its special kind of magic on raw, rough-hewn cedar.

Or you can call Masonite Canada Ltd., and order new Woodsman Lap Siding now.

Woodsman has the honest character of real weathered cedar, right down to its deep-etched grain and natural texture.

It takes Mother Nature years to create this rugged effect.

It takes Masonite just a couple of days.

MASONITE
CANADA LTD

182. Advertisement for "Masonite" shaped like clapboarding and textured like weathered cedar.

In so using mimetic textures to make a house a home, popular/commercial arts do for our society what the traditional art of architecture has done for societies throughout history. Why did early settlers in the New World go to such troublous lengths to reproduce in their new wilderness the material textures of their homes in Old Europe? For that same reason, assuredly. It would have been so much more logical to copy Amerind modes and manners of using the abundant forests for housing, so much easier than re-learning near-obsolescent European modes and techniques of wood-building.[33] Yet building with traditional European techniques in stone and brick began in the midst of a land so covered with trees that no building could be begun without first clearing its site of timber![34] Yearning for continuity through familiar and remembered textures can explain not only how shapes and prototypes from the early European Middle Ages[35] reappeared in the first settlements of North America, but why mobile homes in our time look as they do. Arts serving mankind's needs produced both, in comparable ways.[36]

Although mimetic textures are extraordinarily profuse in mobile homes and related highway building types (motels, diners and automobile accessories, etc.), it would be mistaken to imagine that they are rare elsewhere. They can be found everywhere—in posh suburban settings quite as often as in trailer parks. Mimetic textures are in fact rare only in avant-garde buildings, where they are used for expressive purposes, not for maintaining continuity with any past.[37] That popular/commercial architecture perpetuates not only mimetic materials associated with earlier times, but also traditional proportions and eclectic styles, is demonstrated by the example here (182): besides the mimetic weathered cedar effect, such a house offers windows mullioned by an 18th-century geometric ratio long ago provided to be a satisfying common denominator of taste amongst North American people, and a style derived from 17th-century New England house-types. Popular/commercial suburban housing has been so maintaining human continuity for almost a century now.

Familiar, and hence meaningful, proportions in built environments and living space are not fixable by fashions of any school or the sensitivities of any architect, but come about over many generations in response to atavistic psychic needs; finding traditional proportions, as popular/commercial builders do, is thus to promote human continuity.

If folk art seems dead, it need only be realized that the engineer who denies art has internalized the repetitive-symmetrical aesthetic and when he creates a 'purely functional' object he usually activates not the organic functionalist philosophy but the same traditional aesthetic as did his great-grandfather, the house carpenter or the wheelwright.

If folk art seems insignificant, ponder the reinforcing effect on the Western child raised in an immediate environment where most things—the furniture, the windows and doors, the houses along the street—are symmetrical. He will grow into a man who will place great value on repetition, control, equilibrium. He will, as farmer or city planner, try to draw nature into symmetry. He will, as scientist, try to draw empirical data into symmetrical models. He will, as old-time craftsman or industrial engineer, create objects that are apparently artless but that are actually—as if Mondrian and Klee never existed—products of the traditional repetitive-symmetrical aesthetic.[38]

Perhaps the most outstanding example of the principle here so nicely enunciated by Henry Glassie, are development houses— i.e., houses built by commercial developers, for mass sale.

The first "development houses" were perhaps Nicholas Barbon's in London after the Great Fire of 1666, well known in North America because Penn used them in his "boom town" of Philadelphia.[39] Comparable housing was built all through 18th and 19th-century America (183, 185). The difference between these and modern popular/commercial development houses is that ours usually come into being without benefit of architectural consultation, whereas in earlier times pattern books written by architects, often of outstanding stature, were almost invariably relied upon.[40] Why? Not for any lack of avant-garde interest in producing designs for mass market. Corbusier's failure to understand elementary conditions of mass housing, in the mid-1920s Pessac project outside Bordeaux, is the classic example, but examples abound from every decade.[41] The examples here are typical (183). However different the outward forms of A, B, and D, all have in common a set of proportions which might be called, following Glassie, an inherited folk aesthetic. 183C is quite differently proportioned—and this is the only one of the four that

183. Examples of speculative housing from John E. Rickert, "House Fashions of the Northeast United States: A Tool of Geographical Analysis," *Annals of the American Association of Geographers,* 57, 2, June 1967. A and B, "Cape Cod" and "Neo-English Colonial" are continuing types from c1900. "Flat Roofed Functional" (C) is a post-1945 appearance, while the "Cubic" (D) has largely disappeared, its greatest popularity occurring c1900-1910.

never established itself as a successful mass-produced housing model. Put it another, simpler, way: A, B, and D "look right" to prospective buyers. C looks "wrong" or "funny."

    Homesteads always were designed and built by substantially this same process: selection by unconscious taste of certain proportions over others, by unconscious preference for one spatial system or another.

The conviction that families ought to be founded, and land is what you found them on, goes too deep in Western (perhaps in all) civilizations to be killed by 20th-century technological changes. They only changed its manifestations. Now the family estate is measured more by what can be earned in salaries than from farming—secondary rather than primary production. But it is still a joint enterprise, to which everyone—husband, wife, older children—contributes. Now the visual metaphor of the successful family is suburbanized. But it remains a substantial house on a piece of land. And what determines its "look" is the "rightness" (familiarity, if you like) of certain proportions (the mimetic materials as well, oftentimes) generation after generation, which thus relate the builders to ancestors of whom they may never have heard, of whose existence they are quite unconscious.

No matter how primitive technologically, a building once accepted by its community as "looking right," and being sited "right," becomes a metaphor of community values—i.e., of "rightness." Thus a Huron Indian village may (184B) be built only of bark and saplings, but constitute a compelling metaphor of rightness inasmuch as the proportions of huts and their relations to each other depend upon community acceptance of how "things ought to be done"; likewise African mud huts, as Labelle Prussin has shown.[41] It follows that when you find the characteristic proportions and behavioral spaces of one culture being adopted by another, you may conclude that this other culture is dying, no matter how many anthropologists and civil rights leaders rush forward to prop it up. And it follows further that buildings which perpetuate community values of this sort are images of persuasion/conviction, whether consciously or no.

In high phases of civilization there is conscious awareness of proportions and of their ethical qualities. This is one of the reasons why "art" as a deliberate or conscious art has so often been said to have originated in Greece; for there you find the same work "kalos" which means beautiful in a visual sense also meaning "ethically right," and there we find the most deliberate beautification practised (q.v., Sect. VI et al.). Twentieth-century designers too have been aware of this correlation and avant-garde apologists were fond of talking about academic or bourgeois art as "immoral." They all too often failed to realize

184A. Text figure from Henry C. Glassie, *Patterns in the Material Folk Culture of the Eastern United States* with the following caption: "This cabin, inhabited by a Choctaw Indian, is located south of Philadelphia, Neshoba County, Mississippi (November, 1963). It displays many of the features common to folk houses of the Deep South: it has a front porch and rear kitchen shed; its roof extends to over the external gable end chimney of brick; it is supported by piers rather than a full foundation, and it is built of small pine logs, split in half, the round side facing outwards with boards nailed vertically to the insides of the logs in lieu of chinking."

B. Village of Huron Indians near Georgian Bay (Midland, Ontario) reconstructed by the iversity of Western Ontario, under direction of Wilfrid Jury.

that neither community ethics nor community aesthetics are qualities to be invented by individual geniuses and then imposed upon the populace, like those personal religions invented by Akbar in Moghul India, Ikhenaton in New Kingdom Egypt, the Webbs in Britain, and so fatuously on and on.

Whether conscious or not, the moment buildings begin to function as metaphors of community standards of rightness, they cease to be utilitarian structures and become architecture—hence we may speak of architecture beginning in the 4th millennium with perpetuation of familiar (revered) shapes and textures by mimesis, and familiar (revered) proportions. Conversely, wherever and whenever buildings similarly function, they represent architectural art no matter what intellectual fashion chooses to designate them.[42] Whence another reason for the significance of popular/commercial architecture—in it is the chief reservoir for our times of proportions transmitted from times immemorial in folk building and High Architecture alike.

For it was precisely these proportions and the sense of "rightness" that went with them, that avant-garde Form-Givers jettisoned in their rise to dominance. They were not concerned with finding proportions familiar and comfortable to their users. Their intent was to impose forms of their own invention on the human environment, so as to mould it into their own image. I am quite prepared to believe that their motive generally was less obsessive egotism than genuine belief that by so restructuring environments they could create a better world—"radiant cities" whose new proportions were one among many signs of a new order whence sin and pain, crime and corruption had been banished forever. Avant-garde sincerity in believing it not only acceptable to do away with all those inherited sets of proportions, but positively desirable that ancient notions of rightness deriving from time-honored usage be obliterated, is not in question. The problem is, radiant cities didn't result. We got Pruitt-Ingoes instead.

Yet still today, familiar and traditional proportions give character to our landscape and so humanize it. Go from France into Germany, or across the channel into England—not to mention from Europe into Asia Minor, or from Asia Minor into

Iran or Uzbekistan, or thence to China or Vietnam—or even from the Hudson Valley into Pennsylvania and thence into Maryland—and significant changes in basic proportions and material textures signal transitions from one culture to another. For this, surviving folk building is accountable only in part; mostly it is modern popular/commercial architecture of all sorts, following proportional systems inherited therefrom. Primorial traditions of right proportion and appropriate materials continue in popular/commercial, as in ancestral folk building, to provide basic metaphors of rightness, of Practical Reason, of Natural Law.[42] These stand as three-dimensional images of How Things Are; what the old Chinese called the *Tao,* the Way of the Universe[43]; what in Christian formulas is phrased: "As it was in the beginning is now and ever shall be, world without end"; the basic and fundamental signification of the word Right in every Indo-European language; (*recht* in Germanic and *dharma* in Sanskrit, *droit* in French and *ortho* in Greek, *pravda* in Slavic[44]— what the ancient Sumerians called sšu and the ancient Egyptians called *ma'at*)

Ma'at was the cosmic force of harmony...the order of created things, physical and spiritual, established at the beginning and valid for all time...the just and proper relationship of cosmic phenomena, including the relationship of the rulers and the ruled...things true not because they were susceptible of testing and verification, but because they were recognized as being in their true and proper places in the order created and maintained by the gods. As an Old Kingdom text says, '*Ma'at* is great and its effectiveness is lasting; it has not been disturbed since the time of Him who made it—it is the right path before him who knows nothing....[45]

Perhaps it is no more than far-fetched coincidence that the physical disintegration of American cities coincided with widespread adoption of Corbusian-type high-rise urban redevelopments on proportional systems totally different from anything before. But the thought does occur—was urban blight entirely caused by economics aggravated by bad planning, or were these vast new housing projects also rendered psychically uninhabitable by their proportional systems?

Nothing was commoner—indeed, practically *de rigeur* in architectural writings over the first six decades of this century, than ridicule of 19th-century "stylistic jackets"—i.e. provisions of different sets of ornamental details to cover the same basic

185. Typical urban house-types (A) from the mid-19th century and (B) from the 1890s in the Lincoln Park area of Chicago (from the Chicago Historical and Architectural Landmarks Commission booklet. *Mid-North Chicago*, 1974).

framework, to accommodate diverse tastes in eclectic historic styles. The point of such ridicule was usually to promote a conviction that the 20th-century should have a style of its own. All too often forgotten was that in this kind of designing a basic unity did exist—the unity of a common set of proportions. A city street displaying half a dozen different styles in eclectic ornament could nevertheless be consistently scaled and proportioned throughout. The resultant humane quality was often realized only when it was lost, by the introduction of architecture scaled and proportioned differently—alleged to be more organically honest, insofar as it had no "fake" ornament; but breaking up the unity of city streets and areas far more catastrophically than any diversity of eclectic ornament ever had. Then, thus, and often too late, came awareness of how the 19th century's despised eclectic architecture had in fact preserved and transmitted comfortable proportions which created a humane built environment; and that one of the ways to restore such an environment was to rediscover traditional proportional systems:

The skins of houses are shallow things that people are willing to change, but people are most conservative about the spaces they must utilize, and in which they must exist. Build the walls of anything, deck them out with anything, but do not change the arrangement of the rooms or their proportions. In these volumes—bounded by surfaces from which a person's senses rebound to him—his psyche develops; disrupt them, and you disrupt him.[46]

Three diverse examples may help make this point decisive:

(1) *Zürich*[47]

On a street called Dolderthal in Zürich are three houses: Nos. 7, 11 and 15. No. 7 was for many years occupied by Siegfried Giedion, premier propagandist for avant-garde architecture, charter member of CIAM.[48] There he wrote *Space Time & Architecture,*[49] the (for all intents and purposes) compulsory text in most architectural schools during the decades when "mechanization took command;[50] thence he tirelessly promoted the International Style generally, in a kind of *troika* apexed by himself, Corbusier and Gropius. It's an old house, built about 1901, like dozens of others in this neighborhood of Zürich, vaguely 19th-century Baroquish, vaguely Art-Nouveauish, what the Europeans call "Romantic Nationalist" in style, supposed to evoke *gemütlichkeit* by generous proportions, high ceilings, rambling effects. Nos. 11 and 15 Dolderthal are blatantly different. They were built in the mid-1930s by Alfred Rott and Marcel Breuer, also prime movers in the modern movement. (Breuer was with Giedion on the 1933 CIAM Mediterranean cruise that produced Corbusier's belated "Athens Charter.") Nos. 11 and 15 incorporate all the latest features Giedion preached and promoted: strip windows, concrete slab, pilotis, grandiose proportions *à la Modulor.* Mechanization has taken command of them; they are *machines à habiter.* The arrangement was that Giedion was to move into one of them when it was finished. But when it was finished, Giedion refused to budge. He liked his familiar house. Its ornament was execrable, indeed everything about it was precisely what he spent his writing days decrying and denouncing. But in the crunch he liked it. He stayed put. With his feet—to steal a metaphor from another distinguished sometime resident of Zurich—he voted No. 7 most liveable of the three. But from this divergence between personal taste and public principles, neither Giedion nor anyone else seemed to draw conclusions—at least not published ones. Nor from the fact that Corbusier and Mies also chose to live and work in old 19th-century buildings while engaged upon their task of restructuring the 20th-century world for its own good.

(2) *Kyoto:*

Kyoto has for so many centuries been Japan's cultural heartland that it was entirely appropriate for Sachio Otani, winner of an open competition to design an International Conference Hall in Kyoto in 1962, should draw preeminently upon traditional motifs.[51] To judge whether the proportional system is correspondingly traditional goes beyond the competence of one whose own traditions of behavioral space are non-Japanese, but (to venture a personal comment) there does seem a disconcertingly familiar feeling of those grandiose International Style a-human proportions in this Hall's interior spaces generally. Conversely, popular/commercial development houses in the Kyoto area seem to perpetuate proportions of traditional Japanese houses.

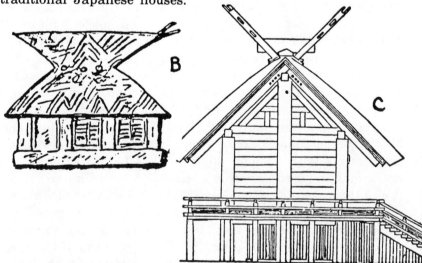

Among traditional models drawn upon for the design are 186B. Jomon pit burial house, represented on a 3rd-century A.D. mirror. 186C. great shrine (dai-jingu) at Ise, front elevation. The latter reputedly has been rebuilt exactly every twenty years since the time of the first Japanese Emperors, two thousand years ago.

Perhaps a big conference center demands comparably big-scaled spaces? Not necessarily; 16th- and 17th-century castles in this same area demonstrate that it's quite possible to construct a big Japanese building out of small units based upon familiar traditional shapes and proportions, for they are simply composed of basic regional peasant house-types assembled in varying combinations.

186A. Kyoto International Conference Hall, completed 1966 on a pond north of Kyoto in a setting of traditional Japanese gardens and waterways, on a design by Sachio Otani. Interior rooms are of diverse sizes and colors to accommodate diverse international gatherings.

(3) Dale, Indiana
About the "Americanness" of Frank Lloyd Wright's architecture, Norris Smith once wrote,[53]

A moment's thought will reveal to us that the stature of the position we have accorded Wright, who is widely regarded as having been the greatest of American architects, has been based in large measure upon his own evaluation of himself...rather than...in reference to the shape of the American world at large....Wright's works are so peripheral, both in their locations and in their relation to generally prevailing conventions that the overwhelming majority of Americans have never beheld an example of his architecture and would be quite baffled by the idea that his was the genuinely American style....

But the "Americanness" of Wright's architecture is not necessarily refuted by his rejection of, or by, an avant-garde Establishment dominated by German refugees to the United

187. "Stone's Best Western Motel," Dale, Indiana. Postcard. Built c1965, typical of motel architecture across United States.

States, and the consequent fact that most plums of corporate commissions in big American cities from the 1940s onwards went to Breuers and Mieses and Gropiuses. It's a question of whose style is closer to the mainstream. Whose style has proportions and behavioral spaces descended from two centuries of traditional building in North America? One look at everyday building common throughout North America and the question answers itself. The designers of "Stone's Best Western Motel" (187) in Dale, Indiana, may never have actually beheld a specimen of Wright's own building, as Norris says; likewise a thousand other popular/commercial designers. But all their architecture clearly comes from a common matrix. It all shares a common tradition—as Mies' and Gropius' never did and never could. Wright's architecture is, as he said, American architecture because it was based upon that common matrix and tradition. Had Wright not been seduced by the cult of Architect as Culture-Hero, he might have realized even better his early ambition to create a truly popular and truly great American architecture. Now it looks as if that must be done by someone working from the other end of the axis, from a popular/commercial base.

A third traditional way of investing architecture with meaningful symbolism has been by borrowing forms which, by whatever means, have accumulated symbolic values in past contexts, and putting them to some present use—i.e., deliberate eclectic styling for persuasive/conviction.

The idea of eclecticism as a meaningless Battle of the Styles was true, by and large, for the end of the 19th century, and examples of it can still be found now. But "Moderns" were largely responsible for making it so. Observing how so much eclectic ornament was being indiscriminately applied, they proposed to abolish all of it, to create a New architecture of sparse purity which would be the mirror image of overdecorated bourgeois building. In the process, they lost that human continuity which down through the centuries it had been the historical social function of eclectic architecture to provide.

And once lost, that continuity is not easily recovered. Despite Lewis Mumford's elequent calls for architectural environments which will be a home for Man, and warnings of the menace and meaninglessness of environments which aren't, he cannot bring himself to face the truth that of the several possible ways in which architecture historically has in fact maintained the human continuity which makes enrivonments humane, the most effective, deliberate and systematic instrument has been eclecticism. And in this respect he is not unique among critics of the modern movement, only typical. Reassessment of eclecticism is only beginning.[54] But there are interesting intimations.

(1) *The Split-Level-Colonial-Ranch American Image.*

"Eclecticism" means *ek lektos,* "out of the best," and involves borrowing and perpetuation—not only of proportions and mimetic shapes and textures, but also details and ornaments of all sorts associated with earlier kinds of building, from doorknobs to lamps and shutters. To talk about the "historical styles" of popular/commercial eclectic buildings in the literal sense is misleading. There never was any such thing as the typical American development house in "split-level-colonial-ranch" form. Even its so-called "colonial" style mixes elements from all sorts of periods and places both before and after the American Revolution. It's not archaeologically scientific; not scholarly— but not therefore, as often intimated, necessarily contemptible.

For few eclectic styles ever were literally correct, in strict art-historical terms (least of all that "Renaissance" age for which adulation remains more or less obligatory in aesthetic line-of-progress art history!). Popular/commercial colonial (and other) styles recall the past in the only sense really effective.

"Minimally eclectic" is how you might best describe small development houses of the Levittown type. But of course their Cape Cod model was minimally eclectic too. So was the ultimate model of them all, the pit-saw-boarded and thatched early dwellings of Plymouth Plantation.

For this kind of historical association, minimal detail is all you need. Such architecture is historical in the same sense as

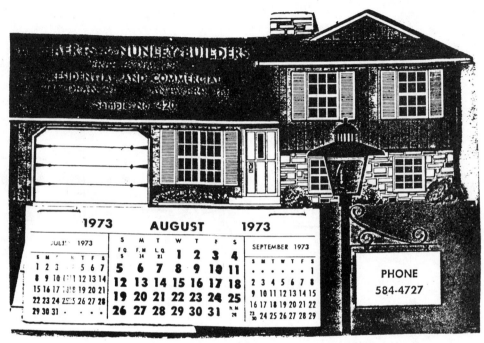

188. Advertising calendar distributed by a contractor in Antwerp, Illinois, 1973.

language. Its every form, like every word we speak, is traceable
back through many earlier generations and so "feels right" when
used. Exactness in imitating earlier buildings is, then, irrelevant.
What matters is not whether people in the past lived in house-
types exactly like these, but that people nowadays recall the past
when they see such houses, and find historical associations
thereby. They appeal, let us say, to owners' subconscious
concepts of themselves as harassed commuters only by
temporary accident—in fact, beneath the forced veneer, sturdy
woodsmen still; independent pioneers, maybe, capable any time,
should need arise, of trekking confidently off in Conestoga
wagons to settle far lands (a fancy which, inverted, no doubt

189A. Small house in Levittown, N
York, c1960. B. "Cape Cod cottag
vernacular Georgian type, Provincetow
Mass., c1760. C. Hut/cabin from t
restored pioneer village at Plymou
Massachusetts, c1630.

assisted their children's yens and fantasies for communes and deserts, vagabondage in Kabul and Katmandu, infatuations with the romantic Che and the sturdy peasant Mao.) Aluminum siding and plastic eaves, asphalt shingles imitating cedar shakes and removeable muntin bars, shutters nailed to the walls forever unshut and celluloid grates never consumed (like Moses' burning bush), all contribute to this image, and make such houses function as images of persuasion/conviction—in the historic way architecture proper has always functioned in and for society. Such a "colonial style," stubbornly perpetuated in the face of all sophisticated opinion, is persuasive in the traditional sense, reinforcing ideological associations.

(2) "The People's Palace": New York to Moscow and back.

There is much talk about us; it is said that like lightning we have swept from the surface of the earth the palaces of the bankers, landowners, and czars. All this is true. But let us build in their place the palace of the workers and laboring peasants....
Comrades! Maybe the European proletariat...when it beholds this enchanted palace of the workers and peasant will realize that we are here to stay....
...On new, splendid, magnificent, and revolutionary earth we, the workers, born in miserable hovels, will leave those hovels in comradely ranks to enter our enchanted palaces to the strains of the great "Internationale."

The speaker was Sergei Kirov; the occasion, his address to the First Congress of the Soviets in December 1922. Anatole Kopp, who reports the speech in *Town and Revolution* comments that it

revealed all the importance that he attached to the architecture as well as the illusions that he cherished with regard to its ideological impact. His speech also contained the germ of certain ideas which were later to divert Soviet architecture along the path of empty monumentalism....

"Empty monumentalism" was indeed how the results of enthusiasms like Kirov's looked from the vantage-point of the entrenched avant-garde Establishment of 1966. And worse. For the Soviet leaders took as their archetype of "enchanted palace" the great skyscrapers of American capitalism in its golden age, from the 1880s to 1917—how ironic! "We are baffled," wrote a typical progressive in the *Architectural Record* for 1937, "by the

190A. Oakland, California, City Hall, 1911 (Palmer, Hornbostel, and Jones, architects).

190B. Lenigrad Hotel on Komsomol Square, Moscow, 1949-53 (Poliakov and Boretskii, architects). (From *Journal of the Society of Architectural Historians*, XXIV, 1965, 1.)

so-called new Soviet architecture which beginning in 1932 bears the stamp of genuine Fascism. Could it be that Bolshevism and Fascism have much in common in their doctrines?" Hardly the point. What Nazi and Soviet architecture of the '30s had in common was a concern for the social function, an awareness that architecture is a public art which necessarily makes statements about the institutions of the State—an understanding of the historic art of architecture, that is to say, which avant-garde critics had lost.[55] From that traditional point of view, appropriating skyscrapers for symbols of the triumphant proletarian made perfect sense. Always, architectural forms borrowed from past eras proclaim current values and achievements. Romanesque styles proclaimed the ties of the Holy Roman Empire to the times of Constantine, first "holy" Roman emperor. Renaissance eclectic forms proclaimed the rebirth of true, i.e., secular, states emulating those of classical Antiquity. Gothic Revival forms proclaimed the continuity of 19th-century British culture with its past, "freedom slowly broadening down from precedent to precedent," as Tennyson stated it, without revolution. Why not employ the classical skyscraper, a symbol of capitalism known to every Russian through pictures and movies, to proclaim how workers have now, thanks to the Party, taken over those enchanted palaces from banished landlords and cremated czars?

One may deplore the particular value systems of Nazi or Soviet states, without denying the validity of the architectural principles they employed. Quite the contrary: more and more critics are at last coming to see the importance of democratic states having an architecture which creates visual metaphors of *their* convictions, instead of mere art works dedicated to ethical relativism.

Musical chairs? The Soviets finally, at long last, abandon American classical or Gothic skyscrapers in favor of steel-and-glass houses, so ethically relative, so eminently suitable therefore to a state which proclaims official morality to be relative to Party dictate. At the same moment, a variant of old McKim-Mead-&-White skyscraper types—what many alarmed observers have called "a gigantic Chippendale chest" threatens to reappear in New York under the aegis of a Master Builder. What it means remains fully to be seen. Possibly no more than a Picasso-type publicity gimmick. Possibly a profound shift in the direction of American architecture. One thing is sure: it may be a "cunning blow to the whole sprawling body of American architecture"[57]as perceived from architectural schools by architecture critics, but it is by no means the astonishing radical novelty so many seem to think. Precisely where Philip Johnson got his idea for the AT&T building he's not telling. But he wouldn't have to look far. The nearest one of Emilio Capaldi's Independence Malls would do.

191. Proposed AT&T tower, New York, designed by Philip Johnson, 1978. According to *Progressive Architecture* (6.78), the "tower would rise 660 feet and cover entire block front...clad in pinkish granite, with details of more or less Renaissance Revival character, which are still being refined. Only 37 office floors would occupy shaft between tall colonnade at base and briken pediment at roof, which would conceal mechanical equipment."

All these traditional means of infusing architectural forms with communal significance can be employed in a "post-modern" architecture—if High Architects are willing to return in some degree to their former role of Form-Finders as well as, instead of, Form-Givers.

Mimetic forms and textures, familiar proportions, eclecticism, all these traditional devices have been preserved in popular/commercial building and can easily, as Philip Johnson's AT&T project has just demonstrated, be re-absorbed into the fabric of High Architecture (which is not to say, of course that Johnson's design has accomplished this difficult feat—its proportions alone obviously need critical refinement). Always assuming, however, architects would be willing to use mimetic shapes and materials not only for expressive ends but also with appropriate associative meanings. Always assuming that architects would take their proportions from the users, not the "Creators' ", experience; that they forgot the dismal kind of arrogance displayed at Chandigarh by Corbusier who as Sten Nilsson described it, "late or early,

...experienced no...doubts. He did not come to learn but to teach. Although he had not set foot in India previously, the principles he represented were universal and well thought out. He was ready to start work immediately 'in perfect gear, a combine harvester at work on the Chandigarh harvest.'... Le Corbusier had counted on the huge human labour force as part of the local resources in Chandigarh.... LeCorbusier boasted that he had been able to carry out the most advanced projects under these primitive conditions.... But his appreciation of the Indians did not extend to accepting them on their own terms. A little episode from the work on the Assembly will serve to illustrate this. The boys whose job it was to lead the donkeys up and down, had begun to draw on the just finished concrete wall. It would have been very easy to preserve these graffiti, a genuine art brut, but Le Corbusier adopted a different approach. He had them copied and then used them as a basis for his *own* drawings of fish, camels, and the *Modulor*, which were pressed into the concrete. This is the way a formgiver works.

Always assuming architects are willing to renounce the Hero-Savior role CIAM cast them in, to remember, as Stanislaus von Moos admonished so cogently in his article on the ship as a metaphor of modern architecture, that buildings are not supposed to remain forever under the orders of some Great Captain who designed them and then, like the Deists's God, went off to some other part of the universe leaving his machine to run forever under the rules He laid down,[59] not a curtain color to be altered, not a shrub to be planted, not a sparrow's nest on any ledge contrary to His will.

Eclecticism's proper social function needs clearly to be understood, as to establish continuity with the past, to transmit values and attitudes from one generation to the next. Whatever and whenever eclecticism fails to fulfil that function, it is worthless and just the kind of dishonest veneer early pioneers of early design said it was.

When the angry young men of the 1880s and '90s wanted to point to the wickedness and corruption of 19th-century bourgeois architecture, they could always find plenty of examples of buildings loaded with a miscellaneous assemblage of decorative motifs applied at random, meaningless, muddled, vulgar. "All drawn from some monstrous tyranny, some oppression by kings and priests," as Sullivan used to rant. One need not go far to find comparable examples today of popular/commercial architecture using eclectic styles without proper purpose.

Anyone objecting to eclecticism as any answer to our present dilemma can point to things like this: "Here's where we came in!" Avant-garde architecture triumphed in the early 20th century precisely because so much late Victorian architecture had become a cluttered chaos of empty decorative forms drawn by whimsy from anywhere or everywhere, applied indiscriminately, for eye-appeal alone. How infinitely better to have a plain building honestly exposing materials and structure than some such fake picturesque pastiche as dreamed up by the Chamber of Commerce of Leavenworth, Washington, in the late 1950s!

So posed, the question is hard to answer—impossible to meet, indeed, on its own metaphysical grounds of virtuous honesty and straightforward exposure versus cynical cover-ups of the true nature of structure. One could point out: if de-decorated buildings were indeed all so well constructed of such attractive materials that exposing them would feast the eyes, that's one thing; but most structures in most places in most parts of the world are just as well covered by something, and why not by something picturesque? Is it such a crime against humanity to house a drugstore in a chalet or turn decrepit Hotel Chisholm into the Edelweiss, even though there's no particular demonstrable connection between Leavenworth and Bavaria?

Leavenworth, Washington 1953

Leavenworth, Washington — The Bavarian Village

192. Before-and-after postcards of Leavenworth, Washington: "...picture taken in 1953 shows how the little city looked before the conversion to Bavarian Alpine architecture," and "the Bavarian Village of Leavenworth, Washington, 1965."

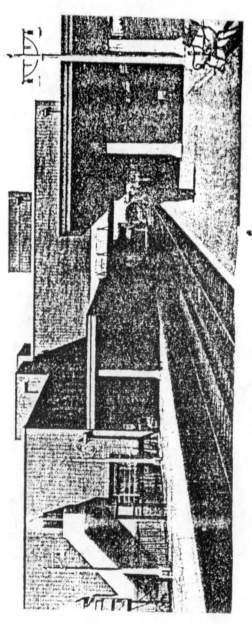
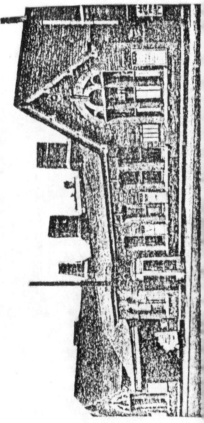

193. New (1938-9) and old railroad stations at Luton in the British Midlands, from H. Holland, *Travellers' Architecture.*

However, the real defense of eclecticism can't rest on these grounds. It's defensible only when the style used has associations with the background and history and present life of the community on whose built environment it is employed. And then it is very defensible—can indeed be promoted in entire good heart.

Holland's *Travellers' Architecture*[60] was typical of avant-garde Establishment mentality (the author may well have changed his view by now!). Replacement of the "old station, built in the style of the Gothic Revival," by a new one designed insofar as possible entirely for physical and mechanical efficiency, is seen as an unmixed good. No recognition of a building "symptomatic of the style of many of the old Midland stations" being thereby related to its region and thence to the great stations of the metropolis like St. Pancras, thence to great Gothic Revival monuments like the Westminster New Palace of the 1830s and Windsor Castle of the 1920s, thereby proclaiming the continuity of British institutions and national character, in distinction to and implicit rebuttal of the American and French revolutionary breaks with the past and adoption of Classical Revival style in proclamation thereof (q.v. 56). No: appreciation of how the old railroad station's style thereby made travellers part of a human heritage and inheritors of a humane environment rather than the faceless cogs in a *machine à voyager* which the new station turns them into. Or perhaps there is awareness of it now. New planning everywhere in Britain is emphasizing old traditions, village greens, humane scale, and the like. The newer railroad stations may too. Sure we need new stations periodically. But they need not be new in the sense of different entirely from the old. They can be new in the sense of renewed, as our bodies grow new skin and new hair. That's the stuff of continuity.

It has been in the name of a better future that modern architecture has repudiated the past. But concern for parents and ancestors is just as much an axiom of Practical Reason as concern for children and futurity is.

It seems to have become fashionable to maintain what while meaningful environments are undeniably desirable, and undeniably not being created by modern architectural means, to ask for them at this time in the world's history is to ask for the impossible. Nowadays, the argument runs, we have no broadly held firm convictions, as in the days of the Pharaohs, or even as in Baroque Europe. Consequently modern architects could not create a meaningful environment no matter how much they might want to. Forms functioning as metaphors of commonly held and understood values simply don't exist, because such values are gone.

> As we move up...to the so-called 'significant' buildings, large commercial complexes, religious edifices, government and other institutional structures, we run into another curious fact: nobody seems to believe, with much conviction, in any of the institutions.

So said George Nelson, speaking to the Harvard Graduate School of Design in 1972.[61] The logical conclusion is faced very honestly. Traditional architecture consisted of meaningful visual metaphors. The avant-garde cannot find any meaning in society and therefore any search for meaningful visual metaphors is useless. Therefore avant-garde architecture has come to an end. Or more exactly, to vary an inelegant metaphor, you can't tell avant-garde buildings from holes in the ground. If not caves, they are mirrors. Either way, they disappear. Architecture disappears. It is, from the avant-garde point of view, all over.

The solution? According to this typical spokesman: "The real problem for the designer is not only to find clients [who have understandably, in such circumstances, dwindled]: he must *first* [and this is italicized in the article] *determine what a humane environment really is.*" Mumford had said the same, back in 1968:"Unless we retain human continuity, our technological accomplishments are not merely meaningless, but menacing." And again, easier said than done.

Let's begin by observing that the notion of past eras where everyone marched to the beat of the same drummer, everyone in society held exactly the same kind of convictions, has long been shown to be false, a simplistic product of romantic nationalist thinking. Meaning in historic architecture, whether Pharaonic or Baroque or whatever, was never a reflection of convictions universally held throughout societies. Architecture historically made its most powerful statements when the institutions it stood for were under attack.[62] Its visual metaphors were means of establishing, transmitting and above all reinforcing convictions. Architecture both proclaimed and persuaded. Architects created dramatic statements of mass conviction as much because people didn't hold them as because they did: their job was precisely to do this and so ensure orderly continuity of society of civilization. The notion that architects ought to be, or could be, revolutionaries has been disastrous not only to humane continuity but even more to the architectural profession itself.

And more basically: those visual metaphors of "institutionalized patterns of human relatedness," which it was the historic business of architecture to create, rested upon the Nature of Things, upon ultimate premises, Practical Reason, whatever name you give the basic ground of thought, on which all argument must rest—including any argument that society has no such convictions. For without that ground no communication would be possible. ("The world is meaningless." "Does that include what you've just said, or not? If so, your statement is meaningless. If not, on what grounds do you exclude your thought from the general meaninglessness of all the rest of the world...?")

A concrete case: Lethbridge University, chosen not because it is bad—far from it—but because it is so typical of the problem avant-garde theory has landed architecture in.[63] Arthur Erickson is unquestionably Canada's most famous designer, and what he does is always interesting and provocative. For the new Simon Fraser University at Burnaby (British Columbia) in the mid-1960s he created the architectural image of public educational institutions as temples for rites capable of transforming humanity. Lethbridge is an essay along the same lines, though rather more subtle and sophisticated, and without Simon Fraser's Arts-&-Crafts undertones. It is also much more highly personal. Indeed the architect provided a viewpoint at his own expense—"Aperture," a giant sculptural keyhole, functioning rather like Velasquez's optical focus in *Las Meniñas* whereby the monarch's eyeball determines how everything shall be seen.

194. Main building of the University of Lethbridge, Alberta, completed in 1971 on the designs of Arthur Erickson. Built principally of concrete, the building is 98 feet high and 912 feet long—some corridors stretching the entire length, their two converging rows of identical office doorknobs producing startling effects of one-point perspective. It is isolated from the town on 450 acres across a coulee or gulch formed by the Oldman River.

General air view showing the Academic-Reside building lengthwise, and the canvas "worm" covered passageway winding up the coulees without which access to the small Physi Education/Fine Arts building would be next impossible in the fierce winds that blow winter a summer over this exposed flat land.

Erickson's Lethbridge epitomizes the basic premise of modernism in architecture: we owe a duty to posterity—to our children and to remote futurity—to make a "better world." In the name of the future we are justified in sacrificing anything and everything else. Erickson's design has nothing to do with the present community, which sits in the Palisser Triangle, a mini-dustbowl in southern Alberta. By great labor and with much civic pride Lethbridge citizens have carved out a small green oasis of little brick and wood houses shaded by carefully nurtured trees. They hoped that their new university might have a somewhat similar shape—a series of smallish buildings set in a treed environment. Of their wishes the new university took no account whatever. It sits haughtily on the farther edge of a great coulee or gully, some miles away from the town, giving a visual impression (intended by its designer) of a vessel riding the waves of the desert. *Magnifique, mais ce n'est pas l'architecture*—at least, not the traditional architectural art of creating visual metaphors meaningfully associated with the present, with values and attitudes held by the people for whom it was allegedly built. Totally unrelated to Lethbridge as it presently exists, this design presents a vision of the future, when this small prairie town will become part of the larger mechanized, scientifically organized and perfected North American technological empire.

It's the future, then, that justifies jettisoning the past. Every slight to present needs and tastes, too, can be forgiven on grounds, "We have a duty to provide our descendants with a better environment than ours has been." Yet even assuming that what we're providing is in fact better (and it's far from demonstrably true that an environment inculcating a machine-like philosophy of education is in fact better than architecture symbolizing education for citizenship), *why* are we under that obligation to the future? Obviously not for ourselves personally; none of us will be around in 2050 to care. Because experience shows that criminals are bred in poor environments, and we don't want our children to grow up in a criminal world? But there is no conceivable way to get from "This action would do you (or me, or us, or our children) good (or harm, or whatever), to "You [or I, or we] ought to do this." Neither is there any way to prove by reason that society ought to be preserved, or even that I (or you, or we) have any right to life at all, good or bad. These are axioms of Practical Reason; only after taking them for granted, as self-evident standards, can we proceed to deduce what good or bad actions may be.

The same Practical Reason which enjoins concern for future welfare on architects also equally enjoins concern for human continuity; if we deny responsibility for the past then we cannot justify any concern for the future either.

Our concern for the future is a matter of justice—justice in the sense of the first premise of Justinian's Code of Roman Law: "...The settled and permanent intention of rendering every person proper and natural rights." (*Constitutions* I,1), in the sense of the Declaration of Independence's "Every person is endowed by the Creator with certain inalienable rights." It's a matter of rightness accepted beyond question, like the "right proportions" of vernacular architecture. The principal justification by which the avant-garde claimed its right to acceptance and power has been that its architecture worked toward a better, honester, opener society. That claim is meaningless without a working definition of justice, held as an axiom of Practical Reason. Any and all demands for a more humane environment rest upon an axiomatic assumption that the living have a duty to work for the good of the yet-to-be-born, and a self-evident notion of what "good" implies: a proposition which is beyond reason, a proposition taken for granted so that reasoning can begin. No moralist can escape it, not even moralists denying morality: Hegel, Marx, Engels, Stirner, Nietzche, all "in order to comment upon what would constitute qualitatively better arrangements [in society]...are forced to return to ethics, with its subjectivist foundations," as Habermas, Caroll, and assorted other sociologists and political analysts have been pointing out for some time.[64]

Despite the claims of avant-garde Founding Fathers to be bringing into being something historically unprecedented, in fact any validity, even any sense of the New Spirit and its New Architecture depends upon a system of values that goes back to the beginning of the world.

The most obvious visual metaphor of social values and institutions which 20th-century architecture has created—however subconsciously, perhaps; however mixed up with other considerations—is an image of the Good Society to Come, in the form of tall big buildings which proclaim beautiful, plentiful,

195. "Hope for the Depressed": illustration from a pamphlet put out by the Revere Copper Company in 1943 showing a tenement family's hopes and dreams for "after the war." Shades of Tony Garnier, Corbusier, CIAM and Stadtkrone. (From Architese, Zurich, 1975).

gleaming steel, radiant glass, honest good grey concrete. With such premises has avant-garde theory consistently justified its often too one-sided technological obsessions, its university buildings that look like factories programmed to churn out X% of engineers, biologists, psychologists, chemists on demand. That all should be concerned with, and should pay for, building a better world in some remote future is taken as self-evident. And rightly: that we should be concerned for the future welfare of mankind is an axiom always held by all reasonable creatures, at all times and places. It is one of what the old philosophers called the principles of Practical Reason. They showed—and their arguments still hold—how this concern for remote futurity derives from the most immediate concern of Practical Reason, namely, that obligation which all reasonable beings accept, to beget, rear or otherwise care for children.

But alongside this concern for children and posterity, Practical Reason has always implied, and rational beings have always taken for granted, an obligation to be concerned for the carefree futures though their scientific construction and the frank expression of materials created by and through applied science: care and welfare of parents. Both belong to the category of humanity in general. Derived from this axiom, inseparable from concern for the future is concern for ancestors, traditions—the past in general. One obligation can't be escaped without denying the other. Both are equally and inexorably derived from Practical Reason. Both equally and obviously belong in that body of self-evident truths which are not themselves subject to reason but are the grounds of reason itself—truths that all civilized and rational beings have accepted from the beginning of time. And you cannot pick and choose among them. That same Practical Reason which makes care for children a self-evident obligation also self-evidently obligates you to care for parents. That same Practical Reason which justifies architecture being concerned with the future also demands that architecture take into account the past and transmission of traditions from earlier generations and past ages. If you deny one, you deny the other. If you accept one as a working premise, you must accept the other.

Just as personal expression was always combined with, and subordinate to, creation of visual metaphors of social values in the great architecture of past ages, so in the great architecture of past ages appeal to present and future was always balanced against and grew out of respect for tradition, continuity, permanence. Here is the basis for rethinking the direction our architecture has been taking. And for some rewriting of architectural history, too.

For responsibility toward the past has been frequently neglected, overlooked, derided even, by those very same radicals and progressives most volubly and conspicuously concerned for future welfare. Avant-garde architecture, so largely their enthusiasm, evidences their attitude. It deliberately eschews all reference to the past. Accordingly, its metaphors of social value tend to be completely one-sided, having to do mostly with the future, a little with the present, nothing with the past.

Not that popular/commercial architecture is much better. It errs in the opposite direction. Its concern is too much with the present and the immediate, so that popular/commercial eclecticism tends to be a means of using the past to propagandize the present. The future it ignores, except when it suits immediate purposes to borrow avant-garde cliches to satisfy some science-fiction fashion of the moment.

The conclusion to be drawn is plain. Significant architecture must be created, and can only be created, by looking to the future while retaining past precedent. Or in other words: the best of avant-garde sensibility and the best of popular/commercial communication. Eclecticism in the effective sense.

Concern for the past and for human continuity, so crucial to a humane environment and indeed to civilization itself, is manifested in two ways: preservation/conservation, "the architecture of the 1980s"; and popular/commercial arts, especially architecture. Study of these should be a major preoccupation in post-modern architectural education.

If and when eclecticism becomes respectable in a post-modern architecture, it will only help create a humane environment if used with intelligent awareness of how historic architecture worked, how it performed its historical social functions, so that similar principles can be applied to the architecture we build tomorrow. Some changes in architectural education will be requisite. Courses in historic architecture and in eclectic styling will need to be re-introduced; but they should not be the old kind of courses that were dropped in the 1940s, teaching what might be called the Bannister Fletcher or Leavenworth type of eclecticism (q.v. 192), where historic styles are put on and off like costume accessories. The social function of these forms needs to be understood.

For the purpose, two main sources are available. First, there is historic architecture itself. Preservation/restoration has often been called "the architecture of the '80s," not only because there has been so much interest in it, but also because only in this field do architects get much chance to work on monumental buildings: on city halls that look like city halls, court houses that evoke the majesty of the Law, and so forth. Here the methodology of social function plays a double role. It's not only essential to understand in order to restore intelligently, but it's also an essential criterion for deciding *what* to restore.

Now that awareness of eclectic forms as a major factor in humanizing environments is becoming more widespread, on what basis do we insist that this building be preserved but reluctantly let that one go? We can't preserve the *whole* built environment. If we say "Beauty is the criterion," then there'll always be somebody who thinks a threatened building is beautiful—and remember, furthermore, how notoriously fickle taste is! In 1860 John Ruskin called the Doge's palace the most beautiful building ever erected in the history of the world. Just a hundred years before, Edward Gibbon said it was "the ugliest building I ever saw." Thirty years ago Beaux-Arts was the ugliest of ugly words. Now it's trendy to admire. If we say "the criterion is Historic Association," then it all depends on how history is evaluated at the moment. Restoration becomes a game of musical chairs, with buildings patched up or torn down like images of Richard Nixon removed from waxworks museums after Watergate, or Cape Kennedy's name quietly restored to Cape Canaveral.

Much sounder and most lasting is to decide on the basis of social function. How important to the endurance of the State, the family, civilization, was this work of architecture? How effectively did it function as a visual metaphor or social value?[65] An outstanding example has been the restoration of war-ruined German cities.

Should ruined cities be rebuilt along lines prescribed by Corbusier, Gropius and the CIAM Co.—expressions of the New Spirit of steel and scientism? Or should they be rebuilt more or less as they had been? Rotterdam opted for Modernismus; its faceless Binnenweg was the result. German cities opted for restoration, on a biological model: "healing" the destroyed city by restoring not merely single cells but the whole organism—"a vitalistic metaphor," according to Jürgen Paul,[66] "which reveals an antirationalistic philosophy of life, with romantic features antipathetic to the whole tenor of Positivism, Materialism, and Faith in Progress which infused the 19th century and has been embodied in the functional and technological aesthetic of 20th-century architecture." The choice was for human continuity, for continuance of German national life. Those forms were a link, not only to the immediate pre-War period, but to pre-Hitler times, to what some like to think of as the "real Germany," land of poets, philosophers, mystics, crusaders, scholars. The social function of eclectic styles was thus self-evident, and self-evidently important. The choice to restore eclectically was indubitably the right one.

196. Restored buildings around the Munster in Freilburg-im-Breisgau. (L) Kornhalle; (R) Kaufhaus. Completion of a plan begun by Joseph Schlippe in 1946, c1976. In thirty years devastated Freilburg was rebuilt and rejuvenated, often in modern materials, but preserving the old "cultural lifeline" forms.

Its soundness is attested to not merely by avoidance of those difficulties and disasters experienced by American urban rebuilding projects which swallowed Radiant City doctrine too raw, but by its steady progress toward ever greater archaeological accuracy. Whereas in the earliest restorations only general features of old Germanic gables and rooflines were preserved, often in cast concrete (no more unnatural a way of using concrete, of course,than "brute" forms—the material goes into any mould!), in the latest restorations of whole sections of Freiburg-im-Breisgau, or Hildesheim, in the early '70s, a very high degree of fidelity to the original was insisted upon. Truly, eclecticism by the back door! Humane environment by a roundabout route.

There is a more direct route. Popular/commercial building has provided an eclectic built environment all around us. It preserves the historic social functions of architecture too, usually in a banal, trivial, mawkish way. It too could benefit by a more intelligent understanding of the principles of social function, and certainly by some admixture of the sensitivity to space, materials, composition and psychological experience of our avant-garde architecture.

Or in a word: learning to *see,* by understanding how popular/commercial arts—the *other* arts of our century—work, is not an exercise in idle appreciation. It's important. It's urgent. It's vital.

Notes to Section V: Persuasion/Conviction

[1]Cf. Fgr. 18. On abstract causal thought in relation to historic arts see further Section VI, and *On Parallels in Universal History,* pp. 74-83.

[2]Cf. Suzi Gablik, *Progress in Art* (London, 1976). She correctly realizes that avant-garde creation requires a mental process corresponding to Piaget's final phase (q.v., Sect. VI). But in claiming that Pollock or Barnett Newman therefore represents a culmination of all the ages, she fails to see that the modern avant-garde Establishment is merely secularizing, trivializing, and making an end in itself of a new dimension of thought which appeared two thousand years earlier—that it is, in its way, another demonstration of Karl Löwith's *Meaning in History:* "...Philosophy of history originates with the Hebrew and Christian faith in a fulfilment and...ends with the secularization of its eschatalogical pattern."

[3]"Notes on the Way," *Collected Essays, Journalism, & Letters of George Orwell* (London, 1968), II, pp. 15, 18.

[4]I reduced this to a table published along with "Taste and Ideology: Principles for a New American Art History," *The Shaping of Art & Architecture in 19th-Century America* (New York, Metropolitan Museum of Art, 1972, pp. 156-187.

[5]Juan Larrea, *Guernica* (New York, 1940), p. 35.

[6]James Johnson Sweeney [sometime director, Museum of Modern Art] "Mondrian, the Dutch and De Stijl, *Art News*, L, summer 1951.

[7]This is the reason for artists historically being able to do their art for widely different types of commissions. Purcell, it's said, was the last musician who could compose impartially for James II and for William and Mary who deposed James. Not so, I think; most modern popular/commercial groups would go on performing irrespective of who paid them. The sculptor Canova could call his group of Herakles and Nessus "Liberty hurling Monarchy into Oblivion" when he was an enthusiast for the French Revolution, and "Authority Hurling Licentious Liberty into the Sea" when enamoured of Napoleon. Beethoven similarly dedicated and un-dedicated compositions to Napoleon.

[8]An argument developed by George Grant, *Technology and Empire* (Toronto, 1969), Ch. XI. He begins with budget allocations within Universities: by their allocations and not by their pious pronouncements ye shall know where educators' values are, is his line. Whence one can extrapolate: it's obvious that sizeable allocations first began to be made for Art at universities and all other levels of education after c1955. This corresponds exactly to the moment when art became unteachable, by its own definition. A paradox? Not if you think in terms of "bread and circuses." Why support art which is unintelligible and uninteresting to 99% of the population? You can justify it to the peasants by claiming "Art will do you Good"— they're too dumb to understand that this is a 19th-century approach long disregarded by the Art Establishment—and at the same time castrate any possible subversion from artists themselves: they caper about in funny hats and make vulgar noises imagining that they are making some sort of bohemian protest, quite harmlessly—nothing will ever come of it.

[9]Not surprisingly, perhaps, little serious research has been done on advertising. Rich research but trivialized treatment characterizes Diana and George Hindley, *Advertising in Victorian England, 1837-1901* (London, 1972). Frank Presbrey, *The History and Development of Advertising* (New York, 1929, repr. 1968) contains useful factual material but little attempt is made to analyze it. E.S. Turner, *The Shocking History of Advertising* (London, 1952) is similarly without footnotes or bibliography.

[10]"In 1928, L.W. Ray, the man in charge of our building activities at that time, succeeded in designing and getting a patent on a moveable all-metal building, the structural framework of which was cold-rolled steel channels of special design, to which could be attached porcelain enamel panels on the outside in such a way that no water could penetrate. The lining on the inside was of porcelain enamel sheets, and the space between the walls was filled with rock wool for insulation.

"As far as we have been able to learn, this building represented the first successful use of porcelain enamel as an architectural material...."
(C.W. Ingram, *"All This from a 5-Cent Hamburger": The Story of the White Castle System,* Newcomen Society, New York/Downington/Princeton/Portland, 1970).

[11]*Ibid.*

[12]It's claimed that this attitude is now being amended. Cf. Merle Curti, "The Changing Concept of 'Human Nature' in the Literature of American Advertising," *Business History Review*, XLI, 4, 1967 (an analysis of *Printer's Ink*, first journal of American advertising, from 1888 to 1954). Duncan Farnan, a talented graduate student from Victoria now (1978) at York (Toronto) is doing a thesis on this problem, which is eagerly to be awaited.

[13]References and an extended treatment of political cartooning generally can be found in *The Unchanging Arts*.

[14]Donald D. Egbert, *Social Radicalism and the Arts in Western Europe* (New York, 1970, distributed by ISUH, Watkins Glen, N.Y., Box 363).
[15]Camilla Gray, *The Great Experiment: Russian Art 1863-1922* (London, 1962).
[16]Cf. Wolf von Eckhardt, *Back to the Drawing Board* (Washington, 1978), and my review in *Inquiry* (San Francisco), 10 Dec. 1978.
[17]XVII, February 1973, p. 14 f.

[18]Adolf Max Vogt, *Russische und französische Revolutionsarchitektur 1917/1789: Zur Einwirkung des Marxismus und des Newtonismus auf die Bauweise* (Koln, 1874), Sect. v, "Das Motif der Arbeit."

[19]Egbert, *Social Darwinism*, p. 268. Garnier was born at Lyon, a city which "even before the Revolutionary year of 1848 has been a chief center of French socialism, and he was raised in a socialist family . . . the *Cité Industrielle* was a modern utopia in the tradition of Fourier's phalanstery." Typical of the inexhaustible mine of facts on the interrelations of social/political radicalism and modernism in the arts in Egbert's book is the casual reference at the end of the section on Garnier to the fact that Auguste Perret was born in Belgium because his father had been a Communard in 1871.
[20]Quoted in *Images of American Living,* p. 416.

[21]Norris K. Smith, "Millenary Folly: The Failure of an Eschatology," *On Art and Architecture in the Modern World* (ALF, Watkins Glen, N.Y., 1971). In the *Ville Radieuse* there will be no night: 'there will be no death, neither sorrow nor crying, neither shall there be any more pain; there are no homes for the aged, no hospitals, no orphanages, no insane asylums, no houses of correction, no jails—for the former things have passed away. And I saw no temple therein, St. John reports, 'for the Lord God Almighty and the Lamb are the temple of it.' So it is with the *Ville Moderne;* there are no churches, no synagogues, no lodge halls, no buildings that can be associated with business corporations; there are no private homes; there are no subsidiary institutions of any kind, for the city itself provides the one basis for binding together all men, who will live here without sin and in timeless harmony with one another, beyond even the reach of death. For LeCorbusier, as earlier for Auguste Comte, the Age of Science, bringing with it the totally engineered environment, was to be the final age, when ignorance and darkness would forever be dispelled and when history would cease." (p. 70)

[22]Cf. Göran Lindahl, "Von der Zukunftskathedrale bis zur Wohnmaschine," *Figura: Uppsala Studies in the History of Art,* New Series I (Stockholm, 1960)
[23](New York, 1969/reprinted Watkins Glen, ALF, 1979), pp. 8, 9, 10.
[24]*Ibid.,* p. 137.

[25]For information about and a tour of popular/commercial housing developments in Sweden, as well as a supply of literature about it, I'm indebted to Lena Johanneson of Uppsalas Konstvetenskapliga Institut. Prophecies of the imminent disappearance of popular/commercial building and its replacement by avant-garde architecture continue unabated, of course; witness the October 1978 issue of *Esquire* which contains an article informing us that by the mid-1980s we'll all be living in totally engineered environments. *Déjà vu:* Garnier, Corbusier, Fuller. Don't wait up for it.
[26](Philadelphia, 1978). Cf. my review in *Inquiry* Oct., 1978.
[27]Review in *Time,* 27 Dec., 1971.
[28]A point expanded in my *Inquiry* review of 11 Dec., 1978.

[29]Reference to model for Jefferson Expansion Memorial in *Time,* 2 July 1956, "The Maturing Modern: "Eero's entry was an audacious . . . arch that looked like a giant, glistening

croquet wicket, which he had conceived while bending a wire and wool pipe cleaner." (p.34). In the same article we read how "Last week, as his wife watched with fascination, he casually turned over his breakfast grapefruit, began carving out elliptical parabolic arches which he then carried off to the office to see if they might do as an idea for the office model of TWA's new terminal at Idlewild...." (p. 32)

[30]Cf. E. Baldwin Smith, "An Introduction of Architectural Symbolism," *Architectural Symbolism of Imperial Rome and the Middle Ages* (Princeton, 1956), p. 3.

[31]I have been unable to discover any information about the designer of this monument, let alone his/her intentions. For all I can learn, it might as well have sprung from the ground from a tossed-out toothpick. The immediate occasion was to commemorate federal financing of the Trans-Canada Highway.

[32]Cf. Fn. II-76.

[33]Cf. Fred Kniffen, "Folk Housing: Key to Diffusion," *Annals of the American Association of Geographers,* LV, 4, Dec., 1965:
"One is struck by the strong influence of European precedent over early building in both mode of construction and form. Framing, the use of vertical and horizontal logs and timbers, even the first sod-covered "wigwams" of Plymouth assuredly stem from European sources, as did all the early house and barn types. Even the rail fence is European in all its several forms, probably including the snake or worm fence, which latter has been reported from Tirol. I have every confidence that this typologically primitive form will eventually be fully established as Old World in origin. In reflecting on European antecedents, it may be pointed out that materials and manners of construction, notably those employing a great deal of wood, that were actually vestigial in western Europe, enjoyed a rebirth and a long life in the New World."

[34]Cf. Hugh Morrison, *Early American Architecture* (New York, 1952):
"In general, brick construction became far more widespread in seventeenth-century Virginia than it did in New England. The reason for this may be sought, perhaps, in the fact that the settlers of New England were predominantly from the southeastern counties of England, where there was very little brick building, whereas the settlers of Virginia came from all parts of England, including regions where brick was a favored material." (p. 140)

[35]Walter Sage, *Europa vor Karl dem Grosse* (Cologne, 1974) has excellent examples of primaeval European house-types and conditions of life.

[36]There are innumerable other examples. Liking for mimetic texture no doubt explains a good deal about the transmission of textural sorts of motifs, like Teutonic or Celtic "ornament," e.g. (Cf. 137A, B, C). Emile Mâle, *La Fin du Paganisme en Gaule* (Paris, 1949), pp, 312ff discusses the survival of a Teutonic "S" motif, originally a sun-symbol, in Merovingian arts of Auverge. It assuredly had lost its original meaning centuries before its use was abandoned; what happened is presumably that surfaces so treated, in appropriately ceremonial places, "looked right" somehow.

[37]Texturing concrete by form-boards expresses the nature of the material, specifically its ability to take whatever form it is cast into. This is not traditional mimesis. Neither is the emphasis on texture for visual effect, as for example in one building I know which has a kind of triple-mimesis treatment: a wooden building, treated to look like a concrete building which has been cast in rough form-boards to express the nature of concrete. Such design has nothing to do with human continuity.

[38]Henry Glassie, "Folk Art," in *Folklore and Folklife, an Introduction* (Chicago, 1972), Richard M. Dorson, ed. pp. 278, 279.

[39]Illustrations in *Images of American Living,* pp. 82, 83.

[40]It's striking how many of the listings in H.R. Hitchcock, *American Architectural Books...published in America before 1895* (2nd edition, Minneapolis, 1962) are "pattern" books by established architects.

[41]"An Introduction to Indigeneous African Architecture," *Journal of the Society of Architectural Historians,* XXXIII, 3, 1974.

[42]A considerable body of theory holds that unconscious value systems can be written into design of all kinds, including architecture, through unconscious preferences for certain kinds of shapes, materials and proportions. Some examples of writing about influences of spatial proportions, and behavioral psychology generally would include Edward T. Hall, *The Hidden Dimension*, 1968; Gerald Adler, *Studies in Analytical Psychology* (New York, 1969); Carl G. Jung, *Mysterium Conjunctionis;* Bollingen Series 14, Princeton, Princeton University Press, 1963; and *Symbols of Transformation*, Princeton, Princeton University Press, 1956; Claude Levi-Strauss, *The Savage Mind* (Chicago University Press, 1962); Abraham H. Maslow, *Motivation and Personality* (New York, 1954); Charles Morris, *Signification and Significance*, Cambridge, MIT, 1964; Talcott Parsons, *Societies: Evolution and Comparative Perspectives*, Englewood Cliffs, New Jersey, 1966; and *The Social System*, New York, 1951; John Weir Perry, *The Self in Psychotic Process*, Berkeley, UCP, 1953; P.D. Ouspensky, *The Psychology of Man's Possible Evolution*, New York, 1954; Karl E. Scheibe, *Beliefs and Values*, New York, 1970.

[43]Cf. W.S.M. Knight, *The Life and Works of Hugo Grotius* (London, 1925), pp. 211, 212: "Natural Law deals not only with things made by Nature herself, but also with things produced by the act of man, and is immutable...unchangeable even by God Himself. It is the law of God as disclosed by Nature to the reason of man. It is, in fact, *jus* properly and strictly so called. By this law things are obligatory or forbidden by their very nature, and man can by no means change their inherent characteristics. Its existence is proved, a priori, by showing the agreement or disagreement of anything with the rational and social nature of man, and a posteriori, when by certain or very probable accounts anything is found to be accepted as Natural Law among all nations, or at least among the civilized."
Cf. C.F.Creel, *Chinese Thought* (New York, 1948), "At the beginning of Chinese civilization was the
"Tao—the Way or Road of harmony with the universe, later expanded by Confucius into a rule of right conduct for happiness ('Men can enlarge the Way, but the Way does not [by itself] enlarge the man'), and still further by the Taoists into a mystical concept standing for the primal stuff of the universe or the totality of all things."

[44]In every European language the words for "left" are different; and usually also mean "wrong": "sinister," "gauche," "links," etc. This corresponds to what behavioral scientists call a value system. In contrast to systems of conscious belief, value systems are largely unconscious.

[45]John A. Wilson, *The Burden of Egypt* (Chicago, 1951), pp. 48, 93.

[46]Henry Glassie, "18th-century Cultural Process in the Delaware Valley," *Winterthur Portfolio* (Winterthur, Delaware), 7, 1974.

[47]For this story I am indebted (as for much else) to Stanislaus von Moos of Zürich, whose biography of LeCorbusier is standard.

[48]*Congrès International des Architectes Modernes*, which could be described appropriately as a sort of "steering committee" for the Modern Architectural Party in general and LeCorbusier's planning ideas in particular. Founded in 1927-8 after Corbusier's plan for the League of Nations Building had been turned down.

[49]The big breakthrough for avant-garde architecture occurred with Gropius's appointment to the Harvard Architectural School in 1934, following his years in the wilderness after resigning from the Bauhaus directorship at Dessau in 1928. It was followed, not fortuitously, by an invitation to Giedion to deliver the Charles Eliot Norton lectures for 1938-39, whence *STA*, published by the Harvard University Press in 1941; whence...*heute gehörte uns die Vereinigte:Staaten, morgen die ganze Welt!* Typesetter for *Space Time & Architecture* was Herbert Bayer of the Bauhaus.

[50]The title of Giedion's next book, *Mechanization Takes Command* (Oxford University Press, 1948). More systematic than *STA*, its basic theme is: because we have perfected mechanics we must have a mechanistic architecture in a mechanical world.

[51]*Guide to Japanese Architecture* (Tokyo, 1971, Nobuo Ito and Shinkenchiku staff), p. 152. There are of course other examples of traditional forms to be found in this standard guide: e.g., Myoshin-ji Hanazono Hall by Murano and Mori, or the Tsuyaja Cultural Center of 1966.

[52]The architect of this church was Hijo Fuchino, following directions (in traditional architectural custom) of Rev. Takie Okumura, founder of the church and its pastor 1904-1937. Only the tower, chapel, and lobby were built originally; model was the castle built by Japan's first Christian feudal lord, Hisahide Matsunaga, who had "styled his castle a citadel of peace and order." The Sunday-school building and Christian Education building were finished only in 1960. *Cf* 60th-Anniversary Booklet, Makiki Christian Church, 829 Pensacola, Honolulu.

[53]"Frank Lloyd Wright and the Problem of Historical Perspective," *Journal of the Society of Architectural Historians*, XXVI, 1, 1967, p. 236.

[54]E.g., Walter C. Kidney's *The Architecture of Choice: Eclecticism in America 1880-1930* (New York, 1974), and Norris Smith's review of it in *JSAH*, XXXIV, 4, 1975.

[55]Anatole Kopp, *Town & Revolution: Soviet Architecture and City Planning, 1917-1925.*

[56]This comes out very clearly in a symposium on architecture in the 1930s published in the *Journal of the Society of Architectural Historians*, XXIV, 1, 1965, p. 54 f. Colin St.John Wilson of Cambridge summed matters up succinctly when he said, "I am truly surprised to hear so much talk purely at the level of forms....I don't think the analogy with painting-to-building is so important as the fact that the forms of De Stijl...carried considerable theosophical meaning....All of this has nothing to do with good taste. It was not on stylistic grounds that the Nazis closed the Bauhaus, and not for nothing did LeCorbusier himself refer to futurism as 'bien dangereux'." etc.

[57]John Morris Dixon, editorial in *Progressive Architecture*, June 1978, p. 7.

[58]Sten Nilsson, *The New Capitals of India, Pakistan, and Bangladesh* (Lund, Scandinavian Institute of Asian Studies Monographs No. 12, 1973), pp. 96, 118.

[59]Stanislaus von Moos, "Das Schiff: eine Metapher der modernen Architektur," *Neue Züricher Zeitung*, 23/24 August 1975, no. 194, pp. 49-50. He points out that in taking the ship as a metaphor of modern architecture, Corbusier did not necessarily use the proportions of a ship in the Villa Savoie or anywhere else; rather, he saw it as a model for society. The ship was for him an emblem of architecture as a means of salvation, like the *Aisle Flottant of the Armée du Salut on the Seine.*

[60](London, 1971), pp. 93-95.

[61]"The End of Architecture," *Architecture Plus*, April 1973, pp. 45, 46.

[62]Obviously the theme for a survey of art and especially architectural history according to the methodology of social function. Cases like Versailles and the Baroque generally are self-evident: while building his great monument Louis XIV says, "Après moi, le déluge." What about Gothic cathedrals? Aren't they expressions of the arrogant power formulated by Boniface VIII's "Unam Sanctam"—the Pope is "God on earth" to whom all material and spiritual things are subject? According to Friedrich Heer, *Europäisches Geistesgeschichte* I, 98, not so: That bull was an "act of desperation" attempting to unify Europe and ward off the increasing attacks on the Church and its authority; the fiercer the attacks, the more lavish Gothic became.

[63]Another example, very comparable, is the International School of Sacred Heart University in Tokyo, designed in 1968 by Kenzo Tange: "An attempt to discover a pattern in complicated human mutual relationships and express that pattern spatially. The intention was to stitch together on the axis of the space, zones for both informal and formal gatherings. The device used to achieve this end is called a 'street,' it is a space designed for the sake of traffic that provides connection among individual buildings and individual rooms, and runs the length of the long axis." (from Shinkenchiku *Guide to [Modern] Japanese Architecture*, Tokyo, 1971, p. 94) Here too no specific associations are lacking—with education, with Japan, with Catholicism, or anything else. You—beholder and/or visitor—are to experience nothing except what the Architect provides for you to experience. Precisely as at Lethbridge, where "Aperture" dictates how the campus shall be viewed. Somehow it all sounds familiar—and is: Baroque design "stood on its head."

[64]Cf. John Carrol, *Breakout from the Crystal Palace* (London/Boston, 1974).

[65]Cf. the issue on *Denkmalpflege* (Historic Preservation) of ARCHITHESE (Zurich, XI, 1974).

[66]*Ibid.*, article by Jürgen Paul, "Der Wiederaufbau des Kornhauses in Freiburg im Breisgau und einige Betrachtungen über Architektur und Geschichtsverständnis," pp. 11-20

Toward an Expanded Art History

Counterparts to the Social Functions of Popular/Commercial Arts in the Arts of Primitives, Children and Traditional Historic Arts

Besides popular/commercial arts, primitives and child arts also perpetuate traditional social functions. Child art complements popular/commercial arts as tools for historical study; whereas popular/commercial arts show how arts traditionally functioned in and for society, child art shows how they develop sequentially.

To summarize: in broad historical sweep, four distinct kinds of social function served through arts can be identified (as well as a fifth—artistic expression—less readily circumscribable but real nonetheless), by which arts historically were known, and for which arts historically were admired and valued.[1]

First, arts historically were activities concerned with the making of substitute images. They provided pictures to serve as substitutes for material things, and as symbols for ideas. In very early times, relationships between reality and image were very close, so that early art had a magical quality for its makers. Not until the kind of analytical thought we associate with the Greeks in the first millenium were reality and image decisively separated; still today something of their old close connection can be experienced if you take a small child to a wax museum.

Second, arts illustrated. Substitute images could be arranged in certain coherent sequences, so related to each other as to "relate" a story about something or record an event (the word "relate" indeed has this double meaning in many languages).

Third, arts historically were concerned with beautification. The historic art of beautification did not itself produce objects, but was a technique or skill of so refining and ornamenting them as to produce something more intelligible, more "sensibly" associated with human life and experience. Beautification was a vehicle for creative and mental growth.

Fourth, historic arts were devices for persuasion and conviction. They were used to support, defend, promote, attack or disparage abstract ideas and ideologies. They were not precious pieces in glass cases, but instruments of war for mankind's mind. Modern avant-garde arts still preserve this function, in however inadvertent, allusive and inherently contradictory a way—in theory dedicated to change and revolution, in practise defending an entrenched intellectual and cultural Establishment. But in historic times, when it was taken for axiomatic that innately disorderly human beings needed stable societies for survival, let alone happiness, persuasion/conviction was a deliberate and conscious function of arts. That function, indeed, can be seen as a principal determinant of the last two thousand years' major stylistic revolutions: from Romanesque to Gothic to Renaissance/Baroque to modern.

Implicit in the purposes for which a given society made given artifacts are the basic values and convictions which underlie all its institutions. It follows that artifacts interpreted in these terms throw all sorts of new light on history. It does not follow, unfortunately, that so interpreting artifacts is easy. The problem is that records rarely tell precisely what artifacts of any kind in any given society were made to do because for the makers of architecture, jewelry, costume or whatever the social function of their artifacts was usually self-evident. Only when the purposes of any activity cease to be self-evident does need arise to explain it explicitly, and often then the true or original purpose has already been forgotten or distorted. That is certainly true of historic arts today, when the whole concept of arts having specific social functions has been distorted and forgotten, as witnesses diverse as Picasso and Lord Clark testify.[2]

But! Though traditional social functions may be lost and forgotten in our dominant avant-garde art, that is not the only artistic activity we have. There are others which perpetuate them. Three, to be precise. Primitive, popular/commercial and child art all in diverse ways carry the ends and means of past arts on into our present.

Not all the traditional social functions of historic arts survive in primitive arts—i.e., arts of de- or uncivilized people: savages, naive painters, and the like. Substitute imagery and illustration, certainly. Deliberate (rather than vestigial) beautification is at least debatable. Conscious persuasion/conviction to any significant degree is highly doubtful.[3] Study of primitive arts for deeper comprehension of traditional social functions has correspondingly limited usefulness. The dependence of naïve painters (Grandma Moses, Douanier Rousseau, etc.) for forms and ideas upon High Arts at a considerable cultural remove demonstrates something of the relationships of traditional Low to High Arts. The arts of "savage" peoples demonstrate how much can be done within the bounds of only two obvious social functions, and so suggest how it might be at least theoretically possible for a human society to get along (in however impoverished a way, granted!) without arts serving all the four social functions performed by Western arts over the past two thousand years. And primitive cultures inculcate the lesson— useful in any considerations of universal history—that there is no necessary "line of progress." Despite orthodox Marxist dogma about an inexorable rise from savagery to civilization,[4] logic and data both point to primitive societies being de-civilized, degenerate in the sense of being remnants of regression from some higher civilization.[5] But any such usefulness is largely negated by the obvious rapid disappearance of true primitive art (as distinct from the kind of ersatz primitive artiness taught to Inuits and Amerinds in craft schools, or deliberate avant-garde cultivation of naive attitudes), and the bastardization of what is left, by contact with popular/commercial arts, anthropological students, and the like.

The usefulness for historical study of surviving traditional social functions in popular/commercial arts is far greater, but they also have limitations, because of telling differences between them and traditional arts. All arts produced in this century suffer, as traditional arts did not, from the separation of Art (i.e., arts for art's sake, essentially) from social function. We have two arts, really—one, the avant-garde, all aesthetic sensibility and form, the other all banality and content. They need to be put together if meaningful and fulfilling art is to be restored to our society.

Meanwhile, because popular/commercial arts for all intents and purposes perform only their bare social functions (whenever they attempt more they all too often turn into kitsch—i.e., objects made only as art, in the same way as avant-garde painting or sculpture, only obedient to a different set of tastes!), they can be deceptive guides to understanding traditional arts, where social function, content and expression all collaborated, fruitfully.

Lastly, there is child art. Like popular/commercial and primitive, it is never "pure," it is always contaminated by environment. Like them too it needs to be carefully distinguished from avant-garde expressions (i.e., from the Herbert Read school of *Education Through Art,* based upon the proposition that mankind in general and children in particular are by nature good and by nature creative, hence that full freedom from rules must produce expressive masterpieces).[6] From Viktor Lowenfeld's systematic studies of *Creative and Mental Growth (inter alia)*[7] it is apparent that all four social functions of traditional arts develop sequentially in child art. First comes substitute imagery in various forms. Then illustration, around the age of five. Then beautification, around nine. Finally, somewhere between twelve and fifteen, deliberate persuasion/conviction (if that comes at all—the matter, as we shall see in a moment, is not cut and dried). "Deliberate" is crucial in this phase; a kind of persuasion/conviction is implicit to some degree, and in some sense, in all functions and at all stages of child art. But conscious use of art deliberately to persuade others toward different opinions or to proclaim convictions of one's own or one's society comes only as an adult culmination of the evolutionary process in child art.

It is precisely in this evolution that the peculiar importance of child art for historical study consists. For the successive appearance of these social functions is marked by the successive appearance of forms to carry them. Both functions and forms, in turn, can be correlated to successive levels and kinds of thought; and the function/form/thought pattern so appearing can be correlated further, to stages of creative and mental growth established by studies in developmental psychology, biological anthropology. Compare the resultant paradigm with studies in the intellectual development of early (i.e., 5th-2nd millennium B.C.) man, with the pattern of cultural and mechanical inventions of those ages, but above all the development of art forms comparable to those appearing at successive stages of creative and mental growth in children, and the possibility of an "ontogeny repeats philogeny" paradigm becomes very evident. (Also its difficulties: whereas child art is plentifully and unambiguously available to research, 5th-2nd millennium arts are neither plentiful nor unambiguous.)

Formal Indications of the Successive Stages of Children's Creative and Mental Growth

In children's art, each developmental stage is marked by the appearance of specific forms to carry the new functions. Substitute imagery develops out of scribbling.

The social function of child art at any stage is evidenced either by the forms employed or by the way they are employed, or both. Thus, whenever you look at child art all over the world, you find it beginning with—or more exactly, beginning as—substitute imagery, in the form of scribbling in all its variants (or "emergent diagrams," as Rhoda Kellogg prefers to call it).[8] Scribbling may be in the first instance no more than simple motor activity—tots waving their arms around with pencils in their fists instead of just waving their arms around, period—but soon it is "named," i.e., identified with a spoken name for something. Ball, perhaps; or cat; or mother; or Me. Whatever, scribblings become symbols for simple concepts, a means of communication—conscious substitute imagery in fact, and therefore "art" in the sense of performing the first of the social functions traditional for the activity called "art" throughout history, until modern times.

From scribbling, formal substitute imagery develops as soon as muscle coordination permits. First primaeval naturalism—"primaeval" in the sense of timeless and unpremeditated, "naturalistic" in the sense of literally replicating a known reality in size, material and texture. Primaeval naturalism corresponds in effect most to a waxworks, perhaps, hence in child art you find it most commonly done in plasticene, mud, or snow (again insofar as physiological technique permits). Thence come two-dimensional substitute images—additively composed, frontally conceived, ideationally scaled. Being more effective substitutes for abstract concepts, and far easier to make, than primaevally naturalistic images, two-dimensional images built up for additions of parts each depicted in the aspect most characteristically remembered (though not necessarily "seen") to become the norm, for most intents and purposes around five-six.

Thence illustration becomes possible—substitute images of this kind put together so as to "relate."

197. Varieties and development of scribbling, age 2-4. Left to right: disordered (2½) longitudinal with repeated motions, (3), circular with variations (3), stereotyped (3½), and anmed (4; can be named anything, e.g., "cat," "me walk," etc.). From Lowenfeld. Indicated mental development: from rudimentary to mature conceptual thought, thence to rudimentary analogical thought.

198. Development of substitute imagery from primaeval naturalism (plasticent figures, left, of boy and truck, intended to be as literal as possible) to additive two-dimensional composition ("Me and My Truck," right) of parts which reproduce the most characteristic aspects of the concept. Indicated mental development: mature conceptual thought plus increasing capacity for analogical thinking.

The device which relates substitute images, and hence makes illustration possible, is a base-line—i.e., a line, real or imaginary (actual or understood) to which substitute images are all attached, and by which, therefore, a relationship amongst all of them can be established. Base-lines are not "ground" lines. They do not represent the ground, or anything else material. They correspond in fact most to those particles of speech or prepositions or inflections (suffixes and prefixes) or tones or agglutinations children now acquire and which similarly have no independent value, in themselves describe nothing, but serve the indispensable function of so relating words to one another that coherent "relations"—in the double sense of story-telling and causal interconnection—are effected. In child art the base-line functions comparably to show how substitute images "relate" to each other and so make them into instruments for "relating" stories, illustrating. The social function of illustration is also evidenced by and manifest in the "bigger-the-better" principle of scaling images (establishing relative sizes is, of course, now made possible by base-lines) and by generalized color. For it is importance to a story (from a child-artist's point of view), not visual actualities, that alike dictates relative sizes and absolute colors. (If the story is of "Me Playing Checkers," then I need to show big fingers but legs can be minimized, conversely for "Me Crossing the Street"; if I color roses red and violets blue and grass green, my house yellow and yours white, my story will be most intelligible—just as, the more exactly I pronounce words like the people around me, the better my story will be told.)

Sometime around nine years of age comes beautification: "I have never yet seen a child of this age level (5-7) spontaneously decorating an object with the purpose of identifying it. All such attempts were forced on the child or 'stimulated' by adults," Lowenfeld reported (*Creative & Mental Growth,* p. 63). Beautification does not itself produce artifacts, or relate them; it is a means, rather, of so treating substitute images or illustrations as to make them more meaningful, hence more attractive, to individual beholders.

Beautification is evidenced in a consistent and conscious interest in pattern and space, and by simultaneously refining shapes so as to make their function intelligible to beholders and adding decoration to them which establishes a relationship to

199. The base-line in child art. A: using the bottom edge of a cardboard box, a child 4 years
and 9 months old relates substitute images (composed on additive principle) of Santa Claus,
sleigh, reindeer, snowman and self, to form a record of an event. B: Christmas drawing by the
same child one year later (December 1965). Motor skills have increased, and simple writing is
now mastered; the story too—Santa leaving presents and eating cookies left for him—is more
complicated. In addition to base-line (understood) relating the images, composition is now
controlled on the bigger-the-better principle of scale relative to narrative importance.
Indicated mental processes: conceptual and mature analogical thought, plus rudimentary
analytical thought.

200. Varieties of beautification. A: deliberate sense of arrangement on the page, evidencing
pattern for decorative purposes in drawings about age 8. B: water-color (from Lowenfeld,
Creative and Mental Growth) done in an "art class" at school, by a 9-year old. "Art" is now an
activity recognizably distinct from speech or writing. Here is evidenced a corresponding sense
of the individual "in" a landscape, rather than a landscape constructed around the individual
(or subject of the picture). Independent space is indicated by the device of a second, higher,
base-line; but nothing occupies this space, and the essential relationship among elements
remains controlled by successive base-lines. Also, the bigger-the-better principle persists: in
the swing, in the tagger's hands, etc. Indicated. mental processes: analytical thought,
employing conceptual and analogical thought.

201. Maturity in art comes when forms are understood in and "work" in relation to an outside, abstract system of ideas. A: For four hundred years or so, maturity meant grasping essentials of perspective (here, Durer's treatist *Underweysung der Messung,* Nuremberg 1525, 1538). This system corresponded to the abstract image of a world ordered by Reason, ultimately of divine authority, which enabled all members of the class-structured State to understand its rationale and to accept "that place to which it hath pleased Providence to call me." B: Product of an art school c1965 teaching Abstract Expressionism—again forms intelligible in terms of an ideology which holds that Mankind is by nature good, creative, just and that in consequence ideal, if not perfect, worlds are producible by giving free expression to the Nature of things—the nature of paint, the nature of life, the Natural Goodness of Man. Mental process involved: conceptual, analogical, analytical thought, all controlled by abstract causality.

makers and users alike—all in their several ways manifestations of a new objective awareness of the world and of the place of individual selves within it.

The last social function to develop in children's art is conscious persuasion/conviction—i.e., use of arts to persuade toward or against sets of ideas. Like beautification, persuasion/conviction is identifiable not by particular forms but by ways of using forms—specifically, by conscious style, by so distinctively handling forms as to deliberately evoke certain desired ideological associations. These techniques are taught in art schools. A generation or two ago, perspective was what artists learned on their way to professionalism; now what they learn is more likely to be some rationale of self-expression. But in either case, they are taught a conscious style, consciously elected for associations with particular values and attitudes and assumptions about what is Real and Important—the old Renaissance/Baroque/bourgeois world-view in the one case, the avant-garde Establishment's in the other.

Correlation of Functions and Forms of Child Art to Successive Levels of Thought

Substitute imagery presupposes capacity for conceptual thought, and for rudimentary analogical thought.[9]

Forms so evidencing social functions also and necessarily manifest evolving mental powers—"creative and mental growth," as Viktor Lowenfeld pointed out long ago—are inseparable.

The first forms of child art—primaeval naturalism in three dimensions, additive representations in two—are all determined by the function of substitute imagery which logically presupposes powers of conceptual thought (197, 198). For, making symbols requires a capacity to conceive them—plus a rudimentary capacity for analogical thought, at least enough to associate material concepts with mental ones. Conceptual plus rudimentary analogical thought constitute a first stage of distinctively human creative and mental growth, distinguishing mankind from animals. Possibly an animal might conceive of itself as "I" in a conscious if not a Cartesian ("remarking that this truth, 'I think, therefore I am,' was so certain and so assured that all...skeptics were incapable of shaking it, I...could receive it without scruple as the first principle of my philosophy") way. Possibly an animal might recognize some shape as a symbol of something else. But that could be proved only by using substitute images as symbols in some way. And this, only human beings do. Only human beings use visual or verbal symbols to communicate.

Thought and speech and art all go together, and all begin with conceptual thoughts related by rudimentary analogies. Child arts from 2-5 manifest also how surprisingly wide a range of mental operations is possible within these mental bounds. Conceptual thought can grasp not only material but also abstract things, for an awareness of "I" necessarily involves awareness of "not-I"—hence perhaps that fear of the dark which many and possibly all tiny children have; hence probably the essential beginnings of all religious experience in recognition of the Numinous; hence demonstrably small children's use of substitute images of abstract concepts. And with rudimentary analogical thought, experiences both material and spiritual can be accumulated—bricks to build a body of knowledge, foundations for more complex mental operations later, just as out of that substitute imagery which manifests conceptual thought later arts of every kind must be built.

Illustration presupposes capacity for mature analogical and rudimentary analytical thought.

Progression to full powers of analogical thought is manifest in appearance of the base-line in child art around the age of five (199). For it is awareness that "this thing is like that thing," which makes a base-line seem necessary, because it makes children discontented with shapes juxtaposed in a spaceless foreground plane, desirous of organizing them into coherent illustrative relationships. Analogical thought is correspondingly and comparably manifested by coherent grammatical story-telling. As the base-line develops in art, so what linguists call deitic terms (i.e., elements which specify time, place and spatial relations) develop in place of long strings of word-prattle. And both manifest powers of analogy developing beyond the rudimentary stage implicit in conceptual arts and thought. In this story-telling, as in children's illustrations, little distinction is made between animate and inanimate objects. What Piaget calls "child animism" prevails. Instead of "I tripped on a stone; it was in the way," the event is told as "This big stone saw me coming and tripped me." Analogical thought processes seem untrammelled at this stage: all similarities are perceived, but ability to analyze counterbalancing differences is feeble or embryonic. There is to be sure some rudimentary analytical thought at this stage; coloring evidences it, for example, in the "roses are red violets are blue" principle, which manifestly involves awareness not only of categories which have certain properities—"this flower called 'rose' is like that flower called 'rose' and both have 'redness'— but also other categories with different properties: "this flower called 'violet' is like that flower called 'violet' and both have 'blueness'." In fact, awareness of categories and cycles is the most obvious result of mental advance around the ages 5-6. Time ceases to be a string of existential events and is experienced via a framework of patterns and cycles: seasons, months, youth-and-age, birth-and-death-and-birth symbolized in ritual acts of various kinds, including stereotyped art symbols. For awareness of societies, races, community ("us" and "them" is the basis of all social organization) appears now in children's art—also connections between and results of actions, which is the beginning of what older philosophers called Natural Law or Practical Reason, foundation of all logic and all ethics, and by extension, of theological speculation as well: if what we "like" to do is a different action from what we "ought" to do, if we cannot by any means get from the proposition "I like to do this" to "I ought to do this," if "good" is therefore not something human beings naturally like or naturally do willingly, then a logical conclusion is that "good" must be something imposed from something outside, something "super-natural." Conversely, as a corollary: all kinds of value judgments become not only possible but inescapable. You cannot deliberately choose good over bad until you have some standards, some "baseline" for distinguishing between them as categories; hence moral judgments and judgments between good and bad arise together. But once you have that standard, you cannot avoid choosing between alternatives; "sin" comes into the child's world.

Analogical thought of the sort evidenced in child arts around the age of 5-7 is essentially negative. It ignores differences between things living and things dead, because it is unable to coordinate the multiple properties of things. Once analytical thought becomes the dominant way of perceiving experience, mythopoeic and animistic perceptions sink (or rise, depending on points of view!) to the level of legend, poetry and mystic insight. That happens around the age of nine or so. It is manifested in awareness of the difference between "art" and ordinary speech communication. Writing becomes the normal mode of communication, "art" becomes "special," something not everybody does (200). Herein is one manifestation of a general insistence on distinguishing between parts and wholes, which now becomes possible with analytical thought. The making of art itself now manifests that process, in-as-much as a new conscious awareness becomes evident of how different parts are related to the same whole in order to make works of art intelligible and meaningful to beholders. But this same awareness points up things that you can do in pictorial language which cannot be done, or done as well, in ordinary speech and writing. You can present things vividly, attractively, pleasingly. Conscious awareness of the difference between word and image also, then, involves conscious awareness of "art" in a specialized sense—of "poetry" or "literature" as distinct from prose, of "dancing" and "acting" and so on.

What makes them different is the process of beautification.

Beautification requires developed capacity for analytical thought, plus rudimentary abstract causal thinking.

Beautification in the historic sense of applying ornament or refining shapes in order to identify use and relate them to human experience, cannot be done without analytical thought. It can only be accomplished by going beyond mere perception of similarities in similar things to perceive relationships among diverse things—precisely that ability to perceive relationships between parts and wholes which is the definition of analytical thinking.

By analytical thought, "beauty" in the visual arts is defined—i.e., by awareness of one object or image performing a function similar to another in society but performing it better, the difference being measurable as "beauty."

Analytical thought likewise identifies artists as distinct from their arts, craftsmen as distinct from their craftsmanship, as part of a general distinguishing of individuals from society collectively.

Or conversely: beautification, third of the great traditional social functions of historic arts to appear in child art, is the manifestation of children's having acquired analytical thought.

Child art at this stage likewise shows awareness of historical time, distinguishing events that took place a few years or generations ago from events centuries old, separating time from legend; this is further evidence for analytical thought. Child artists at this stage can distinguish between those standards set by what "I personally" think good and verified by experience, and standards set by other people; they can correspondingly distinguish between ethics and morals in society as a whole, whereby behavior patterns sanctioned by and relative to the whole can be questioned or challenged by individuals holding different convictions—and in both cases the distinction is made possible by analytical thought. Child art at this stage thus shows capability for perceiving new types of relationships between Numinous experience and the promptings of conscience and Natural Law—new dimensions of religious speculation. In sum: "art" objectively pursued as an activity distinct from mere visual communication is evidence for, and produced by, those new powers of analytical thought which make possible all sorts of other new reasoned comparisons and considered judgments—in history, in morality, in government, in law.

Artistic maturity requires, and is inseparable from, capacity for abstract causal thinking.

Abstract causal thought processes are manifest in the final stage of child art—or more precisely in the transition from child to adult art. That is to say, arts become a specialized adult profession, and develop in response to abstract formulae, by processes of abstract causal thought.

Abstract causality is most obviously manifested in a heightened degree of objectivity, the culmination of a successive development away from subjectivity.

In the art of very small children, each image is an entirely separate concept, subjectively perceived. Construction of baselines to relate analogous concepts, occurring somewhere around 5-6 is essentially subjective. Objectivity begins with awareness of interrelationships among concepts independent of the perceiver, first manifest by the art of beautification. Beautification, that is, implies a natural order which perceptive individuals can analyze, but which does not depend upon their analysis—i.e., an object goes on existing whether or not it is beautified by refinement of shape, applied ornament, or whatever. Full objectivity is realized, however, only with awareness that this natural order in turn may be governed by abstract laws, principles or forces which are so objective, so completely outside an individual's perception or powers to analyze as to be knowable only by their effects. This is an adult way of seeing, and it is manifested in art by all social functions— substitute imagery, illustration and beautification—being consciously determined by relationships to abstract laws or principles; all being fully meaningful only by reference to a body of pure theory independent of any particular images. This relationship, these references, are established by appropriate styles for conveying given bodies of principles and ideas. Such styles are what adult artists chiefly learn in professional training—whether by explicit precept in art schools as now, or by assimilation in the course of apprenticeship, as in earlier times (201).

When abstract systems of thought or standard principles give significance to artistic forms and determine their use, both deliberate persuasion and conscious expressions of conviction become possible. Further—such deliberate use of symbols for persuasion/conviction is only possible through, and hence is a manifestation of, abstract causal thought.

Abstract causal thinking may be defined as a process of postulating a hypothetical world of absolutely uniform conditions, from which abstract laws are deduced, whose validity can then be tested by application to given, specific, concrete situations in the material world. Two thousand years ago abstract causality was best manifested in the theological systems of the great world religions which then appeared, and related earthly events to an abstract, spiritual, idealistic world.

Nowadays it is Science that best exemplifies the processes of abstract causal thought. To explain why matches light when struck, Science does not make analogical comparisons of matches struck in similar ways, nor analyze interrelationships of events or people leading up to the act of match striking; these mental operations, when employed, serve only for observing and accumulating data. Explaining the data is done by first postulating an imaginary world of absolutely uniform conditions of friction, chemicals, velocity, etc., then correlating with those the actual sequence of events in any one case of match-striking. That is to say, particular and concrete things are understood by reference to general and abstract systems—this is the essence of abstract causal thinking, typical of the final stage of evolution from child to adult art.

The function/form/thought pattern so appearing can be correlated yet again to stages of creative and mental growth exhibited in developmental psychology and biological anthropology.

Thus the pattern of successive developments of new social functions in child art is evidenced by successive developments of new forms, and both in turn manifest successive developments of new thought patterns. To this paradigm other patterns can be correlated as well. For example, stages in developmental psychology postulated by Jean Piaget:(1) Sensori-Motor Stage, birth to about 2 years; (2) Pre-Operational or Representational Phrase, about 2-6 years; (3) Concrete Operational Phase, about 7-11 years; (4) Formal Operational Phase, about 12-15 years.[10] Correlatable again is the four-stage pattern of growth in awareness of time, identified by biological anthropologists: (1) Biological Time, rhythms of metabolism for sleeping, waking, eating, such as we become acutely aware of during long jet travels; (2) Social Time, the three to five generations which constitute family units; (3) History Proper, recording events in the last few thousand years; (4) finally, Cosmic Time, the kind of time concepts meant by eternity, light-years, geological epochs—any name is appropriate as long as it implies vastness, not measurable or calculable (the human mind can only postulate "infinity" we cannot really comprehend something that actually has no end).

Correlation of Children's Mental and Creative Growth with Historic Arts of the Ancient World: A Possible Ontogeny-Repeats-Phylogeny Paradigm

Out of all these correlations a table can be composed:

Approx. age	Social functions of child art	Characteristic art forms	Thought processes	Corresponding stages of developmental psychology	Corresponding types of time awareness
		by which social function(s) are carried out	i.e. modes of comprehension manifest by these forms and function(s)	(Piaget)	(Biological Anthropology)
0 –	SUBSTITUTE IMAGERY	SYMBOLS (Abstract or Naturalistic)	CONCEPTUAL (+ ability to use conceptual thought = primitive kind of analogical thought, enough to perceive concepts)	SENSORI-MOTOR (0–2)	BIOLOGICAL
3 +	Substitute Imagery ILLUSTRATION	Symbols (Abstract or Naturalistic) USED WITH BASELINE to tell a story	Conceptual ANALOGICAL (+ ability to use analogical thought to make discoveries = primitive analytical powers)	Sensori-Motor PRE-OPERATIONAL or REPRESENTA-TIONAL (2–6)	Biological SOCIAL
8 +	Substitute Imagery Illustration BEAUTIFICATION	Symbols deliberately refined in shape or decorated as distinctive form of communication	Conceptual Analogical ANALYTICAL (+ ability to use analytical thought for speculation = primitive abstract causality)	Sensori-Motor Pre-Operational CONCRETE OPERATIONAL (7–11)	Biological Social HISTORICAL
11 +	Substitute Imagery Illustration Beautification PERSUASION/ CONVICTION	Symbols, illustration, beautified objects consciously used to persuade or convince re abstract ideologies and value systems	Conceptual Analogical Analytical ABSTRACT CAUSALITY	Sensori-Motor Pre-Operational Concrete Operational FORMAL OPERATIONAL	Biological Social Historical COSMIC

Comparing the paradigm of children's creative and mental growth with studies in the intellectual development of early man (i.e., 5th to 1st millennium B.C.) with the pattern of cultural and mechanical inventions of those ages, but above all with the development of art forms comparable to those appearing at successive stages of children's creative and mental growth, and the possibility of correlation becomes evident. Also objections to it: whereas child art is plentiful, early arts are rare and possibly untypical.

About the existence of roughly four stages of evolutionary development from childhood to adulthood in modern times there can then be little doubt. In the context of historical study, however, three questions come immediately to mind.

First, is this pattern inexorable? Does it proceed from innate psychic process? Or is it something produced or producible by external conditioning—inculcated by rituals of food production, parental suggestion, or whatever? Does it jump from one stage to another, and if so, what triggers the jumps? Or does one level slide imperceptibly up to the next without any outside stimulation, simply by some mindless obedience to chemical processes instituted at the creation of the world?

Obviously a question in part metaphysical, related to the whole basic controversy as to whether "man makes himself" totally—values and ethics as well as tools being part of a mechanistic, impartial, ultimately controllable process—or whether there is some outside, objective frame of reference which makes values absolute and to which Man appeals rather than dictates; and to that extent never conclusively answerable to everyone's satisfaction (or possibly to anyone's!). But insofar as the question is in part merely statistical, the statistic is 100%—no "leap of faith" in scientific causality is required to see that children's proceeding through successive stages of creative and mental growth can no more be blocked than their physical growth can be arrested. The process may be distorted, as children in divers times and places have had their feet bound or foreheads flattened, their height stunted by diet or minds warped by superstition. But it cannot be denied. Adults who pretend to child-like attitudes and innocent thoughts do so by the kind of conscious and deliberate choice that no child ever can make. Peter Pan remains fictional. Nobody can stay in or return to child-like states. Growth to maturity—of some kind and degree—is part of the nature of things, proof that there is an order to the universe which humans belong to and cannot escape. In that sense at least, the question, is evolution in child art inexorable? can be answered straight out as Yes.

Second, is the pattern universal nowadays? Can the four stages of creative and mental growth identified by philosophers and psychologists, biological anthropologists and child educators, be recognized in all parts of the world? Apparently yes; but with a major reservation: in every modern society, some children go through all four stages, but not all children in any society.[11] The significance for historical study is this: disparities in mental ability appear to be inherent, innate, not products of any quality of circumstance whose disappearance can be anticipated in some coming classless state. But this disparity is not apparently racial, since in all advanced societies some people do progress through all four stages; it is simply part of that unequal distribution of abilities and talents among human beings which no amount of denunciation or institution-changing seems able to cure. Despite conditioning and predetermined behavior patterns, history is still affected by individual talents, abilities, character and will.

Third, was this pattern of creative and mental growth universal at all times in history? Has the four-stage development which modern children go through been experienced at least by some members of all generations of *homo sapiens* throughout history? Or to put it in answerable terms, do historic arts always manifest four social functions from the prehistoric caves onward, as normative opinion has held for a century now?[12] Or do they appear successively as in child art, and thus presuppose a corresponding evolution of mental capacities within historical times.[13] Once recall how identifiable forms in child art are invented to serve indentifiable social functions (base-line), and how these forms and functions together evidence the mental processes involved, and some kind of objective answer to the historical question is possible—of particular importance, obviously, in any kind of cross-cultural study.

202. To create art like the painted animals on the ceiling at Altamira cave (a) or the "Venus of Willendorf" (B) nothing beyond conceptual and rudimentary analogical thought would be required; substitute imagery would explain their function in prehistoric society entirely. Everything else attributed to prehistoric art turns out, on rigorous examination, to be read into it by modern observers—it aesthetic qualities, its function for witchcraft, etc. Flecks of red paint are explained with the fewest assumptions—on William of Occam's principle!—as helping make the figure the substitute image for a living body. Furthermore, as Rhoda Kellogg observed, "Prominent in the art of prehistoric man are the abstract and early pictorial motifs commonly found in child art today. Indigenous art also contains these motifs."

Unequivocal evidence of base-line—hence, of illustration, and of analogical thought—is not to be found in prehistoric arts.

Precisely what prehistoric objects like cave paintings, statuettes or incised bones were made for, nobody can say.[14] Guesses vary with intellectual fashions—now sorcery, now sex fethishes, now computation. Questionable even is the assumption that the images related to each other in any very coherent fashion.[15] The only fact beyond dispute is that they are substitute imagery. Whether two-dimensional abstractions or literal primaeval naturalism, they preserve the physical appearance of people and things in such a way as to be recognized by others (including us). For this reason they are properly included in books on art—because substitute imagery is the first demonstrable attribute of activities historically called "arts." The only mental processes that can be conclusively proved from the evidence of prehistoric arts, then, are conceptual and rudimentary analogical thought. Study of children's creative and mental growth shows how much can be done with these processes—enough to account objectively for everything Paleolithic: images of material and abstract concepts, ritual touchings, time calculated by notchings

203A. Rock painting from Jabbaren (Tassili), North Africa, presently dated after 4000 B.C.

203B. Drawings on rock faces of Casulla gorge on the south-east Spanish coast, presently dated 6th to 5th millennium.

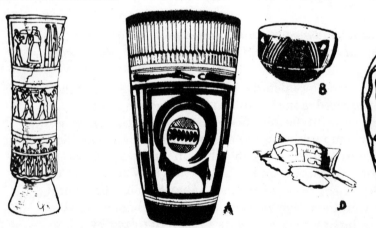

204. Alabaster vase from Warka, 4th millennium. Baghdad, National Museum. CF 71. Indicated mental processes: conceptual plus analogical plus rudimentary analytical thought.

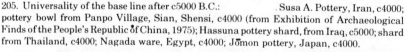

205. Universality of the base line after c5000 B.C.:   . Susa A. Pottery, Iran, c4000; pottery bowl from Panpo Village, Sian, Shensi, c4000 (from Exhibition of Archaeological Finds of the People's Republic of China, 1975); Hassuna pottery shard, from Iraq, c5000; shard from Thailand, c4000; Nagada ware, Egypt, c4000; Jōmon pottery, Japan, c4000.

(additive, existential awareness, i.e.), rudimentary Numinous religion.[16] Study of popular/comercial arts of substitute imagery demonstrate conclusively that such images double as words, so that it is entirely probable that prehistoric images did the same, whence their awesome magical quality sometimes mistaken for modern-type artistic expression:

The farther back language as a whole is traced, the more poetical and animated do its sources appear, until it seems to dissolve at last into a kind of mist of myth.... Words themselves are felt to be alive and to exert a magical influence,

as Owen Barfield put it.[17] It's quite possible that small children gazing in wonder at waxworks recapture just a touch of the ancient awe with which art/words/concepts originally were invested. But as for the rest, "Sistine Chapels of the Ice Age," mute inglorious Picassos, descriptions of hunts and so forth, that must remain subjective speculation.

Deliberate illustration and the beginnings of architecture manifest analogical thought.

The second function identifying activities historically called "arts" was illustration—telling stories or recording events in pictorial form. Illustration was demonstrably in existence by at least 4000 B.C. Demonstrably, that is, by use of a base-line which appears quite suddenly (relatively speaking). For twenty millennia or so human artifacts were in existence without any unequivocal evidence for base-lines; now, within a few thousand years, this device is indisputably in evidence, in North African rock paintings and drawings from the Spanish Levant, and most strikingly of all, in pottery and decorated vessels generally, all across the world.

It could be argued that base-lines at Tassili, Cassula or other earlier sites are accidental. By c4000 B.C. there is no doubt: use of the base-line is conscious and deliberate. You find it on this famous vase, or on Susa A pottery (205) used to relate substitute images of offering-bearers, sacrificial animals and totemic emblems to each other, thus "relating" in the sense of "telling the story" of their participation in ceremonial ritual. What's more, you find base-lines now all over the world, universally.

Quite suddenly, base-lines appear everywhere around the fourth millennium, from Susa to Shensi. A pictorial element not itself imaging anything, but serving only as a device to relate other images to each other in a coherent way, the base-line indicates beyond doubt an intention so to relate them, and hence the existence of analogical thought by this time.

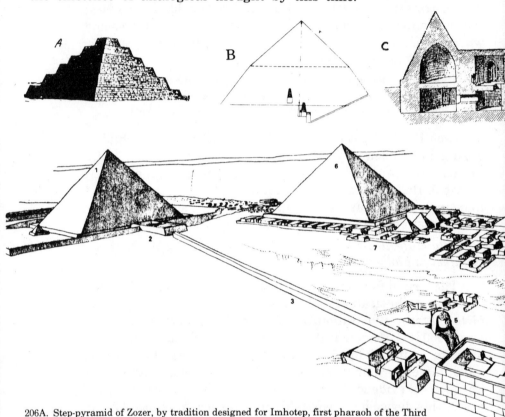

206A. Step-pyramid of Zozer, by tradition designed for Imhotep, first pharaoh of the Third Dynasty of Old Kingdom Egypt, c2700/2650 B.C. (206B) Blunt pyramid at Dashur built for Pharaoh Sneferu, father of Khufu, c2700. (206C) Section through late period pyramid at Abydos (206D Schematic restoration of Great Pyramid complex at Gizeh.

Analogical thought is manifest too in mimesis, the process whereby shapes originating in perishable materials are reproduced because of the associations attaching to that shape from early use as tombs, Great One's houses, granaries, and the like, rather than for any material purpose. Whence the beginnings of architecture: this stone dome is like that round hut of perishable grass used by Great Ones long ago and hence connoting a Sacred and Royal Presence; this colossal pyramid in stone coalesces the symbolic step-pyramid shape of the primaeval hill, the round-house tomb, the ben-ben sun symbol.[18]

In the Great Pyramid complex a great number of different mimetic shapes—each itself the product of an operation of analogical thought—are coalesced by further analogical thought to form an additive (as distinct from an organically or analytically understood) whole. So the developed pyramids contain (without loss of the significance of any!) the "primaeval hill" symbol of life divinely renewed (exemplified by the step-pyramid, which is like the primaeval hill in shape, 296A), and possibly also therein the "divine staircase" connecting Earth and Heaven; certainly the "ben-ben" solar symbol of Eternity (which caps the Blunt Pyramid at Dashur, 296B) and functioned as a sun symbol; and the primaeval round-house/dome tomb form, seen at its clearest in the later pyramids (206C). But analogical thought does not recognize one shape as necessarily independent from others with similar associations; so the whole complex of Pyramids, Sphinx, river temple, mastaba tombs, funeral boat, and other such forms together would undoubtedly, were analogical thought the principal mental process involved, to be taken to constitute a single great image.

But an image of what? Child art can suggest how a civilization dominated by analogical thought might perceive things—Heinrich Shäfer made exhaustive comparisons of ancient Egyptian and modern child art on this level[19]—but it cannot tell us what illustrative arts *do* in and for society. Here however we can turn to the other major perpetuator of traditional social functions: popular/commercial arts. And their evidence is forthright: the function of illustrative arts in society is to reinforce conformity. Conformity, not conservatism; to call popular/commercial arts reactionary in a political or social sense is to misconceive them. They will reinforce community ethics and outlook no matter what these may be; wherever left-liberal attitudes are dominant in society, these will be what comics, movies, television, etc., promulgate. For example: at the moment, most popular/commercial arts assume a widespread faith in Science as a miracle-worker and savior of mankind comparable to the Church in earlier times.[20] What force might command comparable belief in the 3rd millenium? Of course nobody knows with certainty exactly why any 3rd-millenium architecture was built. But the general motivation seems plain enough. Common to pyramids, ziggurats, and megaliths alike are certain general

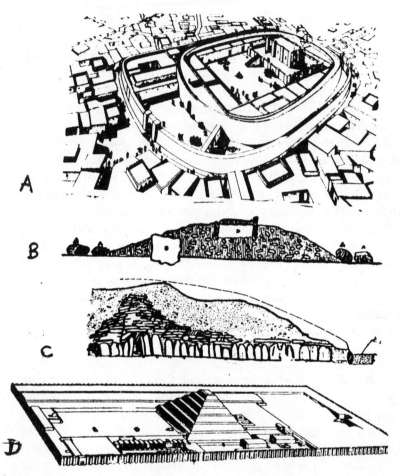

[207A] Eshunna temple complex, Khafaje; (207B) Section of barrow grave over cairn A, Jiwarji, Deccan (from Meadows Taylor, *Megalithic Tombs in the Deccan.* (207C) Section through chambered barrow grave, New Grange, Ireland. (207D) Restoration of Step-Pyramid complex, Saqqara.

indications of function: they all had something to do with an orientation toward celestial bodies; with burials, either in them or around them; and with rituals. That is, they all have to do with cycles: seasons, birth-and-death, seed-time and harvest—or in broadest terms, with the idea of the Nature of Things. An exciting and dramatic revelation when first realized: the foundation of all ethics, all science, all philosophy—existence no longer existential, but ordered, coherent, comprehensible. What the great complex of analogical mimetic symbols at Gizeh probably represented, then, was *ma'at,* the eternal right rhythm of things:

they were "this Eternity which I have made" as an Old Kingdom Pharaoh is recorded as saying.[21]

And as in children around five, ability to coordinate the multiple properties of things is defective, so also it seems to be in the fourth and third millennium: awareness that "this thing is like that thing" is not counterbalanced by a corresponding degree of awareness of differences. Hence the mythopoeic mode of perception which Henri Frankfort identified as characteristic of *The Intellectual Adventure of Early Man;* hence that total identification of image and reality which A. Leo Oppenheimer considered the most baffling aspect for moderns to grasp of religion in *Ancient Mesopotamia.*[22] Hence too the hugeness of early architecture; no sooner has the principle of mimesis become effective and large stone replicas of revered perishable shapes begun to appear than the largest monuments in history are built. Ziggurats in Mesopotamia, megalithic monuments all along the littoral of the Mediterranean and Atlantic, huge earthworks in India and China—they match the Great Pyramids, if not in absolute size, certainly in employing comparably huge percentages of the gross national produce of their societies. What all of them have in common is untrammelled analogical thought.

That is to say, a ziggurat does not merely reproduce the shape of a sacred mountain, it *is* one and the same thing. Stonehenge is one and the same thing as the wooden shape that preceded it. And so on—"the bigger the better" principle runs riot. Analogical thought controlled only by rudimentary powers of analysis, hence unable to coordinate the multiple properties of things, produces buildings of extraordinary hugeness and cost (relative to resources, as well as absolutely), within a few generations of the very beginnings of architecture everywhere.

Indeed these monuments constitute a record of transition from conceptual to analogical thought as the norm of mental operations everywhere. This transition, rather than the use of stone or bronze or iron, marks the real beginnings of civilization everywhere. But it is also the record of an era before analytical thought became effective. There is only what Albright called proto-logical thought.[29]

Analytical thought and beautification not provable before Greek times.

For, although conscious beautification in arts of the fourth and third millennium—and by inference, analytical thought—is often assumed, if not explicitly stated, by scholars about Susa A pottery, for instance; by popularizers about the pyramids; by avant-garde sculptors about megalomonuments like Stonehenge, the facts and the experts both belie it. The discoverer of Susa A pottery, Edmond Pottier, took pains to demolish the notion of its involving conscious beautification; in his excavation report he characterized them not as decorated in the sense of beautified, but written upon, with prophylactic symbols.[23] Baldwin Smith's 1938 *Egyptian Architecture as Cultural Expression* demonstrated that, all Wilhelm-Worringer-type talk about "grand visual masses" and suchlike in Egyptian architecture to the contrary, no evidence exists for any ancient Egyptian ever thinking of them in that way.[24] As for avant-garde pronouncements about menhirs and dolmens being "art," the formula "art is what the artist says it is," allows any pot, pan, or post to be called "art" whenever the mood strikes.

For second-millennium arts like Ikhenaton's from Amarna, or Cretan frescoes, a better case for beautification could be argued. On arts of the Amarna era, Heinrich Schäfer's analysis in *Aegyptischer Kunst,* that Egyptian artists never went beyond children's principles of representations around 5-7, is not as fully convincing as for other periods.[25] But whatever beautification there then was was sporadic, unsystematic and probably not deliberate—at least deliberateness is not provable. Conscious systematic beautification, long cited as one of the classical Greeks' greatest accomplishments, does not appear in any indubitably proven way, before them.[29]

Conscious systematic beautification and analytical thought, is demonstrable c600-400 in Greece, and elsewhere.

Around 600 a systematic development begins to alter the forms of artifacts central to Greek life-style, which cannot be explained by any change in usage or users, nor by any

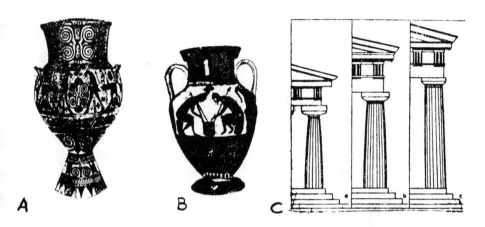

208A,B. Evolution of amphora in shape and ornament, from Melos c650-600 (National Museum, Athens) to Exekias's amphora from Chiusi (Vatican) c550, where abstract and figural ornament are consciously deisgned for unified effect on beholder. (C): Evolution of Doric columns and entablature between 600 and 400 B.C. There is no change in specific shapes, nor in mimetic connotations of those shapes, nor their physical function; what change internal proportional system, making interrelationships of parts more intelligible to individual beholder. (Cf. 49, 50, 144).

improvement in performing the functions of substitute imagery or illustration. Specific shapes remain recognizable (amphoras, Doric columns, etc.): they keep their mimetic associative values; and their physical function remains unaltered likewise. What changes is the internal proportional system, making interrelationships of parts more intelligible to individual beholders. The only obvious purpose of such a development must be to enable individual beholders to relate to objects so refined in terms of their own experience. Thus vases came to look like "better pourers," and columns came to look like "better supporters." A comparably conscious and deliberate development can be traced in decoration applied to vessels, buildings and the like (49, 50, 144), establishing a coherent and meaningful relation of parts to wholes, and wholes to the perception of individual viewers. This art is thus not a producer but a processor of objects—a way of so treating artifacts as to identify their function and relate them generally to human life and to individual users' experience in particular. The greatness of Greek art was not that its forms were absolutely original; none of them in fact were (Greek temple forms are mimetic perpetuations in stone of revered forms originating in wood, most of them common to all Aryan peoples), but consisted in the refinement of those forms by a process of analytical thought. This new power of analytical thought so manifest in Greek arts transformed all aspects of Greek life as well—government, philosophy, mechanics, religion.[26] Of this process, creations like the Temple of Zeus at Olympia are classic examples (128).[27]

But was this new analytical thought peculiar to Greece? Once generally believed, that can be maintained no longer. Look in other contemporary arts for qualities similarly manifesting analytical thought, and they can be found everywhere.

209. Part of the logo for the 1977 Summer Institute in Cross-Cultural Studies (University of Victoria/ISUH). Its purpose was to set forth the theme of study: outward diversity of form, but throughout the age, evidence for the workings of analytical thought on a new mature plane, in (L. to R.):

Late Vedic India (a week's presentation by Partha Mitter, Sussex), Scythia, Urartu (Boris Piotrovsky, Hermitage Leningrad)Late Chou China (David Waterhouse, Toronto), Olmec (Charles Wicke (Mexico) Etruria (John Oleson, Victoria).

Expanded mental capacity is demonstrable by comparative and cross-cultural studies: of the organic way Scythian metalwork is composed, for example; or of the principle of federated government on which the Achaemenid Empire and the Roman republic were organized (and possibly, more than one scholar has speculated, in Olmec polity in the New World too)[28]; or the common concern for the relationship of parts (individuals) to wholes (communities) apparent in the thought and speculations of the Greek sages and the Hebrew prophets, of Confucius and the Buddha, of Zarathustra and Mahendra.

Abstract causal thought, and arts of conviction/persuasion, not demonstrable in arts before the Christian era.

Did the Greeks also have abstract causal thought—at least, more than a rudimentary and occasional use of it? If so, it is not demonstrable from their arts, in any way comparable to its demonstrable operations in arts from the beginnings of the Christian era onwards through the Middle Ages and into modern times. Evidence of all sorts suggests that the Greeks had no more than intimations of this mode of thought.[29] Not least of such evidence is lack of demonstrable persuasion/conviction in historic Greek arts.

Persuasion/conviction is a complex function to identify. All objects that function in any way as counterparts or symbols for some kind of reality involve persuasion/conviction—substitute images of things and ideas, illustrative records of events and experiences, and beautifications thereof to enhance their relationship to people and history. In that sense, persuasion/conviction is the first and oldest of all social functions. But persuasion/conviction as a conscious art appears much later in history.

Conscious persuasion/conviction through arts involves deliberate employment of some distinctive "style"—some combination of forms, voids, spaces, etc., recognizably enough different from another to carry associations with a distinctive set of abstract beliefs. And demonstrable examples of arts persuasive in that sense are not provable much before the Christian era—certainly not in architecture, which is by its collective nature *the* art of conviction.

Not that changes of architectural style never occurred earlier, of course. Obviously they did, whenever conquests of one people by another occurred. Greek temples displaced Minoan sanctuaries. The Canaanite house of Baal on Jerusalem was replaced by Jehovah's permanent home in a different style. Palaces of Persian form superseded Assyrian ones. Architecture and metalwork of Egyptian style spread into Palestine and Syria with Egypt's New Kingdom Empire. But that was no change of style in the sense of something dramatically and consciously different from what people of a previous generation had built—

like Renaissance contrasted to Gothic, or International Style with Victorian. That was just one set of mimetic substitute images replacing another—not because of some change in abstract beliefs or convictions within a given population proclaimed by new styles, but because of invaders overrunning and occupying territories of earlier peoples, and reproducing their own revered shapes in place of the conquered's. Similarly the "new art" at Akhenaton's capital of Amarna involved a new iconography, not a new style, as Heinrich Schäfer demonstrated long ago (1923) in *Aegyptische Kunst*. In Babylonia and Assyria as well as Greece there was in the 5th and 4th centuries B.C. a slow maturing from archaic to stylised forms; but that is a process of refinement of inherited forms, not the sudden appearance of a whole new style. Such a dramatic and conscious change of style is first unequivocally to be demonstrated in the early centuries of the Christian era—most notably, perhaps, in the contrast between the two great basilicas built under Emperor Constantine's administration at Rome in the early 4th century A.D.: the Basilica Nova of Maxentius, and Old St. Peter's.[30]

210A. Conjectural reconstruction of the Basilica Nova of Maxentius, early 4th century, completed by Constantine the Great.

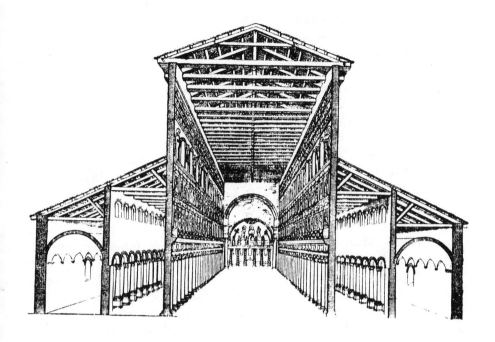

210B. Conjectural reconstruction of Old St. Peter's basilica, completed by Constantine the Great, c330.

Whether 19th or 20th-century restorations, how accurate in detail is irrelevant to the central contrast between late Imperial and early Christian basilicas: they differed deliberately and consciously in style because they derived their ultimate meaning from different sources. The imperial basilica is still composed like the Greek temple, as an organically-related composition of inherited forms with mimetic associations peculiar to the race which built them—i.e., the Romans. Vaster, certainly; technologically different, especially in the use of arches and concrete; but not involving any fundamentally different thinking process. Differences in appearance from earlier structures reflected only that a different kind of relationship to individual beholders had developed, not a different set of abstract ideas. The Basilica Nova was still recognizably the product of the same process of analyzing relationships of parts to wholes which had begun refining traditional Greek mimetic shapes in Greek

494 Learning to See

temples a thousand years before. Now, as a kind of self-defeating climax to that process of analytical refinement, all the parts were so related to the whole as to lose independent existence. In plan and visual effect the Basilica Nova was monospatial. No part had meaning or indeed any real existence independently of the whole: the building was related to spectators in the same way that the State related to its citizens, denying individual initiative, presenting only a single massive collective block.

St. Peter's was an equally major architectural project, but so different in style as usually to be described and located in another historical context entirely. In the typical art-history survey you find the Basilica Nova of Maxentius at the end of the Graeco-Roman section, as culmination (or exhaustion) of the analytical, organic kind of architecture that begins to appear in archaic Greek times—the end of Ancient art history. Old St. Peter's, by contrast, commonly introduces the history of Christian architecture and arts; it is where medieval art history begins. Both placements are correct: what is often distorted or obscured by so separating these two buildings is the fact that they were built at the same time by the same people. No change of race or national artistic tradition was involved; the difference in style between these two basilicas has nothing to do with Germanic or Persian influence. Nor has it anything to do with some patron's personal taste—the same emperor funded both building programs. Nor yet with some influx of foreign taste from workmen—the same corps of imperial builders did the actual construction in both cases. Furthermore, the same people used both buildings—i.e., worshippers in Old St. Peter's on Sundays might find themselves transacting business in the Basilica Nova on Mondays. The change of style at Old St. Peter's was entirely dictated by belief—that is, need for a different kind of visual metaphor to affirm new convictions.

The bishops who set St. Peter's style in collaboration with the first Christian emperor deliberately went back to an earlier model of basilica, from republican Rome—not for aesthetic reasons, but as a deliberate visual metaphor of a new kind of social order. Or more exactly, a metaphorical return to old Roman republican virues. Lost in the corruptions of Imperial times, they were now to return on a higher, transcendant plane, as the basis for a rejuvenated Roman society with new goals capable of enlisting popular enthusiasm. Plain walls and open timbered roof symbolized old Roman austerity and disdain for luxury, now spiritualized. Transcendental effects of mosaics especially proclaimed a fundamental conviction that "the things which are seen are temporal, but the things which are not seen are eternal." And systematic division into hierarchically ordered units in ground plan and spatial organization evoked that divine order of the cosmos which was now to be taken as model for earthly governance.

Sweeping changes of taste motivated by social function of persuasion/conviction produce the great styles of art history—universally.

Such a change in style deliberately proclaimed a change in convictions held, and was intended to persuade others thereto. Henceforth abstract causality governs major arts, and persuasion/conviction is the social function which provides the deep motivation for those sweeping changes in "artistic taste" from Romanesque to Gothic, from Gothic to Renaissance/Baroque, from Renaissance/Baroque to "modern" which constitute later art history.[31] Later art history begins at this point.

But since a comparable shift of style can be observed throughout the world at this time—compare, for example, Buddhist arts in India or Central Asia, China or Japan with preceding styles there (18A-D)—later art history can no longer be limited merely to the line-of-progress from Rome to Middle Ages to Us. So study of popular/commercial arts leads to parallels in universal history—to a new art history, based upon the methodology of social function.

Footnotes to Section VI: Toward an Expanded Art History

[1]Parts of this chapter have appeared in other forms: in the *Proceedings of the 1977 Summer Institute in Cross-Cultural Studies* (Victoria: ISUH & University of

Victoria, 1978), pp. 7-17; in "Popular Arts and Historic Artifacts," *Popular Architecture* (Bowling Green, M. Fishwick and J.M. Neil, eds), 1973, pp. 87-105; *On Parallels in Universal History* (Watkins Glen, 1974); and in *Art History*

[2]"Today we are in the unfortunate position of having no order or canon whereby all artistic production is submitted to rules. They—the Greeks, the Romans, the Egyptians—did. Their canon was inescapable because beauty, so-called, was, by definition, contained in those rules. But as soon as art had lost all link with tradition, and the kind of liberation that came in with Impressionism permitted every painter to do what he wanted to do, painting was finished. When

they decided it was the painter's sensations and emotions that mattered, and every man could recreate painting as he understood it from any basis whatever, then there was no more painting; there were only individuals. Sculpture died the same death."

So no less representative a modern than Picasso put the case for our modern concept of "art" being different from historic arts (quoted in Francoise Gilot and Carlton Lake, *Life with Picasso,* 1964, pp. 74-75). The same point was made in a different way by Lord Clark, commenting on the beginnings of art history in the movement to authenticate Italian paintings (*The New Review of Books,* 24 November 1977):

"This movement had one serious defect; it did not begin to look at works of art in their historical context. Berenson and Bode never considered what contemporary patrons, guilds, princes or ecclesiastical bodies wanted from their artists. And one reason for this was that Renaissance patrons of all sorts wanted something almost incredibly different from what we want today. Instead of an aesthetic specimen in a glass case they wanted a symbol, or complex of symbols, which should express their thoughts and aspirations. By the mid-nineteenth century no one (except Ruskin) thought symbolically...."

[3]As was established by Franz Boas decades ago in *The Mind of Primitive Man* (New York, 1938), this is not due to any racial inferiority, of course.

[4]Based specifically on Lewis Morgan, *Human Societies* (New York, 1877), beloved of Marx and Engels, and generally upon historical materialism, explaining evolution from amoeba to superman by mechanistic organic causality alone.

[5]Simple logic alone would suggest that primitives must be different from prehistoric peoples in some very fundamental ways. As early as 1897 this point was being insisted upon against some of the more zealous and doctrinaire anthropologists:

"A great deal can be learned about early man by studying peoples who are savages and consequently nearer than others to the first humans; but never forget that most of these have themselves come, whether by their own efforts or by contact with more advanced peoples, to a state of development which true primitives in the historic sense of that word never arrived at." (Alexander Conze, "Uber den Ursprung der bildenden Kunst," *Sitzungsberichte der Akademie der Wissenschaft,* Berlin, 1897, p. 105.)

A less scholarly, but in its own day more famous statement of the same principle occurs in G.K. Chesterton's *Everlasting Man* of 1927: "Modern savages cannot be exactly like prehistoric men, because they are not prehistoric. Modern savages are not ancient because they are modern.... it has appeared to a good many intelligent and well-informed people...probable that the experience of the savages has been that of a decline from civilisation. Most of those who criticise this view do not seem to have any very clear notion of what a decline from civilisation would be like. Heaven help them, it is likely enough that they will soon find out. They seem to be content if cave-men and cannibal islanders have some things in common, such as certain particular implements. But it is obvious on the face of it that any peoples reduced for any reason to a ruder life would have some things in common. If we lost all our firearms we should make bows and arrows; but we should not necessarily resemble in every way the first men who made bows and arrows.

"It is therefore absurd to argue that the first pioneers of humanity must have been identical with some of the last and most stagnant leavings of it. There were almost certainly some things, there were probably many things, in which the two were widely different or flatly contrary." (pp. 63-67)

[6]Published by Faber & Faber in 1936, *Education Through Art* had an influence on art education comparable to Giedion's *Space, Time & Architecture* (Charles Eliot Norton lectures, 1938-39, published 1941) on architectural education.

[7]First published in 1947, it went through four editions to 1954. In the fifth, after Lowenfeld's death, material began to be added which substantially contradicted both the data and conclusions Lowenfeld presented (!).

[8]Rhoda B. Kellogg, *Analyzing Children's Art* (Washington, National Press, 1969), identifies "twenty basic scribbles" as the "building blocks of art." Diversity of opinion and nomenclature for these stages, and opinions about them, is irrelevant to the central argument here, that child art develops in demonstrable and analyzable stages.

[9]My thanks to Professor John Robinson of the Department of Psychology, University of Louisville, for suggestions regarding the terminology in this section.

[10]E.g., Jean Piaget, *The Child and Reality, Problems of Genetic Psychology* (New York, 1973)—especially the first chapter on "Time and the Intellectual Development of the Child": *The Growth of Logical Thinking* (with Barbel Inhelder) (New York, 1953).

[11]Such at least is the conclusion of Pierre R. Dasen, "Cross-Cultural Piagetian Research: A Summary," *Journal of Cross-Cultural Psychology* (III, 1, March 1972, pp. 23-40.

[12]The idea of an evolution in human intelligence has been the subject of many essays, of which Carl Sagan's *Dragons of Eden* is the most popular recently. It was preceded by Robert Rudolf Schmidt, *The Dawn of the Human Mind* (London, 1936), which argued that "every human life repeats, in its psychical and mental

development, the conceptual forms of the stages of human evolution"—assuming, however, that all stages had been gone through long before cave-painting prehistoric men appeared. Actually the idea of Mankind repeating stages in individual evolution goes back at least to Augustine; our idea of creative and mental growth is, as usual, a secularization of *tanquam in uno quodam homine diffuso toto orbe terrarum et succrescente per volumina saeculorum (Ennar.* in Ps. 118, 16, 6), repeated by Pascal in *Fragment du Traité du Vide:* "All men progress together as the universe ages, for the same thing occurs in the succession of man's generations as in the successive ages of one man." Cf. Henri Irenée Marrou, *Théologie d'histoire* (Paris, 1968).

[13]This view occurs much less often, for obvious reasons; one recent example is Julian Jaynes, *The Emergence of Consciousness in the Breakdown of the Bicameral Mind* (Princeton, 1976 [New York, 1977] which argues that consciousness in the modern sense appears only around the 2nd millennium B.C.

[14]*Cf.* Peter J. Ucko and Andrée Rosenfeld, *Palaeolithic Cave Art* (London, 1968): "Perhaps the most important single barrier to an understanding of the significance of Palaeolithic parietal art is the ignorance which still surrounds the use of caves by Palaeolithic man. Until it is known exactly what Palaeolithic man was doing inside caves, apart from painting and engraving on their walls, all interpretations of parietal art can only be tentative hypotheses."

[15]A great advantage of studying history in art is that one does not have to rely upon subjective impressions of beauty in art, or subjective assumptions about the meanings of words (as in philosophy) where there is internal evidence. Thus all sorts of writers about caves wax lyrical about their beauty and their narrative qualities, &c. J. Jelinek, *The Pictorial Encyclopedia of the Evolution of Man* (London, 1975) informs us that "it seems almost certain that this is an account of an event that took place," *à propos* of the famous man and bison at Lascaux (p. 294). E. Adamson Hoebel in his popular textbook *Anthropology, The Study of Man* (New York, 1958, repr. 1966), p. 184, talks about how art "was also an end in itself. The Upper Palaeolithic artist produced not merely images, but beautiful images. He not only strove to produce magically efficacious representations of the goals of his desires but also developed artistic skill for the intrinsic pleasure it gave him...." Nary a "possibly" or a "probably" throughout. Yet we can look at the works thus being extolled and expounded, and we can see for ourselves that there is no scale and no base line; that animals are painted one on top of the other and obviously at different times by different people (even if Marshak's *Roots of Civilization* had not proved it), and we can see that words like Jelinek's "unified composition" applied to what he is talking about are like criticism read in art magazines, mere words, unattached to any possible meaning, merely expressing a writer's admiration for what he sees; he knows what he likes. This is not to be confused with analytical study of arts as evidence for history.

[16]Alexander Marshack, *Roots of Civilization* (New York, 1972) showed by microscopic analysis that cave art was *used* in the most literal sense of being touched, felt, handled—over and over again, generation after generation. He suggested that it was used to keep records—much (we might extrapolate) as prisoners in windowless cells try to record the passage of days by notching a stick every dinner-time. There is evidence for inability or unwillingness to calculate by

cycles. Although Marshack's findings indicated some fairly complicated communal activities, simple conceptual thought could account for all of it. Or in other words: prehistoric arts could be explained as the kind of work a clever three-year-old might do if he/she had adult motor skills.

[17]*History in English Words* (London, 1953/Grand Rapids, 1967).

[18]The foregoing is obviously a simplistic generalization from presentations of an enormously complex and controversial field; cf. E. Baldwin Smith, *The Dome* (Princeton, 1950) and *Egyptian Architecture as Cultural Expression* (New York, 1938/Watkins Glen, 1968); Henri Frankfort, &c., *The Intellectual Adventure of Ancient Man, et al.*

[19]Heinrich Schäfer, *Von ägyptischer Kunst* (Wiesbaden, 1965).

[20]Cf. Brian Ash (ed.) *The Visual Encyclopedia of Science Fiction* (New York, 1977); also, for specific illustrations, my article "The Popular Arts & Universal History: New Principles for Historical Study," *Festschrift Klaus Lankheit* (Koln, 1973), pp. 78-95.

[21]John A. Wilson, *The Burden of Egypt* (Chicago, 1951), pp. 48-49.

[22](Chicago, 1964), Sect. IV, "Why a 'Mesopotamian religion' should not be written," pp. 172-82.

[23]Edmond Pottier, "Sur les vases peintes de l'acropole de Suse," *Mémoires de la délégation en Perse,* 1912.

[24]*op cit.,* pp. 240ff.

[25]*Op. cit.,* pp. 345ff; having argued that even in Amarna Egyptian art never departed from its timeless formulae, he can conclude: "Through the Greeks came a demarcation in pictorial arts all across the world. Wherever their spirit was not operative—as in Egypt—the principles or representing Nature remained the same for the simplest adult, child or greatest artist...."

[26]Again a simplisitically generalized summary of a fearfully complicated subject. One citation must do; from Barfield's *History in English Words (op. cit.,)*, p. 110: "Perhaps the most significant of all those words which are first found in Aristotle's treatise on *Logic* is *analytic.* Here is indeed a new word made to express a new kind of thinking.... The *analytical* method of thought led naturally in Alexandria to the actual dissection of bodies...."

[27]Q.v. Fns. III-127, 128.

[28]*Proceedings* of the 1977 Summer Institute in Cross-Cultural Studies are available from ISUH, Box 363, Watkins Glen, N.Y. 14891.

[29]It must be self-evident that no movement in history, least of all development of thought, occurs all at once. Likewise any new movement in thought begins with scattered intimations long before it gets focused in one place and for one cause. Examples of early intimations of abstract causality in Greece would of course include Plato's metaphor of the cave, and self-conscious archaism of the late Hellenistic age, such as the archaizing Athena in Naples, and possibly the temple at Paestum.

This was accepted as full abstract causality by William Foxwell Albright, whose *From the Stone Age to Christianity: Monotheism and the Historical Process* (Baltimore 1940, repr. 1957 Doubleday Anchor) came to my attention after this typescript was set in type. Here was set forth on philological and linguistic grounds three phases or levels of mental development roughly corresponding to what in this text are called conceptual, analogical, and analytical thought. In his chapter "Towards an Organismic Philosophy of History" he identifies "prelogical, corporative thinking," then a "protological" stage, an "empirical stage of logical thinking, where the highest thought is quite logical as a rule, but draws its sanctions from the results of experience and not from formal canons of thinking."

Finally "personalism tends to replace corporatism" in classical Greek times, whereafter "for the past 2500 years civilized man has thought in much the same fundamental ways" (pp. 122-123). The Hebrews and everybody else, he insisted learned logical thinking from the Greeks. (p. 3: "I still insist on the basic character of the Greek revolution in higher culture, and deny the possibility of definition of concepts, logical classification of data, and deductive reasoning among the Hebrews before the third century B.C." (p.3). This complements the art-historical evidence adduced by Schäfer (q.v.) But   that there is a stage of thought or a mental level higher than logical thinking he did not even discuss. I don't know why. Perhaps philological and linguistic history doesn't deal with or require an awareness of it. He did not reject the idea ; he never considered it at all.

[30]I owe this example (and much else) to Norris K. Smith, Cf. *Medieval Art* (Dubuque, 1967).

[31]One might have supposed that an explanation of the change of style from classical to Byzantine by ideological persuasion, would have had *prima facie* appeal for Byzantine scholars. "Hellenistic" survivals in the frescoes of Sta. Maria Antique were considered by C.R. Morey and his school to be products of some artistic backwater, probably Alexandria (much as one might have said, in the 1920s, that narrative easel painting survived in backwaters remote from Paris and die Brücke). Ernst Kitzinger in 1934 showed that this "Hellenistic" style in fact originated in Constantinople itself. Yet only Per Jonas Nordhagen had the temerity to point out the obvious conclusion: "In what I think is a little masterpiece of fiction I have suggested that the 'Hellenistic style' came into being as part of the political reconstruction of the Emperor Heraclius and his dynasty," rather than some artistic quirk. (symposium, Nationalmesuem, Stockholm, "Fornkristen och bysantinsk konst," 20 November 1968, *Byzantina* (Stockholm) II, 1973, pp. 8-11.

Index I
Arts and Architecture

Arts, Avant-Garde and Fine

abstract causal thought in, 367f
advertising devices in, 384
architecture, appeal of, 26; definition
    of, 397, 401-2; Establishment of 433,
    6; by capitalism, 361, 392; in 1930s,
    460; origins, 285, 397, 400-401;
    formalism of 407-8; mimetic effects
    in, 459, rejection of ornament, 260,
    435; Bauhaus, 265; brute, 285;
    International Style, 6; Japanese,
    430f.
beauty not objective of, 33
borrowings from popular/commercial,
    360
cinema, 154; American, 35 fn45
comics, underground, 165
Constructivism, 265
denunciations of, 406
design, auto, 334; distinguished from
    traditional beautification, 292,
    297f., and from aesthetics, 292;
    ship, 345-8
distinguished from traditional &
    historic, 15, 17; failure to so
    distinguish and fals analogies
    resulting, 23f, 31, 362
Fine Art, product of obsolescence, 156;
    in underground comics, 165-6; in
    games, 221; comparisons with
    popular/commercial, 193
furniture, 348
inverted religiosity, 405
monotony, 406
monuments, 458
moral mission of, 260, 287-8, 424-5
origins, in Fine art, 156; remote, 286
pacifism in, 215
painting, relation to photography, 141;
    Rembrandt precursor of, 35 fn42;
    see also Oldenberg, Courbet, &c.
political ineffectiveness of, 457
"pop," distinguished from popular/
    commercial, 24, 142, 387

pornography, relation to, 191
principles: art-as-art, 19, 23; Beaux-Arts
    inversion, 287; egalitarian, 196, 302;
    ethical relativism, futuristic
    premises, 447-9; godlike artist, 247,
    248, 286-369; honesty in design, 418;
    non-choice, 355-6; personal, private
    & secret language, 369-370; rejec-
    tion of traditional social functions,
    19, 33, of "meaning" 446; utopian,
    220, 348, 350, 447-9
protest in, 370.
support of: by capitalism, 361, 372; by
    government, 96;

Arts, Traditional and Historic

abstract, 40f
African arts, 147; architecture, 459,
    sculpture, 93;
allegorical, 71f
American, study of 12; colonial style,
    395; see also capitols, state and
    U.S., development houses, New
    England meeting houses &c.,
Amerind, 55, *56, 425,* 458, 464; see also
    teepee, &c.
architecture: force for continuity, 421;
    early, 89, fundamentals, 400-401;
    humanizing capacity, 227; eclecti-
    cism in, 405; mural painting in,
    265f., via prints, 273, medieval,
    274; origins of, 106, 110-11, 139,
    483, 495; play metaphor in, 150;
    stabilizing force, 419f.; symbolism,
    mimetic, 416; visual metaphors
    created by, 407
Art Nouveau, 358
Baroque, theory of, 270
Buddhist, 641, *264,* 288. See also (e.g.)
    Bamiyan, Gandhara
Byzantine (Early Christine) arts,

501

Arts, Popular/Commercial

Index II
General Index

Q: quoted from

abstract causality defined, 476; early intimations of, 498; in child art, 475f; necessary for printing, 147 fn. 62; 367, 456, 470, 494
Abstract Expressionism, *470*, (by Rajah)
abstraction, movement towards, 40f
Ackerman, James S. Q10, 30, 33
Adams, John, 36, Q on art, 266
Addams, Charles, 170-172
advertising, see ARTS, POPULAR/ COMMERCIAL
Aeneid, 67, 144
Aeschylus, 284
aesthetics, discipline of, 290f., and Fine Arts, 357
Afghanistan, Buddha figures at Bamiyan, 64f
Agra, Taj Mahal, 91, *92,* 123, 128, 145
airplanes, design of, 360
Akhenaton, Pharaoh, 487, 490
Albany, N.Y., State Capitol, 125
Alberti, Leon Battista, 18
Albright, William Foxwell, 487, 499
Alexander the Great, statue, 143
Alice in Wonderland, 196, 197, 199, *200,* 283, 300
All in the Family, 283
allegorical arts, 71f.
Allendale Nativity (Natl. Gall., Washington), 30
Altamira, 36, *38,* 50
Ambasz, Emilio, Q348, 350
Amerinds, origins, of 284; stereotypes of 136f; techniques unadopted, 458; see further ARTS, TRADITIONAL
Amos 'n' Andy, 175
analogical thought in illustration, 153, 296, 367; in Pyramids, 484, 469, 470, 471, 473
analytical thought in beautification, 296f., 367; early unproved intimations

of, 485-7; in Greece, 275f., 326f., 485f. 498, 469-70; 473-4
animals, anthropomorphic, 196, 286; totemic, 208f; worshipped in Egypt 209f.
animated cartoons, evolution of, 198; nature of, 280, see also ARTS P/C
Aquinas, St. Thomas, 123
Aristotle, 498
Armi, Clement Edson, 330, Q332
Armstrong, Neil, 158
Ars Moriendi, 289
art history, surveys of 4-8, 25, 70; unused by historians, examples 28f.
Art Nouveau, 358
Asche, Kurt, 147
Assyrian arts, 278, 289, *364*
Asterix, 218f., *219*
Athena, Pheidias' status of ,60
Athens, Parthenon, 60, 70, 115, *116,* model for 19th-century architecture, 115
Auerbach, Ernst, 32, 148
Augustine, St., 496
automobiles, design of, 327f.; history of, 359; racing, 222
axes, 314; design of *315*

Bamiyan, great Buddhas, 64-5, *66,* 263
Barasch, Frances K., 284
Barfield, Owen, Q33, Q482-3, Q498
Barks, Carl, 280
Barnum, P.T., 372, 374
Baroque art, nature of, 270; see also ARTS, TRADITIONAL
base-line, 468; universal, 483
baseball, 220
Baudelaire, Charles, 281
Bauhaus, 302, 400; see also ARTS, AVANT-GARDE
Baum, L. Frank, 94, 252

504